MONTRÉAL &
QUÉBEC CITY

Where to Stay and Eat
for All Budgets

Must-See Sights
and Local Secrets

Ratings You Can Trust

Fodor's Travel Publications   New York, Toronto, London, Sydney, Auckland
www.fodors.com

FODOR'S MONTRÉAL & QUÉBEC CITY 2005
Editor: John D. Rambow

Editorial Production: Jacinta A. O'Halloran
Editorial Contributors: Tracey Ariel, Chris Barry, Collin Campbell, Mark Cardwell, Satu Hummasti, Mary Ann Simpkins, Julie Waters, Paul Waters
Maps: David Lindroth, *cartographer;* Bob Blake and Rebecca Baer, *map editors*
Design: Fabrizio La Rocca, *creative director;* Guido Caroti, *art director;* Moon Sun Kim, *cover designer;* Melanie Marin, *senior picture editor*
Cover Photo (Summer nightlife on Grande Allée, Québec City): Yves Tessier/Productions Tessima Ltée
Production/Manufacturing: Robert B. Shields

SPECIAL SALES
This book is available for special discounts for bulk purchases for sales promotions or premiums. Special editions, including personalized covers, excerpts of existing books, and corporate imprints, can be created in large quantities for special needs. For more information, write to Special Markets/Premium Sales, 1745 Broadway, MD 6-2, New York, New York 10019, or e-mail specialmarkets@randomhouse.com.

AN IMPORTANT TIP & AN INVITATION
Although all prices, opening times, and other details in this book are based on information supplied to us at press time, changes occur all the time in the travel world, and Fodor's cannot accept responsibility for facts that become outdated or for inadvertent errors or omissions. So **always confirm information when it matters,** especially if you're making a detour to visit a specific place. Your experiences—positive and negative—matter to us. If we have missed or misstated something, **please write to us.** We follow up on all suggestions. Contact the Montréal & Québec City editor at editors@fodors.com or c/o Fodor's at 1745 Broadway, New York, New York 10019.

PRINTED IN THE UNITED STATES OF AMERICA

10 9 8 7 6 5 4 3 2 1

DESTINATION MONTRÉAL & QUÉBEC CITY

M ontréal andQuébec City share a language and a river, but, like jealous sisters, the two cities rarely see eye to eye. Montréal, the younger and edgier of the two, is a brassy island metropolis where commercial towers overshadow the domes of its several major faiths and whose bars and cafés buzz with many languages. Québec City, on the other hand, is more solidly French, moving at a slower, more bureaucratic pace (it is the provincial capital, after all). It's also the more graceful of the two, a walled city out of a fairy tale, with mansard roofs, dormer windows, and winding cobbled streets. The differences run deep, but Québec City and Montréal do complement each other. Visit only one and you miss half the story of French Canada.

Tim Jarrell, Publisher

CONTENTS

Maps

CloseUps

ABOUT THIS BOOK

There's no doubt that the best source for travel advice is a like-minded friend who's just been where you're headed. But with or without that friend, you'll have a better trip with a Fodor's guide in hand. Once you've learned to find your way around its pages, you'll be in great shape to find your way around your destination.

SELECTION

Our goal is to cover the best properties, sights, and activities in their category, as well as the most interesting communities to visit. We make a point of including local food-lovers' hot spots as well as neighborhood options, and we avoid all that's touristy unless it's really worth your time. You can go on the assumption that everything you read about in this book is recommended wholeheartedly by our writers and editors. Flip to On the Road with Fodor's to learn more about who they are. It goes without saying that no property mentioned in the book has paid to be included.

RATINGS

Orange stars ★ denote sights and properties that our editors and writers consider the very best in the area covered by the entire book. These, the best of the best, are listed in the Fodor's Choice section in the front of the book. Black stars ★ highlight the sights and properties we deem Highly Recommended, the don't-miss sights within any region. Fodor's Choice and Highly Recommended options in each region are usually listed on the title page of the chapter covering that region. Use the index to find complete descriptions. In cities, sights pinpointed with numbered map bullets ❶ in the margins tend to be more important than those without bullets.

SPECIAL SPOTS

Pleasures & Pastimes focuses on types of experiences that reveal the spirit of the destination. Watch for Off the Beaten Path sights. Some are out of the way, some are quirky, and all are worth your while. If the munchies hit while you're exploring, look for Need a Break? suggestions.

TIME IT RIGHT

Wondering when to go? Check On the Calendar up front and chapters' Timing sections for weather and crowd overviews and best days and times to visit.

SEE IT ALL

Use Fodor's exclusive Great Itineraries as a model for your trip. For a good overview of the entire destination, mix regional itineraries from more than one chapter. In cities, Good Walks guide you to important sights in each neighborhood; ▶ indicates the starting points of walks and itineraries in the text and on the map.

BUDGET WELL

Hotel and restaurant price categories from ¢ to $$$$ are defined in the opening pages of each chapter; expect to find a balanced selection for every budget. For attractions, we always give standard adult admission fees; reductions are usually available for children, students, and senior citizens. Want to pay with plastic? AE, D, DC, MC, V following restaurant and hotel listings indicate whether American Express, Discover, Diner's Club, MasterCard, or Visa are accepted.

BASIC INFO	Smart Travel Tips lists travel essentials for the entire area covered by the book; city- and region-specific basics can also be found at the end of each chapter. To find the best way to get around, see the transportation section; see individual modes of travel ("Car Travel," "Train Travel") for details. We assume you'll check Web sites or call for particulars.
ON THE MAPS	Maps throughout the book show you what's where and help you find your way around. Black and orange numbered bullets ❶ ① in the text correlate to bullets on maps.
BACKGROUND	In general, we give background information within the chapters in the course of explaining sights. The vocabulary at the end of the book can be invaluable.
FIND IT FAST	The first two chapters of the book focus on the cities: "Montréal" and "Québec City." They're mostly arranged by neighborhood. The rest of the province of Québec is covered in the third chapter; it's divided into small regions, within which towns are covered in logical geographical order; attractive routes and interesting places between towns are flagged as En Route. Heads at the top of each page help you find what you need within a chapter.
DON'T FORGET	Restaurants are open for lunch and dinner daily unless we state otherwise; we mention dress only when there's a specific requirement and reservations only when they're essential or not accepted—it's always best to book ahead. Hotels have private baths, phones, TVs, and air-conditioning and operate on the European Plan (a.k.a. EP, meaning without meals), unless otherwise noted. We always list facilities but not whether you'll be charged extra to use them, so when pricing accommodations, find out what's included.

SYMBOLS

Many Listings

★ Fodor's Choice
★ Highly recommended
⊠ Physical address
✢ Directions
🕮 Mailing address
☎ Telephone
🖷 Fax
⊕ On the Web
✍ E-mail
🎫 Admission fee
☉ Open/closed times
▶ Start of walk/itinerary
Ⓜ Metro stations
▭ Credit cards

Outdoors

🏌 Golf
⛺ Camping

Hotels & Restaurants

🏨 Hotel
🛏 Number of rooms
♨ Facilities
🍴 Meal plans
✕ Restaurant
🍴 Reservations
👔 Dress code
🚭 Smoking
🍷 BYOB
✕🏨 Hotel with restaurant that warrants a visit

Other

🐣 Family-friendly
🔌 Contact information
⇨ See also
⊠ Branch address
☞ Take note

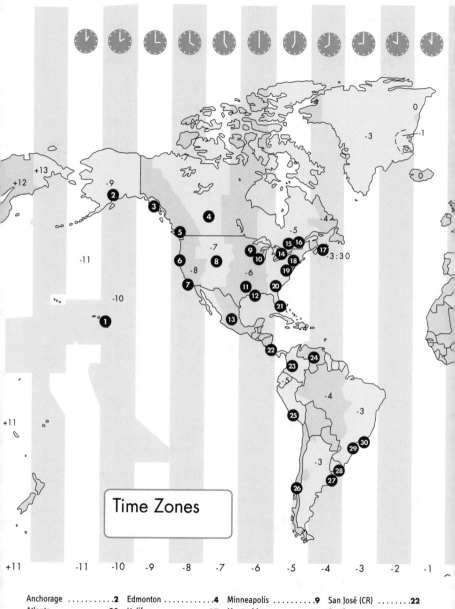

Time Zones

Montréal & Québec City

Lac Kempt

CANADA

QUÉBEC

Montréal   Québec City

Parc National de la Mau

St-Michel-des-Saints

Parc du Mont Tremblant

117

Labelle

Lac Gagnan

Papineau

Lac Simon

323

St-Jovite

117

Ste-Agathe-des-Monts

125

131

50

Joliette   Tracy

Sorel

31

40

133

158

25

St-Jérome

Lachute

158

15

148

Boloeil

148

Hawkesbury

17

34

30

116

Montréal

13

Chambly

10

ONTARIO

417

Alexandria

34

Monckland

40

40

Châteaugay

St-Jean   Iberville

20

Lac St-François

Salaberry-de-Valleyfield

15

138

Lac Champlain

401

St. Lawrence

Cornwall

NEW YORK

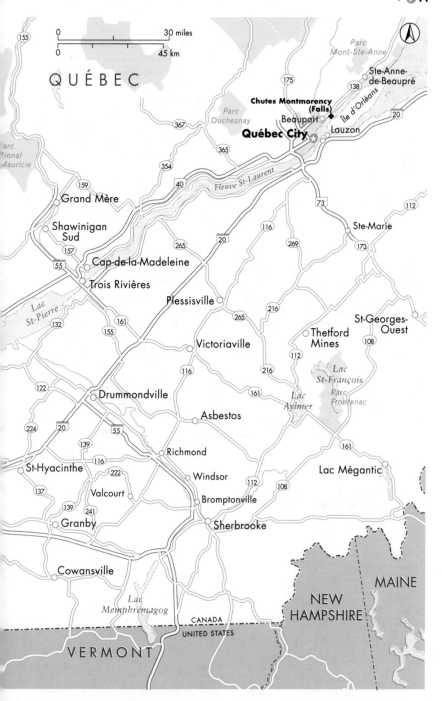

ON THE ROAD WITH FODOR'S

A trip takes you out of yourself. Concerns of life at home completely disappear, driven away by more immediate thoughts—about, say, what marvels will beguile the next day, or where you'll have dinner. That's where Fodor's comes in. We make sure that you know all your options, so that you don't miss something that's around the next bend just because you didn't know it was there. Because the best memories of your trip might well have nothing to do with what you came to Montréal and Québec City to see, we guide you to sights large and small all over the region. You might set out to tour Montréal's Olympic Park or stroll Québec City's Plains of Abraham, but back at home you find yourself unable to forget sharing coffee and pastries at a neighborhood *marché,* exploring narrow cobblestone streets, or sampling maple-syrup treats. With Fodor's at your side, serendipitous discoveries are never far away.

Our success in showing you every corner of Montréal and Québec is a credit to our extraordinary writers. Although there's no substitute for travel advice from a good friend who knows your style, our contributors are the next best thing—the kind of people you would poll for travel advice if you knew them.

Independent writer Tracey Ariel, who has called Montréal home since 1993, loves covering the city and its people for various magazines and newspapers. She's also authored three books, including hiking and cross-country skiing guides to Ontario. Tracey updated the Smart Travel Tips and the Montréal A to Z sections.

Native Montrealer Chris Barry, who writes a weekly column for the *Montreal Mirror,* has contributed to scores of publications over the years. He updated the Eastern Townships section and portions of Montréal.

A native of Ontario, freelance journalist and writer Mark Cardwell has lived in the Québec City area for the past 20 years. He travels frequently in the area, and has learned to love the people and places of this culturally diverse, naturally stunning corner of Canada.

Travel writer and screenwriter Mary Ann Simpkins has lived in France, Mexico, the United States, and other parts of Canada. In 2003 she moved from Québec City to Ottawa, enabling her to continue writing about the province and other parts of the world for numerous publications, including the *Montréal Gazette.* She is the author of *Travel Bug Canada* and co-author of *Ottawa Stories.*

Paul Waters and Julie Waters are a travel-writing team from Montréal, which they cover for Fodor's. Paul is an editorial-board member at the *Montréal Gazette;* Julie works for various trade travel magazines.

(1) Montréal

Montréal and the island on which it stands both take their name from Mont-Royal, a stubby plug of tree-covered igneous rock that rises just 330 feet above the surrounding cityscape. Although its height is unimpressive, "the mountain" forms one of Canada's finest urban parks, and its summit offers visitors a grand overview of what North America's only French-speaking metropolis has to offer. To the south are the shops, museums, and office towers of the Golden Square Mile and downtown. Beyond them, along the St. Lawrence River, are the narrow, cobbled streets of Vieux-Montréal, and still farther out are the green sanctuaries of îles Notre-Dame and Ste-Hélène. Spreading out from Mont-Royal's eastern flank are the polyglot neighborhoods of the Quartier-Latin and Plateau Mont-Royal, abuzz with restaurants, nightclubs, and cafés. In the distance, rising like some futuristic launch site, is the tower of the Olympic Stadium. Much of the city is easily accessible on foot; the rest can be reached via the métro system. The grid layout is easy to navigate, once you remember that street numbers run north from the river and that the long spine of Boulevard St-Laurent splits Montréal neatly into east and west sides.

(2) Québec City

Québec City is widely considered to be the most French city in North America; nearly 95% of the people who live here claim French as their mother tongue. The only walled city north of Mexico is split into two tiers, separated by steep rock against which are more than 25 *escaliers* (staircases). Along the banks of the St. Lawrence River is the Lower Town, or Basse-Ville, the oldest neighborhood in North America. Its time-worn streets brim with up-to-the-minute shops, charming restaurants, and art galleries, as well as touristy stores, all housed in former warehouses and residences. You can see the rooftops of the Lower Town from the Terrasse Dufferin boardwalk in Vieux-Québec's Upper Town, or Haute-Ville. The most prominent buildings of Québec City's earliest European inhabitants stand here. One often-photographed landmark is the castle-like Fairmont Le Château Frontenac, a hotel with copper-roofed towers and a commanding view of the St. Lawrence River. Many military sites—fortifications and battlements—and a number of museums and other attractions encircle the city. Beyond the town walls, old and new government buildings intermingle with the structures of a modern metropolis that grew up in the 20th century.

(3) Province of Québec

The province is huge—at 600,000 square mi (1,500,000 square km), it's nearly three times the size of France—and its staggeringly varied landscape stretches from pastoral valleys at its southern edge to arctic tundra in the far north. The Charlevoix region has valleys and plateaus, and cliffs cut by waterfalls, and mountains that brush the St. Lawrence River. The province's vast maple forests bring brilliant color to fall and sweetness to spring, when sap is boiled into syrup, a mainstay of Québecois dishes. The wildlife is as varied as the terrain: caribou, black bear, and moose live on the Gaspé Peninsula and in other parts; a massive colony of gannets summers on Île Bonaventure, off the peninsula's tip; and blue, beluga, and other whales come to feed and breed in the Saguenay River and at the mouth of its fjord. The Laurentians encompass thousands of miles of wilderness, but for many people the draw is Mont-Tremblant and its world-class slopes. And if being 3,150 feet high doesn't make you feel close enough to the heavens, you can turn your attention to the stars at the Eastern Townships' Mont-Mégantic observatory.

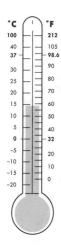

°C		°F
100		212
40		105
37		98.6
30		90
25		80
20		70
15		60
10		50
5		40
0		32
-5		20
-10		10
-15		0
-20		

Montréal and Québec City are best in summer, when the weather is warm and festivals kick in by the dozen. Nights can be chilly. The long winter is cold, snowy, and slushy. In Montréal, it's a good opportunity to explore the underground malls that run beneath the city. In Québec City, do as the locals do: bundle up and get on with your business. Winter festivals, some of the best in the world, help take the edge off the season. (Be careful of ice on sidewalks, tall buildings, bridges, and roadways, which can be quite hazardous.) Spring is short and normally chilly, while fall can be either beautifully crisp or gray, dull, and rainy.

Hilly and mountainous regions, such as the Eastern Townships and the Laurentians, tend to be colder and windier than Montréal, as befits their higher elevations.

Eastern Canada's two finest downhill-skiing destination villages are within easy driving distance of the cities (Tremblant to Montréal; Mont St-Anne to Québec City). You should wear as many layers as you can and find the best outerwear possible to fend off the sometimes brutal cold in these areas.

Climate
The following are average daily maximum and minimum temperatures for Montréal. Because of its northerly position, Québec City tends to be as much as 10°F colder, especially in winter.

🄵 Forecasts **Weather Channel Connection** ☎ 900/932–8437, 95¢ per minute from a Touch-Tone phone.

MONTRÉAL

Jan.	23F	− 5C	May	65F	18C	Sept.	68F	20C
	9F	−13C		48F	9C		53F	12C
Feb.	25F	− 4C	June	74F	23C	Oct.	57F	14C
	12F	−11C		58F	14C		43F	6C
Mar.	36F	2C	July	79F	26C	Nov.	42F	6C
	23F	− 5C		63F	17C		32F	0C
Apr.	52F	11C	Aug.	76F	24C	Dec.	27F	−3C
	36F	2C		61F	16C		16F	−9C

ON THE CALENDAR

Québec has always been able to find a reason to party. Québec City celebrates one of the world's most brutal winters with a carnival that includes a boat race across an ice-choked river. Throughout the province, the rest of the year is full of festivals celebrating jazz, international folklore, film, classical music, fireworks, comedy, and hot-air balloons. The provincial tourist board has more information about these and other festivals.

WINTER

Jan.–Feb.

La Fête des Neiges (☎ 800/797–4537 ⊕ www.fetedesneiges.com) is Winter Carnival in Montréal. It lasts about two weeks and takes place at Parc Jean Drapeau on the river, in the east end of the city.

Québec City's Carnaval de Québec (⊕ www.carnaval.qc.ca), a festival of winter-sports competitions, ice-sculpture contests, and parades, spans three weekends. The Plains of Abraham are the main stage.

Festival Montréal en Lumière (⊕ www.montrealhighlights.com), a festival of mostly classical music, takes place on Montréal's Place des Artes during the last two weeks of February.

SPRING

April

Sugaring-off parties celebrate the maple-syrup season throughout the province, but especially north and east of Montréal.

SUMMER

June

The Fringe Festival (⊕ www.montrealfringe.ca) brings world-renowned playwrights, acting troupes, dancers, and musicians to Montréal.

July

Festival International de Jazz de Montréal (☎ 514/790–1245 or 800/361–4595) draws more than 1,000 musicians from all over the world for an 11-day series.

The 11-day Québec City International Summer Festival (☎ 418/523–4540 ⊕ www.infofestival.com) offers entertainment in the streets and parks of Old Québec City.

Montréal's world-famous Juste pour Rire (Just for Laughs; ☎ 514/845–2322 ⊕ www.hahaha.com) comedy festival hosts international comics, in French and English, from the second through third weeks of July.

At Festival Orford (☎ 888/310–3665 ⊕ www3.sympatico.ca/arts.orford), international artists perform in Orford Park's music center (about an hour east of Montréal) throughout August.

The Coupe Rogers AT&T (⊕ www.rogersattcup.com) tennis tournament brings top professional players to Montréal.

August	Montréal's World Film Festival (☎ 514/848–3883 ⊕ www.ffm-montreal.org) continues to grow in popularity.
	St-Jean-sur-Richelieu's Hot Air Balloon Festival (☎ 450/347–9555 ⊕ www.montgolfieres.com) is the largest gathering of hot-air balloons in Canada.
	In early or mid-August, the Fêtes de la Nouvelle France (☎ 418/694–3319 ⊕ www.nouvellefrance.qc.ca) re-creates the days of the French regime with markets and artisans in the Old Town district of Québec City.
FALL	
September	The Québec International Film Festival (☎ 418/523–3456 ⊕ www.telegraphe.com/fifq) is screened in Québec City.
	The Gatineau Hot Air Balloon Festival (⊕ www.vielle.gatineau.qc.ca), held Labor Day weekend, brings together hot-air balloons from across Canada, the United States, and Europe.
October	Farmers' markets, arts-and-crafts fairs, and activities such as weekend hikes are part of the Festival of Colors, which celebrates autumn throughout the province of Québec.

PLEASURES & PASTIMES

Fine Food

Canadian fine dining really began in Québec, where eating in a good restaurant with a bottle of wine has long been a part of life. Montréal can claim many superb restaurants that serve both classic and innovative French cuisine. The city's varied population has also made it rich in ethnic restaurants, from delis to Asian eateries. Québec City has a narrower range of choices, but good French and Québecois fare is available. In the countryside, a number of inns provide food that can compete with any served in the cities for freshness and creativity. Hearty meat pies, pâtés, and creative uses of maple syrup are traditional throughout the province. When you're in Québec, do as the locals do and order the table d'hôte, a several-course package deal that is often cheaper and may give you a chance to sample some special dishes.

French Heritage

To visit Québec is to encounter more than 450 years of French civilization in North America. The streets of Vieux-Montréal and the Upper and Lower Towns of Québec City hold centuries-old buildings full of historical importance. Churches such as the Basilique Notre-Dame-de-Québec in Québec City, the Basilique Notre-Dame-de-Montréal in Montréal, and the Basilique Ste-Anne-de-Beaupré in Ste-Anne-de-Beaupré tell part of the story. Excellent museums, including the Musée d'Archéologie Pointe-à-Callière in Montréal and the Musée de la Civilisation in Québec City, add further insight. But history is alive in Québec: in the language, the people, and the arts. Whether you're sitting in a café, walking through a botanical garden, or just strolling the city streets, you enter a different culture.

The Great Outdoors

Montréal and Québec City are just a few hours' drive from a wilderness full of rivers, lakes, and mountains, and lovely rural areas are even closer. The Laurentian Mountains are an hour north of Montréal, and the Eastern Townships lie to the city's southeast. The Île d'Orléans, 15 minutes from Québec City, embodies the traditional lifestyle of rural Québec. The lovely villages, mountains, and waterfalls of the Charlevoix stretch along the north shore of the St. Lawrence River from Ste-Anne-de-Beaupré to the Saguenay River.

Native Canadian Art

Interest continues to grow in the highly collectible art and sculpture of the Inuit, or Eskimo. For the best price and a guarantee of authenticity, purchase Inuit and other First Nations crafts in the province where they originate. Many styles attributed to certain tribes are mass-produced for sale in galleries and shops far from their regions of origin. At the very top galleries you can be assured of getting individually crafted pieces, though the prices will be higher than in the provinces of origin. The Canadian government has registered the symbol of an igloo as a mark of a work's authenticity. Check that this government sticker or tag is attached before you make your purchase.

FODOR'S CHOICE

Fodor's Choice
★

The sights, restaurants, hotels, and other travel experiences on these pages are our editors' top picks—our Fodor's Choices. They're the best of their type in Montréal, Québec City, and the rest of the province—not to be missed and always worth your time. All the details are in the chapters that follow.

LODGING

$$$$	**Ritz-Carlton, Montréal.** The city's grandest hotel successfully blends Edwardian style with modern amenities. Also here: the careful and personal attention that the luxury chain is known for.
$$$–$$$$	**Hotel Dominion 1912, Québec City.** Modern and uncluttered, guest rooms in this former warehouse building include special design touches such as swing-out night tables. The lobby seems more like a chic living room than something you'd find in most hotels.
$$$–$$$$	**Hotel Nelligan, Montréal.** Two adjoining 1850s stone buildings on rue St-Paul make up this boutique hotel one block north of the Vieux-Port and a block south of the Basilique Notre-Dame-de-Montréal. In warm weather breakfast is served on the roof terrace.
$$$–$$$$	**Loews Hôtel Vogue, Montréal.** Behind the hotel's facade of polished rose granite and tall windows are elegant rooms with silk upholstery and lacy duvets. Bathrooms have whirlpool tubs, TVs, and phones.
$$–$$$	**Auberge du Vieux-Port, Montréal.** Tall windows and exposed beams lend charm to this inn in an 1880s building in Vieux-Montréal, overlooking the old port. Rooms have brass beds and stone or brick walls.
$$–$$$	**Auberge les Passants du Sans Soucy, Montréal.** Brass beds, stone walls, exposed beams, soft lighting, whirlpool baths, and flowers galore create a romantic mood at this rue St-Paul gem in a former warehouse.

BUDGET LODGING

$	**Aux Berges de l'Aurore, Notre-Dame-des-Bois.** The views from this five-room B&B at the foot of Mont-Mégantic are spectacular, as is the food. Many ingredients are from the inn's garden.
$	**Auberge Knowlton, Knowlton.** Although it was built in 1849, this local landmark keeps up with the times, offering Internet access and other modern amenities while retaining its country charm.

RESTAURANTS

$$$$ **Caprices de Nicolas, Montréal.** The two art nouveau–inspired rooms of this French restaurant are magnificent, but the most romantic tables are in the soaring plant-filled atrium. The food is as exquisite as the setting.

$$$–$$$$ **À la Bastille Chez Bahüaud, Québec City.** Superb sauces accompany French and other international dishes at this restaurant in an old stone house adorned with modern art. A garden provides the setting for outdoor dining.

$$$–$$$$ **L'Eau à la Bouche, Ste-Adèle.** Nouvelle cuisine meets traditional Québecois cooking at the restaurant of this Bavarian-style inn in the lower Laurentians.

$$$–$$$$ **Laurie Raphaël, Québec City.** The eclectic dishes here take classic French fare and add international and local accents for zing—roulade of caribou and duck foie gras, for example, comes with cranberry-port sauce.

$$$–$$$$ **L'Initiale, Québec City.** The eight-course *menu gastronomique* is a meal to remember, but all the French fare here is sophisticated. Gracious service enhances the experience.

$$$–$$$$ **Toqué!, Montréal.** Co-owner Normand Laprise, one of Montréal's celebrity chefs, heads a sometimes whimsical kitchen that takes its inspiration from market-fresh ingredients.

BUDGET RESTAURANTS

$–$$ **Brioche Lyonnaise, Montréal.** A butter brioche here with a bowl of steaming café au lait is one of the finest breakfasts in the city, but this quintessential Quartier Latin café also serves table d'hôte lunches and dinners.

$–$$ **Schwartz's Delicatessen, Montréal.** The smoked meat at this deli is the city's best—it almost melts in your mouth. Don't ask for a menu (there isn't one) and, unless you don't mind long lines, don't go during the prime lunch or dinner hours.

¢   **St-Viateur Bagel & Café, Montréal.** The light, crispy bagels that come out of the wood-fired brick oven here have won over the hearts, and stomachs, of many—including New York City expats.

HISTORY

Basilique Notre-Dame-de-Montréal, Montréal. The 3,800-seat neo-Gothic church has a star-studded blue vaulted ceiling, stained-glass windows from Limoges, a 7,000-pipe organ, and one of the largest bells in North America.

Basilique Ste-Anne-de-Beaupré, Ste-Anne-de-Beaupré. The monumental basilica with two granite steeples, 18 altars, 22 chapels, and more than 200 stained-glass windows draws hordes of pilgrims who come to worship Québec's patron saint.

Maison St-Gabriel, Montréal. In this stone farm structure, a rare example of 17th-century rural architecture, St. Marguerite Bourgeoys trained young orphan French girls to become the wives and mothers of New France.

Plains of Abraham, Québec City. The site of the 1759 French-British battle that decided the fate of New France is now part of a large park overlooking the St. Lawrence River.

Vieux-Québec, Québec City. The immaculately preserved old town, veined with narrow winding streets, is steeped in more than four centuries of history and French tradition.

PARKS & GARDENS

Jardin Botanique, Montréal. The second-largest botanical garden in the world has 181 acres of gardens, 10 greenhouses, one of the best bonsai collections in the West, and the biggest Ming-style garden outside Asia.

Parc Jean-Drapeau, Montréal. Stretching across two islands in the middle of the St. Lawrence River, this urban playground includes a major amusement park, a casino, flower gardens, and a beach.

Parc du Mont-Royal, Montréal. Designed by the co-creator of New York City's Central Park, these 494 acres of forest and paths in the heart of the city are a year-round escape for many city dwellers.

SMART TRAVEL TIPS

Finding out about your destination before you leave home means you won't squander time organizing everyday minutiae once you arrive. You'll be more streetwise when you hit the ground as well, better prepared to explore those aspects of Montréal and Québec City that drew you here in the first place. The organizations in this section can provide information to supplement this guide; contact them for up-to-the-minute details, and consult the A to Z sections that end each chapter for facts on the various topics as they relate to the different regions. Happy landings!

AIR TRAVEL

BOOKING

When you book, look for nonstop flights and remember that "direct" flights stop at least once. Try to avoid connecting flights, which require a change of plane. Two airlines may operate a connecting flight jointly, so ask whether your airline operates every segment of the trip; you may find that the carrier you prefer flies you only part of the way. To find more booking tips and to check prices and make online flight reservations, log on to www.fodors.com.

CARRIERS

When flying internationally, you must usually choose between a domestic carrier, the national flag carrier of the country you are visiting, and a foreign carrier from a third country. National flag carriers have the greatest number of nonstops. Domestic carriers may have better connections to your hometown and serve a greater number of gateway cities. Third-party carriers may have a price advantage.

Of the major U.S. and U.K. airlines, American, British Airways, Continental, Delta, Northwest, and US Airways serve Montréal; United flies to Montréal and Québec City.

More specifically, US Airways has six nonstop flights daily from New York's La-Guardia Airport to Montréal–&Pierre Elliott Trudeau International Airport, Montréal–Trudeau for short. Regularly scheduled flights to Montréal and Québec City are available on Air Canada and the regional feeder airlines associated with it. Air Canada has the most nonstop flights and flies to Montréal–Trudeau and Québec City's Jean Lesage International Airport from some 30 U.S. cities.

Air Canada has dominated Canada's airline industry since the end of 1999 when it took over the smaller, financially troubled Canadian Airlines. Now discount carriers such as WestJet and JetsGo have entered the fray, leaving the national airline with roughly half of the business. Competitor JetsGo also sells tickets only via its Web site. JetsGo and Zip fly only within Canada, but WestJet also flies to Orlando, New York, and Los Angeles.

Within Québec, two Native airlines offer scheduled service from Montréal to northern parts of the province. Air Creebec offers three daily flights to 10 locations; Air Inuit has one daily flight to 16 locations.

From the United Kingdom, Canadian charter line Air Transat offers flights to Montréal, though not in winter. This carrier also flies between many major Canadian cities and to Fort Lauderdale, Orlando, and some European destinations on seasonal schedules.

For regulations and for the locations of airports that allow private flights, check with the regional tourism agencies for charter companies and with the District Controller of Air Services in Québec City. Private pilots should obtain information from the Canada Map Office, which has the "Canada Flight Supplement" (lists of airports with Canada Customs services) as well as aeronautical charts.

🛪 Major Airlines **Air Canada** ☎ 888/247-2262 ⊕ www.aircanada.ca, www.flytango.com. **Air France** ☎ 800/667-2747 ⊕ www.airfrance.ca. **American Airlines** ☎ 800/433-7300 ⊕ www.aa.com. **British Airways** ☎ 800/247-9297, 0845/722-2111 in the U.K. ⊕ www.britishairways.com. **Continental** ☎ 800/525-0280 ⊕ www.continental.com. **Delta** ☎ 800/241-4141 ⊕ www.delta.com. **Northwest** ☎ 800/225-2525 ⊕ www.nwa.com. **United** ☎ 800/241-6522 ⊕ www.united.com. **US Airways** ☎ 800/428-4322 ⊕ www.usair.com.

🛪 Smaller Airlines **Air Creebec** ☎ 800/361-2965 ⊕ www.aircreebec.ca. **Air Inuit** ☎ 800/361-2965 ⊕ www.airinuit.com. **Air Transat** ☎ 877/872-6728 or 866/847-1919 ⊕ www.airtransat.com. **WestJet** ☎ 888/937-8538 ⊕ www.westjet.ca. **JetsGo** ☎ 866/448-5888 ⊕ www.jetsgo.com.

CHECK-IN & BOARDING

Always **find out your carrier's check-in policy.** Plan to arrive at the airport about two hours before your scheduled departure time for domestic flights and 2½ to 3 hours before international flights. You may need to arrive earlier if you're flying from one of the busier airports or during peak air-traffic times. To avoid delays at airport-security checkpoints, try not to wear any metal. Jewelry, belt and other buckles, steel-toe shoes, barrettes, and underwire bras are among the items that can set off detectors.

Assuming that not everyone with a ticket will show up, airlines routinely overbook planes. When everyone does, airlines ask for volunteers to give up their seats. In return, these volunteers usually get a several-hundred-dollar flight voucher, which can be used toward the purchase of another ticket, and are rebooked on the next flight out. If there are not enough volunteers, the airline must choose who will be denied boarding. The first to get bumped are passengers who checked in late and those flying on discounted tickets, so get to the gate and check in as early as possible, especially during peak periods.

Always **bring a government-issued photo I.D.** to the airport; even when it's not required, a passport is best.

U.S. Customs and Immigration maintains an office at Montréal–Trudeau airport. U.S.-bound passengers should arrive early enough to clear customs before their flight. Trudeau Airport also offers self-serve check-in and boarding passes at electronic kiosks throughout the airport. Make sure you arrive at the airport at least two hours before your flight's scheduled departure.

Security measures at Canadian airports are similar to those in the United States. Be sure you're not carrying anything that could be construed as a weapon—a Swiss

Army knife or a toy gun, for example. Arriving passengers from overseas flights might find a beagle in a green coat sniffing their luggage; he's looking for forbidden agricultural products.

CUTTING COSTS

The least expensive airfares to Montréal and Québec City are priced for round-trip travel and must usually be purchased in advance. Airlines generally allow you to change your return date for a fee as long as you do so before your scheduled departure; many airlines void the entire ticket if you fail to make changes prior to your scheduled departure. Most low-fare tickets are nonrefundable. It's smart to call a number of airlines and check the Internet; when you are quoted a good price, book it on the spot—the same fare may not be available the next day, or even the next hour. Always check different routings and look into using alternate airports. Also, price off-peak flights, which may be significantly less expensive than others. Travel agents, especially low-fare specialists (➪ Discounts & Deals), are helpful.

Consolidators are another good source. They buy tickets for scheduled flights at reduced rates from the airlines, then sell them at prices that beat the best fare available directly from the airlines. (Many also offer reduced car-rental and hotel rates.) Sometimes you can even get your money back if you need to return the ticket. Carefully read the fine print detailing penalties for changes and cancellations, purchase the ticket with a credit card, and confirm your consolidator reservation with the airline.

When you fly as a courier, you trade your checked-luggage space for a ticket deeply subsidized by a courier service. There are restrictions on when you can book and how long you can stay. Some courier companies list with membership organizations, such as the Air Courier Association and the International Association of Air Travel Couriers; these require you to become a member before you can book a flight.

Many airlines, singly or in collaboration, offer discount air passes that allow for-

eigners to travel economically in a particular country or region. These visitor passes usually must be reserved and purchased before you leave home. Information about passes often can be found on most airlines' international Web pages, which tend to be aimed at travelers from outside the carrier's home country. Also, try typing the name of the pass into a search engine, or search for "pass" within the carrier's Web site.

🛪 Consolidators **AirlineConsolidator.com** ☎ 888/468-5385 ⊕ www.airlineconsolidator.com; for international tickets. **Best Fares** ☎ 800/880-1234 or 800/576-8255 ⊕ www.bestfares.com; $59.90 annual membership. **Cheap Tickets** ☎ 800/377-1000 or 800/652-4327 ⊕ www.cheaptickets.com. **Expedia** ☎ 800/397-3342 or 404/728-8787 ⊕ www.expedia.com. **Hotwire** ☎ 866/468-9473 or 920/330-9418 ⊕ www.hotwire.com. **Now Voyager Travel** ✉ 45 W. 21st St., Suite 5A New York, NY 10010 ☎ 212/459-1616 🖷 212/243-2711 ⊕ www.nowvoyagertravel.com. **Onetravel.com** ⊕ www.onetravel.com. **Orbitz** ☎ 888/656-4546 ⊕ www.orbitz.com. **Priceline.com** ⊕ www.priceline.com. **Travelocity** ☎ 888/709-5983, 877/282-2925 in Canada, 0870/876-3876 in the U.K. ⊕ www.travelocity.com.

🛪 Courier Resources **Air Courier Association/Cheaptrips.com** ☎ 800/280-5973 or 800/282-1202 ⊕ www.aircourier.org or www.cheaptrips.com; $34 annual membership. **International Association of Air Travel Couriers** ☎ 308/632-3273 ⊕ www.courier.org; $45 annual membership. **Now Voyager Travel** ✉ 45 W. 21st St., Suite 5A, New York, NY 10010 ☎ 212/459-1616 🖷 212/243-2711 ⊕ www.nowvoyagertravel.com.

ENJOYING THE FLIGHT

State your seat preference when purchasing your ticket, and then repeat it when you confirm and when you check in. For more legroom, you can request one of the few emergency-aisle seats at check-in, if you're capable of moving obstacles comparable in weight to an airplane exit door (usually between 35 pounds and 60 pounds)—a Federal Aviation Administration requirement of passengers in these seats. Seats behind a bulkhead also offer more legroom, but they don't have under-seat storage. Don't sit in the row in front of the emergency aisle or in front of a bulkhead, where seats may not recline.

Ask the airline whether a snack or meal is served on the flight. If you have dietary concerns, request special meals when booking. These can be vegetarian, low-cholesterol, or kosher, for example. It's a good idea to pack some healthful snacks and a small (plastic) bottle of water in your carry-on bag. On long flights, try to maintain a normal routine, to help fight jet lag. At night, get some sleep. By day, eat light meals, drink water (not alcohol), and **move around the cabin** to stretch your legs. For additional jet-lag tips consult *Fodor's FYI: Travel Fit & Healthy* (available at bookstores everywhere).

None of the major airlines or charter lines permit smoking.

FLYING TIMES

Flying time (gate-to-gate) to Montréal is 1½ hours from New York, 2 hours from Chicago, 4½ hours from Dallas, 6 hours from Los Angeles, 6½ hours from London, and 22 hours from Sydney.

HOW TO COMPLAIN

If your baggage goes astray or your flight goes awry, complain right away. Most carriers require that you **file a claim immediately.** The Aviation Consumer Protection Division of the Department of Transportation publishes *Fly-Rights,* which discusses airlines and consumer issues and is available online. You can also find articles and information on mytravelrights.com, the Web site of the nonprofit Consumer Travel Rights Center.

🚩 Airline Complaints **Aviation Consumer Protection Division** ✉ U.S. Department of Transportation, Office of Aviation Enforcement and Proceedings, C-75, Room 4107, 400 7th St. SW, Washington, DC 20590 ☎ 202/366-2220 ⊕ airconsumer.ost.dot.gov. **Federal Aviation Administration Consumer Hotline** ✉ for inquiries: FAA, 800 Independence Ave. SW, Washington, DC 20591 ☎ 800/322-7873 ⊕ www.faa.gov.

Canadian Transportation Agency ✉ Air Travel Complaints Commissioner, Ottawa, ON K1A 0N9 ☎ 888/222-2592 🖷 819/953-5686 ⊕ www.cta-otc.gc.ca.

RECONFIRMING

Check the status of your flight before you leave for the airport. You can do this on your carrier's Web site, by linking to a flight-status checker (many Web booking services offer these), or by calling your carrier or travel agent. Always confirm international flights at least 72 hours ahead of the scheduled departure time.

AIRPORTS

Montréal–Pierre Elliott Trudeau International Airport (also known by its previous name, Dorval International Airport, airport code YUL) and Mirabel International Airport (YMX) serve Montréal, and the small Jean Lesage International Airport (YQB) serves Québec City. Mirabel is used for cargo flights, while Dorval handles passenger flights.

🚩 Airport Information **Aéroports de Montréal** ✉ 1100 blvd. René-Lévesque Ouest, Suite 2100, Montréal ☎ 514/394-7200 ⊕ www.admtl.com. **Aéroport de Québec** ✉ 500 rue Principale, Québec ☎ 418/640-2700 ⊕ www.aeroportdequebec.com. **Montréal-Pierre Elliott Trudeau International Airport** ✉ 975 blvd. Roméo-Vachon Nord, Dorval ☎ 514/394-7377. **Jean Lesage International Airport** ✉ 510 rue Principale, Ste-Foy ☎ 418/640-2700. **Montréal-Mirabel International Airport** ✉ 12600 rue Aérogare, Mirabel ☎ 514/394-7377.

BIKE TRAVEL

Despite Canada's harsh climate and demanding landscape, long-distance bicycle travel is very popular, especially in Québec, which has been developing the Route Verte, a 3,500-km (2,170-mi) network of trails covering the southern half of the province. Some terrain is steep and hilly, but it's always a good trip. In many areas, some of the prettiest roads have dirt or gravel surfaces, which make a hybrid bike more practical than a road bike.

Nationally, the Trans-Canada Trail—linking the Atlantic to both the Pacific and Arctic oceans—will allow bicycles along much of its length when the project is finished in the next few years. Cyclists aren't allowed on most multiple-lane, limited-access highways, but much of the Trans-Canada Highway is a two-lane blacktop with broad, paved shoulders that are widely used by bikers crossing the country. Secondary roads that see little traffic (and almost no truck traffic) are plentiful.

Bicycle rentals are readily available in all major cities, in recreational areas (the Québec Laurentians, for example), and in resort towns, usually for $10 to $25 per day.

For maps and information about bicycle routes, consult the provincial tourist information offices.

BIKES IN FLIGHT

Most airlines accommodate bikes as luggage, provided they are dismantled and boxed; check with individual airlines about packing requirements. Some airlines sell bike boxes, which are often free at bike shops, for about $20 (bike bags can be considerably more expensive). International travelers often can substitute a bike for a piece of checked luggage at no charge; otherwise, the cost is about $100. Most U.S. and Canadian airlines charge $40–$80 each way.

BOAT & FERRY TRAVEL

A fast hydrofoil, the *Dauphin,* runs from Montréal to Québec City daily from mid-May to late September. Travel time is two hours each way.

FARES & SCHEDULES

A one-way ticket on the *Dauphin* is C$49–C$89; a round-trip ticket is C$98–C$158. Children's fares (ages 2–12) are C$59 one-way and C$79 round-trip. Although the boat runs daily, the ticket office at Montréal's Quai Jacques-Cartier or Québec's Pointe à Carcy—where the boat departs—is open weekdays 10–6 from May 15 to September 26. You can also call Les Dauphins to reserve a seat.

🚢 Boat & Ferry Information **Les Dauphins du Saint-Laurent** ⊠ Quai Jacques-Cartier, Montréal ☎ 514/288–4499, 514/281–0383, or 877/648–4499 ⊠ Pointe à Carcy, Québec ☎ 418/694–2476 or 877/648–4499 ⊕ www.dauphins.ca.

BUSINESS HOURS

Business hours are fairly uniform throughout the province.

BANKS & OFFICES

Most banks in the province are open Monday through Thursday from 10 until 3 and Friday from 10 until 5 or 6. Some banks are open longer hours and on Saturday

morning. All banks are closed on national holidays. Most banks (as well as most self-serve gas stations and convenience stores) have automatic teller machines (ATMs) that are accessible around the clock.

Government offices are generally open 9–5; some close for an hour around noon. Post offices are open 8–5 weekdays and 9–noon on Saturdays. Postal outlets in city pharmacies—of which there are many in Montréal—may stay open as late as 9 PM, even on Saturdays.

GAS STATIONS

Most highway and city gas stations in the province are open daily (although there's rarely a mechanic on duty Sunday) and some are open around the clock. In small towns, gas stations are often closed on Sunday, although they may take turns staying open.

MUSEUMS & SIGHTS

Hours at museums vary, but most open at 10 or 11 and close in the evening. Some smaller museums close for lunch. Many museums are closed on Monday; some stay open late on Wednesday, often waiving admission.

The days when all churches were always open are gone; vandalism, theft, and the drop in general piety have seen to that. But the major churches in Montréal and Québec City—the Basilique Notre-Dame-de-Montréal, for example—are open daily, usually about 9–6.

PHARMACIES

Most pharmacies in Montréal and Québec City are open until 10 or 11 PM, but a few stay open around the clock. In the rest of the province, pharmacies are generally open 9–5.

SHOPS

Stores and supermarkets usually are open Monday through Saturday 9–6, although in Montréal and Québec City, supermarkets are often open 7:30 AM–9 PM and some food stores are open around the clock. Most liquor stores are closed on Sunday. Shops often stay open Thursday and Friday evenings, most malls until 9 PM. Convenience stores tend to stay open around the clock all week.

BUS TRAVEL

The bus is an essential form of transportation in Québec Province, especially if you're not driving but want to visit out-of-the-way towns that don't have airports or rail lines.

Approximately 10 private bus lines serve the province. Orléans Express is probably the most convenient, as it offers regular service between Montréal and Québec City with a fairly new fleet of clean, comfortable buses. Limocar, another bus line, serves the ski resorts of the Laurentians and Eastern Townships. Greyhound Lines and Voyageur offer interprovincial service and are timely and comfortable, if not exactly plush. Smoking isn't permitted on any buses.

CUTTING COSTS

Most bus companies offer discounts if you book in advance, usually either 7 or 14 days ahead. Discounts are also often available for kids (children ages 15 and under can travel for free on most bus lines if tickets are booked three days in advance), and for companions, who can travel free for a set price.

FARES & SCHEDULES

Bus terminals in Montréal and Québec City are usually efficient operations, with service all week and plenty of agents on hand to handle ticket sales. In villages and some small towns, the bus station is simply a counter in a local convenience store, gas station, or snack bar. Getting information on schedules beyond the local ones is sometimes difficult in these places. In rural Québec, it's a good idea to **bring along a French–English dictionary,** although most merchants and clerks can handle a simple ticket sale in English.

PAYING

In major bus terminals, most bus lines accept at least some of the major credit cards. Some smaller lines require cash or take only Visa or MasterCard. All accept travelers' checks in U.S. or Canadian currency with suitable identification, but it's advisable to exchange foreign currency (including U.S. currency) at a bank or exchange office. Be prepared to use cash to buy a ticket in really small towns.

RESERVATIONS

Most bus lines don't accept reservations for specific seats. You should plan on picking up your tickets at least 45 minutes before the bus's scheduled departure time.
Bus Information Central Bus Station ✉ 505 blvd. Maisonneuve Est Montréal ☎ 514/842-2281. **Gare du Palais Bus Station** ✉ 320 rue Abraham-Martin, Québec ☎ 418/525-3000. **Greyhound Lines** ☎ 800/231-2222, 800/661-8747 in Canada ⊕ www.greyhound.ca. **Limocar** ☎ 450/681-3111 or 866/700-8899 ⊕ www.limocar.ca. **Orléans Express** ☎ 514/395-4000 ⊕ www.orleansexpress.com. **Voyageur** ☎ 514/842-2281 ⊕ www.voyageur.com.

CAMERAS & PHOTOGRAPHY

To catch Québec at its most dramatically beautiful, consider a winter trip. City and country take on a special glamour when they're frosted with snow. The *Kodak Guide to Shooting Great Travel Pictures* (available at bookstores everywhere) is loaded with tips.
Photo Help Kodak Information Center ☎ 800/242-2424 ⊕ www.kodak.com.

EQUIPMENT PRECAUTIONS

Don't pack film or equipment in checked luggage, where it is much more susceptible to damage. X-ray machines used to view checked luggage are extremely powerful and therefore are likely to ruin your film. Try to ask for hand inspection of film, which becomes clouded after repeated exposure to airport X-ray machines, and keep videotapes and computer disks away from metal detectors. Always keep film, tape, and computer disks out of the sun. Carry an extra supply of batteries, and be prepared to turn on your camera, camcorder, or laptop to prove to airport security personnel that the device is real.

CAR RENTAL

Rates in Montréal run from about C$34 to C$50 a day for an economy car with air-conditioning and unlimited kilometers. If you prefer a manual-transmission car, check whether the rental agency of your choice offers stick shifts; many agencies in Canada don't.
Major Agencies Alamo ☎ 800/522-9696 ⊕ www.alamo.com. **Avis** ☎ 800/331-1084, 800/

879–2847 in Canada, 0870/606–0100 in the U.K., 02/9353–9000 in Australia, 09/526–2847 in New Zealand ⊕ www.avis.com. **Budget** ☎ 800/527–0700, 0870/156–5656 in the U.K. ⊕ www.budget.com. **Dollar** ☎ 800/800–6000, 0800/085–4578 in the U.K. ⊕ www.dollar.com. **Hertz** ☎ 800/654–3001, 800/263–0600 in Canada, 0870/844–8844 in the U.K., 02/9669–2444 in Australia, 09/256–8690 in New Zealand ⊕ www.hertz.com. **National Car Rental** ☎ 800/227–7368, 0870/600–6666 in the U.K. ⊕ www.nationalcar.com.

CUTTING COSTS

Weekend rates are usually better than daily rates, but you have to keep the car for at least two days. Rates are also lower if you rent by the week. Rentals at the airports near Québec City and Montréal are usually more expensive than rentals elsewhere in the area.

For a good deal, book through a travel agent who will shop around. Also, price local car-rental companies—whose prices may be lower still, although their service and maintenance may not be as good as those of major rental agencies—and research rates on the Internet. Consolidators that specialize in air travel can offer good rates on cars as well (⇨ Air Travel). Remember to ask about required deposits, cancellation penalties, and drop-off charges if you're planning to pick up the car in one city and leave it in another. If you're traveling during a holiday period, also make sure that a confirmed reservation guarantees you a car.

🚗 Local Agencies **Discount Car Rentals** ✉ Montréal ☎ 514/849–2277 or 800/263–2355 ⊕ www.discountcar.com. **Enterprise** ✉ Montréal ☎ 514/844–9794 or 800/736–8222. **Via Route** ✉ Montréal ☎ 514/521–5221 or 888/842–7688 ⊕ www.viaroute.com.

INSURANCE

When driving a rented car you are generally responsible for any damage to or loss of the vehicle. You also may be liable for any property damage or personal injury that you may cause while driving. Before you rent, see what coverage you already have under the terms of your personal auto-insurance policy and credit cards.

REQUIREMENTS & RESTRICTIONS

You must be at least 19 years old to rent a car in Québec, and some car-rental agencies don't rent to drivers under 25. Most rental companies don't allow you to drive gravel roads. Crossing into the United States is allowed. Child seats are compulsory for children ages 5 and under.

SURCHARGES

In Québec, drivers under age 25 often have to pay a surcharge of C$5 a day.

Before you pick up a car in one city and leave it in another, ask about drop-off charges or one-way service fees, which can be substantial. Also inquire about early-return policies; some rental agencies charge extra if you return the car before the time specified in your contract, while others give you a refund for the days not used. To avoid a hefty refueling fee, fill the tank just before you turn in the car, but be aware that gas stations near the rental outlet may overcharge. It's almost never a deal to buy the tank of gas that's in the car when you rent it; the understanding is that you'll return it empty, but some fuel usually remains.

CAR TRAVEL

Your driver's license may not be recognized outside your home country. International driving permits (IDPs) are available from the American and Canadian automobile associations and, in the United Kingdom, from the Automobile Association and Royal Automobile Club. These international permits, valid only in conjunction with your regular driver's license, are universally recognized; having one may save you a problem with local authorities.

Canada's highway system is excellent. It includes the Trans-Canada Highway, which uses several numbers and is the longest highway in the world—running about 8,000 km (5,000 mi) from Victoria, British Columbia, to St. John's, Newfoundland, using ferries to bridge coastal waters at each end. It passes through Montréal and Québec City.

Distances in Canada are always signed in kilometers.

FROM THE UNITED STATES

The U.S. Interstate Highway System leads directly into Canada: I–91 and I–89 from Vermont to Québec, and I–87 from New York to Québec. Many smaller highways also connect Québec with New York, Vermont, New Hampshire, and Maine.

Drivers must carry owner registration and proof of insurance coverage, which is compulsory in Canada. Québec drivers are covered by the Québec government no-fault insurance plan. Drivers from outside Québec can obtain a Canadian Non-Resident Inter-Provincial Motor Vehicle Liability Insurance Card, available from any U.S. insurance company. The card is accepted as evidence of financial responsibility in Canada, but you're not required to have one. The minimum liability in Québec is C$50,000. If you are driving a car that isn't registered in your name, carry a letter from the owner that authorizes your use of the vehicle.

🚗 Insurance Information **Insurance Bureau of Canada** ☎ 514/288-6015, 800/361-5131 in Québec ⊕ www.ibc.ca. **Société de l'assurance automobile du Québec** ☎ 514/873-7620, 418/643-7620, 800/361-7620 ⊕ www.saaq.gouv.qc.ca

EMERGENCY SERVICES

Dial 911 in an emergency. Contact CAA, the Canadian Automobile Association, in the event of a flat tire, dead battery, empty gas tank, or other car-related mishap. Automobile Association of America membership includes CAA service.

🚗 **CAA** ☎ 800/222-4357 or 514/861-7111 ⊕ www.caa-quebec.qc.ca.

GASOLINE

Gasoline is always sold in liters; 3.8 liters make a gallon. At this writing, gas prices in Canada are fluctuating considerably, ranging from C$0.84 to $C0.98 per liter (this works out to about $2.35 to $2.75 per gallon U.S.). Lead-free gas is called *sans plomb* or *ordinaire*. (Gas stations don't sell leaded gasoline.) Fuel comes in several grades, denoted in Montréal by bronze, silver, and gold colors and in other areas of the province as *reguliere* and *superieure*.

Major credit cards are widely accepted, and often you can pay at the pump. Receipts are provided if you want one—ask for a *facture*.

ROAD CONDITIONS

In Montréal and Québec City, the jumble of bicycle riders, delivery vehicles, taxis, and municipal buses can be chaotic. In the countryside at night, roads are lit at exit points from major highways but are otherwise dark. Roads in the province aren't very good—be prepared for some spine-jolting bumps and potholes, and check tire pressure once in a while. In winter, be aware of changing road conditions: Montréal streets are kept mostly clear of snow and ice, but outside the city the situation deteriorates. Locals are notorious for exceeding the speed limit, so keep an eye on your mirrors.

RULES OF THE ROAD

By law, you are required to wear seat belts even in the back seat. Infant seats also are required. Radar-detection devices are illegal in Québec; just having one in your car is illegal. Speed limits, given in kilometers, are usually within the 90–110 kph (50–68 mph) range outside the cities.

Right turns on red signals are allowed in the province, excluding the island of Montréal, where they're prohibited. Driving with a blood-alcohol content of 0.08% or higher is illegal and can earn you a stiff fine and jail time. Headlights are compulsory in inclement weather. Drivers may use handheld cell phones.

🚗 **Ministère des Transports du Québec** ☎ 888/355-0511 ⊕ www.mtq.gouv.qc.ca.

CHILDREN IN QUÉBEC

Travelers crossing the border with children should **carry identification for them** similar to that required by adults (i.e., passport or birth certificate). Children traveling with one parent or other adult should bring a letter of permission from the other parent, parents, or legal guardian. Divorced parents with shared custody rights should carry legal documents establishing their status. Persons under 18 years of age who are not accompanied by their parents should bring a letter from a parent or guardian giving them permission to travel to Canada.

If you are renting a car, don't forget to arrange for a car seat when you reserve. For general advice about traveling with children, consult *Fodor's FYI: Travel with Your Baby* (available in bookstores everywhere).

For information about fun things for families to do in Montréal, pick up *Montréal Families,* a free newspaper that's available in grocery stores, community centers, and libraries throughout Montréal.

Local Information **Montréal Families** ☎ 514/487-8881.

FLYING

If your children are two or older, ask about children's airfares. As a general rule, infants under two not occupying a seat fly at greatly reduced fares or even for free. But if you want to guarantee a seat for an infant, you have to pay full fare. Consider flying during off-peak days and times; most airlines will grant an infant a seat without a ticket if there are available seats. When booking, confirm carry-on allowances if you're traveling with infants. In general, for babies charged 10% to 50% of the adult fare you are allowed one carry-on bag and a collapsible stroller; if the flight is full, the stroller may have to be checked or you may be limited to less.

Experts agree that it's a good idea to use safety seats aloft for children weighing less than 40 pounds. Airlines set their own policies: if you use a safety seat, U.S. carriers usually require that the child be ticketed, even if he or she is young enough to ride free, because the seats must be strapped into regular seats. And even if you pay the full adult fare for the seat, it may be worth it, especially on longer trips. Do **check your airline's policy about using safety seats during takeoff and landing.** Safety seats are not allowed everywhere in the plane, so get your seat assignments as early as possible.

When reserving, request children's meals or a freestanding bassinet (not available at all airlines) if you need them. But note that bulkhead seats, where you must sit to use the bassinet, may lack an overhead bin or storage space on the floor.

LODGING

Most hotels in Canada allow children under a certain age to stay in their parents' room at no extra charge, but others charge for them as extra adults; be sure to find out the cutoff age for children's discounts.

Several hotels, particularly those within chains, offer child-friendly amenities, such as check-ins with gift packs, indoor pools, babysitting services, free and discounted meals, toy libraries, and specially designed play areas. The Mont-Sainte-Anne Famclub organizes family travel—with accommodation and activities included—to a mountain resort area about 30 minutes north of Québec City.

Best Choices **Delta Montréal** ✉ 475 av. President Kennedy, Montréal H3A 1J7 ☎ 877/286-1986 or 514/286-1986 ⊕ www.deltamontreal.com. **Delta Centre-Ville** ✉ 777 rue University, Montréal H3C 3Z7 ☎ 877/814-7706 or 514/879-1370 ⊕ www.deltahotels.com. **Fairmont The Queen Elizabeth** ✉ 900 blvd. René Lévesque Ouest, Montréal H3B 4A5 ☎ 514/861-3511 ⊕ www.fairmont.com/queenelizabeth. **Stoneham Mountain Resort** ✉ 1420 av. du Hibou, Stoneham G0A 4P0 ☎ 800/463-6888 or 418/848-2411 ⊕ www.ski-stoneham.com. **Mont-Sainte-Anne Famclub** ✉ 2000 blvd. Beaupré, Beaupré G0A 1E0 ☎ 888/827-3434 ⊕ www.famclub.net.

SIGHTS & ATTRACTIONS

Places that are especially appealing to children are indicated by a rubber-duckie icon (☺) in the margin.

CONSUMER PROTECTION

The Consumer Protection Act guarantees that merchants supply goods and services without misleading customers. The *Office de la protection du consommateur* (consumer protection office) collects, mediates, and tracks complaints; merchants with complaints against them within the last two years are listed on its Web site.

Office de la protection du consommateur (☎ 418/646-0495, 888/672-2556 in Canada) ⊕ www.opc.gouv.qc.ca).

Whether you're shopping for gifts or purchasing travel services, **pay with a major credit card** whenever possible, so you can cancel payment or get reimbursed if there's a problem (and you can provide documentation). If you're doing business with a particular company for the first time, contact your local Better Business Bureau and the attorney general's offices in your state and (for U.S. businesses) the company's home state as well. Have any complaints been filed? Finally, if you're buying a package or tour, always consider travel insurance that includes default coverage (⇨ Insurance).

⟦f⟧ BBBs Canadian Council of Better Business Bureaus ⊠ 44 Byward Market Sq., Suite 220, Ottawa, ON K1N 7A2 ☎ 613/789–5151 ⎙ 613/789–7044 ⊕ www.canadiancouncilbbb.ca. **Council of Better Business Bureaus** ⊠ 4200 Wilson Blvd., Suite 800, Arlington, VA 22203 ☎ 703/276–0100 ⎙ 703/525–8277 ⊕ www.bbb.org.

CRUISE TRAVEL

While many operators offer cruises along sections of the 3,058-km (1,900-mi) St. Lawrence River as it flows from Lake Ontario to the Gulf of St. Lawrence and then the Atlantic Ocean, only three companies offer cabin cruises. Two—Navigation Madeleine (C.T.M.A.) and Relais Nordik—offer cargo cruising between Montréal and the Iles-de-la-Madeleine and between Rimouski and Blanc-Sablon. Écomertours NordSud offers ecology-learning cruises from Carleton, in the Baie des Chaleurs, in summer and from Montréal to the Saguenay River in fall.

To learn how to plan, choose, and book a cruise-ship voyage, consult *Fodor's FYI: Plan & Enjoy Your Cruise* (available in bookstores everywhere).

⟦f⟧ Cruise Lines Écomertours Nord-Sud ⊠ 260 rue de l'Évêché Est, Rimouski ☎ 418/724–6227 or 888/724–8687 ⊕ www.ecomertours.com. **Navigation Madeleine (C.T.M.A.)** ⊠ 313 chemin du Quai C.P. 245, Cap-aux-Meules ☎ 418/986–3278 or 888/986–3278 ⊕ www.ctma.ca. **Relais Nordik** ⊠ 17 av. Lebrun, Rimouski ☎ 418/723–8787 or 800/463–0680 ⊕ www.relaisnordik.com.

CUSTOMS & DUTIES

When shopping abroad, keep receipts for all purchases. Upon reentering the country, **be ready to show customs officials what you've bought.** Pack purchases together in an easily accessible place. If you think a duty is incorrect, appeal the assessment. If you object to the way your clearance was handled, note the inspector's badge number. In either case, first ask to see a supervisor. If the problem isn't resolved, write to the appropriate authorities, beginning with the port director at your point of entry.

U.S. Customs and Immigration has preclearance services at Dorval International Airport, which serves Montréal. This allows U.S.-bound air passengers to depart their airplane directly on arrival at their U.S. destination without further inspection and delays.

IN AUSTRALIA

Australian residents who are 18 or older may bring home A$400 worth of souvenirs and gifts (including jewelry), 250 cigarettes or 250 grams of cigars or other tobacco products, and 1,125 ml of alcohol (including wine, beer, and spirits). Residents under 18 may bring back A$200 worth of goods. Members of the same family traveling together may pool their allowances. Prohibited items include meat products. Seeds, plants, and fruits need to be declared upon arrival.

⟦f⟧ Australian Customs Service ⌂ Regional Director, Box 8, Sydney, NSW 2001 ☎ 02/9213–2000 or 1300/363263, 02/9364–7222 or 1800/020–504 quarantine-inquiry line ⎙ 02/9213–4043 ⊕ www.customs.gov.au.

IN CANADA

American and British visitors may bring in, duty-free, for personal consumption 200 cigarettes; 50 cigars; 7 ounces of tobacco; and 1 bottle (1.1 liters or 40 imperial ounces) of liquor or wine or 24 355-ml (12-ounce) bottles or cans of beer. Any alcohol and tobacco products in excess of these amounts is subject to duty, provincial fees, and taxes. You can also bring in gifts up to a total value of C$750.

A deposit is sometimes required for trailers (refunded upon return).

Cats and dogs must have a certificate issued by a licensed veterinarian that clearly identifies the animal and vouches that it has been vaccinated against rabies during the preceding 36 months. Certificates aren't necessary for seeing-eye dogs. Plant material must be declared and inspected. There may be restrictions on some live plants, bulbs, and seeds. You may bring food for your own use, as long as the quantity is consistent with the duration of your visit and restrictions or prohibitions on some fruits and vegetables are observed.

Canada's firearms laws are significantly stricter than those in the United States. All handguns and semiautomatic and fully automatic weapons are prohibited and cannot be brought into the country. Sporting rifles and shotguns may be imported provided they are to be used for sporting, hunting, or competition while in Canada. All firearms must be declared to Canada Customs at the first point of entry. Failure to declare firearms will result in their seizure, and criminal charges may be made. Regulations require visitors to have a confirmed Firearms Declaration to bring any guns into Canada; a fee of C$50 applies, good for one year. For more information, contact the Canadian Firearms Centre.

🛂 **Canada Border Services Agency** ✉ 2265 St-Laurent Blvd., Ottawa, ONT K1G 4K3 ☎ 800/461-9999 in Canada, 204/983-3500, 506/636-5064 ⊕ www.cbsa-asfc.gc.ca.

Canadian Firearms Centre ☎ 800/731-4000 ⊕ www.cfc-ccaf.gc.ca.

IN NEW ZEALAND

All homeward-bound residents may bring back NZ$700 worth of souvenirs and gifts; passengers may not pool their allowances, and children can claim only the concession on goods intended for their own use. For those 17 or older, the duty-free allowance also includes 4.5 liters of wine or beer; one 1,125-ml bottle of spirits; and either 200 cigarettes, 250 grams of tobacco, 50 cigars, *or* a combination of the three up to 250 grams. Meat products,

seeds, plants, and fruits must be declared upon arrival to the Agricultural Services Department.

🛂 **New Zealand Customs** ✉ Head office: The Customhouse, 17–21 Whitmore St., Box 2218, Wellington ☎ 09/300-5399 or 0800/428-786 ⊕ www.customs. govt.nz.

IN THE U.K.

From countries outside the European Union, including Canada, you may bring home, duty-free, 200 cigarettes, 50 cigars, 100 cigarillos, or 250 grams of tobacco; 1 liter of spirits or 2 liters of fortified or sparkling wine or liqueurs; 2 liters of still table wine; 60 ml of perfume; 250 ml of toilet water; plus £145 worth of other goods, including gifts and souvenirs. Prohibited items include meat and dairy products, seeds, plants, and fruits.

🛂 **HM Customs and Excise** ✉ Portcullis House, 21 Cowbridge Rd. E, Cardiff CF11 9SS ☎ 0845/010-9000 or 0208/929-0152 advice service, 0208/929-6731 or 0208/910-3602 complaints ⊕ www.hmce. gov.uk.

IN THE U.S.

U.S. residents who have been out of the country for at least 48 hours may bring home, for personal use, $800 worth of foreign goods duty-free, as long as they haven't used the $800 allowance or any part of it in the past 30 days. This exemption may include 1 liter of alcohol (for travelers 21 and older), 200 cigarettes, and 100 non-Cuban cigars. Family members from the same household who are traveling together may pool their $800 personal exemptions. For fewer than 48 hours, the duty-free allowance drops to $200, which may include 50 cigarettes, 10 non-Cuban cigars, and 150 ml of alcohol (or 150 ml of perfume containing alcohol). The $200 allowance cannot be combined with other individuals' exemptions, and if you exceed it, the full value of all the goods will be taxed. Antiques, which U.S. Customs and Border Protection defines as objects more than 100 years old, enter duty-free, as do original works of art done entirely by hand, including paintings, drawings, and sculptures. This doesn't apply to folk art or handicrafts, which are in general dutiable.

You may also send packages home duty-free, with a limit of one parcel per addressee per day (except alcohol or tobacco products or perfume worth more than $5). You can mail up to $200 worth of goods for personal use; label the package PERSONAL USE and attach a list of its contents and their retail value. If the package contains your used personal belongings, mark it AMERICAN GOODS RETURNED to avoid paying duties. You may send up to $100 worth of goods as a gift; mark the package UNSOLICITED GIFT. Mailed items do not affect your duty-free allowance on your return.

To avoid paying duty on foreign-made high-ticket items you already own and will take on your trip, register them with Customs before you leave the country. Consider filing a Certificate of Registration for laptops, cameras, watches, and other digital devices identified with serial numbers or other permanent markings; you can keep the certificate for other trips. Otherwise, bring a sales receipt or insurance form to show that you owned the item before you left the United States.

For more about duties, restricted items, and other information about international travel, check out U.S. Customs and Border Protection's online brochure, *Know Before You Go.*

U.S. Customs and Border Protection ✉ for inquiries and equipment registration, 1300 Pennsylvania Ave. NW, Washington, DC 20229 ⊕ www.cbp.gov ☎ 877/287-8667, 202/354-1000 ✉ for complaints, Customer Satisfaction Unit, 1300 Pennsylvania Ave. NW, Room 5.2C, Washington, DC 20229.

DISABILITIES & ACCESSIBILITY

Some facilities in Canada aren't easy to use in a wheelchair—the subway system in Montréal, for example, and city buses just about everywhere. However, thanks to increased awareness and government incentive programs, most major attractions—museums, churches, theaters—are equipped with ramps and lifts to handle wheelchairs. National and provincial institutions—parks, public monuments, and government buildings—almost always are accessible.

The Canadian Paraplegic Association National Office has information about touring in Canada. Kéroul, which was founded by travelers with disabilities to promote tourism in Québec among people in similar circumstances, rates hotels and attractions, organizes trips, and lobbies for improved facilities.

To file a complaint about transportation obstacles at Canadian airports (including flights), railroads, or ferries, contact the Director, Accessible Transportation Directorate, at the Canadian Transportation Agency.

Local Resources Canadian Paraplegic Association National Office ✉ 1101 Prince of Wales Dr., Ottawa, ON K2C 3W7 ☎ 800/720-4933 or 613/723-1033 ⊕ www.canparaplegic.org. **Kéroul** ✉ Box 1000, Branch M, Montréal, QC H1V 3R2 ☎ 514/252-3104 ⊕ www.keroul.qc.ca.

RESERVATIONS

When discussing accessibility with an operator or reservations agent, ask hard questions. Are there any stairs, inside *or* out? Are there grab bars next to the toilet *and* in the shower/tub? How wide is the doorway to the room? To the bathroom? For the most extensive facilities meeting the latest legal specifications, opt for newer accommodations. If you reserve through a toll-free number, consider also calling the hotel's local number to confirm the information from the central reservations office. Get confirmation in writing when you can.

TRANSPORTATION

Complaints Aviation Consumer Protection Division (⇨ Air Travel) for airline-related problems. **Departmental Office of Civil Rights** ✉ for general inquiries, U.S. Department of Transportation, S-30, 400 7th St. SW, Room 10215, Washington, DC 20590 ☎ 202/366-4648 ☎ 202/366-9371 ⊕ www.dot.gov/ost/docr/index.htm. **Disability Rights Section** ✉ NYAV, U.S. Department of Justice, Civil Rights Division, 950 Pennsylvania Ave. NW, Washington, DC 20530 ☎ ADA information line 202/514-0301, 800/514-0301, 202/514-0383 TTY, 800/514-0383 TTY ⊕ www.ada.gov. **U.S. Department of Transportation Hotline** ☎ for disability-related air-travel problems, 800/778-4838 or 800/455-9880 TTY.

TRAVEL AGENCIES

In the United States, the Americans with Disabilities Act requires that travel firms serve the needs of all travelers. Some agencies specialize in working with people with disabilities.

▲ Travelers with Mobility Problems **Access Adventures/B. Roberts Travel** ✉ 206 Chestnut Ridge Rd., Scottsville, NY 14624 ☎ 585/889-9096 ⊕ www.brobertstravel.com ✐ dltravel@prodigy. net, run by a former physical-rehabilitation counselor. **CareVacations** ✉ No. 5, 5110-50 Ave., Leduc, Alberta, Canada, T9E 6V4 ☎ 780/986-6404 or 877/ 478-7827 🖷 780/986-8332 ⊕ www.carevacations. com, for group tours and cruise vacations. **Flying Wheels Travel** ✉ 143 W. Bridge St., Box 382, Owatonna, MN 55060 ☎ 507/451-5005 🖷 507/451-1685 ⊕ www.flyingwheelstravel.com.

DISCOUNTS & DEALS

Be a smart shopper and compare all your options before making decisions. A plane ticket bought with a promotional coupon from travel clubs, coupon books, and direct-mail offers or purchased on the Internet may not be cheaper than the least expensive fare from a discount ticket agency. And always keep in mind that what you get is just as important as what you save.

DISCOUNT RESERVATIONS

To save money, look into discount reservations services with Web sites and toll-free numbers, which use their buying power to get a better price on hotels, airline tickets (⇨ Air Travel), even car rentals. When booking a room, always **call the hotel's local toll-free number** (if one is available) rather than the central reservations number—you'll often get a better price. Always ask about special packages or corporate rates.

When shopping for the best deal on hotels and car rentals, look for guaranteed exchange rates, which protect you against a falling dollar. With your rate locked in, you won't pay more, even if the price goes up in the local currency.

▲ Airline Tickets **Air 4 Less** ☎ 800/AIR4LESS; low-fare specialist.

▲ Hotel Rooms **Accommodations Express** ☎ 800/444-7666 or 800/277-1064 ⊕ www.acex. net. **Hotels.com** ☎ 800/246-8357 ⊕ www.hotels.

com. **Quikbook** ☎ 800/789-9887 ⊕ www. quikbook.com. **Steigenberger Reservation Service** ☎ 800/223-5652 ⊕ www.srs-worldhotels. com. **Turbotrip.com** ☎ 800/473-7829 ⊕ www. turbotrip.com.

PACKAGE DEALS

Don't confuse packages and guided tours. When you buy a package, you travel on your own, just as though you had planned the trip yourself. Fly/drive packages, which combine airfare and car rental, are often a good deal. In cities, ask the local visitors bureau about hotel and local transportation packages that include tickets to major museum exhibits or other special events.

EATING & DRINKING

French-Canadian fast-food follows the same concept as American fast-food, though roasted chicken is also popular. Local chains to watch for include St-Hubert, which serves rotisserie chicken, and La Belle Province, Lafleur, and Valentine, all of which serve hamburgers, hot dogs, and fries. As an antidote, try the Montréal chain Le Commensal—it's completely vegetarian, and it's excellent.

Poutine (fries topped with gravy and cheese curds) is a wildly popular provincial specialty. In Montréal, other notable specialties include sandwiches of house-smoked brisket similar to pastrami, offered by numerous small delis, and bagels, which are quite different from those made elsewhere. In general, the restaurant scene in Montréal offers extraordinary diversity, reflecting the city's multicultural heritage.

A trip to Québec in late March or early April isn't complete without a visit to a *cabane à sucre* (sugar shack). These rustic, family-run dining halls (many close to cities) offer a look at the tradition and cuisine of French-Canadian maple-syrup producers. The multicourse meals are always concluded with the mother of all Québecois desserts, *tarte au sucre* (sugar pie). The price may include a horse-drawn sleigh ride through the maple stands before the meal.

The restaurants we list are the cream of the crop in each price category. Properties indicated by a ✕⊞ are lodging establishments whose restaurant warrants a special trip.

MEALTIMES

Unless otherwise noted, the restaurants listed in this guide are open daily for lunch and dinner.

RESERVATIONS & DRESS

Reservations are always a good idea; we mention them only when they're essential or not accepted. Book as far ahead as you can, and reconfirm as soon as you arrive. (Large parties should always call ahead to check the reservations policy.) We mention dress only when men are required to wear a jacket or a jacket and tie.

WINE, BEER & SPIRITS

Beer lovers rejoice at the selection available from highly regarded local microbreweries, such as Unibroue (Fin du Monde, U, U2), Brasseurs du Nord (Boreale), and McAuslan (Griffon, St. Ambroise). You may find these and other microbrews bottled in local supermarkets and on tap in bars. The local hard cider P. O.M. is also excellent. Caribou, a traditional concoction made from red wine, vodka (or some other liquor), spices, and, usually, maple syrup, is available at many winter events and festivals throughout the province, such as Québec City's winter carnival. Small bars may also offer the drink in season.

The province's liquor stores, SAQ, stocks a wide choice of wines and is also the only place you can buy hard liquor; most SAQ stores are open regular business hours. Supermarkets and convenience stores carry lower-end wines, but they can sell wine and beer until 11 PM all week (long after SAQ stores have closed). The minimum legal age for alcohol consumption is 19.

EMBASSIES & CONSULATES

All embassies are in Ottawa. Emergency information is given at the end of each chapter. The U.S. consulate in Montréal is open weekdays 8:30–noon; additionally it's open 2–3:30 Wednesday.

🚩 Australia **Australian High Commission** ✉ 50 O'Connor St., Suite 710, Ottawa, ONT ☎ 613/236-0841 ⊕ www.ahc-ottawa.org.

🚩 New Zealand **New Zealand High Commission** ✉ 99 Bank St., Suite 727, Ottawa, ONT ☎ 613/238-5991 ⊕ www.nzhcottawa.org.

🚩 United Kingdom **British High Commission** ✉ 80 Elgin St., Ottawa, ONT ☎ 613/237-1530 ⊕ www.britainincanada.org.

🚩 United States **U.S. Consulate General** ✉ 1155 rue St-Alexandre, Montréal, QC H27 1Z2 ☎ 514/398-9695 ✉ 2 pl. Terrasse Dufferin, behind Château Frontenac, Québec QC G1R 4T9 ☎ 418/692-2095. **U.S. Embassy** ✉ 490 Sussex Dr., Ottawa ON K1N 1G8 ☎ 613/238-5335 ⊕ www.usembassycanada.gov.

GAY & LESBIAN TRAVEL

Canada is generally a tolerant country, and same-sex couples should face few problems in major metropolitan areas. Montréal actively and avidly competes for gay visitors, and has a large, visible, and active gay and lesbian community. In Québec, same-sex couples are afforded the same rights as married heterosexual couples, which has further enhanced the reputations of both Montréal and Québec City as progressive and accepting communities.

Montréal's gay community is centered in Le Village, a cluster of bars, restaurants, boutiques, and antiques shops in the once run-down area between rues Amherst and Papineau. The annual Parade de la Fierté Gaie et Lesbienne, held the first weekend in August, is one of the city's biggest parades and ends a week of gay cultural activities. The community also holds an annual gala ball during the Black and Blue Festival, which occurs in October on Canada's Thanksgiving Day. The community supports three magazines—*Fugues, RG,* and *Gazelle.*

In Québec City, although the lesbian and gay community isn't as large as that in Montréal, a number of bed-and-breakfast and club owners cater to gay travelers. In late August the city's historic district comes alive with Fierté Québec (Pride Québec), drawing participants and spectators from near and far. Gaybek (⊕ www.gaybek.com) is an excellent on-line guide to gay and lesbian travel in Québec City.

🚩 Gay- & Lesbian-Friendly Travel Agencies **Different Roads Travel** ✉ 8383 Wilshire Blvd., Suite 520, Beverly Hills, CA 90211 ☎ 323/651-5557 or 800/

429-8747 (Ext. 14 for both) 🖷 323/651-5454
✎ lgernert@tzell.com. **Kennedy Travel** ✉ 130 W.
42nd St., Suite 401, New York, NY 10036 ☎ 212/840-
8659, 800/237-7433 🖷 212/730-2269 ⊕ www.
kennedytravel.com. **Now, Voyager** ✉ 4406 18th St.,
San Francisco, CA 94114 ☎ 415/626-1169 or 800/
255-6951 🖷 415/626-8626 ⊕ www.nowvoyager.
com. **Skylink Travel and Tour/Flying Dutchmen
Travel** ✉ 1455 N. Dutton Ave., Suite A, Santa Rosa,
CA 95401 ☎ 707/546-9888 or 800/225-5759
🖷 707/636-0951; serving lesbian travelers.

HOLIDAYS

Canadian national holidays are as follows: New Year's Day (Jan. 1), Good Friday (late March or early April), Easter Monday (the Monday following Good Friday), Victoria Day (late May), Canada Day (July 1), Labour Day (early September), Thanksgiving (mid-October), Remembrance Day (November 11), Christmas, and Boxing Day (December 26). St. Jean Baptiste Day (June 24) is a provincial holiday.

INSURANCE

The most useful travel-insurance plan is a comprehensive policy that includes coverage for trip cancellation and interruption, default, trip delay, and medical expenses (with a waiver for preexisting conditions).

Without insurance you'll lose all or most of your money if you cancel your trip, regardless of the reason. Default insurance covers you if your tour operator, airline, or cruise line goes out of business—the chances of which have been increasing. Trip-delay covers expenses that arise because of bad weather or mechanical delays. Study the fine print when comparing policies.

U.K. residents can buy a travel-insurance policy valid for most vacations taken during the year in which it's purchased (but check preexisting-condition coverage). British and Australian citizens need extra medical coverage when traveling overseas.

Always **buy travel policies directly from the insurance company**; if you buy them from a cruise line, airline, or tour operator that goes out of business you probably won't be covered for the agency or operator's default, a major risk. Before making

any purchase, review your existing health and home-owner's policies to find what they cover away from home.

🔢 Travel Insurers In the U.S.: **Access America** ✉ 2805 N. Parham Rd., Richmond, VA 23294 ☎ 800/284-8300 🖷 804/673-1491 or 800/346-9265 ⊕ www.accessamerica.com. **Travel Guard International** ✉ 1145 Clark St., Stevens Point, WI 54481 ☎ 715/345-0505 or 800/826-1300 🖷 800/955-8785 ⊕ www.travelguard.com.

🔢 Insurance Information In the U.K.: **Association of British Insurers** ✉ 51 Gresham St., London EC2V 7HQ ☎ 020/7600-3333 🖷 020/7696-8999 ⊕ www.abi.org.uk. In Canada: **RBC Insurance** ✉ 6880 Financial Dr., Mississauga, ON L5N 7Y5 ☎ 800/668-4342 or 905/816-2400 🖷 905/813-4704 ⊕ www.rbcinsurance.com. In Australia: **Insurance Council of Australia** ✉ Insurance Enquiries and Complaints, Level 12, Box 561, Collins St. W, Melbourne, VIC 8007 ☎ 1300/780808 or 03/9629-4109 🖷 03/9621-2060 ⊕ www.iecltd.com.au. In New Zealand: **Insurance Council of New Zealand** ✉ Level 7, 111-115 Customhouse Quay, Box 474, Wellington ☎ 04/472-5230 🖷 04/473-3011 ⊕ www.icnz.org.nz.

LANGUAGE

Although Canada has two official languages—English and French—the province of Québec has only one. French is the language you hear most often on the streets here; it is also the language of government, businesses, and schools. Only in Montréal, the Ottawa Valley (the area around Hull), and the Eastern Townships is English more widely spoken. Most French Canadians speak English as well, but learning a few French phrases before you go is useful. Canadian French has many distinctive words and expressions, but it's no more different from the language of France than North American English is from the language of Great Britain.

LANGUAGES FOR TRAVELERS

A phrase book and language-tape set can help get you started. *Fodor's French for Travelers* is available at bookstores everywhere.

LODGING

In Montréal and Québec City, you have a choice of luxury hotels, moderately priced modern properties, and small older hotels with perhaps fewer conveniences but more charm. Options in small towns and in the country include large, full-service resorts; small, privately owned hotels; roadside motels; and B&Bs. Even outside the cities you need to make reservations at least on the day on which you plan to pull into town.

Expect accommodations to cost more in summer than in the colder months (except for places such as ski resorts, where winter is high season). When making reservations, ask about special deals and packages. Big-city hotels that cater to business travelers often offer weekend packages, and many city hotels offer rooms at up to 50% off in winter. If you're planning to visit Montréal or Québec City or a resort area in high season, book well in advance. Also be aware of any special events or festivals that may coincide with your visit and fill every room for miles around. For resorts and lodges, remember that winter ski-season is a period of high demand, and plan accordingly.

The lodgings we list are the cream of the crop in each price category. We always list the facilities that are available, but we don't specify whether they cost extra; when pricing accommodations, always ask what's included and what costs extra. Properties are assigned price categories based on the range between their least and most expensive standard double rooms at high season (excluding holidays). Properties marked ✕☑ are lodging establishments whose restaurants warrant a special trip.

Assume that hotels operate on the European Plan (EP, with no meals) unless we specify that they use the Continental Plan (CP, with a Continental breakfast), Breakfast Plan (BP, with a full breakfast), Modified American Plan (MAP, with breakfast and dinner), or the Full American Plan (FAP, with all meals).

APARTMENT & HOUSE RENTALS

If you want a home base that's roomy enough for a family and comes with cooking facilities, consider a furnished rental. These can save you money, especially if you're traveling with a group. Home-exchange directories sometimes list rentals as well as exchanges.

The *Gazette* (⊕ www.montrealgazette. com), Montréal's English-language daily, has the best rental listings in town. *Hour* (⊕ www.hour.ca), a good weekly free paper in Montréal, also has rental listings.

🔲 International Agents **Hideaways International** ⊠ 767 Islington St., Portsmouth, NH 03801 ☎ 603/ 430-4433 or 800/843-4433 🖷 603/430-4444 ⊕ www.hideaways.com, annual membership $145.

BED & BREAKFASTS

B&Bs can be found in both the country and the cities. For assistance in booking these, contact the provincial B&B association. Be sure to check out B&B Web sites, although many are not as up-to-date as they should be. Room quality varies from house to house as well, so **ask to see a few rooms before making a choice.**

🔲 Reservation Services **Québec Provincial Association of B&Bs** ☎ 418/522-6354 ⊕ www. bbbonjourquebec.com

CAMPING

Campgrounds in Québec range from rustic woodland settings far from the nearest paved road to facility-packed open fields full of sleek motor homes next to major highways. Some of the best sites are in national and provincial parks—well cared for, well equipped, and close to plenty of nature and activity programs for both children and adults. The campgrounds in the coastal regions of Québec are particularly beautiful. Campers tend to be working- or middle-class families with a fair sprinkling of seniors, but their tastes and practices are as varied as the campsites they favor. Some see camping simply as a way to get practical, low-cost lodgings on a road trip, while other, more sedentary campers move into one campground with as much elaborate equipment as they can and set up for a long stay. Wilderness camping for hikers and canoeists is available in national and provincial parks.

HOME EXCHANGES

If you would like to exchange your home for someone else's, join a home-exchange organization, which will send you its updated listings of available exchanges for a year and will include your own listing in at least one of them. It's up to you to make specific arrangements.

🏠 Exchange Clubs **HomeLink International** 🏠 Box 47747, Tampa, FL 33647 ☎ 813/975-9825 or 800/638-3841 🖷 813/910-8144 ⊕ www.homelink. org; $110 yearly for a listing, online access, and catalog; $70 without catalog. **Intervac U.S.** ✉ 30 Corte San Fernando, Tiburon, CA 94920 ☎ 800/756-4663 🖷 415/435-7440 ⊕ www.intervacus.com; $125 yearly for a listing, online access, and a catalog; $65 without catalog.

HOSTELS
No matter what your age, you can save on lodging costs by staying at hostels. In some 4,500 locations in more than 70 countries around the world, Hostelling International (HI), the umbrella group for a number of national youth-hostel associations, offers single-sex, dorm-style beds and, at many hostels, rooms for couples and family accommodations. Membership in any HI national hostel association, open to travelers of all ages, allows you to stay in HI-affiliated hostels at member rates; one-year membership is about $28 for adults (C$35 for a two-year minimum membership in Canada, £14 in the U.K., A$52 in Australia, and NZ$40 in New Zealand); hostels charge about $10–$30 per night. Members have priority if the hostel is full; they're also eligible for discounts around the world, even on rail and bus travel in some countries.

🏠 Organizations **Hostelling International–USA** ✉ 8401 Colesville Rd., Suite 600, Silver Spring, MD 20910 ☎ 301/495-1240 🖷 301/495-6697 ⊕ www. hiusa.org. **Hostelling International–Canada** ✉ 205 Catherine St., Suite 400, Ottawa, ON K2P 1C3 ☎ 613/237-7884 or 800/663-5777 🖷 613/237-7868 ⊕ www.hihostels.ca. **YHA England and Wales** ✉ Trevelyan House, Dimple Rd., Matlock, Derbyshire DE4 3YH, U.K. ☎ 0870/870-8808, 0870/770-8868, 0162/959-2600 🖷 0870/770-6127 ⊕ www.yha.org.uk. **YHA Australia** ✉ 422 Kent St., Sydney, NSW 2001 ☎ 02/9261-1111 🖷 02/9261-1969 ⊕ www.yha.com.au. **YHA New Zealand** ✉ Level 1, Moorhouse City, 166 Moorhouse Ave., Box 436, Christchurch ☎ 03/379-9970 or 0800/278-299 🖷 03/365-4476 ⊕ www.yha.org.nz.

HOTELS
Canada doesn't have a national rating system for hotels, but Québec's tourism ministry rates the province's hotels; the stars are more a reflection of the number of facilities than of the hotel's performance. Hotels are rated zero to three stars, with zero stars representing minimal comfort and few services, and three stars being the very best. All hotels listed have private bath unless otherwise noted.

🏠 Toll-Free Numbers **Best Western** ☎ 800/528-1234 ⊕ www.bestwestern.com. **Choice** ☎ 800/424-6423 ⊕ www.choicehotels.com. **Clarion** ☎ 800/424-6423 ⊕ www.choicehotels.com. **Comfort Inn** ☎ 800/424-6423 ⊕ www.choicehotels.com. **Days Inn** ☎ 800/325-2525 ⊕ www.daysinn.com. **Hilton** ☎ 800/445-8667 ⊕ www.hilton.com. **Holiday Inn** ☎ 800/465-4329 ⊕ www.ichotelsgroup.com. **Inter-Continental** ☎ 800/327-0200 ⊕ www.ichotelsgroup.com. **Marriott** ☎ 800/228-9290 ⊕ www.marriott.com. **Omni** ☎ 800/843-6664 ⊕ www.omnihotels.com. **Quality Inn** ☎ 800/424-6423 ⊕ www.choicehotels.com. **Radisson** ☎ 800/333-3333 ⊕ www.radisson.com. **Ramada** ☎ 800/228-2828, 800/854-7854 international reservations ⊕ www.ramada.com or www.ramadahotels.com. **Renaissance Hotels & Resorts** ☎ 800/468-3571 ⊕ www.renaissancehotels.com. **Ritz-Carlton** ☎ 800/241-3333 ⊕ www.ritzcarlton.com. **Sheraton** ☎ 800/325-3535 ⊕ www.starwood.com/sheraton. **Wyndham Hotels & Resorts** ☎ 800/822-4200 ⊕ www.wyndham.com.

MAIL & SHIPPING
In Canada you can buy stamps at the post office or from vending machines in most hotel lobbies, railway stations, airports, bus terminals, many retail outlets, and some newsstands. If you're sending mail to or within Canada, **be sure to include the postal code** (a combination of six digits and letters). Note that the suite number often appears before the street number in an address, followed by a hyphen.

The postal abbreviation for Québec is QC.

POSTAL RATES
Within Canada, postcards and letters up to 30 grams cost 49 Canadian cents; between 31 grams and 50 grams, the cost is 80 Canadian cents; and between 51 grams and 100 grams, the cost is 98 Canadian cents. Letters and postcards to the United States cost 80 Canadian cents for up to 30 grams, 98 Canadian cents for between 31

and 50 grams, and C$1.60 for up to 100 grams. Prices include GST (goods and services tax).

International mail and postcards run C$1.40 for up to 30 grams, C$1.96 for 30 to 50 grams, and C$3.20 for 51 to 100 grams.

RECEIVING MAIL
Visitors may have mail sent to them c/o General Delivery in the town they are visiting, for pickup in person within 15 days, after which it is returned to the sender.

SHIPPING PARCELS
Many shops ship purchases home for you; when they do, you may avoid having to pay the steep provincial taxes. By courier, a package takes only a few days, but via regular Canada Poste mail, packages often take a week—or longer—to reach the United States. Be sure to address everything properly and wrap it securely.

MEDIA
NEWSPAPERS & MAGAZINES
*Maclean's, Walrus,*and *Saturday Night* are Canada's main general-interest magazines. All three cover arts and culture as well as politics. Canada has two national newspapers, the *National Post* and the *Globe and Mail*—both are published in Toronto and are available at newsstands in major foreign cities, especially the big weekend editions, which are published on Saturday. The arts-and-entertainment sections of both papers have advance news of major events and exhibitions across the country. Montréal's English daily newspaper is the *Montréal Gazette*; Québec's French-language daily is *Le Soleil*. For entertainment listings, try the *Montréal Mirror* (⊕ www.montrealmirror.com) or *Voir* (⊕ www.voir.ca), a French-language newspaper that publishes Montréal and Québec City editions.

RADIO & TELEVISION
U.S. television dominates Canada's airwaves. In border areas—where most Canadians live—Fox, PBS, NBC, CBS, and ABC are readily available. Canada's two major networks, the state-owned Canadian Broadcasting Corporation (CBC) and the private CTV, and the smaller Global Network broadcast a steady diet of U.S. sitcoms and dramas in prime time with only a scattering of Canadian-produced dramas and comedies. The selection of Canadian-produced current-affairs programs, however, is much wider. The CBC also has a parallel French-language network, Radio-Canada. Canadian cable subscribers have the usual vast menu of specialty channels to choose from, including the all-news outlets operated by CTV and CBC.

The CBC operates the country's only truly national radio network, in both French and English and on AM and FM. The daily schedule is rich in news, current affairs, discussion programs, and classical music.

MONEY MATTERS
Throughout this book, all prices, including those for dining and lodging establishments, are given in Canadian dollars. The price of a cup of coffee ranges from less than C$1 to C$2.50 or more, depending on how upscale or downscale the place is; beer costs C$3 to C$7 in a bar; a smoked-meat sandwich costs about C$5 to C$6; and museum admission can cost anywhere from nothing to C$15.

Prices throughout this guide are given for adults. Substantially reduced fees are almost always available for children, students, and senior citizens. For information on taxes, *see* Taxes.

ATMS
ATMs are available in most bank, trust-company, and credit-union branches across the province, as well as in most convenience stores, malls, and self-serve gas stations.

CREDIT CARDS
Throughout this guide, the following abbreviations are used: **AE,** American Express; **D,** Discover; **DC,** Diners Club; **MC,** MasterCard; and **V,** Visa.

🔌 Reporting Lost Cards **American Express** ☎ 800/528-4800. **Diners Club** ☎ 800/234-6377. **MasterCard** ☎ 800/307-7309. **Visa** ☎ 800/336-8472.

CURRENCY

U.S. dollars are accepted in much of Canada, especially in communities near the border. Traveler's checks (some are available in Canadian dollars) and major U.S. credit cards are accepted in most areas.

The units of currency in Canada are the Canadian dollar (C$) and the cent, in almost the same denominations as U.S. currency ($5, $10, $20, 1¢, 5¢, 10¢, 25¢, etc.). The $1 and $2 bill are no longer used in Canada; they have been replaced by $1 and $2 coins (known as a "loonie," because of the loon that appears on the coin, and a "toonie," respectively).

CURRENCY EXCHANGE

At this writing, the exchange rate is US$1 to C$1.34, £1 to C$2.42, €1 to C$1.61, A$1 to 99 Canadian cents, and NZ$1 to 86 Canadian cents.

For the most favorable rates, **change money through banks.** Although ATM transaction fees may be higher abroad than at home, ATM rates are excellent because they're based on wholesale rates offered only by major banks. You won't do as well at exchange booths in airports or rail and bus stations, in hotels, in restaurants, or in stores. To avoid lines at airport exchange booths, get a bit of local currency before you leave home.

🗺 Exchange Services **International Currency Express** ✉ 427 N. Camden Dr., Suite F, Beverly Hills, CA 90210 ☎ 888/278-6628 orders 🖷 310/278-6410 ⊕ www.foreignmoney.com. **Travel Ex Currency Services** ☎ 800/287-7362 orders and retail locations ⊕ www.travelex.com.

PACKING

If you plan on camping or hiking in the deep woods in summer, carry insect repellent, especially in June, which is black-fly season. Winters are snowy and cold; bring plenty of layers, including sweaters and thermal underwear, as well as boots, gloves, and a hat.

In your carry-on luggage, pack an extra pair of eyeglasses or contact lenses and enough of any medication you take to last a few days longer than the entire trip. You may also ask your doctor to write a spare prescription using the drug's generic name, as brand names may vary from country to country. In luggage to be checked, **never pack prescription drugs, valuables, or undeveloped film.** And don't forget to carry with you the addresses of offices that handle refunds of lost traveler's checks. Check *Fodor's How to Pack* (available at online retailers and bookstores everywhere) for more tips.

To avoid customs and security delays, carry medications in their original packaging. Don't pack any sharp objects in your carry-on luggage, including knives of any size or material, scissors, nail clippers, and corkscrews, or anything else that might arouse suspicion.

To avoid having your checked luggage chosen for hand inspection, don't cram bags full. The U.S. Transportation Security Administration suggests packing shoes on top and placing personal items you don't want touched in clear plastic bags.

CHECKING LUGGAGE

You're allowed to carry aboard one bag and one personal article, such as a purse or a laptop computer. Make sure what you carry on fits under your seat or in the overhead bin. Get to the gate early, so you can board as soon as possible, before the overhead bins fill up.

Baggage allowances vary by carrier, destination, and ticket class. On international flights, you're usually allowed to check two bags weighing up to 70 pounds (32 kilograms) each, although a few airlines allow checked bags of up to 88 pounds (40 kilograms) in first class. Some international carriers don't allow more than 66 pounds (30 kilograms) per bag in business class and 44 pounds (20 kilograms) in economy. On domestic flights, the limit is usually 50 to 70 pounds (23 to 32 kilograms) per bag. In general, carry-on bags shouldn't exceed 40 pounds (18 kilograms). Most airlines won't accept bags that weigh more than 100 pounds (45 kilograms) on domestic or international flights. Expect to pay a fee for baggage that exceeds weight limits. Check baggage restrictions with your carrier before you pack.

Airline liability for baggage is limited to $2,500 per person on flights within the United States. On international flights it amounts to $9.07 per pound or $20 per kilogram for checked baggage (roughly $640 per 70-pound bag), with a maximum of $634.90 per piece, and $400 per passenger for unchecked baggage. You can buy additional coverage at check-in for about $10 per $1,000 of coverage, but it often excludes a rather extensive list of items, shown on your airline ticket.

Before departure, itemize your bags' contents and their worth, and label the bags with your name, address, and phone number. (If you use your home address, cover it so potential thieves can't see it readily.) Include a label inside each bag and **pack a copy of your itinerary.** At check-in, make sure each bag is correctly tagged with the destination airport's three-letter code. Because some checked bags will be opened for hand inspection, the U.S. Transportation Security Administration recommends that you leave luggage unlocked or use the plastic locks offered at check-in. TSA screeners place an inspection notice inside searched bags, which are re-sealed with a special lock.

If your bag has been searched and contents are missing or damaged, file a claim with the TSA Consumer Response Center as soon as possible. If your bags arrive damaged or fail to arrive at all, file a written report with the airline before leaving the airport.

◪ Complaints **U.S. Transportation Security Administration Contact Center** ☎ 866/289-9673 ⊕ www.tsa.gov.

PASSPORTS & VISAS
When traveling internationally, carry your passport even if you don't need one (it's always the best form of I.D.) and **make two photocopies of the data page** (one for someone at home and another for you, carried separately from your passport). If you lose your passport, promptly call the nearest embassy or consulate and the local police.

U.S. passport applications for children under age 14 require consent from both parents or legal guardians; both parents must appear together to sign the application. If only one parent appears, he or she must submit a written statement from the other parent authorizing passport issuance for the child. A parent with sole authority must present evidence of it when applying; acceptable documentation includes the child's certified birth certificate listing only the applying parent, a court order specifically permitting this parent's travel with the child, or a death certificate for the nonapplying parent. Application forms and instructions are available on the Web site of the U.S. State Department's Bureau of Consular Affairs (⊕ travel.state.gov).

ENTERING CANADA
Citizens and legal residents of the United States don't need a passport or visa to enter Canada, but other proof of citizenship (a birth certificate) and some form of photo identification is requested. Naturalized U.S. residents should carry their naturalization certificate. Permanent residents who aren't citizens should carry their "green card." U.S. residents entering Canada from a third country must have a valid passport, naturalization certificate, or "green card."

Citizens of the United Kingdom need only a valid passport to enter Canada for stays of up to six months.

PASSPORT OFFICES
The best time to apply for a passport or to renew is in fall and winter. Before any trip, check your passport's expiration date, and, if necessary, renew it as soon as possible.

◪ Australian Citizens **Passports Australia** Australian Department of Foreign Affairs and Trade ☎ 131-232 ⊕ www.passports.gov.au.
◪ New Zealand Citizens **New Zealand Passports Office** ☎ 0800/22-5050 or 04/474-8100 ⊕ www.passports.govt.nz.
◪ U.K. Citizens **U.K. Passport Service** ☎ 0870/521-0410 ⊕ www.passport.gov.uk.

SENIOR-CITIZEN TRAVEL
To qualify for age-related discounts, mention your senior-citizen status up front when booking hotel reservations (not when checking out) and before you're

seated in restaurants (not when paying the bill). Be sure to have identification on hand. When renting a car, ask about promotional car-rental discounts, which can be cheaper than senior-citizen rates.

🎓 Educational Programs **Elderhostel** ✉ 11 Ave. de Lafayette, Boston, MA 02111-1746 ☎ 877/426-8056, 978/323-4141 international callers, 877/426-2167 TTY 🖷 877/426-2166 ⊕ www.elderhostel.org. **Interhostel** ✉ University of New Hampshire, 6 Garrison Ave., Durham, NH 03824 ☎ 603/862-1147 or 800/733-9753 🖷 603/862-1113 ⊕ www.learn. unh.edu.

SHOPPING

Montréal has some of the most varied shopping in Canada. The city owes its founding to the fur trade and is still the fur capital of Canada; it's also a good place to hunt for antiques and to buy clothes direct from manufacturers.

Some smaller regions and towns have become known for particular products. Farmers in rural Québec, who produce more than 75% of the world's supply of maple syrup, often have roadside stands where you can buy sugar, taffy, and syrup.

SMART SOUVENIRS

Québec pop and folk music is linguistically distinctive, and French-Canadian stars range from rock hunk Roch Voisine to passionate chansoniers Félix Leclerc and Gilles Vigneault. Cistercian monks in the Lac St-Jean area of northern Québec make chocolate-covered blueberries (*chocolat au bleuets* in French) in summer. They're available all over the province but vanish almost as quickly as they're made. However, you can purchase other, less-perishable blueberry products from this area year-round.

WATCH OUT

Americans should note that it is illegal for them to buy Cuban cigars in Canada and bring them home.

SPORTS & OUTDOORS

BICYCLING

Cycling is wildly popular in Montréal and throughout the province. The biking asso-

ciation Vélo Québec is a good source for information. You can rent a bicycle almost anywhere, and bike lanes and touring itineraries are common not only in Montréal but even in small towns. The Route Verte, a 3,500-km (2,170-mi) network of trails, covers the southern half of the province.

🚴 Association **Canadian Cycling Association** ✉ 702-2197 Riverside Dr., Ottawa, ON K1H 7X3 ☎ 613/248-1353 🖷 613/248-9311 ⊕ www. canadian-cycling.com. **Vélo Québec** ✉ 1251 rue Rachel Est, Montréal QC H2J 2J9 ☎ 800/567-8356 or 514/521-8356 ⊕ www.velo.qc.ca.

CANOEING & KAYAKING

The provincial tourism office can be of assistance, especially in locating an outfitter to suit your needs. You may also contact the Canadian Recreational Canoeing Association.

🚣 Association **Canadian Recreational Canoeing Association** 🖃 Box 398, Merrickville, ON K0G 1N0 ☎ 613/269-2910 or 888/252-6292 🖷 613/269-2908 ⊕ www.paddlingcanada.com.

CLIMBING/MOUNTAINEERING

🧗 Association **Alpine Club of Canada** 🖃 Box 8040, Canmore, AB T1W 2T8 ☎ 403/678-3200 🖷 403/678-3224 ⊕ www.alpineclubofcanada.ca. **Fédération Québécoise de la Montagne et de l'Escalade** ✉ 4545 av. Pierre-De Coubertin, C.P. 1000, Succursale M, Montréal, QC H1V 3R2 ☎ 866/204-3763 or 514/252-3004 ⊕ www.fqme.qc.ca.

GOLF

Locals golf fanatically in almost any weather, but the summer is short here, and most courses don't stay officially open very long; you may have trouble getting a tee time on a summer weekend as a result. Call ahead. Courses and practice ranges can be found everywhere, from mountains and lakes to the city. The Laurentians are a favorite destination of golfers in the province.

⛳ Association **Royal Canadian Golf Association** ✉ 2070 Hadwen Rd., Mississauga, ON L5K 2T3 ☎ 905/849-9700 🖷 905/845-7040 ⊕ www.rcga. org. **Québec Golf Association** ✉ 415 av. Bourke, Suite 110, Dorval QC H9S 3W9 ☎ 514/633-1088 ⊕ www.golfquebec.org.

HIKING

⛰ Association Fédération Québécoise de la Marche (Québec Walking Federation) ✉ 4545 av. Pierre-de-Coubertin, Montréal QC H1V 3R2 ☎ 514/252-3157, 866/252-2065 in Québec.

STUDENTS IN CANADA

⛰ I.D.s & Services STA Travel ✉ 109 Clarence St., Ottawa, ON K1N 5P5 ☎ 613/562-2722, 800/777-0112 24-hr service center 🖷 613/562-4569 ⊕ www.sta.com. **Travel Cuts** ✉ 187 College St., Toronto, ON M5T 1P7, Canada ☎ 416/979-2406, 866/246-9762 in Canada, 800/592-2887 in the U.S. 🖷 416/979-8167 ⊕ www.travelcuts.com ✉ Québec branch: Voyages Campus, 2085 rue Union, Montréal, QC ☎ 514/864-5995, 866/832-7564 in Québec 🖷 514/864-0932 ⊕ www.travelcuts.com.

STA Travel ✉ 10 Downing St., New York, NY 10014 ☎ 212/627-3111, 800/777-0112 24-hr service center 🖷 212/627-3387 ⊕ www.sta.com. **Travel Cuts** ✉ 187 College St., Toronto, ON M5T 1P7, Canada ☎ 800/592-2887 in the U.S., 416/979-2406 or 866/246-9762 in Canada 🖷 416/979-8167 ⊕ www.travelcuts.com.

TAXES

A goods and services tax (GST) of 7% applies on virtually every transaction in Canada except for the purchase of basic groceries. In addition to imposing the GST, Québec levies a sales tax of 6% to 12% on most items purchased in shops, at restaurants, and on hotel rooms.

Departing passengers in Montréal pay a C$17 airport-improvement fee that's included in the cost of an airline ticket.

GST REFUNDS

You can **get a GST refund** on purchases taken out of the country and on short-term accommodations of less than one month, but not on food, drink, tobacco, car or motor-home rentals, or transportation; rebate forms, which must be submitted within 60 days of leaving Canada, may be obtained from certain retailers, duty-free shops, customs officials, or from the Canada Customs and Revenue Agency. Instant cash rebates up to a maximum of C$500 are provided by some duty-free shops when you leave Canada, and, in most cases, goods that are shipped directly by the vendor to the purchaser's home aren't taxed. Refunds are

paid out in U.S. dollars for U.S. citizens, euros for E.C. citizens that use that currency, Australian dollars for Australians, New Zealand dollars for New Zealand residents, and Canadian dollars for everyone else. Always save your original receipts from stores and hotels (not just the credit-card receipts), and be sure the name and address of the establishment are shown on the receipt. Original receipts aren't returned, unless you request them. To be eligible for a refund, receipts must total at least C$200, and each receipt must show a minimum purchase of C$50.

⛰ Canada Customs and Revenue Agency ✉ Visitor Rebate Program, Summerside Tax Centre, 275 Pope Rd., Suite 104, Summerside, PE C1N 6C6 ☎ 902/432-5608, 800/668-4748 in Canada ⊕ www.ccra-adrc.gc.ca.

PROVINCIAL TAX REFUNDS

Québec offers a sales-tax rebate system similar to the federal one. For provincial tax refunds, call the provincial toll-free visitor information lines for details (⇨ Visitor Information). Most provinces don't tax goods shipped directly by the vendor to the visitor's home address.

TIME

Montréal and Québec City are both in the Eastern Standard Time zone. Los Angeles is three hours behind local time and Chicago is one hour behind. Sydney is 14 hours ahead; London is five hours ahead.

TIPPING

Tips and service charges aren't usually added to a bill in Canada. In general, tip 15% of the total bill. This goes for waiters and waitresses, barbers and hairdressers, and taxi drivers. Porters and doormen should get about C$2 a bag. For maid service, leave at least C$2 per person a day (C$3 to C$5 in luxury hotels).

TOURS & PACKAGES

Because everything is prearranged on a prepackaged tour or independent vacation, you spend less time planning—and often get it all at a good price.

BOOKING WITH AN AGENT

Travel agents are excellent resources. But it's a good idea to collect brochures from several agencies, as some agents' suggestions may be influenced by relationships with tour and package firms that reward them for volume sales. If you have a special interest, find an agent with expertise in that area; the American Society of Travel Agents (ASTA; ⇨ Travel Agencies) has a database of specialists worldwide. You can log on to the group's Web site to find an ASTA travel agent in your neighborhood.

Make sure your travel agent knows the accommodations and other services of the place being recommended. Ask about the hotel's location, room size, beds, and whether it has a pool, room service, or programs for children, if you care about these. Has your agent been there in person or sent others whom you can contact?

Do some homework on your own, too: local tourism boards can provide information about lesser-known and small-niche operators, some of which may sell only direct.

BUYER BEWARE

Each year consumers are stranded or lose their money when tour operators—even large ones with excellent reputations—go out of business. So check out the operator. Ask several travel agents about its reputation, and try to **book with a company that has a consumer-protection program.** (Look for information in the company's brochure.) In the United States, members of the United States Tour Operators Association are required to set aside funds ($1 million) to help eligible customers cover payments and travel arrangements in the event that the company defaults. It's also a good idea to choose a company that participates in the American Society of Travel Agents' Tour Operator Program; ASTA will act as mediator in any disputes between you and your tour operator.

Remember that the more your package or tour includes, the better you can predict the ultimate cost of your vacation. Make sure you know exactly what is covered, and beware of hidden costs. Are taxes, tips, and transfers included? Entertainment and excursions? These can add up.

🖪 Tour-Operator Recommendations **American Society of Travel Agents** (⇨ Travel Agencies). **National Tour Association** (NTA) ✉ 546 E. Main St., Lexington, KY 40508 ☎ 859/226-4444 or 800/682-8886 🖷 859/226-4404 ⊕ www.ntaonline.com. **United States Tour Operators Association** (USTOA) ✉ 275 Madison Ave., Suite 2014, New York, NY 10016 ☎ 212/599-6599 🖷 212/599-6744 ⊕ www.ustoa.com.

THEME TRIPS

The companies listed below offer multiday tours in Canada. Additional local or regionally based companies that have different-length trips with these themes are listed in each chapter, either with information about the town or in the A to Z section that concludes the chapter.

🖪 Adventure **Gorp Travel** ✉ 6707 Winchester Circle, Suite 101, Boulder, CO 80301 ☎ 303/516-1153 or 877/440-4677 🖷 303/635-0658 ⊕ www.gorptravel.com.

🖪 Bicycling **Backroads** ✉ 801 Cedar St., Berkeley, CA 94710-1800 ☎ 510/527-1555 or 800/462-2848 🖷 510/527-1444 ⊕ www.backroads.com. **VBT** ✉ 614 Monkton Rd., Bristol, VT 05443 ☎ 800/245-3868 or 802/453-4819 🖷 802/453-4806 ⊕ www.vbt.com. **Les Voyages du Tour de l'Île** ✉ 1251 rue Rachel Est, Montréal, QC H2J 2J9 ☎ 514/521-8356 or 800/567-8356 in summer only 🖷 514/512-5711 ⊕ www.velo.qc.ca.

🖪 Walking/Hiking **New England Hiking Holidays** 🖃 Box 1648, North Conway, NH 03860 ☎ 603/356-9696 or 800/869-0949 in the U.S. ⊕ www.nehikingholidays.com.

TRAIN TRAVEL

Amtrak has daily service from New York City's Penn Station to Montréal, although the train sometimes arrives too late to make any connecting trains that evening. Connections are available, often the next day, to Canadian rail line VIA Rail's Canadian routes. The ride takes up to 10 hours, and one-way tickets cost $55 to $68. VIA Rail trains run from Montréal to Québec City often, and take three hours. Smoking isn't allowed on these trains.

CUTTING COSTS

The 30-day North American RailPass, offered by Amtrak and VIA Rail, allows unlimited coach-economy travel in the United States and Canada. You can either indicate your itinerary when purchasing the pass or confirm it as you travel. The cost is $1,000 from early June to mid-October, $711 at other times. VIA Rail also offers a Canrail pass (for travel within Canada) and a Corridor Pass (for travel anywhere between Windsor, Ontario and Québec City. Senior citizens (60 and older), children (18 and under), and students are entitled to an additional 10% discount off all rates.

FARES & SCHEDULES

🚆 Train Information **Amtrak** ☎ 800/872-7245 ⊕ www.amtrak.com. **VIA Rail Canada** ☎ 888/842-7245 or 514/989-2626 ⊕ www.viarail.ca.

TRANSPORTATION AROUND QUÉBEC

A car allows you to explore the province fully. If you're traveling only to Montréal or Québec City, however, a car isn't necessary. Buses can transport you between cities and towns, but they make many stops. Train service is efficient but it doesn't go everywhere in the province and it's expensive, as is short-hop air service.

TRAVEL AGENCIES

A good travel agent puts your needs first. Look for an agency that has been in business at least five years, emphasizes customer service, and has someone on staff who specializes in your destination. In addition, **make sure the agency belongs to a professional trade organization.** The American Society of Travel Agents (ASTA)—the largest and most influential in the field with more than 20,000 members in some 140 countries—maintains and enforces a strict code of ethics and will step in to help mediate any agent-client disputes involving ASTA members if necessary. ASTA (whose motto is "Without a travel agent, you're on your own") also maintains a Web site that includes a directory of agents. (If a travel agency is also acting as your tour operator, *see* Buyer Beware *in* Tours & Packages.)

In Québec, all travel agencies have to pay a bond to obtain a permit from the *Office de la protection du consommateur* (consumer protection office), which in turn protects travelers if they become stranded.

🚆 Local Agent Referrals **American Society of Travel Agents** (ASTA) ✉ 1101 King St., Suite 200, Alexandria, VA 22314 ☎ 703/739-2782 or 800/965-2782 24-hr hotline 🖷 703/684-8319 ⊕ www.astanet.com. **Association of British Travel Agents** ✉ 68-71 Newman St., London W1T 3AH ☎ 020/7637-2444 🖷 020/7637-0713 ⊕ www.abta.com. **Association of Canadian Travel Agencies** ✉ 130 Albert St., Suite 1705, Ottawa, ON K1P 5G4 ☎ 613/237-3657 🖷 613/237-7052 ⊕ www.acta.ca. **Australian Federation of Travel Agents** ✉ Level 3, 309 Pitt St., Sydney, NSW 2000 ☎ 02/9264-3299 or 1300/363-416 🖷 02/9264-1085 ⊕ www.afta.com.au. **Travel Agents' Association of New Zealand** ✉ Level 5, Tourism and Travel House, 79 Boulcott St., Box 1888, Wellington, 6001 ☎ 04/499-0104 🖷 04/499-0786 ⊕ www.taanz.org.nz.

VISITOR INFORMATION

Learn more about foreign destinations by checking government-issued travel advisories and country information. For a broader picture, consider information from more than one country.

🚆 Tourist Information **Canadian Tourism Commission** ✉ 55 Metcalfe St., Suite 600, Ottawa ON K1P 6L5 ☎ 613/946-1000 ⊕ www.travelcanada.ca. **Infotourisme Québec** ✉ 1255 rue Peel, Bureau 400, Montréal, H3B 4V4 ☎ 877/266-5687 or 514/873-2015 ⊕ www.bonjourquebec.com.

🚆 In the U.K. **Destination Québec** ✉ Aurora Marketing Ltd., Suite 11-16, 35-37 Grosvenor Gardens House, London SW1 W0BS ☎ 020/7233-8011. **Visit Canada Center** ✉ Box 170, Ashford, Kent TN24 0ZX ☎ 0906/871-5000, 60p per minute ⊕ www.travelcanada.ca.

🚆 Government Advisories **U.K. Foreign and Commonwealth Office** ✉ Travel Advice Unit, Consular Division, Old Admiralty Building, London SW1A 2PA ☎ 0870/606-0290 or 020/7008-1500 ⊕ www.fco.gov.uk/travel. **Australian Department of Foreign Affairs and Trade** ☎ 300/139-281 travel advice, 02/

6261-1299 Consular Travel Advice Faxback Service ⊕ www.dfat.gov.au. **New Zealand Ministry of Foreign Affairs and Trade** ☎ 04/439-8000 ⊕ www.mft.govt.nz.

WEB SITES

Do check out the World Wide Web when planning your trip. You'll find everything from weather forecasts to virtual tours of famous cities. Be sure to visit Fodors.com (⊕ www.fodors.com), a complete travel-planning site. You can research prices and book plane tickets, hotel rooms, rental cars, vacation packages, and more. In addition, you can post your pressing questions in the Travel Talk section. Other planning tools include a currency converter and weather reports, and there are loads of links to travel resources.

MONTRÉAL

1

HEAR THE ROAR OF 7,000 PIPES
At the organ mass at the Basilique
Notre-Dame-de-Montréal ⇨*p.12*

RELAX WITH A CAFÉ AU LAIT
At the Brioche Lyonnaise ⇨*p.54*

BRING HOME A SALAMI
From Schwartz's Delicatessen ⇨*p.56*

SPLURGE ON A ROMANTIC MEAL
In the soating atrium at Caprices
de Nicolas ⇨*p.49*

SEE WHERE A SAINT DID HER WORK
In the Maison St-Gabriel ⇨*p.17*

STRIKE A WORLDLY POSE
At the Loews Hôtel Vogue bar ⇨*p.63*

GET A BIRD'S-EYE VIEW
From atop Mont-Royal ⇨*p.38*

WALK BENEATH THE CITY
At the Musée d'Archéologie et d'Histoire
Pointe-à-Callière ⇨*p.18*

By Paul and
Julie Waters

CANADA'S MOST ROMANTIC METROPOLIS, Montréal is an island city
that seems to favor grace and elegance over order and even prosperity,
a city full of music, art, and joie de vivre. In some ways it resembles Vi-
enna—past its peak of power and glory, perhaps, but still a vibrant and
beautiful place full of memories, dreams, and festivals.

That's not to say Montréal is ready to fade away. It may not be so young
anymore, but it remains Québec's largest city and an important port and
financial center. Its office towers are full of young Québecois entrepreneurs ready and eager to take on the world. The city's four universities—two English and two French—and a host of junior colleges
add to this zest. (A 1999 study by local McGill University showed that
Montréal's population had the highest proportion of students of any
city in North America—4.38 per hundred, just a whisker ahead of
Boston's 4.37.)

Montréal is the only French-speaking metropolis in North America and
the second-largest French-speaking city in the Western world, but it's
a tolerant place that over the years has made room for millions of immigrants who speak dozens of languages. About 14% of the 3.3 million people who live in the metropolitan area claim English as their
mother tongue, and another 19% claim a language that's neither English nor French.

The city's grace, however, has been sorely tested. Since 1976, Montréal
has twice endured the election of a separatist provincial government, a
law banning all languages but French on virtually all public signs and
billboards, and three referenda on the future of Québec and Canada—
the last the cliffhanger of 1995, in which just 50.58% of the population voted to remain part of Canada. Montréal, where most of the
province's Anglophones and immigrants live, bucked the separatist
trend and voted nearly 70% against independence.

The drama has since cooled, and in 2003 the province elected the fed-
eralist Liberals to power. Indeed, Montréal has emerged stronger and
more optimistic. And why not? Founded by the French, conquered by
the British, and occupied by the Americans, it's a city that's used to tur-
moil. Montréal has a long history of reconciling contradictions.

It remains a city of contrasts. The glass office tower of La Maison des
Coopérants, for example, soars above a Gothic-style Anglican cathedral
that sits gracefully in its shadow. The neo-Gothic facade of the Basilique
Notre-Dame-de-Montréal glares across Place d'Armes at the pagan
temple that serves as the head office of the Bank of Montréal. And while
pilgrims still crawl up the steps of the Oratoire St-Joseph on one side
of Mont-Royal, thousands of their fellow Catholics line up to get into
the Casino de Montréal on the other side—not necessarily what the earnest
French settlers who founded Montréal envisioned when they landed on
the island in May 1642.

Those 54 pious men and women under the leadership of Paul de Chomedey,
sieur de Maisonneuve, and Jeanne Mance, a French noblewoman, hoped
to create a new Christian society. They named their settlement Ville-Marie

Getting a real feel for this bilingual, multicultural city takes some time. An ideal stay is seven days, but even three days of walking and soaking up the atmosphere is enough time to visit Mont-Royal, explore Vieux-Montréal, do some shopping, and perhaps visit the Parc Olympique. It also includes enough nights for an evening of bar-hopping on rue St-Denis or rue Crescent and another for a long, luxurious dinner at one of the city's excellent restaurants.

If you have 3 days

Any visit to Montréal should start with the peak of Mont-Royal, the city's most enduring symbol. Afterward wander down to avenue des Pins and then through McGill University to downtown. Make an effort to stop at the Musée des Beaux-Arts de Montréal and St. Patrick's Basilica. On Day 2, explore Vieux-Montréal, with special emphasis on the Basilique Notre-Dame-de-Montréal and the Musée d'Archéologie Pointe-à-Callière. On Day 3 you can either visit the Parc Olympique (recommended for children) or stroll through the Quartier Latin.

If you have 5 days

Start with a visit to Parc du Mont-Royal. After viewing the city from the Chalet du Mont-Royal, visit the Oratoire St-Joseph. You should still have enough time to visit the Musée des Beaux-Arts before dinner. On Day 2, get in some shopping as you explore downtown, with perhaps a visit to the Centre Canadien d'Architecture. Spend all of Day 3 in Vieux-Montréal, and on Day 4 stroll through the Quartier Latin. On Day 5, visit the Parc Olympique and then do one of three things: visit the islands, take a ride on the Lachine Rapids, or revisit some of the sights you missed in Vieux-Montréal or downtown.

If you have 7 days

A week gives you enough time for the five-day itinerary, above, while expanding your Vieux-Montréal explorations to two days and adding a shopping spree on rue Chabanel and a visit to the Casino de Montréal.

---

in honor of the Blessed Virgin, and set out to convert the native people. The heroism of Jeanne Mance and Marguerite Bourgeoys, who came 11 years later, marked those early years. Mance established the Hôpital Hôtel-Dieu de St-Joseph, still one of the city's major hospitals. In 1659 she invited members of a French order of nuns to help her in her efforts. That order, the Religieuses Hospitalières de St-Joseph, now has its motherhouse in Montréal and is one of the oldest groups of nuns in the Americas. Marguerite Bourgeoys, with Mance's help, established the colony's first school and taught both French and native children how to read and write. Bourgeoys also founded the Congrégation de Notre Dame, a teaching order that still has schools in Montréal, elsewhere in Canada, and around the world. Canonized by the Roman Catholic Church in 1982, she became Canada's first female saint.

Piety wasn't Ville-Marie's only raison d'être, however. At the confluence of two major transportation routes—the St. Lawrence and Ottawa rivers—the settlement soon emerged as the leading center for the lucrative trade in beaver pelts that underpinned the whole economy of New France. The beaver's dense underfur was used to make the felt hats that were a staple of European fashion for a century. The fur-induced prosperity led to the development of other domestic industries, including iron smelting, farming, quarrying, and some mining. Through it all, the city's religious roots were never forgotten. Until 1854, long after the French lost possession of the city, the island of Montréal remained the property of the Sulpicians, an aristocratic association of French priests. The Sulpicians were initially responsible for administering the colony and for recruiting colonists. They still run the Basilique Notre-Dame-de-Montréal and train priests for the Roman Catholic archdiocese.

The French regime in Canada ended with the Seven Years' War—what Americans call the French and Indian War. British troops took Québec City in 1759, and Montréal fell less than a year later. The Treaty of Paris ceded all of New France (the French colonies in North America) to Britain in 1763, and soon English and Scottish settlers poured into Montréal to take advantage of the city's geography and economic potential. By 1832, Montréal was a leading colonial capital of business, finance, and transportation and had grown far beyond the walls of the old settlement. Much of that business and financial leadership has since moved to Toronto, the upstream rival Montrealers love to hate.

EXPLORING MONTRÉAL

The Île de Montréal (Island of Montréal) sits in the St. Lawrence River and is 51 km (32 mi) long and 14 km (9 mi) wide. The island takes its name from 764-foot-high Mont-Royal, which provides the only rise in the landscape and which is known by residents simply as "the mountain." The 24 suburbs on the island were absorbed into the city of Montréal in 2002, forming one megacity and dismaying many suburbanites: over half of the 24 suburbs later voted to "demerge." A belt of off-island suburbs is on the south shore of the St. Lawrence, and just to the north across the narrow Rivière des Prairies, on an island of its own, sits Laval, a suburb that's now the second-largest city in the province.

The countryside is never far away. The pastoral Eastern Townships, first settled by Loyalists fleeing the American Revolution, are less than an hour's drive away, and the Laurentians, an all-season playground full of lakes and ski hills, are even closer.

For a good overview of the city, head for the lookout at the Chalet du Mont-Royal in the Parc du Mont-Royal. You can drive most of the way, park, and walk ½ km (¼ mi), or hike all the way up from chemin de la Côte-des-Neiges or avenue des Pins. Look directly out—southeast—from the semicircular lookout to see, at the foot of the hill, the McGill University campus and, surrounding it, the skyscrapers of downtown Montréal. Just beyond, along the bank of the river, are the stone houses of Vieux-Montréal. Hugging the south shore on the other side of the river are Îles Ste-Hélène and Notre-Dame, sites of La Ronde amusement park, the Biosphère, and the Casino de Montréal; acres of parkland; and

Faith & History

Reminders of the city's long history are found everywhere, including in its churches. Some buildings in Vieux-Montréal (Old Montréal) date to the 17th century. Other parts of the city are full of Victorian architecture. Institutions such as the Musée McCord de l'Histoire Canadienne, the Musée d'Archéologie Pointe-à-Callière, and the Stewart Museum in the Old Fort on Île Ste-Hélène attest to the city's fascination with its past.

1

Montréal's two most popular attractions are the oratory dedicated to St. Joseph on the north side of Mont-Royal and the Basilique Notre-Dame-de-Montréal, dedicated to his wife, in Vieux-Montréal. These are just two of dozens of churches built in the days when the Québecois were among the most devout Roman Catholics. Other gems include St. Patrick's Basilica and the Chapelle Notre-Dame-de-Lourdes. The parish churches in some poor neighborhoods can be as grand as some cathedrals.

Nightlife

Montréal's reputation as a place to visit for a night on the town dates at least to Prohibition days, when hordes of Americans would flood the city every weekend to eat, drink, and be merry (and not necessarily in that order). African-American jazz musicians and singers particularly loved the place because they could stay, dine, and imbibe where they wanted, free of most of the discriminatory restrictions they faced back home. Dozens of dance and jazz clubs and bistros line downtown streets, and the city has hundreds of bars where you can argue about sports, politics, and religion until the wee hours of the morning. Much of the action takes place along rue St-Denis and adjacent streets in the eastern part of the city or on rues Bishop, Crescent, and de la Montagne in the downtown area. The scene is constantly shifting; last year's hot spot can quickly become this year's has-been. The best and easiest way to figure out what's in is to stroll along rue St-Denis or rue Bishop at about 10:30 PM and look for the place with the longest line and the rudest doorman.

Shopping

Thanks to the development of the Cité Souterrain (Underground City), shopping is a year-round sport in Montréal. Subterranean passageways and the Métro link a vast complex that includes two major department stores, at least a dozen huge shopping malls, and more than 1,000 boutiques. Antiques, hand-crafted jewelry, avant-garde fashions, vintage clothing, leather goods, sleek home furnishings—the variety of goods keeps things interesting above and below ground. Add to this Montréal's status as one of the fur capitals of the world and it's easy to see why the city is a shopping destination. For Americans there's the added bonus of the U.S. dollar's continued strength against Canadian currency.

---

the Lac de Î'le Notre-Dame public beach—all popular excursions. To the east are rue St-Denis and the Quartier Latin, with its rows of French and ethnic restaurants, bistros, chess hangouts, designer boutiques, antiques shops, and art galleries. Even farther east you can see the flying-saucer-shape Olympic Stadium and its leaning tower.

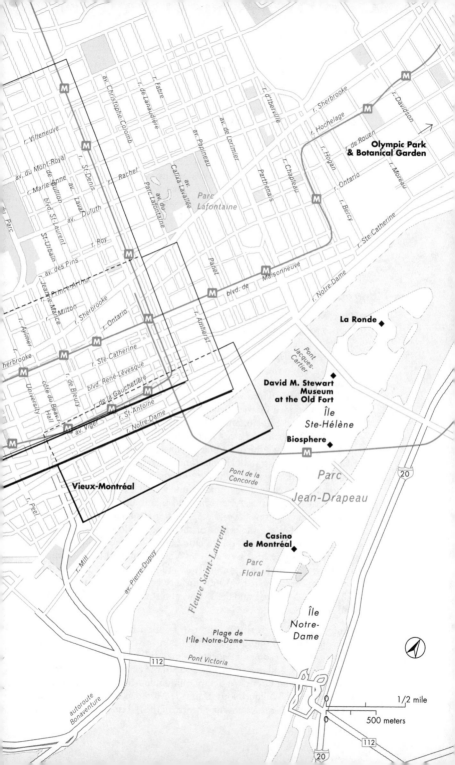

If you're planning to visit several museums, look into the city's museum pass (available at museums and Centre Info-Touriste).

Numbers in the text correspond to numbers in the margin and on the chapter's maps.

Getting Your Bearings

Montréal is easy to explore. Streets, subways, and bus lines are clearly marked. The city is divided by a grid of streets roughly aligned east–west and north–south. (Montréal takes its directions from the flow of the river rather than the compass, so this grid is tilted about 40 degrees off—to the left of—true north, meaning that west is actually southwest and so on.) North–south street numbers begin at the St. Lawrence River and increase as you head north; east–west street numbers begin at boulevard St-Laurent, which divides Montréal into east and west halves. The city is not so large that seasoned walkers can't see all the districts around the base of Mont-Royal on foot. Nearly everything else is easily accessible by Montréal's clean and quiet bus and Métro (subway) system.

Vieux-Montréal

When Montréal's first European settlers arrived by river in 1642, they stopped to build their houses just below the St. Lawrence River's treacherous Lachine Rapids that blocked the way upstream. They picked a site near a former Iroquois settlement on the bank of the river nearest Mont-Royal. In the decades after the founding, Montréal consisted of a handful of wood houses clustered around a pair of stone buildings, all flimsily fortified by a wood stockade. For almost three centuries this district—bounded by rues Berri and McGill on the east and west, rue St-Jacques on the north, and the river to the south—was the financial and political heart of the city. Government buildings, the largest church, the stock exchange, the main market, and the port were here. The narrow but relatively straight cobblestone streets were lined with solid, occasionally elegant houses, office buildings, and warehouses—all made of stone. In the early days a thick stone wall with four gates protected the city against Native Americans and marauding European powers. Montréal quickly grew beyond the bounds of its fortifications, however, and by World War I the center of the city was closer to Mont-Royal. Dominion Square (now Square Dorchester) became the new heart of Montréal. For the next two decades Vieux-Montréal (Old Montréal), as it became known, was gradually abandoned, the warehouses and offices emptied. In the early 1960s the city began studying ways to revitalize Vieux-Montréal, and the area went through a period of renovations and restorations.

Today Vieux-Montréal is a center of cultural life and municipal government. Most of the summer activities revolve around Place Jacques-Cartier, which becomes a pedestrian mall full of street performers and outdoor cafés, and the Vieux-Port, one of the city's most popular recreation spots. The Orchestre Symphonique de Montréal performs summer concerts at Basilique Notre-Dame-de-Montréal, and English-language plays are staged in the Centaur Theatre in the old stock exchange building. This district has museums devoted to history, religion, and the arts. It also has a growing number of boutique hotels.

Take the Métro to the Square-Victoria station and follow the signs to the rue St-Antoine exit. After emerging via a genuine Parisian métro entrance, you are on **Square Victoria ❶** ⌐, a two-block-long strip of trees and grass dominated by a bronze statue of the Queen herself. Cross rue St-Antoine, turn left and cross rue McGill and walk south to No. 747, the entrance to the **Centre de Commerce Mondial de Montréal ❷**, one of the city's more appealing enclosed spaces, with a fountain and frequent art exhibits. Exit on the north side of the complex onto rue St-Antoine and turn right. The grassy park across the street is **Place Jean-Paul Riopelle ❸**, named for one of the city's most important modern artists. The building with the multicolor translucent plastic panels just to the east is the Palais des Congrès, a 1½-million-square-foot convention center that sprawls across the Ville Marie Expressway and fills six city blocks. Turn right on rue St-Pierre, walk south to **rue St-Jacques.** The pale-yellow stone building with the third-story columns to the right, on the southwest corner, is the former headquarters of the **Royal Bank of Canada ❹**. It remains a bank branch. Walking east, you see the Victorian office buildings of the country's former financial center. The area can seem deserted on weekends, when the business and legal offices close down, but things get livelier closer to the waterfront.

Walk the few blocks to **Place d'Armes ❺**, a square that was the site of battles with the Iroquois in the 1600s and later became the center of Montréal's Haute-Ville, or Upper Town. Horse-drawn calèches are available at the south end of the square; on the north side is the **Bank of Montréal ❻**, a domed, temple-like building with Corinthian columns. The **Basilique Notre-Dame-de-Montréal ❼**, one of the most beautiful churches in North America, dominates the south end of Place d'Armes. The low, more retiring stone building behind a wall to the west of the basilica is the 17th-century **Vieux Séminaire ❽**, Montréal's oldest building. Unlike the basilica, it is not open to the public. To the east of the basilica is **rue St-Sulpice,** one of the first streets in Montréal, and catercorner from it stands the art deco Aldred Building, the first building in Montréal to exceed 10 stories. Next to that is a nine-story red-stone tower built in 1888 by a New York life-insurance company. One block farther east on rue Notre-Dame, just past boulevard St-Laurent and on the left, rises the black-glass-sheathed 1971 **Palais de Justice ❾**, the courthouse. The large domed building at 155 rue Notre-Dame Est is the mid-19th-century **Vieux Palais de Justice ❿**. The imposing Beaux Arts building across the street with the stately columns and grand bronze doors is the **Cour d'Appel du Québec ⓫**. The Vieux Palais de Justice abuts the small **Place Vauquelin ⓬**, named after an 18th-century French naval hero. North of this square is **Champ-de-Mars ⓭**, a former military parade ground and now a public park crisscrossed by archaeologists' trenches. The ornate building on the east side of Place Vauquelin is the Second Empire–style **Hôtel de Ville ⓮**, or City Hall, built in 1878.

The castle-like structure right across rue Notre-Dame from the Hôtel de Ville is **Musée du Château Ramezay ⓯**, built as the residence of the

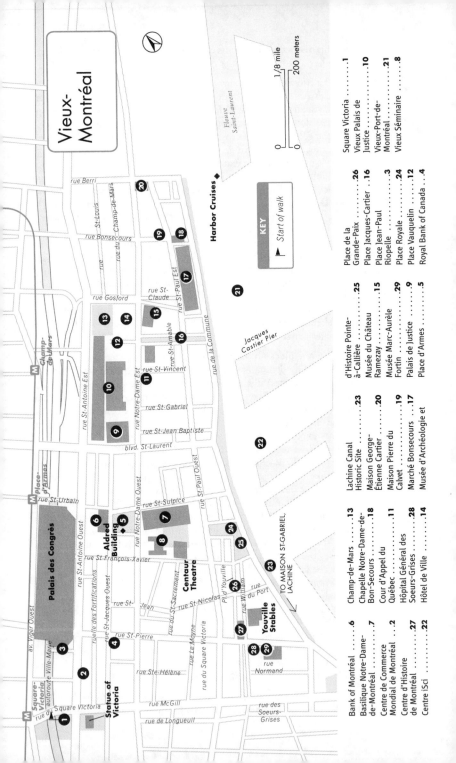

Vieux-Montréal

KEY

▲ Start of walk

Harbor Cruises ◆

0 1/8 mile
0 200 meters

11th governor of Montréal, Claude de Ramezay, and now a museum. To the west of the château is **Place Jacques-Cartier** ⑯, the heart of Vieux-Montréal. This lively square, lined with restaurants and sidewalk cafés, is dominated by a statue of Admiral Horatio Nelson. From spring to late fall, the one-block **rue St-Amable**, near the bottom of the square, becomes a marketplace for jewelers, artists, and other craftspeople.

Just past rue St-Amable, turn left onto **rue St-Paul**, a narrow, gently curving cobblestone street of art galleries, restaurants and souvenir shops. The long, domed building on the right a block and a half east of Place Jacques-Cartier is the **Marché Bonsecours** ⑰, a public market with exhibits on Montréal in the hall upstairs and boutiques specializing in regional crafts and Québecois fashions downstairs. Just beyond it is the **Chapelle Notre-Dame-de-Bon-Secours** ⑱, founded Montréal's first schoolteacher. Across from the chapel on the northeast corner of rue Bonsecours is the historic **Maison Pierre du Calvet** ⑲, an 18th-century house where Benjamin Franklin was a frequent guest.On your left just before you reach rue Berri are the two mid-19th-century houses that make up the **Maison George-Étienne Cartier** ⑳, a museum honoring one of the leading figures in the founding of the Canadian federation in 1867. The front entrance is on rue Notre-Dame, but you can enter from the back gardens.

When you come out of the museum, walk south on rue Berri to rue de la Commune, which runs along the waterfront. At rue Bonsecours, cross the street and enter the **Vieux-Port-de-Montréal** ㉑, one of Montreal's most popular parks. It is home to the **Centre iSci** ㉒, Montréal's state-of-the-art science center. At the western end of the port area is the entrance to the **Lachine Canal Historic Site** ㉓, a canal-turned-park that has the city's most popular bicycle path. The Promenade du Vieux-Port offers a panoramic view of the Vieux-Montréal skyline with the skyscrapers of the modern city rising behind it.

Backtrack along rue de la Commune to **Place Royale** ㉔, the oldest public square in Montréal. On the north side of Place Royale is the Old Customs House, now the gift shop and offices of the **Musée d'Archéologie et d'Histoire Pointe-à-Callière** ㉕, Montréal's premier museum of history and archaeology. The main exhibits are in the modern, shiplike building just across Place d'Youville. After visiting the museum, walk 1½ blocks down **Place de la Grande-Paix** ㉖, past a monument raised to the first settlers, to the Flemish-style fire station that houses the **Centre d'Histoire de Montréal** ㉗, a museum that focuses on the city's multicultural nature. Walk south on rue St-Pierre toward the harbor, past the ruins of the **Hôpital Général des Soeurs-Grises** ㉘, which served as a shelter for homeless children in the 18th and 19th centuries. Next to the ruins is the **Musée Marc-Aurèle Fortin** ㉙, a gallery dedicated to the works of one of Québec's most distinctive landscape artists.

You can end your walk either by heading back to the Vieux-Port for a harbor excursion or a daring ride on the Lachine Rapids, or you can return to the Centre de Commerce Mondial and Square-Victoria Métro by walking north on rue St-Pierre. If it's evening, take a detour by turning left on rue Le Moyne and then right on **rue Ste-Hélène**, Montréal's only gaslit street.

TIMING   If you walk briskly and don't stop, you can get through this route in less than an hour. A more realistic and leisurely pace takes about 90 minutes (still without stopping), or longer when the streets are icy. Comfortable shoes are a must for the cobblestone streets.

The Basilique Notre-Dame, one of Montréal's most famous landmarks, deserves at least a 45-minute visit, as does the Musée du Château Ramezay. The Pointe-à-Callière museum could keep an enthusiastic history buff occupied for a whole day, so give it at least two hours. If you do visit any museums, call ahead for seasonal hours.

What to See

❻ Bank of Montréal. The head office of Canada's oldest chartered bank is a tribute to business and finance. It's housed in a neoclassical structure built on Place d'Armes in 1847 and remodeled by the renowned New York architectural firm McKim, Mead & White in 1905. The central dome and Corinthian columns give it the air of an ancient Greek or Roman sanctuary, in sharp contrast to the Gothic glory of the Catholic Basilique Notre-Dame-de-Montréal across the square. The bank's interior is even more templelike—in the main entrance, a 20-foot statue stands like an ancient goddess amid a forest of dark marble columns supporting an intricate coffered ceiling. Representing Patria—"homeland"—the statue stands as a memorial to the war dead of 1914–18. The bank's tellers work in an immense room surrounded by more marble columns. A one-room museum recounts the early history of banking in Canada. ✉ *119 rue St-Jacques, Vieux-Montréal* ☎ *514/877–7373* ✆ *Free* ✆ *Weekdays 9–3* Ⓜ *Place-d'Armes.*

❼ Basilique Notre-Dame-de-Montréal (Our Lady of Montréal Basilica). James O'Donnell, the Protestant architect who designed this 3,800-seat temple, was so pleased with his handiwork that he became Catholic. Everything about the basilica, which opened in 1829, is on a grand scale. The twin towers of its neo-Gothic facade are 228 feet high, and the western tower holds Le Gros Bourdon, the largest bell in North America at 11,240 kilograms (just over 12 tons). The interior isn't so much Gothic as neo-Romanesque, with stained-glass windows, pine and walnut carvings, and a blue vaulted ceiling studded with thousands of 24-karat gold stars. The stained-glass windows are from Limoges and commemorate episodes of Montréal's history. Life-size wooden carvings of Ezekiel and Jeremiah sit under the opulently decorated pulpit, which has an intricately twisting staircase. Those honored in the side altars include St. Marguerite d'Youville, Canada's first native-born saint; St. Marguerite Bourgeoys, Canada's first schoolteacher; and a group of Sulpician priests martyred in Paris during the French Revolution.

FodorsChoice
★

The northwest corner of the church has been glassed off to make a small prayer room away from the noise of the visiting hordes, and as a result the magnificent baptistery, decorated with frescoes by Ozias Leduc, is difficult to see. With more than 7,000 pipes, the Casavant pipe organ is one of the largest on the continent. If you want to hear the organ roar, drop in for the solemn 11 AM Sunday mass, and pay special attention to the music played at the end. Behind the main altar is the **Sacré-Coeur**

Chapel (Sacred Heart Chapel), destroyed by fire in 1978 and rebuilt in five styles. Its dominant feature is the huge modern bronze sculpture that forms the backdrop for the altar. The chapel is often called the Wedding Chapel: hundreds of Montrealers get married in it every year. The wedding of pop diva Céline Dion to her manager in 1994, however, filled the main church, as did the state funeral of hockey great Maurice "Rocket" Richard in May 2000, and that of former prime minister Pierre Elliot Trudeau four months later (honorary pallbearers Fidel Castro and Jimmy Carter shared the front pew on the left). In the evening, the darkened nave is transformed into a backdrop for La Lumière Fut (There Was Light), a state-of-the-art light-and-sound show that depicts the history of Montréal and showcases the church's extraordinary art.

Notre-Dame is an active house of worship, so dress accordingly (i.e., no shorts or bare midriffs). The main church is closed to tours during Sunday masses (at 9AM, 11AM, 12:30PM, and 4:30PM), and the chapel can't be viewed during the 12:15PM and 5&PM weekday masses. ⊠ 116 rue Notre-Dame Ouest, Vieux-Montréal ☎ 514/849–1070 ⊕ www. basiliquenddm.org ⊠ C$2, including guided tour; C$10 for La Lumière Fut ☉ Daily 7–5; 20-min tours in French and English every hr 8–4 July–Sept., every 2 hrs (or by prior arrangement) Oct.–June Ⓜ Place-d'Armes.

❷ Centre de Commerce Mondial de Montréal (Montréal World Trade Center). The narrow, soaring atrium houses boutiques, a food court, frequent art exhibits, and Montréal's own chunk of the Berlin Wall, complete with graffiti. Photographers often use the fountain and reflecting pond at the west end as a backdrop for fashion shoots and wedding groups. The statue of Amphitrite (Poseidon's wife) overlooking the fountain is an 18th-century piece removed from the municipal fountain of St-Mihiel-de-la-Meuse in France. The complex covers a block of the ruelle des Fortifications, a narrow lane that marks the place where the city walls once stood. Developers glasse-in the lane and sandblasted and restored 11 of the 19th-century buildings that lined it. One of them—the Nordheimer, at the southeastern end of the complex and now part of the Inter-Continental Montréal hotel—is worth a look. To see it, climb the stairs to the hotel lobby and cross the footbridge. The building's dark woodwork and Celtic-style mosaics reflect the romantic tastes of the Scottish businessmen who ran Victorian Montréal. The building once housed a small concert hall where such luminaries as Sarah Bernhardt and Maurice Ravel performed. ⊠ 380 rue St-Antoine Ouest, Vieux-Montréal ☎ 514/982–9888 Ⓜ Square-Victoria.

🐾 ㉗ Centre d'Histoire de Montréal (Montréal History Center). The best thing about this modest little museum is the handsome Flemish-style former fire station that houses it. The ground-floor gallery uses photos, pictures, artifacts, and audio clips to give a quick survey of the city's story. On the 2nd floor are a series of screens showing Montrealers of various ethnic backgrounds talking about their city. One floor up, the glassed-in walkway leading to the temporary-exhibit room affords a good view of the old city. ⊠ 335 pl. d'Youville, Vieux-Montréal ☎ 514/872–3207

⊕ *www2.ville.montreal.qc.ca/chm/chm.htm* ✉ *C$6.50* ◷ *Tues.–Sun. 10–5* Ⓜ *Place-d'Armes or Square-Victoria.*

🕐 ㉒ **Centre iSci.** Montréal's interactive science center fills more than 600,000 square feet on the old King Edward Pier. The center's two main exhibition halls—Eureka and Technocity—use puzzles, quizzes, games of strategy and skill, demonstrations, and hands-on experiments to explore various aspects of medicine, aerospace, computers, communications and media, natural resources, and engineering. The center also encompasses three IMAX film theaters and the giant-screen, interactive Immersion Studios theater, in which audience members use touch screens to vote on the twists and turns of the story. The center also includes Porto Fiorentino, a 1,000-seat family restaurant that overlooks the harbor and presents interactive culinary activities and piano concerts. In the neighboring food court, staff members give lessons about nutrition and agriculture. ✉ *Quai King Edward, Vieux-Montréal* ☎ *514/496–4724 or 877/496–4724* ⊕ *www.isci.ca* ✉ *Exhibit halls and Immersion Studios C$10; IMAX C$12; exhibit halls, Immersion Studios, and IMAX C$17* ◷ *Daily 9–5* Ⓜ *Place-d'Armes or Champ-de-Mars.*

⓭ **Champ-de-Mars** (Field of Mars). This acre-size green space was a parade square for local regiments until 1924, as well as a place where fashionable Montrealers would take walks in the evenings. In 1991, archeologists excavated the space here, uncovering the foundations of a long stretch of the city's stone walls, built between 1717 and 1745.

⓲ **Chapelle Notre-Dame-de-Bon-Secours** (Our Lady of Perpetual Help Chapel). St. Marguerite Bourgeoys had a chapel built on this waterfront site in 1657 to house a statue of Notre-Dame-de-Bon-Secours (Our Lady of Perpetual Help), credited with the rescue of those in peril at sea. Fire destroyed that structure, and the present stone one was erected in 1771 with the rescued statue enshrined in a side altar to the left of the main one. The chapel has always had a special place in the hearts of mariners, and is usually referred to simply as the Église des Matelots, or the Sailors' Church. A larger-than-life statue of the Virgin graces the steeple of the present building, facing the river with arms outstretched in welcome. Mariners who survived the perils of ocean crossings in the 18th and 19th centuries often came to the church to thank the Virgin for her help and to leave votive lamps in the shape of small model ships—many of them still hang from the ceiling. You may climb the steeple to the "aerial," a tiny chapel where mariners came to pray for safe passage. A renovation project in 1998 revealed beautiful 18th-century murals that had been covered up with more-recent pictures. The adjacent **Musée Marguerite Bourgeoys** explores the life of the saint and the history of Montréal, with an emphasis on education. ✉ *400 rue St-Paul Est, Vieux-Montréal* ☎ *514/282–8670* ⊕ *www.marguerite-bourgeoys.com* ✉ *Chapel free, museum C$6* ◷ *May–Oct., daily 10–5; Nov.–mid-Jan. and mid-Mar.–Apr., daily 11–3:30; mid-Jan.–mid-Mar., open only for Sun. mass at 10:30 (in French)* Ⓜ *Champ-de-Mars.*

⓫ **Cour d'Appel du Québec** (Québec Court of Appeals). Ernest Cormier, the architect who designed Canada's Supreme Court building in Ottawa and one of the country's leading exponents of the Beaux Arts style, designed this columned building in 1926 as the city's main criminal court. Its massive bronze doors are richly carved, and the vast main hall has dome-shape skylights and travertine facing. ✉ *100 rue Notre-Dame Est, Vieux-Montréal* ☎ *No phone* ⊙ *Weekdays 9–6* Ⓜ *Champ-de-Mars.*

㉘ Hôpital Général des Soeurs-Grises (General Hospital of the Gray Nuns). These ruins of the hospital the Frères Charon established in 1694 have been preserved as a memorial to Canada's first native-born saint, Marguerite d'Youville (1701–71), who took over the hospital in 1747 and ran it until it burned down in 1765. St. Marguerite founded the Soeurs de la Charité, better known as the Soeurs Grises, or Gray Nuns. The bare stone walls once formed the west wing and the transept of the chapel. The gold script on the wall facing the street is a copy of the letters signed by Louis XIV establishing the hospital. In the shadow of the hospital is the **Maison de Mère d'Youville,** which houses a small retreat operated by the Gray Nuns as well as some remarkable reminders of St. Marguerite's days, such as the old kitchen where she worked, with its enormous fireplace and big stone sink; the stone floor of the room that served as North America's first external clinic; and the room where St. Marguerite died. The house isn't open to the general public, but guided tours can be arranged. Donations are accepted. ✉ *138 rue St-Pierre, Vieux-Montréal* ☎ *514/842–9411 for tours of Maison de Mère d'Youville (ask for Sr. Marguerite D'Aoust)* Ⓜ *Square-Victoria.*

⑭ Hôtel de Ville. President Charles de Gaulle of France marked Canada's centennial celebrations in 1967 by standing on the central balcony of Montréal's ornate City Hall on July 24 and shouting *"Vive le Québec libre"* ("Long live free Québec"), much to the delight of the fledgling separatist movement. Perhaps he got carried away because he felt so at home: the Second Empire–style city hall, built in 1878, is modeled on the one in Tours, France. Free guided tours are available daily 9–5 in June, July, and August, and the main hall is used for occasional exhibitions. ✉ *275 rue Notre-Dame Est, Vieux-Montréal* ☎ *514/872–3355* 🖼 *Free* ⊙ *Main hall, daily 9–5* Ⓜ *Champ-de-Mars.*

---

off the
beaten
path

LACHINE – This district's name began as a joke. In the 17th century, Robert Cavalier de La Salle, the first seigneur to hold land west of the Lachine Rapids, was obsessed with finding a westward passage to Asia. His persistent and unsuccessful attempts led his fellow colonists to refer to his lands derisively as "La Chine," or China.

Lachine has the oldest standing house on the Île de Montréal: the Maison LeBer–LeMoyne, built by Montréal merchants Jacques LeBer and Charles LeMoyne between 1669 and 1685. Now the **Musée de Lachine** (Lachine Museum), it houses historical collections, including colonial-era artifacts and documents. The house and its outbuildings also serve as a showcase for local and regional artists. ✉ *1 chemin du Musée, Lachine* ⊕ *lachine.ville.montreal.qc.ca/musee* ☎ *514/ 634–3471 Ext. 346* 🖼 *Free* ⊙ *Wed.–Sun. 11:30–4:30.*

An old stone warehouse on the Lachine waterfront that dates from 1802 is now the **Fur Trade in Lachine National Historic Site.** This museum re-creates the salad days when Lachine's position upstream from the rapids made it an important center in the fur trade: the site is stocked with bales of pelts ready for shipment to England, and trade goods—blankets, flour, tea, axes, guns—for the area trappers. ⊠ *1255 blvd. St-Joseph, Lachine* ☎ *514/637–7433 or 514/283– 6054* ⊕ *www.parkscanada.gc.ca* ⊠ *C$2.50* ☉ *Apr.–mid-Oct., Mon. 1–6, Tues.–Sun. 10–12:30 and 1–6; mid-Oct.–late Nov., Wed.–Sun. 9:30–12:30 and 1–5.*

★ ☾ ㉓ **Lachine Canal Historic Site.** It was a group of prescient French priests who first tried to dig a canal to move cargo around the treacherous Lachine Rapids, but they had neither the royal approval nor the money to finish the job. That didn't happen until 1825, when the Lachine Canal opened, linking Montréal's harbor to Lac St-Louis and the Ottawa River. The canal remained one of Canada's most vital waterways until 1959, when the St. Lawrence Seaway rendered it obsolete by allowing large cargo ships to travel between the Atlantic and the Great Lakes. The Lachine Canal was subsequently closed to navigation and became an illicit dumping ground for old cars and the victims of underworld killings, while the area around it degenerated into an industrial slum.

In 1988, however, the federal government planted lawns and trees along the old canal and transformed it into a long, thin park linking the Vieux-Port to Lachine, one of the island's oldest municipalities and the spot where the St. Lawrence widens to become Lac St-Louis. In spring, summer, and fall, hundreds of Montrealers ride or skate the 9-mi bicycle path to picnic in Lachine's lakefront park or dine in one of the century-old buildings along the waterfront. The path, which in winter hosts cross-country skiers, is the first link in the more than 60 mi of bike trails that make up the **Pôle des Rapides** (☎ 514/364–4490).

The canal is open to pleasure craft, and you can take a shuttle boat between Vieux-Montréal and Lachine. The canalside factories and warehouses—most now abandoned or converted into offices or housing—provide an insight into the city's early industrial development. A permanent exhibition at the **Lachine Canal Interpretation Centre** explains the history and construction of the canal. The center, on the western end of the canal, is free and open daily (except Monday morning) mid-May to September 1, 10–noon and 1–6. ⊠ *Lachine* ☎ *514/ 637-7433* ⊕ *www.parkscanada.gc.ca* ⊠ *Free* ☉ *Sunrise–sunset.*

㉔ **Maison George-Étienne Cartier.** The two houses of this museum explore the private and public life of George-Étienne Cartier, the statesman who persuaded French-speaking Québecois to join the Canadian federation when it was formed in 1867. In the east house, which focuses on Cartier's political career, you can listen to recordings of him and his contemporaries arguing the pros and cons of confederation or learn about Cartier's major role in getting the colony's first railways built. Next door, where the Cartier family lived in the 1860s, you can listen to portions of taped conversation from "servants" gossiping about the lives of their master and mistress. The residence is furnished in the opulently fussy style favored by the 19th-century bourgeois. From mid-November to mid-December, Victorian holiday decorations festoon the home. ✉ *458 rue Notre-Dame Est, Vieux-Montréal* ☎ *514/283–2282 or 800/463–6769* ⊕ *www.parkscanada.gc.ca* 🖃 *C$3.25* ☉ *Late May–early Sept., daily 10–6; early Sept.–mid-Dec. and Apr.–late May, Wed.–Sun. 10–noon and 1–5* Ⓜ *Champp-de-Mars.*

⑲ Maison Pierre du Calvet. The thick fieldstone walls and multipane casement windows mark this as one of Vieux-Montréal's oldest residences, built in 1725 by a prosperous merchant. A fan of Voltaire and a fierce supporter of the American Revolution, du Calvet often entertained Benjamin Franklin during the 1775–76 American occupation. The house is now occupied by a restaurant and a small but opulent bed-and-breakfast (called Pierre du Calvet AD1725). ✉ *405 rue Bonsecours, Vieux-Montréal* ☎ *514/282–1725* ⊕ *www.pierreducalvet.ca.*

FodorśChoice **Maison St-Gabriel.** The spirit of New France comes to life in this stone-
★ walled compound deep in the working-class Pointe-St-Charles neighborhood. Its 17th-century stone farmhouse, with its complex roof beams and huge attics, has been restored to the way it was when St. Marguerite Bourgeoys and her religious order used it to teach household arts to the *filles du roy* (daughters of the king): young orphans sent from France to be the wives and mothers of New France. In the summer there are demonstrations on the museum's ample grounds in such skills as lace-making and candle-making. The kitchen is equipped with a rare kind of granite sink and an ingenious wastewater-disposal system. Several items that belonged to St. Marguerite are on display, including a writing desk she used. It's best to take a cab here; the ride takes about 10 minutes from Vieux-Montréal. ✉ *2146 pl. Dublin, Pointe St-Charles* ☎ *514/935–8136* ⊕ *www.maisonsaint-gabriel.qc.ca* 🖃 *C$7* ☉ *Late June–Labor Day, Tues.–Sun. 10–5 (guided tours every hr); early Sept.–late Dec. and mid-Feb.–late June, Tues.–Sat. 1:30–3:30 and Sun. 1–5.*

⑰ Marché Bonsecours (Bonsecours Market). The domed, neoclassical building that dominates the waterfront of Vieux-Montréal was built in the 1840s to serve as the city's main market. The main entrance, on rue St-Paul, has a portico supported by six cast-iron Doric columns imported from England. Two rows of meticulously even, sashed windows and a silvery dome complete the gray-stone building's distinctive features. Because of the slope of the land, the building's waterfront side appears more massive than its long, low frontage along rue St-Paul. The market building became municipal offices in the early 1960s, and a late-'90s refurbishing transformed it into a public space with an exhibition hall (usually open Tuesday–Sunday 10–7) on the 2nd floor for history and culture displays. The bright, airy ground floor facing rue St-Paul, and the lower floor facing the waterfront, house restaurants, as well as shops and boutiques with a focus on local crafts and fashions. ✉ *350 rue St-Paul Est, Vieux-Montréal* ☎ *514/872–7730* ⊕ *www.marchebonsecours.qc.ca* Ⓜ *Champ-de-Mars.*

★ **㉓ Musée d'Archéologie et d'Histoire Pointe-à-Callière** (Pointe-à-Callière Archaeology and History Museum). This imposing, shiplike building is built right over the excavated remains of structures that date from Montréal's beginnings. Visits usually start with an audiovisual show that gives an overview of the area's history from the Ice Age to the present. When that's over, you descend deep below street level to the bank of the Rivière St-Pierre, which flowed past the site. It was here that the first settlers built their homes and traded with the Native American inhabitants. One of the most impressive finds unearthed here was the city's first Catholic cemetery, with some tombstones still intact. From there, you wander through the stone foundations of an 18th-century tavern and a 19th-century insurance building. Filmed figures representing past inhabitants appear on ghostly screens. For a spectacular view of the Vieux-Port, the river, and the islands, ride the elevator to the top of the tower, or stop for lunch in the museum's glass-fronted café.

The museum's excellent gift shop, full of books on Montréal's history as well as pictures and reproductions of old maps, engravings, and other artifacts, is in the Old Customs House, a neoclassical gray-stone building erected in 1836. An industrial exhibit is housed in the 1915 Youville Pumping House, across the street from the main building. In summer, there are re-creations of period fairs and festivals on the grounds near the museum. ⊠ *350 pl. Royale, Vieux-Montréal* ☎ *514/872–9150* ⊕ *www.pacmuseum.qc.ca* ⊠ *C$10* ⊙ *July–Aug., weekdays 10–6, weekends 11–5; Sept.–June, Tues.–Fri. 10–5, weekends 11–5* Ⓜ *Place-d'Armes.*

 ⓯ Musée du Château Ramezay. With its thick stone walls, steeply pitched roof, and dormer windows, the building has the air of a Norman castle. Two squat stone towers added in the late 18th century contribute to the effect. French governors, British conquerors, and American occupiers have all lived here. The 11th governor of Montréal, Claude de Ramezay, built the château in 1702, and the Compagnie des Indes Occidentales (the French West Indies Company) took it over in 1745 and stored furs in the basement vaults. The British used it as headquarters after their conquest in 1760, and so did the American commanders Richard Montgomery and Benedict Arnold, whose troops occupied the city during their 1775–76 campaign to conquer Canada. Benjamin Franklin, who came north in a failed attempt to persuade the Québecois to join the American Revolution, stayed here during that winter adventure.

The building became a museum of city and provincial history in 1895 and has been restored to the style of Governor de Ramezay's day. The public rooms on the ground floor include the Salon Nantes, with 18th-century Louis XV–style mahogany paneling. The main-floor displays are somewhat staid—uniforms, documents, and furniture—but a series of tableaux in the basement vividly depicts the everyday lives of the city's early European settlers, and the château's garden has been planted in a typical colonial fashion. The museum's collection is eclectic, however. One of its most prized possessions, for example, is a bright-red automobile that was produced at the turn of the 20th century by the De Dion-Bouton company for the city's first motorist. ⊠ *280 rue Notre-Dame Est, Vieux-Montréal* ☎ *514/861–3708* ⊕ *www.chateauramezay.qc.ca*

✉ C$7 ◷ June–Sept., daily 10–6; Oct.–May, Tues.–Sun. 10–4:30 Ⓜ Champ-de-Mars.

---

need a break?

In summer, few places are livelier than **Place Jacques-Cartier,** just around the corner from the Musée du Château Ramezay. You can stop at a *terrasse* (sidewalk café) for a beer or a coffee, or just sit on a bench amid the flower vendors and listen to the street musicians. You might also want to give *poutine* a try. Québec's contribution to junk-food culture, it's made of french fries covered with cheese curds and smothered in gravy.

★ ㉙ **Musée Marc-Aurèle Fortin.** Heavy clouds, higgledy-piggledy villages, and lush, fantastic trees crowd the painted landscapes in this little museum dedicated to the work of Marc-Aurèle Fortin (1888–1970), one of the local pioneers of modern art. Fortin experimented wildly with different techniques. He painted some of his works on canvases that he'd pre-painted gray to emphasize the warm light of the countryside; others he painted on black backgrounds to create dramatic contrasts. Fortin painted some cityscapes, but he is best known for his rich and bountiful landscapes of the Laurentians, the Gaspé, and the Charlevoix region. ✉ 118 rue St-Pierre, Vieux-Montréal ☎ 514/845–6108 ✉ C$5 ◷ Tues.–Sun. 11–5 Ⓜ Square-Victoria.

❾ **Palais de Justice** (Courthouse). Lawyers in elaborate gowns and cravats and judges in scarlet-trimmed robes decide points of law in this black-glass tower built in 1971 as the main courthouse for the judicial district of Montréal. Criminal law in Canada falls under federal jurisdiction and is based on British common law, but civil law is a provincial matter. Québec's is based on France's Napoleonic Code, which governs all the minutiae of private life—from setting up a company and negotiating a mortgage to drawing up a marriage contract and registering the names of children. Although there are no tours of the building, you can drop in to any courtroom and see how justice is dispensed. Proceedings are usually in French—defendants in criminal cases can choose which official language they wish to be tried in. ✉ 1 rue Notre-Dame Est, Vieux-Montréal Ⓜ Place-d'Armes or Champ-de-Mars.

❺ **Place d'Armes.** Montréal's founder, Paul de Chomedey, slew an Iroquois chief in a battle here in 1644 and was wounded in return. His statue stands in a fountain in the middle of the pleasant, cobblestone square surrounded by shrubs and flowers. Tunnels beneath the square protected the colonists from the winter weather and provided an escape route; unfortunately they are too small and dangerous to visit. ✉ Bordered by rues Notre-Dame Ouest, St-Jacques, and St-Sulpice, Vieux-Montréal Ⓜ Place-d'Armes.

㉖ **Place de la Grande-Paix.** The narrow strip of grass and trees on Place d'Youville just east of Place Royale marks the spot where a little stream used to flow into the St. Lawrence. It was on this point of land between the two bodies of water that the colonists landed their four boats on May 17, 1642. An obelisk records the names of the first settlers. A favorite of local office workers, the park is named for the peace treaty the French signed in 1701 with representatives of dozens of Indian nations. ⊠ *Between Place d'Youville and rue William, Vieux-Montréal* Ⓜ *Place-d'Armes.*

★ ⑯ **Place Jacques-Cartier.** Musicians, magicians, and acrobats entertain the summer crowds that congregate in this historic square in the heart of Vieux-Montréal. The restaurants lining the square serve escargot as well as poutine to their patrons, who sit in open-air terrasses watching the passing scene. The 1809 monument at the top of the square was the first monument in the British Empire erected to honor Lord Nelson's victory over Napoléon Bonaparte's French navy at Trafalgar. The campaign to raise money for it was led not by patriotic British residents of Montréal but by the Sulpician priests, who didn't have much love for the Corsican emperor either—the priests were engaged in delicate land negotiations with the British government at the time and were eager to show what good subjects they were. ⊠ *Bordered by rues Notre-Dame Est and de la Commune, Vieux-Montréal* Ⓜ *Champ-de-Mars.*

❸ **Place Jean-Paul-Riopelle.** Jean-Paul Riopelle (1923–2002) was one of the leaders of the *mouvement automatiste* that turned Québec's art world on its ear in the 1940s. He created the dramatic fountain at the north end of this grassy little park, where fanciful steel figures are set in a "ring of fire." ⊠ *Bordered by rue St-Antoine and av. Viger and Place Jean-Paul-Riopelle and rue de Bleury.*

㉔ **Place Royale.** The oldest public square in Montréal, dating to the 17th century, was a public market during the French regime and later became a Victorian garden. The neoclassical Vielle Douane (Old Customs House) on its south side serves as the gift shop for the Pointe-à-Callière Archaeology and History Museum. ⊠ *Bordered by rues St-Paul Ouest and de la Commune, Vieux-Montréal* Ⓜ *Place-d'Armes.*

⑫ **Place Vauquelin.** The statue in this small square represents Admiral Jacques Vauquelin, a naval hero of the French regime. In summer, foot-weary strollers often soak their feet in the fountain. ⊠ *Between rues St-Antoine Est and Notre-Dame Est, near rue Gosford, Vieux-Montréal* Ⓜ *Champ-de-Mars.*

❹ **Royal Bank of Canada.** The last landmark of Montréal's gilded age is this 22-story tower in pale-yellow stone, designed by New York architects York & Sawyer. The building's main banking hall has a coffered ceiling and is decorated with the coats-of-arms of the eight provinces that made up Canada when the bank was built in 1928. It's now used for a branch of the Royal and for various other offices. ⊠ *360 rue St-Jacques, Vieux-Montréal* ☎ *514/874–2959* ⌨ *Free* ⊙ *Weekdays 10–4* Ⓜ *Place-d'Armes.*

Rue St-Amable. In summer this tiny street linking Place Jacques-Cartier and rue St-Vincent turns into an open-air market where artists, photographers, and caricaturists display their wares.

Rue St-Jacques. Popular with filmmakers, the stretch of rue St-Jacques between rue McGill and boulevard St-Laurent is often decked out as Main Street U.S.A., complete with American flags, signs in English, and period cars. Stone nymphs, angels, and goddesses decorate the Victorian office buildings lining this stretch, which once served as the financial heart of Canada.

Rue St-Sulpice. A plaque at No. 445 (near rue St-Paul) on rue St-Sulpice—one of the oldest streets in Montréal—marks the spot where Jeanne Mance built the Hôpital Hôtel-Dieu de St-Joseph, the city's first hospital, in 1644.

▶ ❶ **Square Victoria.** An 1872 bronze of the Queen-Empress overlooks this two-block-long park of trees, benches, and fountains. The modern Bourse de Montréal (Stock Exchange) and the IATA headquarters on the west side of the square contrast nicely with the fine examples of early 1900s business buildings on the east side. The art nouveau Métro entrance north of rue St-Antoine is, in fact, an authentic one from Paris. It was a gift from the French capital's transit commission. ⊠ *rue Square Victoria.*

❿ **Vieux Palais de Justice.** This former courthouse, a domed building in the Classical Revival style, was built in 1857 to house the civil courts, but is now a warren of city offices. The sculpture group on the lawn at the west end of the building depicts St. Marguerite Bourgeoys, Montréal's first schoolteacher, playing with a group of children. ⊠ *155 rue Notre-Dame Est, Vieux-Montréal* Ⓜ *Champ-de-Mars.*

★ ☾ ㉑ **Vieux-Port-de-Montréal** (Old Port of Montréal). In warm weather, skateboarders, strollers, bicyclists, and street performers crowd the revitalized old port, where you can take harbor cruises and raft rides on the Lachine Rapids. (Bicycles and in-line skates are available for rent at shops along rue de la Commune.) A ferry takes pedestrians to the park on Île Ste-Hélène. In winter, you can skate on a huge outdoor rink in the Vieux-Port. The **King Edward Pier** is the site of iSci, Montréal's science center. If you feel up to it, climb the 192 steps to the top of the **Clock Tower** for a good view of the waterfront and the islands; it was erected at the eastern end of the waterfront in memory of merchant mariners killed during World War I. Every couple of years or so, Montréal's Cirque du Soleil comes home to pitch its blue-and-yellow tent in the Vieux-Port. ⊠ *Vieux-Montréal* ☎ *514/496-7678 or 800/971-7678* ⊕ *www.oldportofmontreal.com* Ⓜ *Place-d'Armes or Champ-de-Mars.*

❽ **Vieux Séminaire** (Old Seminary). Montréal's oldest building was built in 1685 as a headquarters for the Sulpician priests who owned the island of Montréal until 1854. It's still a residence for the Sulpicians who administer the basilica. The clock on the roof over the main doorway is the oldest (pre-1701) public timepiece in North America. Behind the seminary building is a garden that is closed to the public, as is the seminary itself. ⊠ *116 rue Notre-Dame Ouest, behind wall west of Basilique Notre-Dame-de-Montréal, Vieux-Montréal* Ⓜ *Place-d'Armes.*

Downtown

On the surface, Montréal's downtown, or *centre-ville,* is much like the downtown core of many other major cities—full of life and noisy traffic, its streets lined with department stores, boutiques, bars, restaurants, strip clubs, amusement arcades, and bookstores. In fact, however, much of the area's activity takes place beneath the surface, in Montréal's Cité Souterrain (Underground City). Development began in 1966 when the Métro opened. Now it includes seven hotels, more than 1,500 offices and 1,600 boutiques, 30 movie theaters, 200 restaurants, three universities, two colleges, two train stations, a skating rink, 40 banks, a bus terminal, an art museum, a complex of concert halls, the home-ice arena of the Montréal Canadiens, and a cathedral. All this is linked by Métro lines and more than 30 km (19 mi) of well-lighted, boutique-lined passages that protect shoppers and workers from the chill of winter and the heat of summer. A traveler arriving by train could book into a fine hotel and spend a week shopping, dining, and going to a long list of movies, plays, concerts, sports events, and nightclubs without once stepping outside.

a good walk

The start of this walk is designed for moles—it's underground—but it gives you an idea of the extent of the Underground City. Start at the McGill Métro station, one of the central points in the Underground City. It's linked to office towers and two of the "Big Three" department stores, Simons and La Baie (the third is Ogilvy). Passages also link the station to major shopping malls such as Le Centre Eaton, Les Promenades de la Cathédrale, and Place Montréal Trust.

Follow the signs from the station to Le Centre Eaton and then descend yet another floor to the tunnel that leads to **Place Ville-Marie** ❶ ▶. The mall complex below the skyscraper was the first link in the Underground City. From here head south via the passageways toward Fairmont Le Reine Elizabeth hotel, which straddles the entrance to the Gare Centrale (Central Station). Walk through the station and follow the signs marked MÉTRO/PLACE BONAVENTURE until you see a sign for Le 1000 rue de la Gauchetière, a skyscraper that houses the **Atrium le Mille de la Gauchetière** ❷, which has an indoor ice rink. Return to the tunnels and again follow signs to the Bonaventure Métro station and then to the Canadian Pacific Railway Company's historic **Windsor Station** ❸. The station and the Place Bonaventure Métro station below it are all linked to **Centre Bell** ❹, the home of the Montréal Canadiens.

By now you're probably ready for some fresh air. Exit the Underground City at the north end of Windsor Station and cross rue de la Gauchetière to **St. George's** ❺, the prettiest Anglican church in the city. Just to the east, across rue Peel, is the **Place du Canada** ❻ park. Cross the park and rue de la Cathédrale to **Cathédrale Marie-Reine-du-Monde** ❼, modeled after St. Peter's Basilica in Rome. People sometimes call the gray granite building across boulevard René-Lévesque from the cathedral the Wedding Cake, because it rises in tiers of decreasing size and has lots of columns, but its real name is the **Sun Life Building** ❽. The park just north of boulevard René-Lévesque and facing the Sun Life Building is **Square Dorchester** ❾, for years the heart of Montréal. The Dominion Square Building at the north end of the park houses the Centre-Infotouriste, the main center for visitor information about the city and the province. Walk west across the park to rue Peel and then walk north to rue Ste-Catherine—this intersection is the heart of downtown.

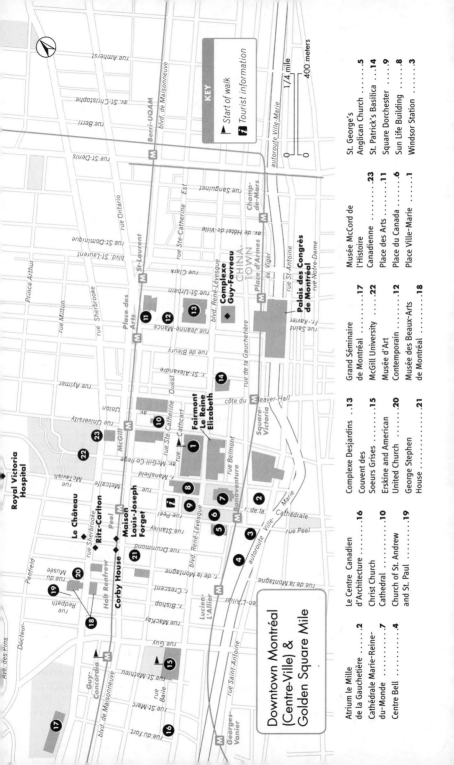

Downtown Montréal (Centre-Ville) & Golden Square Mile

KEY

▲ Start of walk

ℹ Tourist information

0	1/4 mile
0	400 meters

Atrium le Mille
de la Gauchetière **2**

Cathédrale Marie-Reine-
du-Monde **7**

Centre Bell **4**

Le Centre Canadien
d'Architecture ..**13**

Christ Church
Cathedral **10**

Church of St. Andrew
and St. Paul **19**

Complexe Desjardins ..**13**

Couvent des
Soeurs Grises **15**

Erskine and American
United Church **20**

George Stephen
House **21**

Grand Séminaire
de Montréal **17**

McGill University **22**

Musée d'Art
Contemporain **12**

Musée des Beaux-Arts
de Montréal **18**

Musée McCord de
l'Histoire
Canadienne **23**

Place des Arts **11**

Place du Canada **6**

Place Ville-Marie **1**

St. George's
Anglican Church **5**

St. Patrick's Basilica ...**14**

Square Dorchester **9**

Sun Life Building **8**

Windsor Station **3**

Turn right and walk east along rue Ste-Catherine, pausing to admire the view at the corner of avenue McGill College. Looking north up this broad boulevard, you can see the Victorian-era buildings of the McGill University campus, with Mont-Royal looming in the background. The grim-looking gray castle high on the slope to the right is the Royal Victoria Hospital. One block farther east brings you to Le Centre Eaton, where this whole walk started, and **Christ Church Cathedral** ⑩, the main church of the Anglican diocese of Montréal.

Unless you want to end your stroll here, continue six blocks farther east on rue Ste-Catherine to **Place des Arts** ⑪, Montréal's main theater complex. **Musée d'Art Contemporain** ⑫, the modern-art museum, is also part of the complex. While still in Place des Arts, follow the signs to the tunnel below rue Ste-Catherine to **Complexe Desjardins** ⑬, headquarters of Québec's credit-union movement. Walk through the complex's bright, airy mall to boulevard René-Lévesque. Here you have a choice: go east and then south on boulevard St-Laurent to explore **Chinatown,** or turn right and walk west for four blocks to visit **St. Patrick's Basilica** ⑭, mother church of the city's English-speaking Roman Catholics.

TIMING Walking this route at a brisk pace takes at least 90 minutes. The Musée d'Art Contemporain is worth at least two hours, so set aside at least half a day and preferably a full day.

What to See

🕒 ❷ **Atrium le Mille de la Gauchetière.** Skating is a passion in Montréal, and you can do it year-round in this skyscraper atrium. During daylight hours, natural light illuminates the indoor ice rink, which is surrounded by cafés, a food court, and a winter garden. Skate rentals and lockers are available. There are skating lessons Friday and Saturday, disco skating Friday night, ice dancing Saturday night, and scheduled ice shows. To find the rink once you're inside the building, keep in mind that a skating rink is called *une patinoire* in French. ⊠ *1000 rue de la Gauchetière, Downtown* 🕾 *514/ 395–0555* ⊕ *www.le1000.com* ⊠ *C$5.50, skate rental C$4.50* ⊙ *Canadian Thanksgiving (2nd Mon. in Oct.)–Easter, Sun.–Thurs. 11:30–9, Fri. 11:30–7, Sat. 10 AM–midnight; Easter–Canadian Thanksgiving, Sun. and Tues.–Fri. 11:30–6, Sat. 10–10* Ⓜ *Bonaventure.*

❼ **Cathédrale Marie-Reine-du-Monde** (Mary Queen of the World Cathedral). When Roman Catholic bishop Ignace Bourget (1799–1885) picked this site in the heart of the city's Protestant-dominated commercial quarter, many of his co-religionists thought he was crazy. But the bishop was determined to assert the Church's authority—and its loyalty to Rome—in the British-ruled city. So he built a quarter-scale replica of St. Peter's Basilica, complete with a magnificent reproduction of Bernini's ornate baldachin (canopy) over the main altar and an ornately coffered ceiling. The figures on the roof don't represent the apostles, but instead the patron saints of the Montréal parishes that contributed to the construction.

Victor Bourgeau, the architect who created the interior of Basilique Notre-Dame in Vieux-Montréal, thought the idea of the cathedral's design terrible but completed it after the original architect proved incompetent. All of Montréal's bishops are entombed in the mortuary chapel on the east side of the nave, where a reclining figure of Bishop Bourget holds place of honor. One last symbol of the bishop's loyalty to the Roman pontiff is a pair of plaques on two pillars in the northeast corner honoring local residents who went to Italy to defend the Papal States from the nationalist Garibaldi. A huge accompanying painting shows the Papal Zouaves fighting off a nationalist attack. ☒ *1071 rue de la Cathédrale (enter through main doors on blvd. René-Lévesque), Downtown* ☎ *514/866–1661* ☒ *Free* ☉ *Daily 7–7* Ⓜ *Bonaventure or Peel.*

❹ **Centre Bell.** The Montréal Canadiens, the hockey team fans call simply *les Glorieux,* have been playing in this brown-brick building since 1996. Guided tours include a visit to the Canadiens' dressing room when possible. ☒ *1260 rue de la Gauchetière Ouest, Downtown* ☎ *514/925–2582 for tours, 514/925–5656 for tickets* ☒ *Tour C$8* ☉ *Tours daily at 11:15 and 2:45 in English, and 9:45 and 1:15 in French* Ⓜ *Bonaventure.*

off the beaten path

EXPORAIL – The west end of the Centre Bell serves as the Lucien-L'Allier suburban train station. On several summer Saturdays, rail buffs can take the Museum Express to Exporail in the South Shore town of Saint-Constant. Canada's largest railway museum, it opened in the summer of 2004 after a major refurbishment. On display are more than 150 locomotives and dozens of rail cars of all kinds, including sleepers, business cars, and even one that served as a mobile classroom. An old Montréal sight-seeing tram takes visitors around the site to visit the various areas. ☒ *110 rue St-Pierre, St-Constant J5A 1G7* ☎ *(450) 632-2410* ⊕ *www.exporail.org* ☒ *C$12; with Museum Express excursion, C$32* ☉ *End of June–Labor Day, daily 10–6; early Sept.–Oct., Wed–Sun 10–5; Nov.–Apr., weekends 10–5. Museum Express leaves Lucien L'Allier Station at 11 AM on certain Saturdays in July and Aug. and returns at 4 PM.*

Chinatown. Chinese first came to Montréal in large numbers after 1880, following the construction of the transcontinental railroad. They settled in an 18-block area between boulevard René-Lévesque and avenue Viger to the north and south, and near rue de Bleury and avenue Hôtel de Ville on the west and east. The area is full of mainly Chinese and Southeast Asian restaurants, food stores, and gift shops. Ⓜ *Place-d'Armes.*

need a break?

Pho Bang New York (☒ 970 blvd. St-Laurent, Chinatown ☎ 514/954–2032) is the best of the small Vietnamese restaurants on the edge of Chinatown that specialize in traditional noodle soups. For less than C$5 (cash only), you get soup, a plate of crispy vegetables, and a small pot of tea. The iced coffee with condensed milk is especially good.

❿ **Christ Church Cathedral.** The gargoyles and grand Gothic entrance of the seat of Montréal's Anglican bishop are a welcome break in the unrelenting strip of commercial rue Ste-Catherine. The structure was built in 1859 and patterned on Snettisham Parish Church in Norfolk, England. Inside, the pillars that support the cathedral's Gothic arches are crowned with carvings of the types of foliage growing on Mont-Royal at the time the church was built. At the four corners of the nave are sculpted heads representing the four Evangelists. The stained-glass windows behind the main altar, installed in the early 1920s as a memorial to the dead of World War I, show scenes from the life of Christ. On the wall just above and to the left of the pulpit is the Coventry Cross; it's made of nails taken from the ruins of Britain's Coventry Cathedral, destroyed by bombing in 1940.

Christ Church has had its problems: it was built on unstable ground, and in 1927 the stone steeple had to be pulled down because it was sinking fast. Thirteen years later, church leaders erected a much lighter structure, with aluminum plates molded to simulate stone. In 1988 the diocese assured the stability of both its soil and its finances by leasing its land and air rights to developers, who then built **La Maison des Coopérants,** a 34-story office tower behind the cathedral, and a huge retail complex, **Les Promenades de la Cathédrale,** below it. ✉ *635 rue Ste-Catherine Ouest, Downtown* ☎ *514/843–6577* ⊕ *www.montreal. anglican.org/cathedral* 🎟 *Free* ☉ *Daily 8–6* Ⓜ *McGill.*

⑬ Complexe Desjardins. The devoutly Catholic Alphonse Desjardins founded Québec's credit-union movement early in the 20th century to rescue his impoverished compatriots from debt and misery. The "peoples' bank" has grown into a major financial institution with headquarters in the towers above this boutique-rich mall. The large galleria on the ground floor hosts everything from displays of law-enforcement technology to gospel singing. ✉ *150 rue Ste-Catherine Ouest, Downtown* ☎ *514/845–4636 or 514/281–1870* ⊕ *www.complexedesjardins.com* Ⓜ *Place-d'Armes or Place des Arts.*

☾ ⑫ Musée d'Art Contemporain (Museum of Contemporary Art). In 1948 a group of Québec artists led by Paul-Émile Borduas (1905–60) and Jean-Paul Riopelle (1923–2002) signed *Le Refus Global,* a manifesto that renounced the political and religious establishment of the day and revolutionized art in the province. The spirit of these "Automatistes," as they called themselves, is at the heart of this museum, which includes 72 Borduas paintings and 80 Riopelle paintings in its permanent collection of more than 5,000 works. Exhibits explore many different kinds of media—paintings, sculptures, installations, multimedia. The museum often has weekend programs, many of which are child-oriented, and almost all are free. Hours for guided tours vary. ✉ *185 rue Ste-Catherine Ouest, Downtown* ☎ *514/847–6226* ⊕ *www.macm.org* 🎟 *C$6; free Wed. after 6 PM* ☉ *Tues. and Thurs.–Sun. 11–6, Wed. 11–9* Ⓜ *Place des Arts.*

⑪ Place des Arts. The government-subsidized complex of five very modern theaters offers guided tours of the halls and backstage to groups of at least 15. These interactive tours are designed to give an idea of how modern theater works, with participants trying their hand at lighting, sound, and other theater activities. ✉ *175 rue Ste-Catherine Ouest, Downtown* ☎ *514/842–2112 tickets, 514/285–4270 information, 514/285–4200 tours* ⊕ *www.pda.qc.ca* 🎟 *C$8.50 per person for groups of 15–25, C$7.50 per person for groups of 25–30* ☉ *Call for tours* Ⓜ *Place des Arts.*

6 Place du Canada. As the name suggests, this pleasant green park in the center of the city celebrates the founding of the Canadian federation in 1867. A statue of Sir John A. Macdonald, the country's first prime minister, stands at the north end of the park—it faces boulevard René-Lévesque, named for Québec's first separatist premier. A major monument to the dead of past wars is a little farther south. Place du Canada is surrounded by an eclectic mishmash of architecture, ranging from neo-Gothic and neoclassical to sleek modern. ⊠ *Bordered by blvd. René-Lévesque and rues de la Gauchetière, Peel, and de la Cathédrale, Downtown* Ⓜ *Bonaventure.*

▶ **1 Place Ville-Marie.** The cross-shape 1962 office tower was Montréal's first modern skyscraper; the mall complex underneath it was the first link in the Underground City. On sunny days, the wide expanse of the building's plaza, just upstairs from the mall, makes a fine place to relax with coffee or a snack from the food court below. Benches, potted greenery, and fine views of Mont Royal make it popular with walkers, tourists, and office workers. ⊠ *Bordered by blvd. René-Lévesque and rues Mansfield, Cathcart, and University, Downtown* ☎ 514/866–6666 Ⓜ *McGill or Bonaventure.*

5 St. George's Anglican Church. The dim interior of this pretty church from 1872 seems a world away from Centre Bell, the modern temple to professional ice hockey just across the street. On the other hand, several prominent National Hockey League players regularly drop in for a few minutes of quiet meditation before joining the action on the ice. The double hammer-beam roof is one of the largest of its type in the world, and the column-free interior, which combines elements of both English and French Gothic styles, is embellished with English wood carving and illuminated with fine stained-glass windows. ⊠ *1101 rue Stanley, Downtown* ☎ *514/866–7113* 💵 *Free* ☉ *Tues.–Sun. 8:30–4:30; Sun. services at 9 and 10:30* AM Ⓜ *Bonaventure.*

14 St. Patrick's Basilica. Rarely visited by sightseers, this 1847 church is one of the purest examples of the Gothic Revival style in Canada. It is to Montréal's anglophone Catholics what the Basilique Notre-Dame is to their French-speaking brethren. The church's colors are soft, and the vaulted ceiling glows with green and gold mosaics. The old pulpit has panels depicting the apostles, and a huge lamp decorated with six 6-foot-tall angels hangs over the main altar. The tall, slender columns that support the roof are actually pine logs lashed together and decorated to look like marble. The Canadian poet Émile Nelligan (1879–1941) was baptized in the font installed in front of the side altar on the east side of the sanctuary. The pew used by Thomas Darcy McGee—a father of confederation who was assassinated in 1868—is marked with a small Canadian flag. Visitors named for even a fairly obscure saint might well be able to find their namesake's portrait in the 170 painted panels on the walls of the nave. The church is three blocks east of Place Ville-Marie. ⊠ *460 blvd. René-Lévesque Ouest, Downtown* ☎ *514/866–7379* ⊕ *www.stpatricksmtl.ca* 💵 *Free* ☉ *Daily 8:30–6. Main mass Sept.–June, Sun. 11.* Ⓜ *Square-Victoria.*

9 **Square Dorchester.** Until 1870, a Catholic burial ground occupied this downtown park, and the bodies are still there. The statuary includes a monument to the Boer War and statues of the Scottish poet Robert Burns (1759–96) and Sir Wilfrid Laurier (1841–1919), Canada's first French-speaking prime minister. ⊠ *Bordered by rues Peel, Metcalfe, and McTavish and blvd. René-Lévesque, Downtown* Ⓜ *Bonaventure or Peel.*

8 **Sun Life Building.** During World War II, Britain stored its gold reserves and the crown jewels in the basement under the Montréal headquarters of the Sun Life Assurance Co. At the time, this was the largest building in the British Commonwealth. Stroll past the Corinthian columns for a look at the grand main hall, which has rosy marble walls and brass-door elevators. ⊠ *1155 rue Metcalfe, Downtown* ☎ *514/866–6411* Ⓜ *Bonaventure.*

3 **Windsor Station.** This proud stone building constructed in the late 1800s was once the eastern passenger terminus for the Canadian Pacific Railway, Canada's first transcontinental link. Today it's a trainless shell: the vast, glass-roof concourse, which has a huge patio and a splendid bronze monument to the dead of World War I, serves no other purpose than to shelter a barbershop, a coffee shop, and a barbecue-chicken restaurant. ⊠ *1100 rue de la Gauchetière, Downtown* ☎ *No phone* Ⓜ *Bonaventure.*

Golden Square Mile

As Montréal grew in confidence and economic might in the 19th century, the city's prosperous merchant class moved north, building lavish stone homes on Mont-Royal. In fact, at the turn of the 20th century, the people who lived here, most of them Scottish, controlled 70% of the country's wealth. Their baronial homes and handsome Protestant churches covered the mountain north of rue Sherbrooke roughly between avenue Côte-des-Neiges and rue University.

Humbler residents south of rue Sherbrooke referred to the area simply as the Square Mile, a name immortalized in novelist Hugh MacLennan's *Two Solitudes* (1945). The Square Mile was eventually "gilded" by the newspaper columnist Al Palmer in the 1950s, long after its golden age had passed. (Proud Square Milers like the actor Christopher Plummer still bridle at the extra adjective.) Many of the palatial homes have been leveled to make way for high-rises and office towers, but architectural gems still stud the area, and rue Sherbrooke remains the city's most elegant street.

This walk takes in much of the Square Mile along with an area named Shaughnessy Village, to the southwest (bounded roughly by rues Atwater and Guy to the west and east and rue Sherbrooke and boulevard René-Lévesque to the north and south). The village takes its name from the lush Shaughnessy Mansion on boulevard René-Lévesque, a house that would fit in quite comfortably up the hill in the Square Mile. Although most of the Shaughnessy family's 19th-century neighbors were well-off businesspeople and professionals who lived in elegant and comfortable homes, they weren't wealthy enough to make it into the Square Mile.

a good walk

Start at the ► Guy-Concordia Métro station at the rue Guy exit. The statue just north of the station—on the little triangular slice of land in the middle of boulevard de Maisonneuve—portrays Norman Bethune, a McGill University–trained doctor from Gravenhurst, Ontario, who served with the Loyalists in the Spanish Civil War and died in China in 1939 while serving with Mao's Red Army. Walk south on rue Guy to rue Ste-Catherine and turn right. The long building on the south side of the street used to be a car dealership and bowling alley until it was transformed into the Faubourg Ste-Catherine, an enclosed market selling specialty and ethnic foods, pastries, and bagels.

At rue St-Mathieu, turn left and head south. The huge gray building on the left side of the street is **Couvent des Soeurs Grises** ⑮, the motherhouse of an order of nuns founded by St. Marguerite d'Youville, Canada's first native-born saint. Across from the convent, turn right onto rue Baile and into the heart of Shaughnessy Village. The family mansion the area is named for now forms part of **Le Centre Canadien d'Architecture** ⑯. Many of the area's town houses and mansions were torn down during the 1960s to make way for boxy high-rises, but a few remain. Note, for example, the fine row of stone town houses just across rue Baile from the architecture center.

Turn right on rue du Fort and walk north four blocks to rue Sherbrooke. On the north side of the street is a complex of fine neoclassical buildings in a shady garden. This is the **Grand Séminaire de Montréal** ⑰, which trains priests for Montréal's Roman Catholic parishes. The two stone towers on the property are among the oldest buildings on the island. In 1928, the anticlerical Freemasons built the grand Greek Masonic Temple across the street at No. 1859.

Walk east along stately rue Sherbrooke, past rows of old town houses holding boutiques and galleries, to the **Musée des Beaux-Arts de Montréal** ⑱. The city's main art collection, which includes works from around the world, is housed here, in two buildings facing each other across rue Sherbrooke. Two fine Protestant churches frame the museum's neoclassical Michal and Renata Hornstein Pavilion, which is on the north side of the street. To the west is the neo-Gothic **Church of St. Andrew and St. Paul** ⑲, and to the east is the red-stone **Erskine and American United Church** ⑳. A few blocks east on rue Sherbrooke, at the corner of rue de la Montagne, is the small Holt Renfrew department store. Dozens of popular bars and bistros are in the old row houses lining rue de la Montagne and the two streets just west of it, rues Crescent and Bishop, between boulevard René-Lévesque and rue Sherbrooke. The area once encompassed the playing fields of the Montréal Lacrosse and Cricket Grounds and later became a suburb lined with the houses of millionaires.

One block east on the south side of rue Sherbrooke at rue Drummond is the Ritz-Carlton, the most important hotel in town. Catercorner from the Ritz is Le Château (1926), a huge, copper-roof apartment building that looks something like a cross between a French château and a Scottish castle. It's one of the few examples of gracious living on rue Sherbrooke. Others worth looking at are the Corby House and the Maison

Louis-Joseph Forget, at 1201 and 1195 rue Sherbrooke Ouest, respectively. One of the area's most magnificent homes, however, is on rue Drummond a couple of blocks south of Sherbrooke. The **George Stephen House** ㉑ was built for the founder of the Canadian Pacific Railway and is now the private Mount Stephen Club.

The campus of **McGill University** ㉒ lies on the north side of rue Sherbrooke three blocks east of the Ritz-Carlton. Opposite its main gate is the Banque Commerciale Italienne (888 rue Sherbrooke Ouest), housed in a beautiful neo-Elizabethan house built in 1906 for Dr. William Alexander Molson, a scion of Montréal's most famous family of brewers. Another block east is the **Musée McCord de l'Histoire Canadienne** ㉓, one of the best history museums in Canada.

TIMING   You need at least 90 minutes for a brisk walk, but you could easily spend a day or more in the area, which is rich in cultural sights such as the Musée des Beaux-Arts and the Musée McCord de l'Histoire Canadienne, both of which deserve visits.

What to See

⓰ **Le Centre Canadien d'Architecture** (Canadian Center for Architecture). Phyllis Lambert, an heiress to the Seagram liquor fortune and an architect of some note, was the genius behind this museum dedicated to the art of building. She had a hand in designing the ultramodern U-shape structure of gray limestone and filled it with her vast collection of drawings, photographs, plans, books, documents, and models; the library alone contains more than 165,000 volumes. The center's six large, well-lighted exhibition rooms present a series of rotating exhibits that focus on the work of a particular architect or on a particular style. Some can be forbiddingly academic, but more playful exhibits have been devoted to dollhouses and American lawn culture. The two arms of the center wrap around a grandly ornate mansion built in 1874 as the family home of the president of the Canadian Pacific Railway, Sir Thomas Shaughnessy. Inside the mansion is a remarkable art nouveau conservatory with an intricately decorated ceiling. On a tiny piece of land across the street is a quirky sculpture garden. ⊠ *1920 rue Baile, Shaughnessy Village* ☎ *514/939–7000* ⊕ *www.cca.qc.ca* ✑ *C$6* ☉ *Oct.–May, Wed.–Sun. 11–6, Thurs. until 8; June–Sept., Tues.–Sun. 11–5, Thurs. until 9* Ⓜ *Guy-Concordia or Georges-Vanier.*

⓳ **Church of St. Andrew and St. Paul.** Soaring above the white-stone communion table at the head of the 220-foot nave of this neo-Gothic church is a glorious stained-glass window of the risen Christ, installed as a memorial to the soldiers of the Royal Highland Regiment of Canada (the Black Watch) killed in World War I. The William Morris Co. made two of the side windows, which were designed by Pre-Raphaelite artist Sir Edward Burne-Jones. The 1932 church, which has Montréal's largest organ—a four-manual Casavant with 6,911 pipes—and a fine 50-voice choir, is open for Sunday services. To see it at other times, ask the secretary at the side entrance at 3415 rue Redpath. ⊠ *Rue Sherbrooke Ouest at rue Redpath, Square Mile* ☎ *514/843–3431* ⊕ *www.standrewstpaul.com* ✑ *Free* ☉ *Sun. service at 11 AM; other times by arrangement* Ⓜ *Guy-Concordia.*

▶ **⓯ Couvent des Soeurs Grises** (Convent of the Gray Nuns). The Gray Nuns moved to this rambling gray-stone convent in 1874, after their residence and hospital in Vieux-Montréal burned down. The convent is closed to the public, but those seeking a quiet place to pray are welcome to use the beautiful Romanesque chapel. The order, which still runs hospitals, shelters for battered women, and halfway houses, was not named for the color of their habits. Their founder started looking after the city's down-and-outs after her unhappy marriage to a whiskey trader ended in widowhood. Both her late husband's profession and the condition of many of her clients earned her and her colleagues the term "soeurs grises"—slang for drunk sisters. But the nuns did, indeed, adopt gray habits. ⊠ *1185 rue St-Mathieu, Shaughnessy Village* ☎ *514/937–9501* ⊠ *By donation* ☉ *Tues.–Sun. 1:30–4:30* Ⓜ *Guy-Concordia or Georges-Vanier.*

⓴ Erskine and American United Church. Various marbles adorn the sanctuary of this massive, neo-Romanesque church built in 1894. Its greatest treasures, however, are the 24 windows in the side chapel—the largest collection of Louis Comfort Tiffany–signed stained-glass windows outside the United States. The Musée des Beaux-Arts de Montréal is in the process of buying the church as an exhibition space for religious art. Until then, to see the interior and the Tiffany windows, go to the avenue du Musée entrance, ring the bell, and ask politely. ⊠ *Rue Sherbrooke Ouest at av. du Musée, Square Mile* ☎ *514/849–3286* ⊠ *Free* ☉ *Sun. service at 11 AM; other times by arrangement* Ⓜ *Guy-Concordia.*

㉑ George Stephen House. Scottish-born George Stephen, founder of the Canadian Pacific Railway, spent C$600,000 to build this impressive home in 1883—it was an almost unimaginable sum at the time. He imported artisans from all over the world to panel its ceilings with Cuban mahogany, Indian lemon tree, and English oak and to cover its walls in marble, onyx, and gold. Now the private Mount Stephen Club, the house is open for dinner most Saturdays (pre-show, three-course meal is C$29.95, seven-course dinner is $65) and brunch most Sundays (C$38.95 for a guided tour and a buffet of braised duck or roast beef). Make reservations for both. ⊠ *1440 rue Drummond, Square Mile* ☎ *514/849–7338* ⊕ *www.clubmountstephen.net* ☉ *Sun. by reservation. Closed to non-members mid-July–Aug.* Ⓜ *Peel or Guy-Concordia.*

⓱ Grand Séminaire de Montréal. Education goes way back on this site. In the mid-1600s, St. Marguerite Bourgeoys used one of the two stone towers in the garden as a school for First Nations (Native American) girls while she and her nuns lived in the other. The 1860 seminary buildings behind the towers are now used by men studying for the priesthood. The seminary is private, but in summer there are free guided tours of the towers, the extensive gardens, and the college's beautiful Romanesque chapel. The chapel is open for Sunday mass from September through June. ⊠ *2065 rue Sherbrooke Ouest, Square Mile* ☎ *514/935–1169, ext. 239* 🖷 *514/935–5497* ⊕ *www.gsdm.qc.ca* ☉ *Guided tours mid-June–mid-Aug., Tues.–Sat. at 1 PM and 3 PM; service Sept.–June, Sun. 10:30 AM* Ⓜ *Guy-Concordia.*

🕐 ㉒ **McGill University.** James McGill, a wealthy Scottish fur trader and merchant, bequeathed the money and the land for this institution, founded in 1828, which now has a student body of 29,000. Probably the best English-language university in the nation, McGill is best known for its medical and engineering schools. A tree-lined road leads from the Greek Revival Roddick Gates to the austere neoclassical Arts Building—the university's original building—at the northern end of the campus. The templelike building to the west of the Arts Building houses the delightful **Redpath Museum of Natural History,** which has a collection that includes dinosaur bones, old coins, African art, and shrunken heads. Under the trees to the east of the main drive, a bronze James McGill hurries across campus holding his tricorn hat against the wind. ✉ *859 rue Sherbrooke Ouest, Square Mile* ☎ *514/398–4455, 514/398–6655 guided tours, 514/398–4086 museum* ⊕ *www.mcgill.ca* ✇ *Free* ⊙ *Museum: Sept.–May, weekdays 9–5, Sun. 1–5; June–Aug., Mon.–Thurs. 9–5* Ⓜ *McGill.*

need a break?

The campus of **McGill University** (✉ 859 rue Sherbrooke Ouest, Square Mile ☎ 514/398–4455) is an island of green in a sea of traffic and skyscrapers. On a fine day you can sit on the grass in the shade of a 100-year-old tree and let the world drift by.

★ ⑱ **Musée des Beaux-Arts de Montréal** (Montréal Museum of Fine Arts). The oldest museum in the country was founded by a group of English-speaking Montrealers in 1860. The art collection is housed in two buildings—the older, neoclassical **Michal and Renata Hornstein Pavilion,** on the north side of rue Sherbrooke, and the glittering, glass-fronted **Jean-Noël-Desmarais Pavilion,** across the street. The two buildings, connected by underground tunnels, hold a large collection of European and North American fine and decorative art; ancient treasures from Europe, the Near East, Asia, Africa, and America; art from Québec and other parts of Canada; and Native American and Inuit artifacts. The museum is particularly strong in 19th-century works, and has one of the finest collections of Canadian paintings, prints, and drawings. In 2001 the museum absorbed the collection of the Musée des Arts Décoratifs, including prototypes of Frank Gehry's bentwood furniture for Knoll and designs by Charles and Ray Eames. The museum also has a gift shop, a bookstore, a restaurant, a cafeteria, and a gallery in which you can buy or even rent paintings by local artists. ✉ *1380 rue Sherbrooke Ouest, Square Mile* ☎ *514/285–2000* ⊕ *www.mmfa.qc.ca* ✇ *Permanent collection free, special exhibitions C$12* ⊙ *Tues.–Sun. 11–6, special exhibitions open until 9 Wed.* Ⓜ *Guy-Concordia.*

★ 🕐 ㉓ **Musée McCord de l'Histoire Canadienne** (McCord Museum of Canadian History). A grand attic of a museum, the McCord documents the life of ordinary Canadians, using costumes and textiles, decorative arts, paintings, prints and drawings, and the 450,000-print-and-negative Notman Photographic Archives, which highlight 19th-century life in Montréal. One series of photographs, for example, portrays the members of the posh Montréal Athletic Association posing in snowshoes on the slopes of Mont-Royal all decked out in Hudson Bay coats and woolen hats.

Each of the hundreds of portraits was shot individually in a studio and then painstakingly mounted on a picture of the snowy mountain to give the impression of a winter outing. There are guided tours, a reading room and documentation center, a gift shop and bookstore, and a café. ✉ *690 rue Sherbrooke Ouest, Square Mile* ☎ *514/398–7100* ⊕ *www. mccordmuseum.qc.ca* ✄ *C$8.50* ⊘ *June 25–Labor Day, weekdays 10–6, weekends 10–5; early Sept.–June 24, Tues.–Fri. 10–6, weekends 10–5; call for tour times* Ⓜ *McGill.*

Quartier Latin & Plateau Mont-Royal

In the early 1900s, rue St-Denis cut through a bourgeois neighborhood of large, comfortable houses. The Université de Montréal was established here in 1893, and the students and academics who moved into the area dubbed it the Quartier Latin, or Latin Quarter. The university eventually moved to a larger campus on the north side of Mont-Royal, and the area went into decline. It revived starting in the early 1970s, largely as a result of the 1969 opening of the Université du Québec à Montréal and the launch of the Festival International de Jazz in the summer of 1980. Plateau Mont-Royal, the trendy neighborhood just north of the Quartier Latin, shared in this revival. Residents are now a mix of immigrants and young professionals eager to find houses ripe for renovation that are also close to the city center. Both the Quartier Latin and Plateau Mont-Royal have rows of French and ethnic restaurants, bistros, coffee shops, designer boutiques, antiques shops, and art galleries. When night falls, these streets are full of omnilingual hordes—young and not so young, rich and poor, established and still studying.

Many of the older residences in this area have graceful wrought-iron balconies and twisting staircases that are typical of Montréal. They were built that way for practical reasons. The buildings are what Montrealers call duplexes or triplexes, that is, two or three residences stacked one atop the other. To save interior space, the stairs to reach the upper floors were put outside. The stairs and balconies, treacherous in winter, are often full of families and couples gossiping, picnicking, and partying come summer. If Montrealers tell you they spend the summer in Balconville, they mean they don't have the money or the time to leave town and won't get any farther than their balconies.

a good walk

Begin at the Berri-UQAM Métro stop. The "UQAM" in the subway name (pronounced "oo-kam" by local Francophones and "you-kwam" by local Anglophones) refers to the **Université du Québec à Montréal ❶ ▶**, whose modern but nondescript brick campus fills up much of three city blocks between rues Sanguinet and Berri. A few splendid, stone fragments of an old church—demolished to make way for the school—have been incorporated into the buildings, notably the main steeple, which still chimes out the hours. A more substantial religious monument that has survived intact right in UQAM's resolutely secular heart is the ornate **Chapelle Notre-Dame-de-Lourdes ❷**, on rue Ste-Catherine.

Just west of rue St-Denis is the Cinémathèque Québecoise, which includes one of the largest cinematic archives in the world. Around the

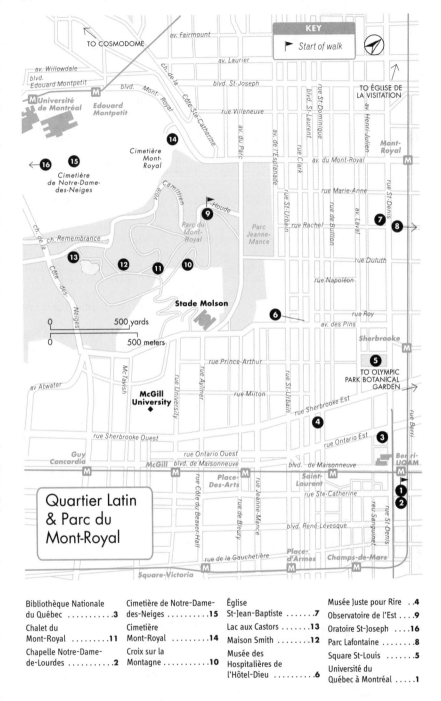

Quartier Latin
& Parc du
Mont-Royal

corner is the headquarters of the National Film Board of Canada, home of a robot-serviced screening room. A half block north on rue St-Denis stands the 2,500-seat Théâtre St-Denis, the city's second-largest auditorium. Continue north on rue St-Denis to the **Bibliothèque Nationale du Québec** ➌, on the left.

Continue north to rue Sherbrooke and turn left. At boulevard St-Laurent turn left again for the **Musée Juste pour Rire** ➍, one of the few museums in the world dedicated to humor. Backtrack east on rue Sherbrooke, turn left on rue St-Denis, and walk north to **Square St-Louis** ➎, a lovely green space.

The stretch of **rue Prince-Arthur** beginning at the western end of Square St-Louis and continuing several blocks west is a center of youth culture. Walk west on rue Prince-Arthur; when you reach **boulevard St-Laurent,** take a right and stroll north. This area was still partly rural in the mid-1800s, with lots of fresh air, and was presumed healthier than overcrowded Vieux-Montréal. In 1861 the Hôpital Hôtel-Dieu, which Jeanne Mance founded in the 17th century, moved into a building at what is now the corner of avenue des Pins and rue St-Urbain, two blocks west of boulevard St-Laurent. Hôtel-Dieu, one of the city's major hospitals, is still here, and next to it is the **Musée des Hospitalières de l'Hôtel-Dieu** ➏, which gives a remarkable picture of the city's early days.

A few blocks north on boulevard St-Laurent, turn right on rue Duluth, an intriguing strip of ethnic restaurants with outdoor terraces, crafts shops, and clothing boutiques. Turn left on avenue Henri-Julien and walk north for a block to see the **Église St-Jean-Baptiste** ➐ on rue Rachel, a neoclassical monument of devotion. Walk east another nine blocks on rue Rachel and you come to **Parc Lafontaine** ➑, at 100 acres the smallest of Montréal's three major parks. After exploring, walk south to rue Sherbrooke Est, turn right, and then walk west on rues Sherbrooke and Cherrier to the Sherbrooke Métro station to complete the walk. Or head farther west to explore Parc du Mont-Royal.

TIMING This is a comfortable afternoon walk, lasting perhaps three hours, or longer if you linger for an hour or so in the Musée des Hospitalières and also spend some time shopping. Note that it's a bit of a climb from boulevard de Maisonneuve to rue Sherbrooke.

What to See

➌ **Bibliothèque Nationale du Québec** (Québec National Library). Québec's official archives have long since outgrown this fine Beaux Arts structure built to house them in 1915, and are scheduled to move to a new, purpose-built building on rue Berri across from the bus terminal in the near future. However, the rooms of this graceful building will likely continue to play host to numerous artistic, cultural, and literary exhibits. ✉ *1700 rue St-Denis, Quartier Latin* ☎ *514/873–1100* Ⓜ *Berri-UQAM.*

Boulevard St-Laurent. Depending on how you look at it, this street is either the division between east and west or it's where east and west meet. After the first electric tramway was installed on boulevard St-Laurent, working-class families began to move in. In the 1880s the first of many waves of Jewish immigrants escaping pogroms in Eastern Europe arrived. They called the street The Main, as in "Main Street." Jews were followed by Greeks, other Eastern Europeans, Portuguese, and, most recently, Latin Americans. The 10 blocks north of rue Sherbrooke are filled with delis, junk stores, restaurants and luncheonettes, and clothing stores, as well as fashionable boutiques, bistros, cafés, bars, nightclubs, bookstores, and galleries. The block between rues Roy and Napoléon is a particularly rich place to investigate. Ⓜ *St-Laurent, Sherbrooke, or Mount-Royal.*

❷ **Chapelle Notre-Dame-de-Lourdes** (Our Lady of Lourdes Chapel). A dazzling mixture of Roman and Byzantine styles, this tiny Roman Catholic chapel is one of the most ornate pieces of religious architecture in the city. Built in 1876, it's decorated with brightly colored murals by the artist Napoléon Bourassa. ⊠ *430 rue Ste-Catherine Est, Quartier Latin* 🕾 *Free* ☉ *Mon.–Sat. 7:30–6; Sun. 9–6* Ⓜ *Berri-UQAM.*

off the beaten path

ÉGLISE DE LA VISITATION DE LA BIENHEUREUSE VIERGE MARIE – Far to the north on the banks of Rivière des Prairies is the oldest extant church on the island of Montréal, the Church of the Visitation of the Blessed Virgin Mary. Its stone walls were raised in the 1750s, and the beautifully proportioned Palladian front was added in 1850. The task of decorating lasted from 1764 until 1837, with stunning results. The altar and the pulpit are as ornate as wedding cakes but still delicate. The church's most notable treasure is a rendering of the Visitation attributed to Pierre Mignard, a painter in the 17th-century court of Louis XIV. Parkland surrounds the church, and the nearby Îles de la Visitation (reachable by footbridge) make for a very good walk. The church is a 15-minute walk north of the Henri Bourassa Métro station, but the trek is worth it. ⊠ *1847 blvd. Gouin Est, Sault-au-Récollet* 🕾 *514/388–4050* 🕾 *Free* ☉ *Daily 10–11:30 and 2–4* Ⓜ *Henri Bourassa.*

❼ **Église St-Jean-Baptiste** (St. John the Baptist Church). The neoclassical facade of this immense parish church hides a sumptuous baroque-revival interior where a baldachin (canopy) of pink marble and gilded wood shelters a white marble altar. The church, dedicated in 1904 to the patron saint of French Canada, seats 3,000 and has a powerful Casavant organ, which makes it popular for concerts and choir recitals. The parishioners who paid for this magnificent church and worshipped in it were largely working-class men and women with large families. The church is only open during mass and for concerts. ⊠ *309 rue Rachel Est, Plateau Mont-Royal* 🕾 *Free* ☉ *Mass Sat. 5 PM, Sun. 10 AM and 11:30 AM* Ⓜ *Mont-Royal.*

❻ **Musée des Hospitalières de l'Hôtel-Dieu.** More than just a fascinating exhibit on the history of medicine and nursing, this museum captures the spirit of an age. France in the 1600s was consumed with religious fervor, and aristocratic men and women often built hospitals, schools, and churches in distant lands. The nuns of the Religieuses Hospitalières de

St-Joseph who came to Montréal in the mid-1600s to help Jeanne Mance run the Hôpital Hôtel-Dieu embodied this fervor, and much of their spirit is evident in the letters, books, and religious artifacts displayed in bilingual exhibits. Pay special attention to the beautiful wooden stairway in the museum's entrance hall. ⊠ *201 av. des Pins Ouest, Plateau Mont-Royal* ☎ *514/849–2919* ⊕ *www.museedeshospitalieres.qc.ca* ✆ *C$5* ⊙ *Mid-June–mid-Oct., Tues.–Fri. 10–5, weekends 1–5; mid-Oct.–mid-June, Wed.–Sun. 1–5* Ⓜ *Sherbrooke.*

> **need a break?** The homey, cash-only **Café Santropol** (⊠ 3990 rue St-Urbain, Plateau Mont-Royal ☎ 514/842–3110) serves hearty soups, cakes, salads, and unusual high-rise sandwiches garnished with fruit (the Jeanne Mance version mixes pineapples and chives in cream cheese). One percent of the profits goes to charity, and the staff runs a meals-on-wheels program.

❹ **Musée Juste pour Rire** (Just for Laughs Museum). The International Comedy Hall of Fame and its film clips of what it believes are the 100 best comics of the last century forms the adult part of this museum, but the rest is pretty much for the kids. ⊠ *2111 blvd. St-Laurent, Quartier Latin* ☎ *514/845–4000* ⊕ *www.hahaha.com* ✆ *C$9 for Hall of Fame* ⊙ *Thurs. and Fri. 9–3, weekends 10–5, Tues. and Wed. by reservation only (minimum 60 people)* Ⓜ *St-Laurent.*

❽ **Parc Lafontaine.** Montréal's two main cultures are reflected in the layout of this popular park: the eastern half is French, with paths, gardens, and lawns laid out in geometric shapes; the western half is English, with meandering paths and irregularly shaped ponds that follow the natural contours of the land. In summer you can take advantage of bowling greens, tennis courts, an open-air theater (Théâtre Verdure) where there are free arts events, and two artificial lakes with paddleboats. In winter the two lakes form a large skating rink. The park is named for Sir Louis-Hippolyte Lafontaine (1807–64), a pioneer of responsible government in Canada. His statue graces a plot on the park's southwestern edge. ⊠ *3933 av. Parc Lafontaine, Plateau Mont-Royal* ☎ *514/872–9800* ⊙ *Daily 9 AM–10 PM* Ⓜ *Sherbrooke or Mont-Royal.*

Rue Prince-Arthur. In the 1960s, the young people who moved to the neighborhood transformed this street into a small hippie bazaar of clothing, leather, and smoke shops. It remains youth-oriented, although it's much tamer and more commercial these days. The city turned the blocks between avenue Laval and boulevard St-Laurent into a pedestrian mall, and the hippie shops have metamorphosed into inexpensive Greek, Vietnamese, Italian, Polish, and Chinese restaurants and neighborhood bars. Ⓜ *Sherbrooke.*

❺ **Square St-Louis.** Nineteenth-century homes built in the large, comfortable style of the Second Empire surround this elegant square, where there's a fountain, benches, and trees. Originally a reservoir, these blocks became a park in 1879 and attracted upper-middle-class families and artists. French-Canadian poets were among the most famous creative types to occupy the houses back then, and the neighborhood today is home to painters, filmmakers, musicians, and writers. On the wall of 336 Square St-Louis you can see—and read, if your French is good—a long poem by Michel Bujold. ⊠ *Bordered by av. Laval and rue St-Denis between rue Sherbrooke Est and av. des Pins Est, Quartier Latin* Ⓜ *Sherbrooke.*

▶ ❶ **Université du Québec à Montréal.** Part of a network of campuses set up by the provincial government in 1969, UQAM encompasses a series of massive, modern brick buildings clogging much of the three city blocks bordered by rues Sanguinet and Berri and boulevards de Maisonneuve and René-Lévesque. The splendid fragments of Gothic grandeur sprouting up among the modern brick hulks are all that's left of Église St-Jacques, built in 1825 and destroyed by fire in 1852. ⊠ *Bordered by rues Sanguinet and Berri and blvds. de Maisonneuve and René-Lévesque, Plateau Mont-Royal* ☎ *514/987–3000* Ⓜ *Berri-UQAM.*

Parc du Mont-Royal

FodorśChoice
★

Frederick Law Olmsted (1822–1903), the codesigner of New York City's Central Park, designed Parc du Mont-Royal, 494 acres of forest and paths in the heart of Montréal. Olmsted believed that communion with nature could cure body and soul. The park follows the natural topography and accentuates its features, in the English style. You can jog, cycle, or stroll the miles of paths, or just scan the horizon from one of two lookouts. Horse-drawn transport is popular year-round: sleigh rides in winter and calèche rides in summer. On the eastern side of the hill stands the 98-foot-tall steel cross that is the symbol of the city. Not far away from the park and perched on a neighboring crest of the same mountain is the Oratoire St-Joseph, a shrine that draws millions every year.

a good tour

Begin by taking the Métro's Orange Line to the Mont-Royal station and transfer to Bus 11 (be sure to get a transfer—*correspondence* in French—from a machine before you get on the Métro). The No. 11 drives right through the Parc du Mont-Royal on the voie Camillien Houde. Get off at the **Observatoire de l'Est ❾** ▶, a lookout with a great view of the Stade Olympique. Climb the stone staircase at the west end of the parking lot and follow the trails to the **Croix sur la Montagne ❿**. From there, you can continue your walk around the top of the mountain by following the road to the **Chalet Mont Royal ⓫**, a baronial building with a terrace that overlooks the skyscrapers of downtown Montréal. From there, continue west to the **Maison Smith ⓬**, which has a display on the history and fauna of the park. From there, walk through the sculpture garden to **Lac aux Castors ⓭**.

Across chemin Remembrance from Lac aux Castors is what looks like one vast cemetery. It is in fact two cemeteries—one Protestant and one Catholic. The Protestant **Cimetière Mont-Royal ⓮** is toward the east in a little valley that cuts off the noise of the city; it's the final resting place of the woman that the heroine of *The King and I* was modeled on. The yellow-brick buildings and tower on the north side of the mountain beyond the cemetery belong to the Université de Montréal, the second-largest French-language university in the world, with nearly 60,000 students. Now head to the Catholic cemetery nearby, the **Cimetière de**

Notre-Dame-des-Neiges 🅕 the final address of many of Québec's leading poets, artists, and politicians.

Wander northwest through the two cemeteries and you eventually emerge on chemin Queen Mary, on the edge of a lively area of street vendors, ethnic restaurants, and boutiques. Walk west on Queen Mary across chemin de la Côte-des-Neiges, and you come to Montréal's most grandiose religious monument, the **Oratoire St-Joseph** 🅖. Across the street is the ivy-covered Collège Notre Dame, where the oratory's founder, Brother André, worked as a porter. Today it's an important coed private school and one of the few in the city that still accept boarders. After visiting the church, retrace your steps to chemin de la Côte-des-Neiges and walk to the Côte-des-Neiges station to catch the Métro.

TIMING   Allot the better part of a day for this tour, longer if you plan on catching some rays or going ice-skating in the park.

What to See

★ ⓫ **Chalet du Mont-Royal.** The view from the terrace here takes in downtown Montréal. In the distance you can see Mont-Royal's sister mountains— Monts St-Bruno, St-Hilaire, and St-Grégoire. These isolated peaks, called the Montérégies, or Mountains of the King, rise dramatically from the flat countryside. Be sure to take a look inside the chalet, especially at the murals depicting scenes from Canadian history. There's a snack bar in the back. ⊠ *Off voie Camillien-Houde, Mont-Royal* 🕾 *No phone* 🖅 *Free* 🕑 *Daily 9–5.*

⓯ **Cimetière de Notre-Dame-des-Neiges** (Our Lady of the Snows Cemetery). The largest Catholic graveyard in the city is the final resting place of hundreds of prominent artists, poets, intellectuals, politicians, and clerics. Among them is Calixa Lavallée (1842–91), who wrote "O Canada," the country's national anthem. Many of the monuments and mausoleums—scattered along 55 km (34 mi) of paths and roadways—are the work of leading artists. There are no tours of the cemetery, but a computer system makes it easy to find graves. ⊠ *4601 chemin de la Côte-des-Neiges, Mont-Royal* 🕾 *514/735–1361* 🌐 *www.cimetierenddn.org* 🕑 *Daily 10–6* Ⓜ *Université de Montréal.*

⓮ **Cimetière Mont-Royal.** The Mont-Royal Cemetery was established in 1852 by the Anglican, Presbyterian, Unitarian, and Baptist churches and is laid out like a terraced garden with footpaths that meander through stands of crab apple trees and past beds of Japanese lilacs. The most famous permanent guest here is Anna Leonowens (1834–1914), who was governess to the children of the King of Siam and the real-life model for the heroine of the musical *The King and I.* ⊠ *1297 chemin de la Forêt, Mont-Royal* 🕾 *514/279–7358* 🌐 *www.mountroyalcem.com/en/cemetery* 🕑 *Daily 10–6* Ⓜ *Edouard Montpetit.*

off the beaten path

COSMODOME – The adventure of space exploration is the focus of this interactive center in suburban Laval, about a 30-minute drive from downtown. It's loaded with such kid-pleasing exhibits as replicas of rockets and space ships and a full-size mock-up of the space shuttle *Endeavor.* There are also films—some of them shown on a 360-degree screen—demonstrations, and games. Next door to the Cosmodome is the **Space Camp** (☎ 800/565–2267), a training center for amateur astronauts nine or older that is affiliated with the U.S. Space Camp in Georgia. ⊠ *2150 autoroute des Laurentides, Laval* ☎ *450/978–3600* ⊕ *www.cosmodome.org* ☲ *C$11.50* ⊙ *Late June–Aug., daily 10–6; Sept.–late June, Tues.–Sun. 10–6.*

❿ **Croix sur la Montagne.** A Montréal landmark since it was erected in 1924, this 98-foot-high steel cross is at the top of Mont-Royal. Lit with hundreds of light bulbs, it can be seen from miles away.

🌼 ⓭ **Lac aux Castors** (Beaver Lake). In summer, children love to float boats in this lake reclaimed from boggy ground. It's a fine skating rink in winter. ⊠ *Off chemin Remembrance, Mont-Royal* Ⓜ *Edouard Montpetit.*

⓬ **Maison Smith.** This stone house was built as the park keeper's residence in 1858. It now houses a small exhibit on the history, flora, and fauna of the park and serves as a gift shop and information center. Hikers who want to make a day of it can pick up maps to the park's extensive network of footpaths. The organization Les Amis de Mont Royal (Friends of Mount Royal) offers various guided walks of the mountains and nearby areas. ⊠ *1260 chemin Remembrance* ☎ *514/843–8240* ⊕ *www. lemontroyal.qc.ca* ⊙ *Weekdays 9–5, weekends 9–7.*

▶ ⑨ **Observatoire de l'Est.** From this lookout you have a spectacular view of the east end of the city and the St. Lawrence River. Snacks are available. ⊠ *Voie Camillien-Houde, Mont-Royal.*

⓰ **Oratoire St-Joseph** (St. Joseph's Oratory). A huge domed church high on a ridge of Mont-Royal, St. Joseph's is the largest shrine in the world dedicated to the earthly father of Jesus (and Canada's patron saint). It's the result of the persistence of a remarkable man named Brother André Besette (1845–1937), a porter in the school run by his religious order. The son of very poor farmers, he dreamed of building a shrine dedicated to St. Joseph and began in 1904 by building a little chapel. Miraculous cures were reported and attributed to St. Joseph's intercession, and Brother André's project caught the imagination of Montréal.

The church's mountainside setting gives it sweeping views over the north of the city, with the Laurentian foothills in the distance. The octagonal copper dome on top of the oratory is one of the biggest in the world. The modern interior is a soaring dim concrete cave full of rows of folding metal chairs and not much in the way of art or color, except for some striking stained-glass windows made by Marius Plamondon. The Montréal sculptor Henri Charlier is responsible for the huge crucifix, the elongated wooden statues of the apostles in the transepts, and the main altar.

In the more modest crypt church at the base of the stairs leading to the main church, a larger-than-life white marble statue of St. Joseph dominates the main altar. Behind the crypt is a room that glitters with hundreds of votive candles lighted in honor of St. Joseph; the walls are hung with crutches discarded by those said to be cured. Just beyond is the simple tomb of Brother André, who was beatified in 1982. His preserved heart is displayed in a glass case upstairs in one of the galleries sandwiched between the crypt and the main church (there are several levels between the two).

High on the mountain, east of the main church, is a beautiful garden commemorating the Passion of Christ with life-size representations of the 14 traditional Stations of the Cross. Carillon, choral, and organ concerts are held weekly in summer, and the church is also home to Les Petits Chanteurs de Mont-Royal, the city's finest boys' choir. The church's front door is 300 steps above street level (many pilgrims climb them on their knees), but a major construction project underway at this writing will link the church to the street-level parking lot with escalators and elevators. ⊠ *3800 chemin Queen Mary, Côte-des-Neiges* ☎ *514/733–8211* ⊕ *www.saint-joseph.org* ✆ *Free* ☉ *Mid-Sept.–mid-May, daily 7–5:30; mid-May–mid-Sept., daily 7 AM–9 PM* Ⓜ *Côte-des-Neiges.*

Olympic Park & Botanical Garden

The giant Stade Olympique and the leaning tower that supports the stadium's roof dominate the skyline of the eastern part of town. But there's much more to the area than the stadium complex, including the Jardin Botanique (Botanical Garden); the Insectarium, the world's largest museum dedicated to bugs; and Parc Maisonneuve, an ideal place for a stroll or a picnic. You can reach the Parc Olympique and the botanical garden via the Pie-IX or Viau Métro stations; a free shuttle links the latter, which is closer to the stadium entrance, with the Jardin Botanique, Biodôme, and Parc Olympique.

a good tour

Start with a ride on the Métro's Green Line and get off at the Viau station, which is only a few steps from the main entrance to the 70,000-seat **Stade Olympique** ❶ ☞, a stadium built for the 1976 summer games. A trip to the top of the **Tour Olympique** ❷, the world's tallest tilting structure, gives you a view up to 80 km (50 mi) on a clear day. The six pools of the **Centre Aquatique** ❸ are under the tower.

Next to the tower is the **Biodôme** ❹, where you can explore both a rain forest and an arctic landscape. Continuing your back-to-nature experience, cross rue Sherbrooke to the north of the park (or take the free shuttle bus) to reach the enormous **Jardin Botanique** ❺. The botanical complex includes the **Insectarium** ❻ and the 5-acre Montréal-Shanghai Lac de Rêve, an elegant Ming-style garden.

After you've looked at the flowers, head to boulevard Pie-IX, which runs along the western border of the gardens. The name of this traffic artery (and the adjoining Métro station) puzzles thousands of visitors every year. The street is named for the 19th-century pope Pius IX, or Pie-IX in French, and it's pronounced pea-neuf. At rue Sherbrooke, cross boulevard Pie-IX and walk west to rue Jeanne-d'Arc past the lavish **Château Dufresne** ❼, a pair of attached mansions built by two brothers in 1916.

TIMING To see all the sights at a leisurely pace, you need a full day.

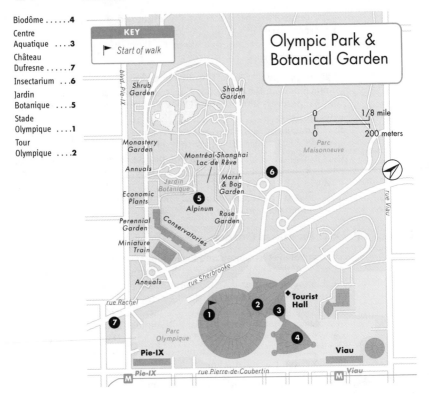

What to See

🖐 ❹ **Biodôme.** Not everyone thought it was a great idea to transform an Olympic bicycle-racing stadium into a natural-history exhibit, but the result is one of the city's most popular attractions, albeit one that's begun to show some wear and tear. Four ecosystems—the boreal forest, tropical forest, polar world, and St. Lawrence River—are under one climate-controlled dome. You follow protected pathways through each environment, observing flora and fauna of each ecosystem. A word of warning: the tropical forest really does feel tropical. If you want to stay comfortable, dress in layers. ✉ 4777 av. Pierre-de-Coubertin, Hochelaga-Maisonneuve ☎ 514/868–3000 ⊕ www.biodome.qc.ca ✇ C$11.75 ⊙ Late June–early Sept., daily 9–6; early Sept.–late June, Tues.–Sun. 9–5 Ⓜ Viau.

🖐 ❸ **Centre Aquatique.** Olympic swimmers competed here in 1976, but now anyone can use four of the six pools. One is for games such as water polo, the others are for laps. Volleyball courts also are available. ✉ 4141 av. Pierre-de-Coubertin, Hochelaga-Maisonneuve ☎ 514/252–4622 ✇ C$3.30 ⊙ Weekdays 2–8, weekends 1–4 Ⓜ Pie-IX or Viau.

❼ **Château Dufresne.** The adjoining homes of a pair of shoe manufacturers, Oscar and Marius Dufresne, provide a revealing glimpse into the lives of Montréal's Francophone bourgeoisie in the early 20th century.

The brothers built this Beaux Arts palace in 1916 along the lines of the Petit-Trianon in Paris and lived in it with their families—Oscar in the eastern half and Marius in the western half. The residences include oak staircases with gilded rails, marble-tile floors, stained-glass windows, and coffered ceilings. Murals by Guido Nincheri, an artist who also decorated many of the city's most beautiful churches, adorn the walls. Worth searching out are the delicate domestic scenes on the walls of the Petit Salon, where Madame Oscar Dufresne entertained her friends. Her brother-in-law, on the other side of the house, relaxed with his male friends in a smoking room decked out like a Turkish lounge. During the house's incarnation as a boys' school in the 1950s, the Eudist priests, who ran the place, covered the room's frieze of frolicking nymphs and satyrs with a modest curtain that their charges lifted at every opportunity. ⊠ *2929 rue Jeanne-d'Arc, Hochelaga-Maisonneuve* ☎ *514/259–9201* ⊕ *www. chateaudufresne.qc.ca* ☐ *C$6* ⊙ *Thurs.–Sun. 10–5* Ⓜ *Pie-IX.*

Ⓒ ⑥ **Insectarium.** Shaped like a bug, this building in the ⇨ **Jardin Botanique** houses more than 250,000 insect specimens. Most are mounted, but colorful butterflies fly free in one room, and there are live ant and bee exhibits, too. In February you can taste such delicacies as deep-fried bumblebees. ⊠ *4581 rue Sherbrooke Est, Hochelaga-Maisonneuve* ☎ *514/872–1400* ⊕ *www.ville.montreal.qc.ca/insectarium* ☐ *May–Oct. C$11.75, Nov.–Apr. C$7.75; price includes Jardin Botanique admission* ⊙ *May–mid-June and Sept. 10–Apr., daily 9–5; mid-June–Sept. 9, daily 9–6* Ⓜ *Pie-IX or Viau.*

Ⓒ ⑤ **Jardin Botanique** (Botanical Garden). With 181 acres of plantings in summer and 10 exhibition greenhouses open all year, this botanical garden founded in 1931 is the second-largest attraction of its kind in the world (after England's Kew Gardens). More than 26,000 species of plants grow here. Among the 30 thematic gardens are a rose garden and an alpine garden; the poisonous-plant garden is a favorite. Traditional tea ceremonies are held in the Japanese Garden, which also has one of the best bonsai collections in the West. The Tree House exhibit center in the arboretum explores the world of the forest. The Jardin des Premier Nations, or the First Nations Garden, includes such indigenous plants and trees as silver birch, maples, Labrador, and jack-in-the-pulpit. Other highlights include the ⇨ **Insectarium** and the 5-acre Montréal-Shanghai Lac de Rêve (Montréal-Shanghai Dream Garden). ⊠ *4101 rue Sherbrooke Est, Hochelaga-Maisonneuve* ☎ *514/872–1400* ⊕ *www.ville.montreal. qc.ca/jardin* ☐ *May–Oct. C$11.75, Nov.–Apr. C$7.75; price includes Insectarium admission* ⊙ *Early Sept.–Oct., daily 9–9; Nov.–late Dec., Tues.–Sun. 9–5; early Jan.–mid-June, daily 9–5; mid-June–early Sept., daily 8–6* Ⓜ *Pie-IX.*

FodorsChoice ★

off the beaten path

MAISONNEUVE – Olympic organizers weren't the first people to have big plans for this socially cohesive but economically depressed neighborhood. At the beginning of the 20th century, when the district was a hard-working, booming industrial center with its own municipal government, civic leaders wanted to transform it into a model city with broad boulevards, grandiose public buildings, and fine homes. World War I and the Depression killed those plans, but a few fine fragments of the grand dream survive, just three blocks south of the Olympic site. The magnificent Beaux Arts public market, which has a 20-foot-tall bronze statue of a farm woman, stands at the northern end of tree-lined avenue Morgan. Farmers and butchers have moved into a modern building next door; the old market is now a community center and the site of summer shows and concerts. Monumental staircases and a heroic rooftop sculpture embellish the public baths across the street. The **Théâtre Denise Pelletier,** at the corner of rue Ste-Catherine Est and rue Morgan, has a lavish Italianate interior; **Fire Station No. 1,** at 4300 rue Notre-Dame Est, was inspired by Frank Lloyd Wright's Unity Temple in suburban Chicago; and the sumptuously decorated **Église Très-Saint-Nom-de-Jésus** has one of the most powerful organs in North America. The 60-acre **Parc Maisonneuve,** stretching north of the Botanical Garden, is a lovely place for a stroll. Ⓜ *Pie-IX or Viau.*

➊ **Stade Olympique.** The stadium, built for the 1976 Summer Olympics, is beautiful to look at but not very practical. It's hard to heat, and the retractable fabric roof, supported by the tower, has never worked properly. It's used for events like Montréal's annual car show. ⊠ *4141 av. Pierre-de-Coubertin, Hochelaga-Maisonneuve* ☎ *514/252–8687* ⊕ *www.rio.gouv.qc.ca* Ⓜ *Pie-IX or Viau.*

➋ **Tour Olympique.** A trip to the top of this 890-foot tower, the world's tallest tilting structure, is very popular; a two-level cable car can whisk 90 people up the exterior of the tower. On a clear day you can see up to 80 km (50 mi) from the tower-top observatory. Daily guided tours of the Olympic complex leave from the **Tourist Hall** (☎ 514/252–8687) in the base of the Tour Olympique. Tours at 12:40 and 3:40 are in English, and tours at 11 and 2 are in French. ⊠ *Av. Pierre-de-Coubertin, Hochelaga-Maisonneuve* ☎ *514/252–4141 Ext. 5246 for tour and tower-ride arrangements* ⊠ *C$10 including tower and tour of Olympic complex; C$5.50 for tour only* Ⓜ *Pie-IX or Viau.*

The Islands

Expo '67—the world's fair staged to celebrate the centennial of the Canadian federation—was the biggest party in Montréal's history, and it marked a defining moment in the city's evolution as a modern metropolis. That party was held on two islands in the middle of the St. Lawrence River—Île Ste-Hélène, formed by nature, and Île Notre-Dame, created with the stone rubble excavated from the construction of Montréal's Métro. Fodor'sChoice The two islands are still a playground. Together they form **Parc Jean-** ★ **Drapeau** (☎ 514/872–4537 ⊕ www.parcjeandrapeau.com/en), named for the visionary mayor who brought the world's fair to Montréal, and encompass a major amusement park, acres of flower gardens, a beach with clean filtered water, and the Casino de Montréal. There's history, too, at the Old Fort, where soldiers in colonial uniforms display the military methods used in ancient wars. In winter you can skate on the old Olympic rowing basin or slide down iced trails on an inner tube.

a good walk

Start at the Jean-Drapeau station on the Métro's Yellow Line. The first thing you see when you emerge is the huge geodesic dome that houses **Biosphère,** an environmental exhibition center. From the Biosphère walk to the northern shore and then east to the Old Fort, now the **Stewart Museum at the Fort.** Just east of the Old Fort past the Pont Jacques-Cartier (Jacques Cartier Bridge) is **La Ronde,** an amusement park.

Now cross over to the island's southern shore and walk back along the waterfront to the Cosmos Footbridge, which leads to Île Notre-Dame. On the way you pass the Hélène de Champlain restaurant, which probably has the prettiest setting of any restaurant in Montréal, and the military cemetery of the British garrison stationed on Île Ste-Hélène from 1828 to 1870.

Île Notre-Dame is laced with a network of canals and ponds, and the grounds are brilliant with flower gardens left from the 1980 Floralies Internationales flower show. Most of the Expo '67 buildings are gone, the victims of time and weather. One that has remained, however, is the fanciful French Pavilion. It and the neighboring Québec Pavilion have been turned into the **Casino de Montréal.** A five-minute walk west of the casino is the Lac de l'Île Notre-Dame, site of **Plage de l'Île Notre-Dame,** Montréal's only beach. In August Île Notre-Dame hosts the Molson Indy automobile race at the **Circuit Gilles Villeneuve.**

After your walk you can return to the Métro or walk back to the city via the Pont de la Concorde (Concord Bridge) and the Parc de la Cité du Havre (Harbor Properties Park) to Vieux-Montréal. If you walk, you can see Habitat '67, an irregular pile of concrete blocks on avenue Pierre-Dupuy that was designed by Moshe Safdie and built as an experiment in housing for Expo '67. The private apartment complex resembles an updated version of a Hopi cliff dwelling.

TIMING   This is a comfortable two-hour stroll, but the Biosphère and the Stewart Museum at the Fort (try to time your visit to coincide with a drill) deserve at least an hour each, and you should leave another half hour to admire the flowers. Children are likely to want to spend a whole day at La Ronde, but in summer the best time to go is in the evening, when it's cooler. Try to visit the casino on a weekday, when crowds are thinnest.

What to See

Biosphère. An environmental center in the huge geodesic dome designed by Buckminster Fuller as the American Pavilion at Expo '67 successfully brings fun to an earnest project—heightening awareness of the St. Lawrence River system and its problems. Water levels in both the river and the Great Lakes have been dropping alarmingly and visitors of all ages—but especially kids—can use games and interactive terminals arranged around a large model of the waterway to explore what that means for shipping, the environment, tourism, water supplies, and hydroelectricity. ⊠ *160 Chemin Tour-de-l'Île, Île Ste-Hélène* ☎ *514/285–5000*

⊕ *www.biosphere.ec.gc.ca/bio* ⊠ *C$9.78* ⊗ *June–Sept., daily 10–6; Oct.–May, Tues.–Fri. noon–5* Ⓜ *Jean-Drapeau.*

★ **Casino de Montréal.** The government has tried to capture the elegance of Monte Carlo here, at what is one of the biggest gambling palaces in the world. The stunning complex—originally the French Pavilion for Expo '67—glitters with glass and murals and has stunning city views. The casino, which is open around the clock, has a dress code that forbids jeans, shorts, and tank tops. There are two keno lounges, more than 3000 slot machines, and 120 tables for playing blackjack, baccarat, roulette, craps, and various types of poker. Also part of the casino are four restaurants, including the formal French eatery Nuances, and a bilingual cabaret theater. Children under 18 are not admitted. ⊠ *1 av. du Casino, Île Notre-Dame* ☎ *514/392–2746 or 800/665–2274* ⊕ *www.casino-de-montreal. com* Ⓜ *Jean-Drapeau (then Bus 167).*

Circuit Gilles Villeneuve. All of the big names in motor sports used to gather at this track for the Grand Prix du Canada Formula 1 event. The track also stages the Molson Indy of Montréal, part of the CART FedEx Championship Series in automobile racing. ⊠ *Île Notre-Dame* ☎ *800/797– 4537* Ⓜ *Jean-Drapeau.*

⟲ **Plage de l'Île Notre-Dame** (Île Notre-Dame Beach). Filtered river water and a pleasant stretch of lawn and trees make this an inviting place for swimming. Lifeguards are on duty, a shop rents swimming and boating paraphernalia, and there are picnic areas and a restaurant. ⊠ *West side of Île Notre-Dame, Île Notre-Dame* ☎ *514/872–4537* ⊠ *C$7.50* ⊗ *Late June–Aug., daily 10–7* Ⓜ *Jean-Drapeau.*

⟲ **La Ronde.** This world-class amusement park, owned by the U.S. company Six Flags, has Ferris wheels, boat rides, and the Monstre, one of the tallest wooden roller coasters in the world, with one section at 132 feet. One of Le Ronde's most thrilling rides is the Vampire, a looping roller coaster that sends riders hurtling upside down at speeds of up to 50 mph. The popular **International Fireworks Competition** (☎ 514/397– 2000, 514/790–1245, 800/361–4595 in Canada) is held here weekends and a couple of weeknights in late June and July. ⊠ *Eastern end of Île Ste-Hélène,* ☎ *514/872–6222* ⊕ *www.laronde.com/en* ⊠ *C$29.95; C$22.60 grounds only* ⊗ *Late May, weekends 10–8; early June–late June, daily 10–8; late June–late Aug., 10 AM–10:30 PM; Sept., weekends 10–7; Oct., Fri. 5 PM–9 PM, Sat. noon–9, Sun. noon–8; call to confirm hrs* Ⓜ *Jean-Drapeau.*

⟲ **Stewart Museum at the Fort.** In summer the grassy parade square of the fine stone Old Fort comes alive with the crackle of colonial muskets fired by reenactors. The French are represented by the Compagnie Franche de la Marine and the British by the kilted 78th Fraser Highlanders, one of the regiments that participated in the conquest of Québec in 1759. The fort itself, built between 1820 and 1824 to protect Montréal from American invasion, is now a museum that tells the story of colonial life in the city through displays of old firearms, maps, and uniforms. The two companies of colonial soldiers raise the flag every day at 11, practice maneuvers at 1, put on a combined display of precision drilling and musket fire at 2:30, and lower the flag at 5. Children can take part. ✉ *Just west of Pont Jacques-Cartier, Île Ste-Hélène* ☎ *514/861–6701* ⊕ *www. stewart-museum.org* 🎟 *$8* ⊗ *Early May–mid-Oct., daily 10–6; mid-Oct.–early May, Wed.–Mon. 10–5* Ⓜ *Jean-Drapeau.*

WHERE TO EAT

Good restaurants can pop up just about anywhere in town, and sometimes they appear in the oddest places. Toqué!, for example, long touted as one of the city's best, is on the ground floor of an office tower in the financial district. That being said, some districts are richer than others. Rue St-Denis and Boul St-Laurent between rues Sherbrooke and Mont-Royal have long been the two hottest dining strips in Montréal, with everything from sandwich shops to high-priced gourmet shrines. The bring-your-own-wine craze started on rue Prince-Arthur and av. Duluth, two noisy, colorful pedestrian streets that remain popular with people looking for a cheap meal and a good time. From the first glimmer of summer until the last hopeful breath of fall, Montrealers love to dine alfresco, at sidewalk tables or on what both French and English speakers call terrasses—private and often tree-shaded decks and gradens. Interesting ethnic restaurants can be found farther north in Little Italy and in the streets around the Marché Jean-Talon. In Downtown, most of the good restaurants are clustered between rues Guy and Peel on the side streets that run between boulevard Dorchester and rue Sherbrooke. Vieux-Montréal, too, has a good collection of restaurants, most of them clustered on rue St-Paul and Place Jacques-Cartier.When you dine out, you can usually order à la carte, but look for the table d'hôte, a two- to four-course package deal. It's usually more economical, often offers interesting specials, and may also take less time to prepare. If you want to splurge on time and money, consider a *menu dégustation,* a five- to seven-course tasting menu executed by the chef. It generally includes soup, salad, fish, sherbet (to cleanse the palate), a meat dish, dessert, and coffee or tea. At the city's finest restaurants, such a meal for two, along with a good bottle of wine, can cost more than C$200 and last four hours.

Menus in many restaurants are bilingual, but some are only in French. If you don't understand what a dish is, don't be shy about asking; a good server will be happy to explain. If you feel brave enough to order in French, remember that in French an entrée is an appetizer and what English speakers call an entrée is a *plat principal,* or main dish.

Dinner reservations are highly recommended for weekend dining.

Prices

WHAT IT COSTS In Canadian dollars				
$$$$	**$$$**	**$$**	**$**	**¢**
AT DINNER over C$30	C$20–C$30	C$12–C$20	C$8–C$12	under C$8

Prices are per person for a main course at dinner (or at the most expensive meal served).

CloseUp

ON THE MENU IN MONTRÉAL

Montrealers are passionate about food. They love to dine on classic dishes in restaurants such as Les Halles and Chez la Mère Michel, or swoon over culinary innovations in places like Toqué! and Area, but they can be equally passionate about humbler fare. They'll argue with some heat about where to get the juiciest smoked meat), the crispiest barbecued chicken, and the soggiest stimés (steamed hot dogs). There's great French food here, but also some of North America's most creative chefs, who seamlessly blend French discipline, Asian and Latin flavors, and the freshest of local ingredients. Immigrants from all over the world—notably Jews from Eastern Europe, Greeks, Thais, Chinese, Portuguese, and especially Italians—have added to the mix, and today the city's restaurants represent more than 75 ethnic groups.

Downtown

Canadian

$–$$ ✕ **Chalet Barbecue.** In the early 1950s, Swiss-born Marcel Mauron and French-born Jean Detanne built a large brick oven in this west-end location and pioneered a Montréal tradition: crispy, spit-barbecued chicken served with a slightly spicy, gravylike sauce and mountains of french fries. There are dozens of imitators all over the city, but no one does it better. Many of the restaurant's customers order their meals to go. ⊠ 5456 rue Sherbrooke Ouest, Notre-Dame-de-Grace ☎ 514/489–7235 ⊟ MC, V Ⓜ Vendôme.

Chinese

$$–$$$$ ✕ **Orchidée de Chine.** Diners feast on such dishes as baby bok choy with mushrooms, spicy spareribs, feather-light fried soft-shell crabs with black-bean sauce, and tender strips of beef served with bell peppers and fried basil leaves. The cream-and-yellow, glassed-in dining room has a great view onto a busy, fashionable sidewalk; a more intimate room is in the back. ⊠ 2017 rue Peel, Downtown ☎ 514/287–1878 ⚐ Reservations essential ⊟ AE, DC, MC, V ☉ Closed Sun. No lunch Sat. Ⓜ Peel.

$–$$$ ✕ **Maison Kam Fung.** This bright, airy restaurant serves Chinatown's most reliable dim sum lunch. Every day from 10 to 3, waiters push a parade of trolleys through the restaurant, carting such treats as firm dumplings stuffed with pork and chicken, stir-fried squid, and delicate shrimp-filled envelopes of pastry. ⊠ 1111 rue St-Urban, Chinatown ☎ 514/878–2888 ⊟ AE, DC, MC, V Ⓜ Place-d'Armes.

Continental

$$$$ ✕ **Beaver Club.** A 2003 makeover softened the fusty-men's-club look of this grand old institution: there are now tapestry banquettes, contemporary First Nations (Native American) prints, and a brown, beige, and cream color scheme. It's still pretty sumptuous, with wing chairs, starched linens, an impeccable staff, and a menu that relies on such classics as roast beef, grilled chops, poached salmon, and Cornish hens. The bar serves the best martini in the city. ⊠ *Fairmont Le Reine Elizabeth, 900 blvd. René-Lévesque Ouest, Downtown* ☎ *514/861–3511* 🏛 *Jacket and tie* 🖃 *AE, D, DC, MC, V* ☺ *Closed Sun. and July. No dinner Mon.; no lunch Sat. and in Aug.* Ⓜ *Bonaventure.*

Delicatessen

¢–$ ✕ **Ben's.** This big, brassy deli is a Montréal institution, with 1950s furnishings and green and yellow walls hung with photos of celebrity customers. Sadly, the food, primarily smoked-meat sandwiches, isn't what it once was, but Ben's remains a good place for a late-night snack. ⊠ *990 blvd. de Maisonneuve Ouest, Downtown* ☎ *514/844–1000* ♧ *Reservations not accepted* 🖃 *MC, V* Ⓜ *Peel.*

French

$$$$ ✕ **Caprices de Nicolas.** Antique furniture, plush seats, stained-glass
FodorsChoice lamps, and dainty china make this restaurant one of Montréal's most
★ luxurious. Its two art nouveau–inspired rooms are magnificent, but the most romantic tables are in the soaring, three-story atrium, reserved for nonsmokers, that's filled with tropical plants. The poached sea bass is exquisite, as is the salmon *pavé* (mousse) with onion preserves and currants. Meatier dishes include organic Québec beef with an herb crust and pistachio gravy. ⊠ *2072 rue Drummond, Downtown* ☎ *514/282–9790* ♧ *Reservations essential* 🖃 *AE, DC, MC, V* ☺ *No lunch* Ⓜ *Peel.*

$$$–$$$$ ✕ **La Rapière.** The musketeer D'Artagnan, dashing master of the rapier
FodorsChoice (or "rapière"), came from Gascony in southwestern France, as do most
★ of this classic little restaurant's specialties. Start with paper-thin slices of the house-smoked goose meat or a portion of delicately pink duck foie gras, followed by a cassoulet of duck, haricot beans, and pork rind. In fact, duck in all its forms is worth trying here. The dessert menu includes nougat ice with custard and hot (oddly enough) crème brûlée, but the cheese plate is so good that it might tempt you to skip the sweet stuff. The room itself is soothing, with terra-cotta-colored walls, tapestries, and stained-glass windows. ⊠ *Sun Life Building, 1155 rue Metcalfe, Downtown* ☎ *514/871–8920* ♧ *Reservations essential* 🖃 *AE, DC, MC, V* ☺ *Closed Sunday, no lunch Saturday* Ⓜ *Peel.*

$$$–$$$$ ✕ **Les Halles.** Trompe l'oeil painted-wood panels and small table lamps give this French restaurant a genuine Belle-Époque glow. Specialties such as Brome Lake duck with hot foie gras and veal with basil and mustard sauce share the menu space with more contemporary dishes, such as flash-broiled salmon fillets and lobster topped with grated coconut. Desserts are classic—the Paris-Brest, a puff pastry with praline cream inside, is one of the best in town. Mirrors, murals, and light colors are part of the Paris-market decor. ⊠ *1450 rue Crescent, Downtown* ☎ *514/844–2328* ♧ *Reservations essential* 🖃 *AE, DC, MC, V* ☺ *Closed Sun. No lunch* Ⓜ *Guy-Concordia or Peel.*

$$$–$$$$ ✕ **Rosalie.** The style is mod bistro—a long blond-wood bar, bare wood tables, tubular steel chairs, and lots of mirrors—and so's the food: roast chicken with a white-wine sauce, braised veal, hot smoked salmon, and perhaps the best steak-frites in town. In summer, the terraces out front

Where to Eat in Montréal

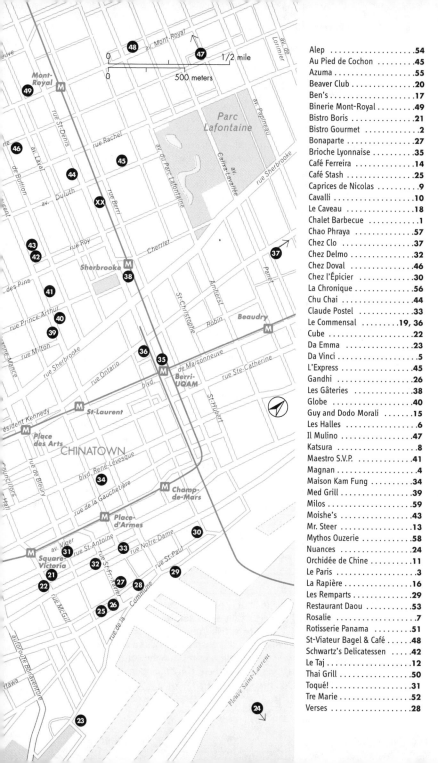

overlooking the street are perfect for lunch and dinner. ⊠ *1232 rue de la Montagne, Downtown* ⊕ *www.rosalierestaurant.com* ☎ *514/392–1970* ☐ *AE, DC, MC, V* Ⓜ *Guy-Concordia.*

$$–$$$$ ✕ **Bistro Gourmet.** This tiny semibasement room could be in 1930s Paris, with its pale-yellow and blue walls. The place is usually so packed that service can be painfully slow, but chef Gabriel Ohana's cooking is worth the wait. His signature dish is duck confit, but his repertoire includes such classics as rack of lamb with garlic, roasted shallots, and a stuffed broiled tomato; fillet of beef in a sauce spiked with blue cheese; and breast of duck over a wine-stewed pear. ⊠ *2100 rue St-Mathieu, Downtown* ☎ *514/846-1553* ☐ *MC, V* ⊗ *No lunch weekends* Ⓜ *Guy-Concordia.*

$$–$$$$ ✕ **Le Caveau.** Among the towers of downtown is an eccentric Victorian house where buttery sauces, creamy desserts, and fairly reasonable prices have survived the onslaught of nouvelle cuisine. The restaurant takes its name from its warm and comfortable cellar, but those who don't like low ceilings can dine on the upper two floors amid sculptures and paintings. A main course might be rabbit cooked with sweet wine, spices, and raisins, or rack of lamb crusted with bread crumbs, mustard, garlic, and herbs. A children's menu, rare in restaurants of Le Caveau's caliber, is available. ⊠ *2063 av. Victoria, Downtown* ☎ *514/844-1624* ☐ *AE, DC, MC, V* ⊗ *No lunch weekends* Ⓜ *McGill.*

$$–$$$$ ✕ **Guy and Dodo Morali.** Color prints, copies of Impressionist paintings, 19th-century portraits, and photographs of Paris decorate the cream-color walls of this comfortable restaurant in the Cours Mont-Royal shopping plaza. In summer, dining spills out onto a little terrace on rue Metcalfe. The daily table d'hôte menu is the best bet, with openers such as lobster bisque followed by lamb in pastry with thyme sauce, or fillet of halibut with leeks. For dessert try the *tarte tatin* (apples and caramel with crème anglaise). ⊠ *Les Cours Mont-Royal, 1444 rue Metcalfe, Downtown* ☎ *514/842-3636* ⊕ *www.guydodo.com* ✍ *Reservations essential* ☐ *AE, DC, MC, V* ⊗ *Closed Sun.* Ⓜ *Peel.*

$$–$$$ ✕ **Le Paris.** Every city should have a Le Paris. Its crowded dining room, with big tables and age-dimmed paint, is as comfortable as the reasonably priced, homey fare that streams out of the kitchen. The *brandade de morue*—salt cod, potatoes, garlic, and cream—is famous, and dishes such as grilled *boudin* (blood sausage), calves' liver meunière, and tripe seem almost soulful. Desserts range from creamy pastries to stewed rhubarb and *île flottant* (meringue floating in a sea of custard). ⊠ *1812 rue Ste-Catherine Ouest, Downtown* ☎ *514/937-4898* ☐ *AE, DC, MC, V* ⊗ *No lunch Sun.* Ⓜ *Guy-Concordia.*

Indian

¢–$ ✕ **Le Taj.** The focus here is on the cuisine of northern India, less spicy and more delicate than that of the south. Tandoori ovens seal in the flavors of the grilled meat and fish. Among the vegetarian choices are *thali*—which includes one vegetable entrée, lentils, and basmati rice—and *saag paneer,* spicy white cheese with spinach. A nine-course lunch buffet costs less than C$10, and at night there's an "Indian feast" for C$20. ⊠ *2077 rue Stanley, Downtown* ☎ *514/845-9015* ☐ *AE, MC, V* Ⓜ *Guy-Concordia.*

Italian

$$$$ ✕ **Cavalli.** The young and the beautiful like to sip cocktails by Cavalli's huge front window, which in summer is open to the passing scene on busy rue Peel. The interior—a pink-and-black illuminated bar, green velvet chairs, and blond-wood paneling—makes an enticing backdrop. And the food? Italian, sort of. Seared tuna comes with bok choy and couscous, and beef carpaccio is served with sliced Minolette cheese and slices of baby peaches preserved with white truffles. ✉ *2040 rue Peel, Downtown* ☎ *514/843–5100* ✍ *Reservations essential* ▭ *AE, DC, MC, V* ☯ *No lunch weekends* Ⓜ *Peel.*

$$–$$$$ ✕ **Da Vinci.** The pioneering owners of Da Vinci were among the first to give Montrealers a taste for anchovies and take-out pizzas. The pizza's no longer on the menu, but you can sit down in the family's romantic Victorian town house and enjoy gnocchi with lamb *ragù* or seafood risotto, followed by cannoli. ✉ *1180 rue Bishop, Downtown* ☎ *514/874–2001* ✍ *Reservations essential* ▭ *AE, DC, MC, V* ☯ *Closed Sun.* Ⓜ *Guy-Concordia.*

Japanese

$$–$$$ ✕ **Katsura.** Stick to the impeccably fresh sushi at this stylish restaurant and you won't go wrong. Try the spicy Kamikaze Roll—salmon, avocado, fried onion, and fish roe—or the *unagi* (grilled eel). ✉ *2170 rue de la Montagne, Downtown* ☎ *514/849–1172* ✍ *Reservations essential* ▭ *AE, DC, MC, V* ☯ *No lunch weekends* Ⓜ *Peel or Guy-Concordia.*

Portuguese

★ **$$–$$$$** ✕ **Café Ferreira.** Antique pottery and bottles of port decorate the pale-yellow walls of this high-ceilinged room—an elegant setting for its "haute" version of Portuguese cuisine. The traditional *caldo verde,* a soup made with kale and sausage, shares space on the menu with grilled fresh sardines; baked salt cod topped with a tomato, onion, and pepper salsa; and *arroz di marisco,* a paella-like dish full of seafood, garlic, and onions. ✉ *1446 rue Peel, Downtown* ☎ *514/848–0988* ▭ *AE, MC, V* ☯ *No lunch Sat.* Ⓜ *Peel.*

Steak

$–$$ ✕ **Mr. Steer.** Several things make this unpretentious restaurant with vinyl booths and plain beige walls worth a visit: a great location in the heart of the downtown shopping district, friendly if brisk service, and the best hamburgers in Montréal. The thick, juicy, almost globular patties, discreetly seasoned and served slightly *saignant* (rare) with a large selection of almost unnecessary dressings and garnishes, are a worthy replacement for steak—although that's available, too, at reasonable prices. ✉ *1198 rue Ste-Catherine Ouest, Downtown* ☎ *514/866–3233* ▭ *MC, V* Ⓜ *Peel.*

Vegetarian

$–$$ ✕ **Le Commensal.** The food at this Montréal-grown chain of vegetarian restaurants—heavy on salads, sandwiches, couscous, and bean dishes—is served buffet style and sold by weight. There are at least seven outlets on the island, all of them big and bright with modern furniture; the nicest is on the 2nd floor of a downtown building with big windows overlooking busy, fashionable rue McGill College. There's also one on rue St-Denis in the heart of the busy nightclub and shopping district, and another on chemin Queen-Mary near the Oratoire St-Joseph. ⊠ *1205 rue McGill College, Downtown* ☎ *514/871–1480* ⊟ *AE, DC, MC, V* Ⓜ *McGill.*

The Islands

French

$$$$ ✕ **Nuances.** The magnificent view of Montréal over the river is the best reason to eat in this formal, paneled restaurant at the Casino de Montréal. The items on the frequently changing menu—such as scallops with shallots and caviar, and caribou loin with a cranberry-enhanced game sauce—are often good, but much pricier than similar fare in town. ⊠ *1 av. du Casino, Île Notre-Dame* ☎ *514/392–2708* ⌂ *Reservations essential* ⊟ *AE, DC, MC, V* ◯ *No lunch* Ⓜ *Jean-Drapeau.*

Olympic Park & Botanical Garden

Canadian

¢–$ ✕ **Chez Clo.** Here, deep in east-end Montréal, where seldom is heard an English word, is authentic Québecois food. A meal in this unpretentious neighborhood diner could start with a bowl of the best pea soup in the city, followed by a slab of *tourtière* (meat pie). The dessert specialty is *pudding au chomeur* (literally, pudding for the unemployed), a kind of shortcake smothered in a thick brown-sugar sauce. The service is noisy and friendly, and the clientele mostly local, but there are often lines. ⊠ *3199 rue Ontario Est, Hochelaga-Maisonneuve* ☎ *514/522–5348* ⊟ *No credit cards* ◯ *No dinner weekends* Ⓜ *Prefontaine or Pie-IX.*

Quartier Latin & Plateau Mont-Royal

Cafés

$–$$ ✕ **Brioche Lyonnaise.** This quintessential Quartier Latin café is in a
Fodor's Choice semibasement with stone walls, across the street from the Théatre St-
★ Denis. A display case holds some of the city's finest pastries, all loaded with butter, cream, fruit, and a dusting of sugar. The butter brioche and a bowl of steaming café au lait make for one of the city's finest breakfasts, but heartier fare is available, too. Table d'hôte meals are served at lunch and dinner, and the place stays open until midnight. The atrium in the back and a terrasse are open in fine weather. ⊠ *1593 rue St-Denis, Quartier Latin* ☎ *514/842–7017* ⊟ *MC, V* Ⓜ *Berri-UQAM.*

$ ✕ **Les Gâteries.** Many writers and artists take their morning espresso in this comfortable little café facing Square St-Louis. The menu is more Montréalais than European, with such local favorites as bagels, muffins, maple-syrup pie, and toast with *cretons* (a coarse, fatty kind of pâté made with pork) sharing space with baguettes and croissants. ⊠ *3443 rue St-Denis, Plateau Mont-Royal* ☎ *514/843–6235* ⊟ *MC, V* Ⓜ *Sherbrooke.*

¢ ✕ **St-Viateur Bagel & Café.** Even expatriate New Yorkers have been
Fodor's Choice known to prefer Montréal's light, crispy, and slightly sweet bagel to its
★ heavier Manhattan cousin. St-Viateur's wood-fired brick ovens have been turning out great bagels since 1959. The dough is boiled in honey-

sweetened water before baking. With coffee and smoked salmon, these bagels make a great breakfast. ⊠ *1127 av. Mont-Royal Est, Plateau Mont-Royal* ☎ *514/528–6361* ⊟ *No credit cards* Ⓜ *Mont-Royal.*

Canadian

$$ ✕ **Au Pied de Cochon.** At the Pig's Foot, Chef Martin Picard reinvents classic comfort foods with a twist—shepherd's pie with venison instead of ground beef, for example, or tourtière made with grain-fed veal from the Charlevoix region rather than the traditional ground pork. He also whips up such hearty classics as pigs'-feet stew, braised in maple syrup or Guinness, or crème caramel. Don't miss the *oreilles-de-crisse* (literally, Christ's ears) appetizer—crispy, deep-fried crescents of pork skin. In summer, the menu lightens up considerably, with a greater emphasis on fish and cold meats. ⊠ *536 av. Duluth, Plateau Mont-Royal* ☎ *514/ 281–1114* ⌂ *Reservations essential* ⊟ *AE, D, DC, MC, V* ⊙ *Closed Sun. and Mon. No lunch* Ⓜ *Sherbrooke or Mont-Royal.*

$ ✕ **Binerie Mont-Royal.** That rarest of the city's culinary finds—authentic Québecois food—is the specialty at this tiny restaurant. The fare includes stews made with meatballs and pigs' feet, various kinds of tourtière, and pork and beans. It's cheap, filling, and charming. ⊠ *367 av. Mont-Royal Est, Plateau Mont-Royal* ☎ *514/285–9078* ⊟ *No credit cards* ⊙ *No dinner weekends* Ⓜ *Mont-Royal.*

Contemporary

★ **$$$$** ✕ **La Chronique.** Red walls with black-and-white photos make an understated backdrop for some of Montréal's most adventurous cooking. Meals seamlessly blend lightened French fare with Japanese, Chinese, and creole touches. Starters like sashimi salmon rubbed with coarsely ground pepper, coriander, and mustard seed might precede pan-fried mahimahi served with thin slices of eggplant filled with goat cheese, for example, or veal sweetbreads with chorizo. Weekend dinners are prix-fixe only—four courses are C$65, and six courses are C$90. ⊠ *99 av. Laurier Ouest, Laurier* ☎ *514/271–3095* ⊕ *www.lachronique.qc.ca* ⌂ *Reservations essential* ⊟ *AE, DC, MC, V* ⊙ *Closed Mon. No lunch* Ⓜ *Mont-Royal.*

★ **$$$–$$$$** ✕ **Globe.** Burgundy leather upholstery, wood paneling, and mirrors decorate this fashionable haunt of diners in their thirties. The vegetables are organic, the meat and poultry free-range, and the portions generous. Slow-cooked meats—rabbit, baby back ribs in red-wine sauce, venison—and the wild chinook salmon are best bets. The menu also includes alphabet soup and home-fried potatoes. ⊠ *3455 blvd. St-Laurent, Plateau Mont-Royal* ☎ *514/284–3823* ⊟ *AE, DC, MC, V* ⊙ *No lunch* Ⓜ *St-Laurent.*

$$$–$$$$ ✕ **Med Grill.** Cherry-color walls, striped chairs, and floor-to-ceiling windows that wrap around two sides of the restaurant makes this one of the most fashionable fishbowls in the city. The food—pepper-crusted tuna with sweetbreads, grilled veal chops with red-grape barbecue sauce and pistachio, and a spectacular molten-chocolate cake—is as adventurous as the vivid surroundings. ⊠ *3500 blvd. St-Laurent, Plateau Mont-Royal* ☎ *514/844–0027* ⊕ *www.medgrill.com* ⌂ *Reservations essential* ⊟ *AE, MC, V* ⊙ *No lunch* Ⓜ *Sherbrooke.*

Delicatessen

$–$$ ✕ **Schwartz's Delicatessen.** The proper name may be the Montréal He-
FodorśChoice brew Delicatessen, but everyone calls it Schwartz's. The smoked and cured
★ meat, prepared in-house, is the city's best, and the tender steaks come
with grilled-liver appetizers. Waiters are briskly efficient, and the furniture is a bit shabby. Don't ask for a menu (there isn't one) and avoid
the lunch and dinner hours—lines are long even on the most brutal winter days. ✉ *3895 blvd. St-Laurent, Plateau Mont-Royal* ☏ *514/842–
4813* ⚅ *Reservations not accepted* ▭ *No credit cards* Ⓜ *Sherbrooke.*

French

$–$$ ✕ **L'Express.** Mirrored walls, a smoky atmosphere, and noise levels that
are close to painful on weekends make this place the closest thing Montréal (and maybe even Canada) has to a Parisian bistro. Service is fast,
prices are reasonable, and the food is good, even if the tiny crowded tables barely have room to accommodate it. Steak tartare with french fries,
salmon with sorrel, and calves' liver with tarragon are marvelous. Jars
of gherkins, fresh baguettes, and aged cheeses make the pleasure last
longer. L'Express has one of the best and most imaginative wine cellars
in town. ✉ *3927 rue St-Denis, Plateau Mont-Royal* ☏ *514/845–5333*
⚅ *Reservations essential* ▭ *AE, DC, MC, V* Ⓜ *Sherbrooke.*

Greek

$$$–$$$$ ✕ **Milos.** Don't let the nets and floats hanging from the ceiling fool you:
this isn't a simple taverna but rather a first-class Greek restaurant with
prices to match. The main dish is usually fish grilled over charcoal and
seasoned with parsley, capers, and lemon juice. Fish are priced by the
pound (C$23–C$32), and you can order one large fish to serve two or
more. You can also eat lamb and veal chops, cheeses, and olives. A $35
table d'hôte menu is available between 5:30 and 6:30 PM. Milos is a healthy
walk from the Laurier Métro. ✉ *5357 av. du Parc, Mile End* ☏ *514/
272–3522* ⊕ *www.milos.ca* ⚅ *Reservations essential* ▭ *AE, D, DC,
MC, V* ◷ *No lunch weekends* Ⓜ *Laurier.*

$$–$$$ ✕ **Mythos Ouzerie.** Scores of fun-seeking diners come to this brick-lined
semibasement every weekend to eat, drink, dance, and be merry in a
Pan-inspired atmosphere of chaos and frenzy. The food is good every
night—moussaka, plump stuffed grape leaves, grilled mushrooms,
braised lamb, grilled squid—but go Thursday, Friday, or Saturday night,
when the live and very infectious bouzouki music makes it impossible
to remain seated. If you want to burn those calories before you have a
chance to digest them, this is the place. ✉ *5318 av. Park, Mile End* ☏ *514/
270–0235* ▭ *AE, DC, MC, V* Ⓜ *Laurier.*

$–$$$ ✕ **Rotisserie Panama.** No one seems to know why this big, noisy Greek
taverna is named for a Latin American country, but who cares? It serves
some of the best grilled meat in Montréal, at reasonable prices. The chicken
and crispy lamb chops are excellent, and on weekends you can order
roasted baby lamb. The more adventurous might try the *kokoretsi*
(organ meats wrapped in intestines and grilled on a spit) or the *patsas*,
a full-flavored tripe soup. Although the chefs specialize in meats, they
are also clever with grilled fish and octopus. Be sure to make reserva-

tions for Fridays and Saturdays. ✉ *789 rue Jean-Talon Ouest, Mile End* ☎ *514/276–5223* 🖃 *AE, MC, V* Ⓜ *Parc.*

Italian

★ **$$$–$$$$** ✕ **Il Mulino.** Nothing about the decor or the location of this family-run restaurant in Little Italy hints at the good things inside. The antipasti alone—grilled mushrooms, stuffed eggplant, pizza, broiled scallops—are worth the trip. The pasta, too, is excellent, especially the *agnolotti* (crescent-shape stuffed pasta) and the gnocchi. Main dishes include simply prepared lamb chops, veal, and excellent fish. ✉ *236 rue St-Zotique Est, Little Italy* ☎ *514/273–5776* ⚐ *Reservations essential* 🖃 *AE, DC, MC, V* ✹ *Closed Sun. and Mon.* Ⓜ *Beaubien.*

★ **$$** ✕ **Tre Marie.** Hearty Italian family fare—think veal stew and *baccala* (salt cod) with polenta, veal tripe with beans and tomato sauce, roast veal in a white wine sauce, and a three-pasta dish that could feed a family of four—is the trademark of this modest but very popular establishment opened in 1966 by sisters Rosina and Maria Fabrizio. The two small rooms, with stucco walls and dark-wood trim, are always full on weekends—often with young couples on dates. ✉ *6934 rue Clark, Little Italy* ☎ *514/277–9859* ⚐ *Reservations essential* 🖃 *AE, DC, MC, V* ✹ *Closed Mon.* Ⓜ *de Castelnau.*

Japanese

$$–$$$ ✕ **Azuma.** The closest thing Montréal has to a Japanese bistro, this lively and friendly restaurant keeps the price of its sushi and sashimi reasonable. You can also get sukiyaki (thin slices of meat cooked in soy sauce), *soba* (buckwheat noodles), and tofu "steak." ✉ *5263 blvd. St-Laurent, Laurier* ☎ *514/271–5263* 🖃 *AE, DC, MC, V* ✹ *Closed Mon.* Ⓜ *Laurier.*

Middle Eastern

$$–$$$ ✕ **Restaurant Daou.** Singer Céline Dion and her husband have enjoyed this casual restaurant, which serves some of the city's best Lebanese food—hummus with ground meat, stuffed grape leaves, and delicately seasoned kabobs. ✉ *519 rue Faillon, Villeray* ☎ *514/276–8310* 🖃 *AE, DC, MC, V* ✹ *Closed Mon.* Ⓜ *Parc.*

$–$$ ✕ **Alep.** Graze on *mouhamara* (pomegranate and walnuts), *sabanegh* (spinach and onions), *fattouche* (salad with pita and mint), and *yalanti* (vine leaves stuffed with rice, chickpeas, walnuts, and tomatoes) in a pleasant, stone-walled room draped with ivy and full of young couples. Kabobs dominate the main courses. ✉ *199 rue Jean-Talon Est, Villeray* ☎ *514/270–6396* 🖃 *MC, V* ✹ *Closed Mon.* Ⓜ *Jean-Talon or de Castelnau.*

Portuguese

$ ✕ **Chez Doval.** Chicken—and sometimes sardines, grouper, and squid—sizzle on the open grill behind the bar. You can eat your meal in the noisy, bright tavern or in the quieter, softly lit dining room. A guitarist works both rooms on weekends. ✉ *150 rue Marie Anne Est, Plateau Mont-Royal* ☎ *514/843–3390* 🖃 *AE, MC, V* Ⓜ *Mont-Royal.*

Seafood

$$–$$$$ ✕ **Maestro S.V.P.** Wine-red walls, etched glass, and a menu on a chalk-board make this seafood restaurant feel like a bistro. The musical instruments on the walls match the playfulness of the cooking. Oysters are the specialty—dozens of kinds from all over the world are available. The rest of the menu is impressive, too, with variations on mussels-and-fries, an excellent poached salmon with mango butter, and a bountiful seafood pot-au-feu in a tomato and basil sauce. Appetizers include tender calamari as well as shrimp dipped in beer batter and rolled in shredded coconut, served with a marmalade and horseradish sauce. ⌂ *3615 blvd. St-Laurent, Plateau Mont-Royal* ☎ *514/842–6447* ⊟ *AE, DC, MC, V* ☉ *No lunch weekends* Ⓜ *Sherbrooke.*

Steak

$$$–$$$$ ✕ **Moishe's.** The Lighter brothers still age their big, marbled steaks in their own cold rooms before charcoal-grilling them, just the way their father did when he opened Moishe's in 1938. There are other items on the menu, such as lamb and grilled arctic char, but people come for the beef. The selection of single-malt Scotches is impressive. ⌂ *3961 blvd. St-Laurent, Plateau Mont-Royal* ☎ *514/845–3509* ⊟ *AE, DC, MC, V* Ⓜ *St-Laurent.*

Thai

$$–$$$ ✕ **Thai Grill.** Dishes range from the fiery—Mussaman curry with beef, and sautéed chicken with cashews, dried red peppers, and onions—to such fragrantly mild delicacies as *gai hor bai toey* (chicken wrapped in pandanus leaves and served with a black-bean sauce). Pale-yellow walls, rich wood trim, and traditional Thai masks decorate the elegant dining room. ⌂ *5101 blvd. St-Laurent, Plateau Mont-Royal* ☎ *514/270–5566* ⊟ *AE, DC, MC, V* Ⓜ *Laurier.*

¢–$$ ✕ **Chao Phraya.** The huge front window of this bright, airy restaurant decorated with subtle Asian accents overlooks fashionable rue Laurier, from which the restaurant draws many of its upscale customers. They come for such classics as crunchy, multiflavored *poe pia* (imperial rolls), *pha koung* (grilled-shrimp salad), and fried halibut in red curry sauce with lime juice. ⌂ *50 rue Laurier Ouest, Laurier* ☎ *514/272–5339* ⌂ *Reservations essential* ⊟ *AE, DC, MC, V* ☉ *No lunch* Ⓜ *Laurier.*

Vegetarian

$–$$ ✕ **Chu Chai.** Vegetarians can usually dine well in any Thai restaurant,
Fodor'sChoice even one that serves plenty of meat and fish dishes. But the chefs at this
★ rigorously vegan restaurant prepare meatless versions of such classic Thai dishes as "duck" salad with pepper and mint leaves, "fish" with three hot sauces, and "beef" with yellow curry and coconut milk, substituting soy and *seitan* (a firm, chewy meat substitute made from wheat gluten) for the flesh. ⌂ *4088 rue St-Denis, Plateau Mont-Royal* ☎ *514/843–4194* ⌂ *Reservations essential* ⊟ *AE, DC, MC, V* Ⓜ *Sherbrooke or Mont-Royal.*

$–$$ ✕ **Le Commensal.** The rue St-Denis branch of Montréal's chain of vegetarian buffets is a bright airy room in the heart of the action. On offer are salads, sandwiches, couscous, and delightful bean dishes. ⌂ *1720* *rue St-Denis, Plateau Mont-Royal* ☎ *514/845–2627* ▭ *AE, DC, MC, V* Ⓜ *St-Laurent.*

Vieux-Montréal

Café

★ **$–$$** ✕ **Claude Postel.** The sandwiches (on first-rate bread), pastries, pâtés, coffees, and a limited selection of prix-fixe meals with entrées such as braised veal, poached salmon, vegetable-and-orange soup make this a popular lunchtime destination with discriminating clerks and lawyers who work in nearby offices. In summer, there's richly flavored ice cream. The place closes at 7 PM. ✉ *75 rue Notre-Dame Ouest, Vieux-Montréal* ☎ *514/844–8750* ▭ *MC, V* Ⓜ *Place-d'Armes.*

Contemporary

★ **$$$–$$$$** ✕ **Cube.** The decor might not sound promising—gray concrete walls, picture windows, and square mirrors—but the low lights and banks of flickering votive candles add a dash of romance to the high-ceilinged room. However, the food, which is unrelentingly modern, keeps center stage. Chef Claude Pelletier likes to serve his appetizers in threes—salmon served marinated, carpaccio, and tartare on one plate, for example, is one of his best. But beware: there's barely a mouthful of each. Main courses aren't huge, either, but fish dishes like roasted striped bass in lemon-herb broth are excellent—as is the homemade ice cream. ✉ *Hôtel St. Paul, 355 rue McGill, Vieux-Montréal* ☎ *514/876–2823* ✍ *Reservations essential* ▭ *AE, DC, MC, V* Ⓜ *Square-Victoria.*

$$$–$$$$
Fodor'sChoice
★ ✕ **Toqué!** Few restaurants in Montréal are as revered as Toqué!, and few chefs as renowned as its co-owner Normand Laprise, so it came as a shock in 2004 when the restaurant moved from a storefront on rue St-Denis to a steel-and-glass tower in the financial district. Toqué! is now more corporate than funky, with widely spaced tables, high glass walls, white and orange curtains, and lots of burgundy, gray, and brown touches. The food, although a little less daring, is still brilliant. Try the smoked salmon with warm bok choy and peperoncino vinaigrette, or Jerusalem artichoke soup with seared foie gras for openers, followed perhaps by roast saddle of deer with house-made gnocchi and a thick garlic cream, or oxtail ravioli. Save room for desserts like crème brûlée and almond-crusted blueberry pie. ✉ *900 Place Jean-Paul-Riopelle, Vieux-Montréal* ☎ *514/ 499–2084* ⊕ *www.restaurant-toque.com* ✍ *Reservations essential* ▭ *AE, DC, MC, V* ⊘ *Closed Mondays. No lunch weekends* Ⓜ *Square-Victoria, Place d'Armes.*

★ **$$$–$$$$** ✕ **Verses.** The setting is certainly romantic; a long stone-walled room looking out on the cobbled streets of Vieux-Montréal. And the food can be poetic—especially such appetizers as mustard soup, and long, thick strips of Angus beef tartare—but the reason for this restaurant's name is that it's housed on the ground floor of Hôtel Nelligan, named after the Romantic Québecois poet Émile Nelligan. For a main course try guinea hen with maple syrup, or sliced duck breast marinated in ginger and served with braised red cabbage. ✉ *Hôtel Nelligan, 100 rue St-Paul Ouest, Vieux-Montréal* ☎ *514/788–4000* ✍ *Reservations essential* ▭ *AE, DC, MC, V* Ⓜ *Place d'Armes.*

French

$$$–$$$$ ✕ **Bonaparte.** A cheerful fireplace and walls richly trimmed in imperial purple and hung with sketches of Napoleonic soldiers set the tone, which complements the menu of traditional French dishes prepared with a light touch. You could start with a wild-mushroom ravioli seasoned with fresh sage and move on to a lobster stew flavored with vanilla and served with spinach fondue, or a roast rack of lamb in port sauce. Lunch is a good value. Upstairs is a small inn. ⊠ *443 rue St-François-Xavier, Vieux-Montréal* ☎ *514/844–4368* ⊕ *www.bonaparte.ca* ⌕ *Reservations essential* ⊟ *AE, DC, MC, V* ☉ *No lunch weekends* Ⓜ *Place-d'Armes.*

★ $$$$ ✕ **Les Remparts.** A stone-walled cellar under the Auberge du Vieux-Port showcases innovative French cooking in surroundings redolent of New France. The restaurant takes its name from an ancient lump of gray stone unearthed during renovations to the building in 1994—it once formed part of the city wall. The cooking is adventurously satisfying, with such appetizers as wontons stuffed with duck confit and goat cheese and perfectly seasoned chicken-liver mousse. For a main dish try the boar—thin slices of rare meat served with shiitake and morel mushrooms—or the grilled smoked salmon with sweet-potato gratin. ⊠ *93 rue de la Commune Est, Vieux-Montréal* ☎ *514/392–1649* ⊟ *AE, DC, MC, V* ☉ *No lunch weekends* Ⓜ *Place d'Armes.*

★ $$$–$$$$ ✕ **Chez l'Épicier.** The name means "The Grocer," and indeed, shelves stocked with such oddball products as Hawaiian sea salt and lobster oil fill the front part of the stone-walled room, along with refrigerated displays of homemade pâtés and terrines. The menu, printed on grocery bags, includes unusual appetizers such as snail shepherd's pie (spiked with roasted garlic) and a delightfully nutty parsnip soup with orange and ginger bits. Main dishes, usually more conservative, might include such delicacies as simply poached Chilean sea bass and veal chops in sherry-vinegar sauce. ⊠ *311 rue St-Paul Est, Vieux-Montréal* ☎ *514/878–2232* ⊕ *www.chezlepecier.com* ⊟ *AE, DC, MC, V* ☉ *No lunch weekends* Ⓜ *Place d'Armes.*

$$–$$$$ ✕ **Bistro Boris.** Behind the restored facade of a burned-out building is one of the best alfresco dining areas in the city. At this huge, tree-shaded terrasse, the bistro fare includes blood pudding, grilled fish, and chops, served with salad or fries. There is an indoor section, as well, which is just fine in winter. ⊠ *465 rue McGill, Vieux-Montréal* ☎ *514/848–9575* ⊟ *AE, D, DC, MC, V* Ⓜ *Square-Victoria.*

Indian

$–$$ ✕ **Gandhi.** Standards like butter chicken, shrimp curry, and lamb vindaloo are served in a pleasant, sunny room with yellow walls and immaculate white linens. ⊠ *230 rue St-Paul Ouest, Vieux-Montréal* ☎ *514/845–5866* ⊟ *AE, MC, V* ☉ *No lunch weekends* Ⓜ *Place-d'Armes.*

Italian

$$–$$$$ ✕ **Da Emma.** Massive stone pillars and wooden beams give this family-run restaurant on the Vieux-Port a genuinely Roman feel. So does the food: seafood antipasto (squid, mussels, shrimp, and octopus drizzled with olive oil), fettuccine with porcini mushrooms, and suckling pig roasted with garlic and rosemary are among the highlights. The homemade tiramasu is excellent. ⊠ *777 rue de la Commune Ouest, Vieux-Montréal* ☎ *514/ 392–1568* ⊟ *AE, D, DC, MC, V* ⊗ *No lunch Sat.* Ⓜ *Square-Victoria.*

Polish

$–$$ ✕ **Café Stash.** On chilly nights many Montrealers turn to Café Stash for sustenance—for pork chops or duck, hot borscht, pierogi, or cabbage and sausage—in short, for all the hearty specialties of a Polish kitchen. Seating is on pews from an old chapel and at tables from an old convent. ⊠ *200 rue St-Paul Ouest, Vieux-Montréal* ☎ *514/845–6611* ⊟ *AE, MC, V* Ⓜ *Place-d'Armes.*

Seafood

$$–$$$ ✕ **Chez Delmo.** Lawyers and businesspeople crowd the long, shiny wooden bar at lunchtime, gobbling up oysters and fish. In the back is a more relaxed and cheerful dining room. The poached salmon with hollandaise is a nice slab of perfectly cooked fish served with potatoes and broccoli. Also excellent are the arctic char and the Dover sole. ⊠ *211–215 rue Notre-Dame Ouest, Vieux-Montréal* ☎ *514/849–4061* ⚎ *Reservations essential* ⊟ *AE, DC, MC, V* ⊗ *Closed Sun., 3 wks in Aug., and Christmas–mid-Jan. No dinner Mon.* Ⓜ *Place-d'Armes.*

Steak

$–$$ ✕ **Magnan.** Everyone from dock workers to corporate executives comes to this tavern in a working-class neighborhood for the unbeatable roast beef and steaks. The salmon pie is a delightfully heavy filler that makes great picnic fare. In summer Magnan adds Québec lobster to its menu and turns its parking lot into an outdoor dining area. Excellent beer from several local microbreweries is on tap. The style is upscale warehouse, with TV sets noisily tuned to sports. ⊠ *2602 rue St-Patrick, Pointe St-Charles* ☎ *514/935–9647* ⊟ *AE, DC, MC, V* Ⓜ *Charlevoix.*

WHERE TO STAY

Montréal's downtown has its share of big, comfortable hotels, but the little inns along the cobbled streets of Vieux-Montréal offer charm as well as a dose of history. There are more than a dozen establishments in the old city, ranging from modern hotels to an 18th-century stone inn that Benjamin Franklin visited.

Keep in mind that during peak season (May through August), finding a bed without making reservations can be difficult. From mid-November to early April, rates often drop, and throughout the year many hotels have two-night, three-day, double-occupancy packages at substantial discounts.

WHAT IT COSTS In Canadian dollars				
$$$$	**$$$**	**$$**	**$**	**¢**
FOR 2 PEOPLE over C$250	C$175–C$250	C$125–C$175	C$75–C$125	under C$75

Prices are for a standard double room in high season; they exclude 7.5% provincial sales tax, 7% goods-and-services tax (GST), and a C$2.30 city tax.

Downtown

$$$$ ⌧ **Le Marriott Château Champlain.** At the southern end of Place du Canada stands this 36-floor skyscraper with distinctive half-moon-shape windows that give the rooms a Moorish look. The furniture is elegant and French. Underground passageways connect the Champlain with the Bonaventure Métro station and Place Ville-Marie. ✉ *1050 rue de la Gauchetière Ouest, Downtown, H3B 4C9* ☎ *514/878–9000 or 800/200–5909* 📠 *514/878–6761* ⊕ *www.marriott.com* 🛏 *611 rooms, 33 suites* ☆ *Restaurant, room service, in-room data ports, minibars, cable TV with movies, indoor pool, gym, health club, sauna, bar, babysitting, concierge, meeting rooms, parking (fee), no-smoking rooms* ▤ *AE, DC, MC, V* ⟉| *EP* Ⓜ *Bonaventure.*

★ **$$$–$$$$** ⌧ **Bonaventure Hilton International.** The large Hilton occupies the top three floors of the Place Bonaventure exhibition center, giving easy access to the Métro and the Underground City. From the outside, the massive building is uninviting, but you step off the elevator into an attractive reception area flanked by an outdoor swimming pool (heated year-round) and 2½ acres of rooftop gardens. Sleek modern furniture and pastel walls decorate the guest rooms. ✉ *1 pl. Bonaventure, Downtown, H5A 1E4* ☎ *514/878–2332 or 800/267–2575* 📠 *514/878–3881* ⊕ *www.hilton.com* 🛏 *360 rooms, 7 suites* ☆ *Restaurant, room service, in-room data ports, minibars, room TVs with movies and video games, pool, gym, bar, shops, concierge, business services, meeting rooms, parking (fee), some pets allowed (fee), no-smoking rooms* ▤ *AE, D, DC, MC, V* ⟉| *EP* Ⓜ *Bonaventure.*

$$$–$$$$ ⌧ **Le Centre Sheraton.** The busy lobby bar of the city's biggest convention hotel is a pleasant forest of potted trees. Rues Crescent and Bishop, lined with clubs and restaurants, are just a few blocks away. The standard rooms are large and airy; those on higher floors have big windows that overlook the mountain or the St. Lawrence River. Furnishings are blandly comfortable, with huge beds, beige walls, and earth-tone accents. ✉ *1201 blvd. René-Lévesque Ouest, Downtown, H3B 2L7* ☎ *514/878–2000 or 888/627–7102* 📠 *514/878–3958* ⊕ *www.starwood.com/sheraton* 🛏 *785 rooms, 40 suites* ☆ *3 restaurants, room service, in-room data ports, minibars, cable TV with movies and video games, indoor pool, gym, health club, hair salon, 2 bars, babysitting, concierge, business services, meeting rooms, parking (fee)* ▤ *AE, D, DC, MC, V* ⟉| *EP* Ⓜ *Bonaventure or Peel.*

$$$–$$$$ ⌧ **Delta Montréal.** With a huge baronial chandelier and gold-colored carpets, the two stories of public space at the Delta look a bit like a French château. Rooms are big, with mahogany-veneer furniture and windows that overlook the mountain or downtown. The hotel has the city's most complete exercise and pool facility and an extensive business center. The Cordial Music bar serves lunch on weekdays. ✉ *475 av. du Président-Kennedy, Downtown, H3A 1J7* ☎ *514/286–1986 or 877/286–1986* 📠 *514/284–4306* ⊕ *www.deltamontreal.com* 🛏 *456 rooms, 4 suites* ☆ *Restaurant, room service, in-room data ports, minibars, cable TV with movies and video games, indoor pool, fitness classes, gym, health club, hot tub, sauna, spa, squash, bar, recreation room, shops, babysitting,* *children's programs (ages 1–13), concierge, business services, meeting rooms, parking (fee), some pets allowed (fee), no-smoking floors* ⊟ *AE, D, DC, MC, V* ⌾| *EP* Ⓜ *McGill or Place des Arts.*

$$$–$$$$ 🏨 **Fairmont Le Reine Elizabeth.** Central Station is right below this hotel, so it's no wonder the lobby resembles a railroad station, with hordes marching this way and that. Upstairs, however, the rooms are modern, spacious, and spotless, with lush pale carpets, striped Regency wallpaper, and chintz bedspreads. The Penthouse floors—20 and 21—have business services, and the Gold Floor has its own elevator, check-in, and concierge. The hotel is the site of many conventions. ⊠ *900 blvd. René-Lévesque Ouest, Downtown, H3B 4A5* ☎ *514/861–3511 or 800/441–1414* 🖶 *514/954–2296* ⊕ *www.fairmont.com* 🛏 *939 rooms, 100 suites* ⚖ *3 restaurants, room service, some in-room data ports, some microwaves, some refrigerators, cable TV with movies and video games, indoor pool, health club, hair salon, 3 bars, babysitting, concierge, concierge floors, business services, meeting rooms, parking (fee), some pets allowed (fee), no-smoking rooms* ⊟ *AE, D, DC, MC, V* ⌾| *EP* Ⓜ *Bonaventure.*

$$$–$$$$ 🏨 **Hôtel de la Montagne.** A naked nymph rises out of the fountain in the lobby, and an enormous crystal chandelier hangs from the ceiling. The large, comfortable rooms are tamer. The hotel has a piano bar and a rooftop terrace, and a tunnel connects it to Thursdays/Les Beaux Jeudis, a popular bar, restaurant, and dance club. Most of the people staying here are in town for the nightlife. ⊠ *1430 rue de la Montagne, Downtown, H3G 1Z5* ☎ *514/288–5656 or 800/361–6262* 🖶 *514/288–9658* ⊕ *www.hoteldelamontagne.com* 🛏 *135 rooms* ⚖ *2 restaurants, room service, in-room data ports, minibars, room TVs with movies and video games, pool, bar, piano bar, cabaret, dance club, shops, babysitting, concierge, meeting rooms, parking (fee), some pets allowed (fee), no-smoking floors* ⊟ *AE, D, DC, MC, V* ⌾| *EP* Ⓜ *Peel.*

★ **$$$–$$$$**   🏨 **Hôtel le Germain.** What was once a dowdy, outdated downtown office building is now a sleek, luxurious boutique hotel with two huge two-story apartments. The earth-tone rooms showcase Québec-designed bedroom and bathroom furnishings in dark, dense tropical woods. All rooms have individual sound systems, three phones, and an iron and ironing board; some have grand views of the skyscrapers along avenue du Président-Kennedy or of Mont-Royal. ⊠ *2050 rue Mansfield, Downtown, H3A 1Y9* ☎ *514/849–2050 or 877/333–2050* 🖶 *514/849–1437* ⊕ *www.hotelgermain.com* 🛏 *99 rooms, 2 suites* ⚖ *Room service, in-room data ports, minibars, cable TV, gym, bar, dry cleaning, concierge, meeting rooms, parking (fee), some pets allowed, no-smoking floors* ⊟ *AE, DC, MC, V* ⌾| *CP* Ⓜ *Peel or McGill.*

$$$–$$$$ 🏨 **Loews Hôtel Vogue.** Tall windows and a facade of polished rose gran-
Fodor$Choice   ite grace this chic hotel in the heart of downtown. The lobby's focal point,
★   L'Opéra Bar, has an expansive bay window overlooking the trendy rue de la Montagne. Guest-room furnishings are upholstered with striped silk, and the beds are draped with lacy duvets. The bathrooms have whirlpool baths, TVs, and phones. ⊠ *1425 rue de la Montagne, Downtown, H3G 1Z3* ☎ *514/285–5555 or 800/465–6654* 🖶 *514/849–8903* ⊕ *www.loewshotels.com* 🛏 *126 rooms, 16 suites* ⚖ *Restaurant, room*

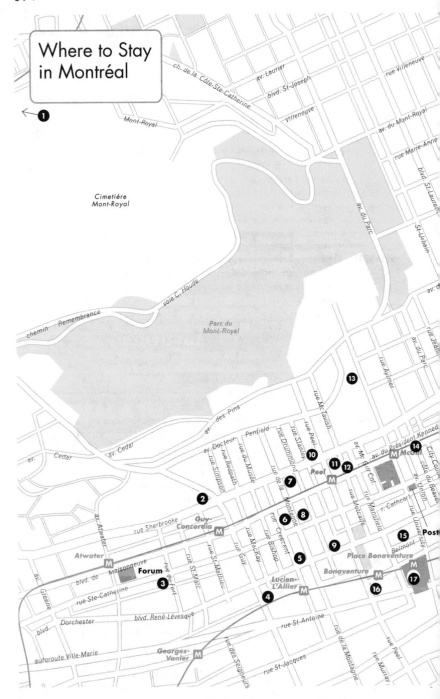

Where to Stay
in Montréal

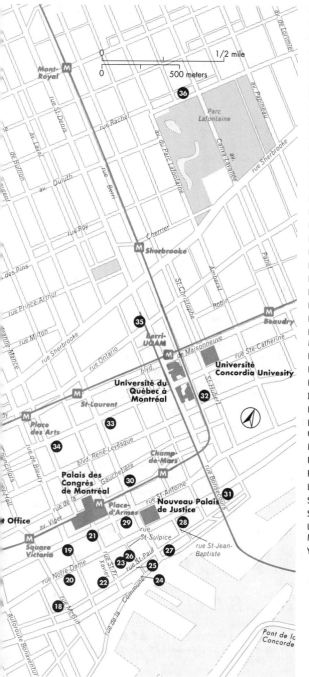

service, in-room data ports, in-room fax, minibars, cable TV, gym, sauna, bar, babysitting, children's programs (ages 1–18), laundry service, concierge, business services, meeting rooms, parking (fee), some pets allowed ⊟ AE, D, DC, MC, V ⦿ *BP* Ⓜ *Peel.*

$$$–$$$$ 🖼 **Hyatt Regency Montréal.** The rooms are bright and comfortable, with floral bedspreads, spacious bathrooms, and good views of downtown, but this 12-story hotel's trump card is location. It's on top of Complexe Desjardins, one of the city's biggest shopping malls and home to a huge, bright, and airy food court. Right across rue Ste-Catherine is Place des Arts and the Musé d'Art Contemporain, and if the weather's wet or cold, you can take the underground links to both as well as to the city's convention center and two Métro lines. Chinatown is a block away and the restaurant strips on rue St-Denis and boulevard St-Laurent are both 10-minute-walks away. Most of the free concerts offered during the International Jazz Festival in July happen right outside the front door. ⊠ *1255 rue Jeanne-Mance, Downtown, H3B 1E5* ☎ *514/982–1234 or 800/233–1234* 🖷 *514/2858–1243* ⊕ *http://montreal.hyatt.com/property* 🛏 *605 rooms, 34 suites* ♿ *Restaurant, in-room data ports, minibars, cable TV with movies, indoor pool, gym, spa, bar, Internet, business services, meeting rooms, parking (fee), no-smoking floors* ⊟ *AE, D, DC, MC, V* ⦿ *EP* Ⓜ *Place des Arts, Place d'Armes.*

$$–$$$$ 🖼 **Holiday Inn Select.** From the two pagodas on the roof to the Chinese garden in the lobby, this Chinatown hotel is full of surprises. The hotel sits catercorner to the Palais des Congrès convention center and is a five-minute walk from the World Trade Center. Its restaurant, Chez Chine, is excellent. An executive floor has all the usual business facilities. The hotel has a small gym, but you also have access to a plush private health and leisure club downstairs with a whirlpool, saunas, a billiards room, and a bar. ⊠ *99 av. Viger Ouest, Chinatown, H2Z 1E9* ☎ *514/878–9888 or 888/878–9888* 🖷 *514/878–6341* ⊕ *www.sixcontinentshotels. com* 🛏 *235 rooms, 6 suites* ♿ *Restaurant, in-room data ports, minibars, cable TV with movies and video games, indoor pool, gym, spa, saunas, bar, business services, meeting rooms, parking (fee), no-smoking floors* ⊟ *AE, D, DC, MC, V* ⦿ *EP* Ⓜ *Place d'Armes.*

$–$$ 🖼 **Hôtel Lord Berri.** Cherrywood-veneer furnishings, huge television sets, and big windows add a splash of comfort to this budget-priced hotel. Near the restaurants and nightlife of the Quartier Latin, the sights of Vieux-Montréal, and the color of Chinatown, the location is also excellent. The hotel restaurant, Il Cavaliere, serves Italian food and is popular with locals. ⊠ *1199 rue Berri, Downtown, H2L 4C6* ☎ *514/845–9236 or 888/363–0363* 🖷 *514/849–9855* ⊕ *www.lordberri.com* 🛏 *148 rooms, 6 suites* ♿ *Restaurant, room service, room TVs with movies, shop, meeting room, parking (fee), no-smoking floors* ⊟ *AE, DC, MC, V* ⦿ *EP* Ⓜ *Berri-UQAM.*

¢–$ 🖼 **YWCA.** One block from rue Ste-Catherine, the YWCA, also open to men, is close to dozens of restaurants. There are single, double, and triple rooms. If you want a room with any amenities, book in advance; not all rooms have a sink and bath. ⊠ *1355 blvd. René-Lévesque Ouest, Downtown, H3G 1T3* ☎ *514/866–9941* 🖷 *514/861–1603* 🛏 *63* *rooms, 30 with bath* & *Café, indoor pool, fitness classes, gym, sauna, shops; no room TVs* ▤ *MC, V* ⏐◯⏐ *EP* Ⓜ *Lucien-L'Allier.*

¢ ⌖ **Hostelling International.** This hostel in the heart of downtown has same-sex dorm rooms that sleep 4, 6, or 10 people. If you're not Canadian, you must have a Hostelling International membership to stay here; however, you have the option of paying C$4.60 a day for temporary membership for up to six days. Members pay C$19 for a dormitory bed, temporary members (Canadians only) C$25. Some rooms are available for couples (C$52 members, C$64 nonmembers) and families. There are kitchen facilities and lockers for valuables. Reserve early for summer lodging. ✉ *1030 rue MacKay, Downtown, H3G 2H1* ☎ *514/843–3317* 🖷 *514/934–3251* ⊕ *www.hostellingmontreal.com* ⇌ *243 beds* & *Café, hair salon, laundry facilities; no a/c in some rooms, no room TVs, no smoking* ▤ *AE, DC, MC, V* ⏐◯⏐ *EP* Ⓜ *Lucien-L'Allier.*

¢ ⌖ **Hôtel l'Abri du Voyageur.** Price and location are this hotel's main selling points, but Hôtel l'Abri du Voyageur also manages to squeeze in some unassuming charm: high ceilings, bare-brick walls, original pine and maple floors, and paintings by local artists. The hotel's three floors are over a restaurant in a commercial building that predates World War I. Each room has a TV and a sink. Studios with a kitchenette and private bath also are available. ✉ *9 rue Ste-Catherine Ouest, Downtown, H2X 1Z5* ☎ *514/849–2922* 🖷 *514/499–0151* ⊕ *www.abri-voyageur.ca* ⇌ *30 rooms, 12 suites with bath* & *Fans, cable TV, parking (fee); no a/c in some rooms* ▤ *AE, MC, V* ⏐◯⏐ *EP* Ⓜ *St-Laurent.*

Quartier Latin & Plateau Mont-Royal

$$–$$$ ⌖ **Auberge de la Fontaine.** This small hotel overlooking Parc Lafontaine sounds wild—contrasting purple and bare-brick walls, red molding, green ceilings—but the place is delightful. Its rooms are in two adjoining turn-of-the-20th-century residences; some have whirlpool baths, and a few have private balconies. You can use the little ground-floor kitchen and take whatever you like from its refrigerator, which is full of snacks. ✉ *1301 rue Rachel Est, Plateau Mont-Royal, H2J 2K1* ☎ *514/597–0166 or 800/597–0597* 🖷 *514/597–0496* ⊕ *www.aubergedelafontaine. com* ⇌ *18 rooms, 3 suites* & *Dining room, cable TV, library, business services, meeting rooms, some free parking, no-smoking rooms* ▤ *AE, DC, MC, V* ⏐◯⏐ *BP* Ⓜ *Mont-Royal.*

$$–$$ ⌖ **Auberge le Jardin d'Antoine.** Patterned wallpaper and antique-reproduction furniture give this small hotel plenty of charm, but its best selling point is its location right on rue St-Denis, among the Quartier Latin's restaurants and nightclubs. The bathrooms are large, and some rooms open onto a narrow, brick-paved terrace. Breakfast is served in a pleasant, stone-walled dining room. ✉ *2024 rue St-Denis, Quartier Latin, H2X 3K7* ☎ *514/843–4506 or 800/361–4506* 🖷 *514/281–1491* ⊕ *www.hotel-jardin-antoine.qc.ca* ⇌ *25 rooms* & *Cable TV, no-smoking rooms* ▤ *AE, D, MC, V* ⏐◯⏐ *BP* Ⓜ *Berri-UQAM.*

¢ ⌖ **Université de Montréal Residence.** The university's student housing accepts visitors from early May to late August. It's on the opposite side of Mont-Royal from downtown and Vieux-Montréal, but next to the Edouard-Monpetit Métro station. Rooms have phones for local calls;

common lounges have microwaves and TVs. For a fee you can use the campus sports facilities. Rates are C$35 per single per night ($C45 for two people in a single, C$50 for a double) or C$210 per week. Those staying here have access to the university's pool and gym facilities. ✉ *2350 blvd. Edouard-Montpetit, Outremont, H3T 1J4* ☎ *514/343–6531* 📠 *514/343–2353* 🌐 *www.resid.umontreal.ca* 🛏 *1,119 rooms with shared bath* 🖃 *MC, V* ⊘ *Closed late Aug.–early May* ⦿ *EP* Ⓜ *Edouard-Monpetit.*

Square Mile

$$$$ 🏨 **Ritz-Carlton.** The guest rooms at Montréal's grandest hotel success-
Fodor's Choice fully blend Edwardian style—all rooms have marble baths, and some
★ suites have working fireplaces—with modern amenities. Careful and personal attention are hallmarks of the Ritz-Carlton's service: your shoes are shined, there's fresh fruit in your room, and everyone calls you by name. Power meals are the rule at Le Café de Paris, where both politicians and businesspeople meet to hash out deals over breakfast, which also serves a formal afternoon tea. ✉ *1228 rue Sherbrooke Ouest, Square Mile, H3G 1H6* ☎ *514/842–4212, 800/363–0366, or 800/241–3333* 📠 *514/842–3383* 🌐 *www.ritzcarlton.com* 🛏 *185 rooms, 45 suites* ⅋ *Restaurant, tea shop, room service, in-room data ports, in-room safes, minibars, cable TV with movies and video games, gym, hair salon, massage, bar, piano bar, shops, babysitting, laundry service, concierge, business services, convention center, parking (fee), some pets allowed (fee)* 🖃 *AE, DC, MC, V* ⦿ *EP* Ⓜ *Peel or Guy-Concordia.*

$$$–$$$$ 🏨 **Hôtel Omni Mont-Royal.** Color, flair, and marble bathrooms dress up this hotel's large, sunny rooms. Le Petit Opus Café and Bar occupies a street-level atrium, which gives it the air of an upscale sidewalk café. A Chinese restaurant, the Zen, is in the basement. An outdoor pool is heated in winter for year-round swimming. ✉ *1050 rue Sherbrooke Ouest, Square Mile, H3A 2R6* ☎ *514/284–1110 or 800/843–6664* 📠 *514/845–3025* 🌐 *www.omnihotels.com* 🛏 *275 rooms, 25 suites* ⅋ *2 restaurants, room service, in-room data ports, in-room safes, minibars, room TVs with movies and video games, outdoor pool, health club, hot tub, sauna, lobby lounge, shops, babysitting, children's programs (ages 3–10), concierge, parking (fee), no-smoking floors* 🖃 *AE, D, DC, MC, V* ⦿ *EP* Ⓜ *Peel.*

$$–$$$$ 🏨 **Hôtel du Fort.** The du Fort is in a residential neighborhood known as Shaughnessy Village, close to shopping at the Faubourg Ste-Catherine and Square Westmount, and just around the corner from the Canadian Center for Architecture. All rooms here have good views of the city, the river, or the mountain. Wooden furniture and pleasantly plump sofas fill the large, airy rooms, which have spacious bathrooms. Breakfast is served in a charming lounge. ✉ *1390 rue du Fort, Shaughnessy Village, H3H 2R7* ☎ *514/938–8333 or 800/565–6333* 📠 *514/938–2078* 🌐 *www.hoteldufort.com* 🛏 *103 rooms, 24 suites* ⅋ *In-room data ports, in-room safes, kitchenettes, cable TV, gym, bar, babysitting, meeting rooms, parking (fee), no-smoking floors* 🖃 *AE, DC, MC, V* ⦿ *CP* Ⓜ *Atwater and Guy.*

$$$ 🏨 **Sofitel Montréal.** Montréal's major museums and shops are just a few steps away from this shiny glass-and-steel tower in the Golden Square

Mile. Floor-to-ceiling windows in the large, airy rooms have grand views of downtown or Mont-Royal. Beige and earth-tone walls are off-set by furniture and trim made from *anegre, a pale and lustrous African wood. Goose-down duvets cover the beds, and original artwork and photographs of Montréal line the walls. ⊠ *1155 rue Sherbrooke Ouest, Square Mile, H3A 2N3* ☎ *514/285–9000 or 800/523–8561* 🖷 *514/289–1155* ⊕ *www.sofitel.com* ⇔ *241 rooms, 13 suites, 4 apartments* ♿ *Restaurant, room service, in-room data ports, in-room safes, minibars, cable TV with movies, gym, sauna, bar, concierge, business services, meeting rooms, parking (fee), some pets allowed (fee), no-smoking floors* ☰ *AE, D, DC, MC, V* ⍟ *EP* Ⓜ *Peel.*

$$–$$$ 🖾 **Château Versailles.** The two mansions that make up this luxury hotel were built at the turn of the 20th century. The sumptuous furnishings reflect the Beaux Arts style of the mansions, with high ceilings and plaster moldings. The marble fireplaces in many of the guest rooms and public rooms still work. ⊠ *1659 rue Sherbrooke Ouest, Square Mile, H3H 1E3* ☎ *514/933–3611 or 888/933–8111* 🖷 *514/933–6867* ⊕ *www.versailleshotels.com* ⇔ *63 rooms, 2 suites* ♿ *Room service, in-room data ports, in-room safes, minibars, cable TV with movies and video games, gym, bar, babysitting, dry cleaning, laundry service, concierge, Internet, business services, parking (fee), no-smoking rooms* ☰ *AE, DC, MC, V* ⍟ *CP* Ⓜ *Guy-Concordia.*

¢ 🖾 **McGill Student Apartments.** From mid-May to mid-August, while McGill students are on summer recess, you can stay in the school's dorms on the grassy, quiet campus in the heart of the city. Nightly rates are C$32 for students, C$38 for nonstudents (single rooms only); some more-expensive rooms include a kitchenette. As a visitor, you may use the campus swimming pool and gym facilities for a fee. The university cafeteria is open during the week, serving breakfast and lunch. Be sure to book early. ⊠ *3935 rue University, Square Mile, H3A 2B4* ☎ *514/398–6367* 🖷 *514/398–6770* ⊕ *www.mcgill.ca/residences* ⇔ *1,000 rooms with shared bath* ♿ *Cafeteria, some kitchenettes, pool, gym; no TV in some rooms* ☰ *MC, V* ⊙ *Closed mid-Aug.–mid-May* ⍟ *EP* Ⓜ *McGill.*

Vieux-Montréal

★ $$$$ 🖾 **Hôtel Gault.** The street is gaslit and the facade is from the 1800s, but the loft-style rooms in this boutique hotel look like something out of a modern-design magazine. Every room is different: some have tile-and-concrete floors brightened by boldly patterned geometric rugs; others have sleek, blond-wood furnishings and contrasting rough-brick walls. Rooms also come with CD and DVD players. Bathrooms have free-standing modern tubs and heated tile floors. ⊠ *449 rue Ste-Hélène, Vieux-Montréal, H2V 2K9* ☎ *514/904–1616 or 866/904–1616* ⊕ *www.hotelgault.com* ⇔ *25 rooms, 5 suites* ♿ *Room service, in-room data ports, in-room safes, minibars, cable TV with movies, gym, bar, business services, parking, some pets allowed, no-smoking floors* ☰ *AE, DC, MC, V* ⍟ *CP* Ⓜ *Square-Victoria.*

★ $$$$ 🖾 **Hôtel Le St. James.** When the Stones rolled into town in 2003, Mick and the boys took over this lavishly furnished luxury hotel, housed in what used to be the Mercantile Bank of Canada. One of the rooms, with

20-foot ceilings and lovingly restored murals of hydroelectric dams and waterfalls, was a boardroom. Guest rooms include large marble bathrooms with separate tubs and showers and have Bang & Olufsen sound systems; some rooms have gas fireplaces. Light meals and afternoon tea are available on the ground floor or the balcony of the two-story lobby bar, which used to be the main banking room. ⊠ *355 rue St-Jacques, Vieux-Montréal, H2Y 1N9* ☎ *514/841–3111 or 866/841–3111* 🖷 *514/ 841–1232* ⊕ *www.hotellestjames.com* ⤶ *23 rooms, 38 suites, 1 apartment* ♧ *Room service, in-room data ports, room TVs with movies, gym, spa, bar, library, concierge, meeting rooms, parking (fee), some pets allowed* ⊟ *AE, D, DC, MC, V* ⫶⊙⫶ *EP* Ⓜ *Place d'Armes.*

★ **$$$$** 🏨 **Le St. Sulpice.** The Basilique Notre-Dame-de-Montréal is next door, and the comfortable lobby lounge and bar open onto a courtyard garden that's one of the rare green spots in Vieux-Montréal's stony landscape. The lodgings—huge suites with queen-size beds, feather duvets, leather armchairs, and casement windows that actually open—are in a structure built in 2002 to blend in with the rest of the neighborhood; the gym and business center are in an adjoining 19th-century building. Some suites have fireplaces and balconies. ⊠ *414 rue St-Sulpice, Vieux-Montréal, H2Y 2V5* ☎ *514/288–1000 or 877/785–7423* 🖷 *514/288–0077* ⊕ *www.lesaintsulpice.com* ⤶ *108 suites* ♧ *Restaurant, room service, in-room data ports, in-room safes, some kitchens, minibars, microwaves, cable TV with movies and video games, gym, massage, babysitting, dry cleaning, laundry service, concierge, business services, meeting rooms, parking (fee), some pets allowed (fee), no-smoking rooms* ⊟ *AE, D, DC, MC, V* ⫶⊙⫶ *BP* Ⓜ *Place-d'Armes.*

$$$–$$$$ 🏨 **Hotel Nelligan.** Verses by Émile Nelligan, Québec's most revered poet,
FodorsChoice decorate the stone and brick walls in this boutique hotel on fashionable
★ rue St-Paul. The hotel takes up two adjoining stone buildings from the 1850s. They're one block north of the Vieux-Port and a block south of the Basilique Notre-Dame-de-Montréal. Some suites have terraces with river views. In summer, breakfast is served on the rooftop terrace, and complimentary wine and cheese are served every afternoon. The four-story, brick-walled atrium bar is an ideal place to sip a cocktail, or you can snag a table near the window overlooking rue St-Paul and watch the world hustle by. ⊠ *106 rue St-Paul Ouest, Vieux-Montréal, H2Y 1Z3* ☎ *514/788–2040 or 877/788–2040* 🖷 *514/788–2041* ⊕ *www. hotelnelligan.com* ⤶ *37 rooms, 27 suites* ♧ *Restaurant, room service, in-room data ports, in-room safes, cable TV, gym, massage, bar, concierge, Internet, business services, meeting rooms, parking (fee), no-smoking floors* ⊟ *AE, D, DC, MC, V* ⫶⊙⫶ *CP* Ⓜ *Place d'Armes.*

★ **$$$–$$$$** 🏨 **Hôtel Place d'Armes.** This ornately Victorian building, once the Canadian headquarters of the Great Scottish Life Insurance Co., has been converted into a comfortable boutique hotel with a fireplace and a bar in the lobby. Furnishings are contemporary, but some of the rooms have brick or stone walls. Bathrooms are tiled in black granite and white marble, and there are four duplex suites. A rooftop terrace with a view of Chinatown and the old city adds a crowning touch. The Basilique Notre-Dame-de-Montréal is just across the square, and the Palais des Congrès convention center is also nearby. ⊠ *701 Côte de la Place d'Armes,*

Vieux-Montréal, H2Y 2X6 ☎ *514/842–1887 or 888/450–1887* 🖷 *514/842–6469* ⊕ *www.hotelplacedarmes.com* ⤴ *44 rooms, 4 suites* ⚖ *Restaurant, room service, in-room data ports, minibars, cable TV, gym, bar, laundry service, concierge, meeting room, parking (fee)* ☰ *AE, DC, MC, V* ⊚ *BP* Ⓜ *Place d'Armes.*

$$$–$$$$ ⊞ **Hotel St. Paul.** Stark white walls and huge shuttered windows give the standard rooms in this converted 19th-century office building a light, ethereal feel. All guest rooms have separate sitting areas with sleek leather furniture. The hotel's Cube restaurant serves some of the city's most innovative food. ⊠ *355 rue McGill, Vieux-Montréal, H2Y 2E8* ☎ *514/380–2222 or 866/380–2222* 🖷 *514/380–2200* ⊕ *www.hotelstpaul.com* ⤴ *96 rooms, 24 suites* ⚖ *Restaurant, room service, in-room data ports, in-room fax, minibars, cable TV with movies, gym, massage, bar, dry cleaning, concierge, business services, parking (fee), no-smoking floors* ☰ *AE, D, DC, MC, V* ⊚ *EP* Ⓜ *Square-Victoria.*

$$$–$$$$ ⊞ **Inter-Continental Montréal.** On the edge of Vieux-Montréal, this luxury hotel is part of the Montréal World Trade Center, a block-long retail and office development. The modern 26-story brick tower is outfitted with fanciful turrets and pointed roofs. Rooms are large, with lush carpets, pastel walls, heavy drapes, and big windows overlooking downtown or Vieux-Montréal and the waterfront. Bathrooms have separate marble tubs and showers. Le Continent restaurant serves fine international cuisine. A footbridge across the Trade Center's mall links the hotel with the 18th-century Nordheimer Building, which houses many of the hotel's public rooms. ⊠ *360 rue St-Antoine Ouest, Vieux-Montréal, H2Y 3X4* ☎ *514/987–9900 or 800/361–3600* 🖷 *514/847–8730* ⊕ *www.montreal.interconti.com* ⤴ *332 rooms, 25 suites* ⚖ *2 restaurants, room service, in-room data ports, minibars, room TVs with movies and video games, indoor pool, health club, sauna, bar, concierge, meeting rooms, parking (fee)* ☰ *AE, D, DC, MC, V* ⊚ *EP* Ⓜ *Square-Victoria.*

★ **$$$–$$$$** ⊞ **Pierre du Calvet** AD **1725.** Merchant Pierre du Calvet—a notorious republican and Freemason—entertained Benjamin Franklin behind the stone walls of this 18th-century home in Vieux-Montréal. Today it's a B&B luxuriously decorated with antique furniture and Oriental rugs. Its Filles du Roy restaurant celebrates nouvelle French cuisine, and the glassed-in garden, filled with flowers and potted plants, is a great place for breakfast. ⊠ *405 rue Bonsecours, Vieux-Montréal, H2Y 3C3* ☎ *514/282–1725* 🖷 *514/282–0546* ⊕ *www.pierreducalvet.ca* ⤴ *1 room, 8 suites* ⚖ *Restaurant, dining room, in-room data ports, library, dry cleaning, laundry service, business services, meeting room, parking (fee), no-smoking rooms; no room TVs* ☰ *AE, D, DC, MC, V* ⊚ *BP* Ⓜ *Champ-de-Mars.*

$$$–$$$$ ⊞ **Springhill Suites.** This modern all-suites hotel with eight stories and plenty of amenities fits seamlessly into one of the narrowest and oldest streets of Vieux-Montréal. Rooms are plain, with pastel walls and nondescript furniture. The Vieux-Port is a five-minute walk to the south, and Place Jacques-Cartier is three blocks east. ⊠ *445 rue St-Jean-Baptiste, Vieux-Montréal, H2Y 2Z7* ☎ *514/875–4333* 🖷 *514/875–4331* ⊕ *www.springhillsuites.com* ⤴ *189 suites* ⚖ *Restaurant, room service, in-room data ports, minibars, microwaves, cable TV with movies, indoor pool, gym, bar, laundry service, meeting rooms, parking (fee)* ☰ *AE, D, DC, MC, V* ⊚ *EP* Ⓜ *Champ-de-Mars.*

★ **$$–$$$** 🖼 **Auberge Bonaparte.** Bonaparte, one of the finest restaurants in Vieux-Montréal, has converted the upper floors of its 19th-century building into an inn. Wrought-iron or Louis Philippe–style furnishings fill the guest rooms, some of which have double whirlpool baths. The back rooms (some with balconies) have views over the private gardens of the Basilique Notre-Dame-de-Montréal. Breakfast is served in your room. ⊠ *447 rue St-François-Xavier, Vieux-Montréal, H2Y 2T1* 🕾 *514/844–1448* 🖷 *514/844–0272* ⊕ *www.bonaparte.ca* 🛏 *30 rooms, 1 suite* ♿ *Restaurant, room service, in-room data ports, cable TV with movies, bar, babysitting, concierge, meeting room, parking (fee), no-smoking rooms* ☱ *AE, D, DC, MC, V* ⍾❘ *BP* Ⓜ *Place d'Armes.*

$$–$$$ 🖼 **Auberge du Vieux-Port.** The rooms' stone and brick walls date to the
Fodor's Choice 1880s, and their tall casement windows overlook either fashionable rue
★ St-Paul or the Vieux-Port. Brass beds and massive exposed beams add to the period feel. In summer, you can watch the fireworks competitions from a rooftop terrace. A full breakfast is served in Les Remparts, the hotel's French restaurant. Rooms in the rue St-Paul annex may be up several flights of stairs; try to check these rooms out in advance. ⊠ *97 rue de la Commune Est, Vieux-Montréal, H2Y 1J1* 🕾 *514/876–0081 or 888/660–7678* 🖷 *514/876–8923* ⊕ *www.aubergeduvieuxport.com* 🛏 *27 rooms* ♿ *Restaurant, room service, in-room data ports, in-room safes, cable TV, massage, babysitting, dry cleaning, laundry service, concierge, business services, parking (fee), some pets allowed (fee); no smoking* ☱ *AE, DC, MC, V* ⍾❘ *BP* Ⓜ *Place d'Armes or Champ-de-Mars.*

$$–$$$ 🖼 **Auberge les Passants du Sans Soucy.** The lobby is an art gallery, the
Fodor's Choice building is a 19th-century fur warehouse, and in winter, burning logs
★ crackle in the fireplace that separates the living and breakfast rooms. The rooms have brass beds, stone walls, exposed beams, soft lighting, whirlpool baths, and lots of fresh-cut flowers. ⊠ *171 rue St-Paul Ouest, Vieux-Montréal, H2Y 1Z5* 🕾 *514/842–2634* 🖷 *514/842–2912* ⊕ *www.lesanssoucy.com* 🛏 *9 rooms, 1 suite* ♿ *Dining room, cable TV, lounge, meeting room; no smoking* ☱ *AE, MC, V* ⍾❘ *BP* Ⓜ *Square-Victoria or Place d'Armes.*

$$ 🖼 **Auberge de la Place Royale.** What was once a 19th-century stone rooming house is now a waterfront B&B overlooking the Vieux-Port. A magnificent old wooden staircase links the floors. Antiques and antique reproductions furnish the spacious guest rooms, some of which have whirlpool baths. In summer a full breakfast is served on a sidewalk terrace; in winter it's served in your room. Service is very attentive. ⊠ *115 rue de la Commune Ouest, Vieux-Montréal, H2Y 2C7* 🕾 *514/287–0522* 🖷 *514/287–1209* ⊕ *www.aubergeplaceroyale.com* 🛏 *9 rooms, 3 suites* ♿ *Restaurant, café, in-room data ports, cable TV, in-room VCRs, babysitting, parking (fee); no smoking* ☱ *AE, DC, MC, V* ⍾❘ *BP* Ⓜ *Place d'Armes.*

NIGHTLIFE & THE ARTS

The "Friday Preview" section of the *Gazette* (⊕ www.montrealgazette.com), the English-language daily paper, has an especially thorough list of events at the city's concert halls, theaters, clubs, dance spaces, and movie houses. The *Mirror* ⊕ www.montrealmirror.com), *Hour* (⊕ www. hour.ca), *Scope*, and *Voir* (⊕ www.voir.ca; in French) also list events and are distributed free at restaurants and other public places.

For tickets to major pop and rock concerts, shows, festivals, and hockey, soccer, and baseball games, you can go to the individual box offices or call **Admission** (☎ 514/790–1245 or 800/361–4595 ⊕ www.admission. com). Tickets to Théâtre St-Denis and other venues are available via **Ticketmaster** (☎ 514/790–1111 ⊕ www.ticketmaster.ca).

The Arts

Circus

Cirque du Soleil (☎ 514/722–7234 or 800/361–4595 ⊕ www. cirquedusoleil.com) is one of Montréal's great success stories. The company began revolutionizing the ancient art of circus when it opened in a blue-and-yellow-striped tent on the Montréal waterfront in 1984. Its shows, now an international phenomenon, combine dance, acrobatics, glorious costumes, and dramatic presentation. Touring companies attract crowds all over North America, Europe, and Asia. Every couple of summers, the circus sets up its tent in the Vieux-Port.

Dance

Traditional and contemporary dance companies thrive in Montréal, though many take to the road or are on hiatus in summer. The leading Québec ballet company is **Les Grands Ballets Canadiens** (☎ 514/849–0269 ⊕ www.grandsballets.qc.ca.), which performs at Place des Arts. Its seasonal offerings mix such classics as *Romeo and Juliet* and *The Nutcracker Suite* with more contemporary offerings. The company also hosts performances by troupes from abroad. The **Ballets Classiques de Montréal** (☎ 514/866–1771), which specializes in classical programs, performs at Place des Arts, the Agora de la Danse, and at dance festivals. **Les Ballets Jazz de Montréal** (☎ 514/982–6771) has done much to popularize modern dance with its free performances at the open-air Théâtre de Verdure in Parc Lafontaine. It also performs at Place des Arts and Théâtre Agora. Casablanca-born choreographer Édouard Lock founded **LaLaLa Human Steps** (☎ 514/277–9090) to explore the boundaries of modern dance. The troupe has a heavy international schedule but also performs at Place des Arts and at Montréal festivals. The **Fondation de Danse Margie Gillis Fondation de Danse** (☎ 514/845–3115 ⊕ www.margiegillis.org) was founded in 1981 to showcase the talents of one of Canada's most exciting and innovative soloists. Gillis works with her own company and guest artists to stage performances at Place des Arts, the Agora de la Danse, and other area venues. Lavish sets and dazzlingly sensual choreography have helped to make **Montréal Danse** (☎ 514/871–4005 ⊕ www. montrealdanse.com) one of Canada's most popular contemporary repertory companies. It has a heavy touring schedule but also performs at Place des Arts, Agora de la Danse, and elsewhere. **Ouest Vertigo Danse** (☎ 514/251–9177) stages innovative, contemporary performances.

Downtown performance and rehearsal space **Agora de la Danse** (✉ 840 rue Cherrier Est, Downtown ☎ 514/525–1500 ⊕ www.agoradanse.com)

FESTIVALS

TEAMS FROM AROUND THE WORLD compete to see who can best light up the sky in a show that combines fireworks and music at the **Concours d'Art International Pyrotechnique** (International Fireworks Competition; ☎ 514/397–2000, 514/790–1245, 800/361–4595 in Canada, 800/678–5440 in the U.S. ⊕ www.montrealfeux.com), held in late June and July (mostly on weekends). Their launch site is La Ronde, on Île Ste-Hélène. A ticket includes an amusement-park pass and a reserved seat with a view, but thousands of Montrealers fill the Jacques-Cartier Bridge to watch the show for free, and hundreds more take their lawn chairs and blankets down to the Vieux-Port or across the river to the park along the south shore and watch the show. They bring radios to pick up the musical accompaniment for the fireworks.

International stars show up for the **Festival International des Films du Monde** (World Film Festival; ☎ 514/848–3883 ⊕ www.ffm-montreal.org), from late August to early September. Films shown compete for the Grand Prix of the Americas. The only competitive North American film festival recognized by the International Federation of Film Producers' Associations, it usually screens about 400 films in a dozen venues, some of them outdoors.

The **Festival International de Jazz de Montréal** (Montréal International Jazz Festival; ☎ 514/790–1245, 800/361–4595 in Canada, 800/678–5440 in U.S. ⊕ www.montrealjazzfest.com), the world's largest jazz festival, brings together more than 1,000 musicians for more than 400 concerts over a period of nearly two weeks, from the end of June to the beginning of July. Big names who have appeared in the past include Count Basie, Ella Fitzgerald, Lauryn Hill, Wynton Marsalis, Chick Corea, Dave Brubeck, Angie Stone, and Canada's most famed singer-pianist, Diana Krall. About three-fourths of the concerts are presented free on outdoor stages for lively audiences who sing, clap, and dance to the music. You can also hear blues, Latin rhythms, gospel, Cajun, and world music. Contact Bell Info-Jazz (☎ 514/871–1881 or 888/515–0515) for information about the jazz festival and travel packages.

Every other September (in odd-numbered years), the **Festival International de Nouvelle Danse** (International Festival of New Dance; ☎ 514/287–1423 tickets) stages events at various venues around town. Tickets always sell quickly.

When **Festival International Nuits d'Afrique** (African Nights International Festival; ☎ 514/499–9329 information, 800/361–4595 tickets ⊕ www.festnuitafric.com) was launched in 1987, 10,000 music lovers showed up. Since then, performances by big names such as Youssou N'Dour, Baaba Maal, Miriam Makeba, and King Sunny Ade have made the 10-day event one of the most important showcases of African and Caribbean culture in North America. These days as many as 120,000 people turn out on warm mid-July nights to hear and see the festival's more than 500 singers, dancers, and musicians.

Montréal en Lumière (Montréal Highlights; ☎ 514/288–9955 ⊕ www.montrealenlumiere.com) is designed to brighten the bleak days of February. For every festival, experts artfully illuminate a few historic buildings. Food, too, is a major ingredient in the fun. Such leading chefs as Paul Bocuse of France come to town to give lessons and demonstrations and to take over the kitchens of leading restaurants. Outdoor and indoor concerts, ice-sculpture displays, plays, dance recitals, and other cultural events take place during the festival.

is affiliated with the Université du Québec à Montréal dance faculty. The Agora de la Danse houses **Tangente**(☎ 514/525–5584 ⊕ www.tangente. qc.ca), which stages weekly performances of experimental dance between September and June. Tangente, which is also an archive for contemporary dance and experimental performance art, fosters national and international exchanges.

Film

Several multiscreen complexes show newly released movies in English and French. At the **Ciné Express Café** (✉ 1926 rue Ste-Catherine Ouest, Downtown ☎ 514/939–2463), you can drop in for a drink, a bistro-style meal, and an old flick. Montréal's main repertory movie theater is **Cinéma du Parc** (✉ 3575 av. du Parc, Downtown ☎ 514/281–1900 ⊕ www. cinemaduparc.com). The **Cinémathèque Québecoise** (✉ 335 blvd. de Maisonneuve Est, Quartier Latin ☎514/842–9763 ⊕www.cinematheque. qc.ca) has a collection of 25,000 Québecois, Canadian, and foreign films, as well as a display of equipment dating from the early days of film.

Fans looking for the best in independent productions—both Canadian and foreign—head for **Ex Centris** (✉ 3536 blvd. St-Laurent, Plateau Mont-Royal ☎ 514/847–3536 ⊕ www.ex-centris.com). Its three comfortable theaters are equipped to screen digital new-media works. Ex Centris is worth a visit just to see the huge rotating clock in the lobby and the bathrooms with reflective metal walls.

The most elaborate of Montréal's cinemas is the **Famous Players Paramount** (✉ 707 rue Ste-Catherine Ouest, Downtown ☎ 514/842–5828). It has two IMAX theaters in addition to 15 rooms with regular screens—all showing Hollywood blockbusters. The stately **Impérial** (✉ 1430 rue Bleury, Downtown ☎ 514/848–0300), where the sumptuous decor of the golden age of movies has been retained after a 2002 renovation, screens foreign and independent productions. At the **NFB Montréal** (✉ 1564 rue St-Denis, Quartier Latin ☎ 514/496–6887 ⊕ www.nfb.ca), cinephiles can browse through the National Film Board of Canada's collection of 6,000 documentaries, dramas, short features, and animated flicks. At the west end of the city is the **Pepsi Forum–AMC** (✉ 2313 rue Ste-Catherine Ouest, Downtown ☎514/904–1274), once the home ice of the Montréal Canadiens. Its 22 screens feature plenty of Hollywood biggies, but the Forum also shows some foreign-language and indie productions. The complex includes several restaurants, a bar, a pool room, coffee shops, and gift shops.

Music

The city has one of the best chamber orchestras in Canada, **I Musici de Montréal** (☎ 514/982–6037). The **Orchestre Métropolitain de Montréal** (☎ 514/598–0870) stars at Place des Arts most weeks during the October–April season. When it's not on tour, the **Orchestre Symphonique de Montréal** (☎ 514/842–9951) plays at the Salle Wilfrid-Pelletier at the Place des Arts. The orchestra also gives Christmas and summer concerts in Basilique Notre-Dame-de-Montréal and pop concerts at the Arena Maurice Richard in Olympic Park. For its free summertime concerts in Montréal's parks, check the *Gazette* listings.

McGill University's **Pollack Concert Hall** (✉555 rue Sherbrooke Ouest, Square Mile ☎ 514/398–4535) presents concerts, notably by the **McGill Chamber Orchestra**. The **Spectrum** (✉ 318 rue Ste-Catherine Ouest, Downtown ☎ 514/861–5851) is an intimate concert hall. The 2,500-seat **Théâtre St-Denis** (✉1594 rue St-Denis, Quartier Latin ☎ 514/849–4211 ⊕ www.theatrestdenis.com), the second-largest auditorium in Montréal (after Salle Wilfrid-Pelletier in Place des Arts), stages a wide range of pop-music concerts performed in English and French, including rock band Wilco, folk singer Rita MacNeil, and Québecois heartthrob Roch Voisine.

Opera

L'Opéra de Montréal (☎ 514/985–2258) stages five productions a year at Place des Arts, as well as opera workshops and a special benefit performance.

Theater

There are at least 10 major French-speaking theater companies in town, some of which have an international reputation. The choices for Anglophones are more limited. The **Théâtre de Quat'Sous** (✉ 100 av. des Pins Est, Downtown ☎ 514/845–7277) performs modern, experimental, and cerebral plays in French. **Théâtre Denise Pelletier** (✉ 4353 rue Ste-Catherine Est, Hochelaga-Maisonneuve ☎ 514/253–8974 ⊕ www.denise-pelletier.qc.ca) puts on a variety of French-language productions in a beautifully restored Italianate hall. **Théâtre du Nouveau Monde** (✉ 84 rue Ste-Catherine Ouest, Downtown ☎ 514/866–8667 ⊕ www.tnm.qc.ca) is the North American temple of French classics. A season's offerings might include works by Shakespeare, Molière, and a modern French playwright. Modern French repertoire is the specialty at **Théâtre du Rideau Vert** (✉ 4664 rue St-Denis, Quartier Latin ☎ 514/844–1793 ⊕ www.rideauvert.qc.ca). Named for one of Québec's best-loved actors, the **Théâtre Jean Duceppe** (☎ 514/842–2112 ⊕ www.duceppe.com) stages major French-language productions in the Place des Arts.

The **Centaur Theatre** (✉ 453 rue St-François-Xavier, Vieux-Montréal ☎ 514/288–3161), Montréal's best-known English theatrical company, stages everything from musical revues to Eugène Ionesco works in the former stock exchange building in Vieux-Montréal. **Place des Arts** (✉ 175 rue Ste-Catherine Ouest, Downtown ☎ 514/842–2112 ⊕ www.pda.qc.ca) is a favorite venue for visiting productions. English-language plays can be seen at the **Saidye Bronfman Centre** (✉ 5170 chemin de la Côte Ste-Catherine, Côte-des-Neiges ☎ 514/739–2301 or 514/739–7944), an arts center for Montréal as a whole and for the Jewish community in particular. Plays in English are presented most of the year, but in May the Yiddish Theatre Group takes over the stage. Touring Broadway productions often can be seen at the **Théâtre St-Denis** (✉ 1594 rue St-Denis, Quartier Latin ☎ 514/849–4211), especially in summer.

Nightlife

Most Montréal bars stop serving around 3:00 AM but stay open until 3:30.

Laser Quest (✉ 1226 rue Ste-Catherine Ouest, Downtown ☎ 514/393–3000) has fog machines, music, and live-action laser-tag games on five levels. It's open until 11 on Friday and Saturday nights, and until 10 Monday through Thursday.

Bars

More than 100 different beers, 30 of them locally brewed, are available at **Bierres & Compagnie** (✉ 4350 rue St-Denis, Plateau Mont-Royal ☎ 514/844–0394), as well as good food—much of it cooked in beer. **Brutopia** (✉ 1219 rue Crescent, Downtown ☎ 514/393–9277) serves good pasta, salads, and steaks. The large selection of draft beer and huge platters of food make it a popular downtown meeting place. **Else's** (✉ 156 rue Roy Est, Plateau Mont-Royal ☎ 514/286–6689) has a good selection of beers and ciders, an eclectic clientele, and a first-rate, friendly staff. It's always packed for Montréal's infamous *cinq-à-sept* (happy hour, literally five-to-seven) on Thursdays and Fridays. Retro is king at the **Gogo Lounge** (✉ 3682 blvd. St-Laurent, Plateau Mont-Royal ☎ 514/286–0882), where those in their twenties and thirties sip martinis with names like Pussycat, LSD, and Yellow Submarine. **Île Noir** (✉ 342 rue Ontario Est, Quartier Latin ☎ 514/982–0866) has a rich wood interior that fits in with its impressive selection of over 100 single-malt whiskeys. **Jello Bar** (✉ 151 rue Ontario Est, Quartier Latin ☎ 514/285–2621) is filled with lava lamps, love seats, and other retro and sleek furnishings. The 52 martini flavors include red lotus, the local favorite. The music ranges from swing and jazz to salsa and R&B, with live performances on weekends.

Sofa (✉ 451 rue Rachel Est, Plateau Mont-Royal ☎ 514/285–1011), as the name suggests, is a comfortable place to sip a port or a Scotch and watch the arty-looking Plateau locals go by. **Stogie's Café and Cigars** (✉ 2015 rue Crescent, Downtown ☎ 514/848–0069) imports cigars directly from Cuba. The relaxed surroundings are ripe for friendly arguments about anything—except the merits of smoking. **Le Swimming** (✉ 3643 blvd. St-Laurent, Plateau Mont-Royal ☎ 514/282–7665) is a vast upscale pool lounge ("pool hall" just isn't genteel enough) with 11 tables and the world's largest table hockey game. The place is very popular with the young and fashionable, and regularly hosts some of the city's best up-and-coming rock, funk, and ska bands. **Wax Lounge** (✉ 3481 blvd. St-Laurent, Plateau Mont-Royal ☎ 514/282–0919) is an intimate upstairs bar specializing in champagne. The couches are excellent for people-watching or just lounging. **Whiskey Café** (✉ 3 rue Bernard West, Plateau Mont-Royal ☎ 514/278–2646) has a superb menu of 20 types of port and over 70 kinds of Scotch. Don't miss the high-tech bathrooms. **Winnie's** (✉ 1459 rue Crescent, Downtown ☎ 514/288–0623), named for Winston Churchill, draws its clientele from among the young professionals and entrepreneurs who work downtown. A favorite with young Anglo-Montrealers, **Ziggy's Pub** (✉ 470 rue Crescent, Downtown ☎ 514/285–8855) has a friendly crowd of regulars and plenty of colorful local personalities to keep you entertained.

Casino

The **Casino de Montréal** (✉ 1 av. du Casino, Île Notre-Dame ☎ 514/392–2746 or 800/665–2274 ⊕ www.casino-de-montreal.com), Québec's first casino, is one of the world's 10 biggest, with over 3,000 slot machines and 120 tables for baccarat, craps, blackjack, and roulette. There are some oddities for those used to Vegas: no drinking on the floor, and no tipping the croupiers. Winners may want to spend some of their gains at Nuances or three other restaurants. The Cabaret de Casino has some of the best shows in town. To get to the casino, which is open around the clock, you can take a C$10 cab ride from downtown, drive (parking is free), or take the Métro to the Jean-Drapeau stop and then board Bus 167.

Comedy

The **Comedy Nest** (⊠ Pepsi Forum, 2313 rue Ste-Catherine Ouest, 3rd fl., Downtown ☎ 514/932–6378) hosts established Canadian and international comedians and is an excellent spot to catch some of the city's funniest up-and-comers. Dinner-and-show packages are available. **Comedyworks** (⊠ 1238 rue Bishop, Downtown ☎ 514/398–9661) is a popular spot upstairs from Jimbo's Pub that books both amateurs and professionals. Acts are more risqué than those at the Comedy Nest.

Dance Clubs

Bar Minuit (⊠ 115 rue Laurier Ouest, Plateau Mont-Royal ☎ 514/271–2110) is open until 3 AM from Wednesday to Saturday and plays an eclectic blend of house, pop, retro, and salsa. The space is often crowded, with Wednesday night happy hour being especially lively. **Club 737** (⊠ 1 pl. Ville-Marie, Downtown ☎ 514/397–0737), a two-level club high atop the city with a sweeping panoramic view and a rooftop terrace, does the disco number every Thursday, Friday, and Saturday night. It has become very popular with the mid-twenties to mid-thirties office crowd. If you find yourself pining for the Decade of Decadence, head to **Electric Avenue** (⊠ 1469 rue Crescent, Downtown ☎ 514/285–8885), where the DJs are unapologetically nostalgic for the 1980s. It's open from 10 PM until last call from Thursday to Saturday. **Newtown** (⊠ 1476 rue Crescent, Downtown ☎ 514/284–6555), one of the city's hottest clubs, is named for its owner, Formula 1 race-car driver Jacques Villeneuve ("Newtown" is the English translation of his name). The tri-level dance club–bar–restaurant caters to a trendy, upscale crowd. Reserve early for the private outdoor terrace table. **Thursdays/Les Beaux Jeudis** (⊠ 1449 rue Crescent, Downtown ☎ 514/288–5656) is the primo downtown bar and disco for the professional set. The dance club opens at 10 PM.

Montréal's love affair with Latin dance is one of long standing, but even before the current craze, the Québecois took dancing seriously. **Cactus** (⊠ 4461 rue St-Denis, Plateau Mont-Royal ☎ 514/849–0349) supplies its patrons with rigorously authentic music, from salsa to merengue. The dance floor is always packed. **Salsathèque** (⊠ 1220 rue Peel, Downtown ☎ 514/875–0016) is one of the most popular Latin clubs in Montréal.

Folk Music

Hurley's Irish Pub (⊠ 1225 rue Crescent, Downtown ☎ 514/861–4111) attracts some of the city's best Celtic musicians, dancers, and storytellers. There's never a cover charge. At **McKibbin's Irish Pub** (⊠ 1426 rue Bishop, Downtown ☎ 514/288–1580), Celtic fiddlers from all over Canada—and, indeed, the world—put in appearances. And the Irish stew is even better than the music. **Old Dublin** (⊠ 1219A rue University, Downtown

☎ 514/861–4448), presents live Celtic bands every night of the week. The menu is made up of standard pub fare, with the notable exception of a few first-rate Indian dishes. **Yellow Door** (✉ 3625 rue Aylmer, Downtown ☎ 514/398–6243), a Montréal folk-music institution since the 1960s and Canada's longest-running coffeehouse, is a basement club showcasing homegrown and international folk and blues acts. There's no alcohol and no smoking.

Gay Bars & Nightclubs

The bars, clubs, and restaurants of the Village, the heart of Montréal's gay and lesbian community, line rue Ste-Catherine between rue Amherst and avenue Papineau. In general, the farther east you walk on rue Ste-Catherine, the greater the emphasis on saunas and strip clubs. *Fugues* (☎ 514/845–7645 ⊕ www.fugues.com), a gay newspaper published in French with a smattering of articles in English, lists events.

Agora (✉ 1160 rue Mackay, Downtown ☎ 514/934–1428) is a casual gay and lesbian hangout in the middle of downtown. It's usually quiet and intimate, apart from Saturday karaoke nights. **Club Bolo** (✉ 960 rue Amherst, Village ☎ 514/849–4777) has a country-and-western theme that attracts both men and women. **Club Parking** (✉ 1296 rue Amherst, Village ☎ 514/282–1199), in the heart of the Village, serves an interesting mix of older leather guys and hip, trendy kids, with the music largely 1980s alternative dance. The upstairs bar has a reputation of being one of the best meeting spots in town.

Club Unity 2 caters to a young, hip crowd of men. Small semi-private lounges are scattered throughout the two-story complex, and the beautiful rooftop terrace is one of the finest in the Village, if not the entire city. Expect to hear some of Montréal's best DJs spinning from Thursday to Saturday. Admission can be C$10 or more, but entrance is free before 11. ✉ *1171 Ste-Catherine Est, Village* ☎ *514/523–4429.*

Le Drugstore (✉ 1360 rue Ste-Catherine Est, Village ☎ 514/524–1960) is a mammoth complex of eight bars on eight floors that in recent years has become an institution of the city's gay scene. In addition to the bars, there are a café, a newsstand, a handsome terrace, and even a couple of shops. Although the crowd includes all ages and types, this is the neighborhood's best hangout for women, who gravitate toward the basement billiards hall and the 2nd-floor lounge.

Sky Pub/Sky Club (✉ 1474 rue Ste-Catherine Est, Village ☎ 514/529–6969) is two hangouts in one, and arguably the busiest gay club in the city, especially among young model types. Downstairs, the Sky Pub is a sprawling, mostly male bar which hosts the neighborhood's busiest happy hour; upstairs, Sky Club is a hip disco with two small dance floors and a mixed crowd of gays and lesbians. Some of the most beautiful cross-dressers in the city gather at **Stereo** (✉ 858 rue Ste-Catherine Est, Village ☎ 514/286–0325) to move on the huge dance floor of this converted theater. It's popular with both men and women. Don't bother arriving before midnight. **Le Stud** (✉ 1812 rue Ste-Catherine Est, Village ☎ 514/598–8243), loud and full of leather, is a men-only hangout that's open until the wee hours.

Jazz & Blues

Biddle's (⊠ 2060 rue Aylmer, Downtown ☎ 514/842–8656) takes its name from the late, great Montréal bassist Charles Biddle, who played here on weekends until just months before he died in 2003. It's still a great spot for jazz, and the ribs and chicken are pretty good, too. The **Upstairs Jazz Club** (⊠ 1254 rue Mackay , Downtown ☎ 514/931–6808) has intimate live jazz: local and imported musicians take the stage seven nights a week. Shark and salmon are two specialties on the good dinner menu.

Reggae, Hip-Hop & World

Aria (⊠ 1280 St-Denis, Quartier Latin ☎ 514/987–6712), one of Montrél's most established after-hours clubs, caters to an urban crowd with local and international DJs and MC's most Friday and Saturday nights. Doors open at 1:30 AM, Saturday and Sunday mornings only. **Le Balattou** (⊠ 4372 blvd. St-Laurent, Plateau Mont-Royal ☎ 514/845–5447), a busy and smoky club, specializes in African and Caribbean music. Performances start late and last even later. **Blue Dog** (⊠ 3958 blvd. St-Laurent, Plateau Mont-Royal ☎ 514/848–7006) has an eclectic musical mix—from reggae to rock—with the real action happening after 11.

Rock

Lovers of blues, punk rock, country, and bluegrass jam into **Barfly** (⊠ 4062A blvd. St-Laurent, Plateau Mont-Royal ☎ 514/284–6665), a tiny but tasteful hole-in-the-wall with some of the cheapest drink prices to be found anywhere on the Main (slang for St-Laurent). **Club Soda** (⊠ 1225 blvd. St-Laurent, Downtown ☎ 514/286–1010), the granddaddy of city rock clubs, is a tall, narrow concert hall with high-tech design and 500 seats—all of them good. The club is open only for shows; phone the box office to find out what's on.

Foufounes Electriques (⊠ 87 rue Ste-Catherine Est, Downtown ☎ 514/844–5539) is the oldest alternative rock venue in the city, having played host to everyone from Nirvana to the Dickies at one time or another. A favorite with punks, it's not for the faint of heart, which should come as no surprise from a club whose name means "electric buttocks." **Spectrum** (⊠ 318 rue Ste-Catherine Ouest, Downtown ☎ 514/861–5851) is the most popular performance venue for rock bands in Montréal.

Jupiter Room is a small and always packed indie rock venue catering to a young crowd. Be prepared to wait in line on the tremendously popular 1980s theme nights every Thursday. ⊠ 3874 blvd. St-Laurent, Plateau Mont-Royal ☎ No phone.

SPORTS & THE OUTDOORS

Most Montrealers would probably claim they hate winter, but the city is rich in cold-weather activities—skating rinks, cross-country-ski trails, and toboggan runs. During warm-weather months, residents head for the tennis courts, miles of bicycle trails, golf courses, and two lakes for boating and swimming. You can even scuba dive in Montréal—in a pool, that is.

Auto Racing

The **Grand Prix du Canada** (☎ 514/350–4731, 514/350–0000 tickets ⊕ www.grandprix.ca) takes place in late June and consistently inspires Montreal's busiest tourist weekend. One of only two venues in North America where one can witness Formula 1 racing, the Canadian Grand Prix takes place at the Circuit Gilles Villeneuve on Île Notre Dame. In late August, Circuit Gilles Villeneuve hosts the **Molson Indy of Montréal** (☎ 514/397–4639), a race sanctioned by the CART FedEx Championship Series.

Biking

Despite the bitter winters (or perhaps because of them), Montréal has fallen in love with the bicycle. More than 350 km (217 mi) of cycling paths crisscross the metropolitan area, and bikes are welcome on the first and last cars of Métro trains during non-rush hours. Ferries at the Vieux-Port take cyclists to Île Ste-Hélène and the south shore of the St. Lawrence River, where riders can connect to hundreds of miles of trails in the Montérégie region. The most popular trail on the island begins at the Vieux-Port and follows the **Lachine Canal** to the shores of Lac St-Louis in Lachine.

Parks Canada (☎ 514/283–6054 or 514/637–7433) conducts guided cycling tours along the Lachine Canal every summer weekend.

Le Pôle des Rapides (☎ 514/364–4490), a network of more than 96 km (60 mi) of bicycle trails that includes the Lachine Canal trail, follows lakefronts, canals, and aqueducts.

Féria du Véle de Montréal (Montréal Bike Fest; ☎ 514/521–8356 ⊕ www.velo.qc.ca), at the end of May, is the biggest such celebration in North America. Cyclists of all ages and conditions take part in a night ride through the streets of the city. Other events include a 22-km (14-mi) ride for children and a couple of challenge races of 100 and 150 km (62 and 93 mi). It all culminates on the last day with as many as 50,000 cyclists taking over the streets for the **Tour de l'Île**, a 50-km (31-mi) ride for all on a route that circles the city.

Le Maison des Cyclistes (✉ 1251 rue Rachel Est, Plateau Mont-Royal ☎ 514/521–8356) rents bikes, and you can drop in to sip a coffee at the Bicicletta café or to browse the maps in the adjoining boutique.

Vélo Aventure (☎ 514/847–0666) rents bicycles at the Vieux-Port. **Velo Montréal** (✉ 3870 Rachel Est, Rosemont ☎ 514/236–8356) is the place to rent bicycles at Parc Jean Drapeau, the site of the 1976 summer Olympics.

Bird-Watching

The 350 bird species in Montréal can be seen from many vantage points. The **Rare Bird Alert** (☎ No phone ⊕ www.pqspb.org) offers information on recent sightings and suggested birding spots.

Boating

In Montréal you can get in a boat at a downtown wharf and be crashing through Class V white water minutes later. **Lachine Rapids Tours**

(✉ 47 rue de la Commune, or quai de l'Horloge, Vieux-Montréal ☎ 514/284–9607) has one-hour voyages for thrill seekers through the rapids in big aluminum jet boats. Heavy-water gear is supplied. You can also choose a half-hour trip around the islands in 10-passenger boats that can go about 100 kph (62 mph). Trips are narrated in French and English. There are five trips daily through the rapids from May through September; the cost is C$55, and reservations are required. Rafting trips are also available.

Football

The 2002 national-champion **Montréal Alouettes** (☎ 514/871–2266 information, 514/871–2255 tickets ⊕ www.alouettes.net) of the Canadian Football League play the Canadian version of the game—bigger field, just three downs, and a more wide-open style—under open skies at McGill University's Molson Stadium from June through October. It's one of the best sporting deals in town.

Golf

Tourisme Québec (☎ 514/873–2015 or 800/363–7777 ⊕ www.bonjourquebec.com) can provide a complete listing of the many golf courses in the greater metropolitan area.

The **Club de Golf Métropolitain Anjou** (Anjou Metropolitan Golf Club; ✉ 9555 blvd. du Golf, Anjou ☎ 514/353–5353 ⊕ www.golfmetropolitainanjou.com), about a 20-minute drive from downtown, has a par-72, 18-hole championship golf course as well as an 18-hole executive course. Rates for 18 holes range from C$34.50 to C$57.50, plus C$30 for an electric cart.

Golf Dorval (✉ 2000 av. Reverchon, Dorval ☎ 514/631–4653 ⊕ www.golfdorval.com), about 20 minutes from downtown by car, encompasses two 18-hole courses (par 70 and 72), a driving range, and two putting greens. Rates for 18 holes range from C$22 to C$41. It costs an additional C$30 for a cart.

Meadowbrook Golf Club (✉ 8370 Côte Saint-Luc, Côte Saint-Luc ☎ 514/488–4875 ⊕ www.clubdegolfmeadowbrook.com) is a somewhat challenging par-75, 18-hole course whose main selling point is its location, only a few kilometers from downtown. The course has a 69.2 rating with a 113 slope. Rates are from C$17 to C$32 for 18 holes. A cart is C$26 more.

Hockey

The **Montréal Canadiens** (✉ 1250 rue de la Gauchetière Ouest, Downtown ☎ 514/932–2582 ⊕ www.canadiens.com), winners of 23 Stanley Cups, meet National Hockey League rivals at the Centre Bell from October through April (and even later if they make the playoffs). Buy tickets in advance to guarantee a seat. College hockey is a bargain alternative for fans who can't get a Canadiens ticket.

The **McGill University Redmen** (✉ 475 av. des Pins Ouest, Downtown ☎ 514/398–7006 ⊕ www.redmenhockey.com) make up in passion what they lack in polish—especially when they take on their cross-city rivals, the Concordia University Stingers.

Ice-Skating

Access Montreal (☎ 514/872–1111) has information on the numerous ice-skating rinks (at least 195 outdoor and 21 indoor) in the city. Outdoor rinks are open from January until mid-March, and admission is free. The rinks on Île Ste-Hélène and at the Vieux-Port are especially large, but there is a $3 admission charge to skate at the latter. You can skate year-round in the **Atrium le Mille de la Gauchetière** (⊠ 1000 rue de la Gauchetière, Downtown ☎ 514/395–1000 or 514/395–0555), a skyscraper atrium. There's disco skating Friday and Saturday nights from October to April, and scheduled ice shows throughout the year. Skate rental is $4.50 per day.

Jogging

Most city parks have jogging paths, and you can also run the trail along the Lachine Canal. For running with a panoramic view, head to the dirt track in **Parc du Mont-Royal** (☎ 514/843–4928).

Skiing/Snowboarding

A "Ski-Québec" brochure is available from **Tourisme Québec** (☎ 514/873–2015 or 800/363–7777 ⊕ www.bonjourquebec.com).

CROSS-COUNTRY   Trails crisscross most city parks, including Parcs des Îles, Maisonneuve, and Mont-Royal, but the best ones are probably the 46 km (29 mi) of trails in the 900-acre **Cap St-Jacques Regional Park** (⊠ 2099 blvd. Gouin Ouest, Pierrefonds ☎ 514/280–6871), on the west end of the island of Montréal, about a half-hour drive from downtown. To get to the park via public transportation, take the Métro to the Henri-Bourassa stop and then the 69 Bus west. Cross-country skiers use the **Lachine Canal** in winter.

DOWNHILL   You don't have to travel far from Montréal to find good downhill skiing, but you do have to travel. **Mont St-Sauveur** (☎ 514/871–0101), with a vertical drop of 700 feet, is the closest decent-size ski hill in the Laurentian Mountains, the winter and summer playground for Montrealers. It's about an hour's drive northwest of Montréal. **Bromont** (☎ 450/534–2200), about a 45-minute drive from the Champlain Bridge, is the closest Appalachian hill, with a 1,329-foot vertical drop. It's in the Eastern Townships, southeast of the city.

Within Montréal, **Parc du Mont-Royal** has a small ski slope. **Mont St-Bruno** (☎ 450/653–3441), on the south shore, has a modest vertical drop of 443 feet, but it includes Québec's biggest ski school and a high-speed lift and also offers night skiing.

Soccer

The Montréal Impact (☎ Tickets 514/790–1245, 800/361–4595, 514/328–3668 ⊕ www.impactmontreal.com) is one of the best sports bargains in town. A consistently strong member of the North American A league, they play from mid-May until mid-September at the **Centre Sportif et des Loisirs Claude-Robillard** (⊠ 1000 av. Emile-Journault, Ahuntsic ☎ 514/872–6900). Tickets are C$15 for reserved seats and C$10 for general admission.

Snorkeling & Scuba Diving

Waddell Aquatics (✉ 6356 rue Sherbrooke Ouest, Westmount ☎ 514/482–1890 or 888/834–8464) offers rentals, lessons in a big pool, and local excursions.

Swimming

Most of the city's municipal outdoor pools are open from mid-June through August. Admission is free weekdays and C$2.75 on weekends and holidays. Contact **Accèss Montréal** (☎ 514/872–1111 ⊕ www.ville.montreal.qc.ca) for details.

You can swim for free at **Bain Schubert** (✉ 3950 blvd. St-Laurent, Plateau Mont-Royal ☎ 514/872–2587), a renovated art deco pool. For a small fee you can swim at one of four indoor public pools at **Centre Aquatique** (✉ 4141 av. Pierre-de-Coubertin, Hochelaga-Maisonneuve ☎ 514/252–4622) at Olympic Park. **Centre Sportif et des Loisirs Claude-Robillard** (✉ 1000 av. Emile-Journault, Ahuntsic ☎ 514/872–6900) has a big (and free) indoor pool. **Plage de Île Notre-Dame** (✉ West side of Île Notre-Dame) is the only natural swimming hole in Montréal. **Vieux Montréal CEGEP** (Junior College; ✉ 255 rue Ontario Est, Quartier Latin ☎ 514/982–3457) has a free indoor pool, open evenings Tuesday through Friday and Saturday 9–3.

Tennis

The Jeanne-Mance, Kent, Lafontaine, and Somerled parks have public courts. For details call **Accèss Montréal** (☎ 514/872–1111 ⊕ www.ville.montreal.qc.ca).

Windsurfing & Sailing

You can rent sailboards and small sailboats at **L'École de Voile de Lachine** (Lachine Sailing School; ✉ 2105 blvd. St-Joseph, Lachine ☎ 514/634–4326).

SHOPPING

Montrealers *magasinent* (shop) with a vengeance, so it's no surprise that the city has 160 multifaceted retail areas encompassing some 7,000 stores. The law allows shops to stay open weekdays 9–9 and weekends 9–5. However, many merchants close evenings Monday through Wednesday and on Sunday. Many specialty service shops are closed on Monday, too. Just about all stores, with the exception of some bargain outlets and a few selective art and antiques galleries, accept major credit cards. Most purchases are subject to a federal goods and services tax (GST) of 7% as well as a provincial tax of 8%. Non-Canadians can claim a refund of some of these taxes, however.

Montréal is one of the fur capitals of the world. If you think you might be buying fur, it's wise to check with your country's customs officials before your trip to find out which animals are considered endangered and cannot be imported.The same caveat applies to collectors of Inuit ivory carvings, which cannot be imported into the United States or other countries. If you do buy Inuit carvings, whether they're made of ivory or soapstone, look for the government of Canada's igloo symbol, which attests to the piece's authenticity.

Some linguistic reminders: A *magasin à rayons* is not a shop selling synthetic fabrics; it's a department store. A *librairie* is a bookstore, not a library (which would be a *bibliothèque.*). *Friperie* (or more colloquially *frip*) is a Québec word used by all language groups to describe secondhand clothes and accessories. *Dépanneur* and *dép* denote a convenience store. *Vente* and more correctly *solde* both mean "sale."

Shopping Districts

Avenue Laurier Ouest, from boulevard St-Laurent to chemin de la Côte-Ste-Catherine, is eight or so blocks dotted with fashionable and trendy shops that carry crafts, clothing, books, and paintings.

Boulevard St-Laurent, affectionately known as the Main, has restaurants, boutiques, and nightclubs that cater mostly to an upscale clientele. Still, the area has managed to retain its working-class immigrant roots and vitality to some degree: high-fashion shops are interspersed with ethnic-food stores, secondhand bookshops, and hardware stores. Indeed, a trip up this street takes you from Chinatown to Little Italy. Shoppers flock to the two blocks of avenue Mont-Royal just east of boulevard St-Laurent for secondhand clothing.

Downtown is Montréal's largest retail district. It takes in rues Sherbrooke and Ste-Catherine, boulevard de Maisonneuve, and the side streets between them. Because of the proximity and diversity of the stores, it's the best shopping bet if you're in town overnight or for a weekend. The area bounded by rues Sherbrooke, Ste-Catherine, de la Montagne, and Crescent has antiques and art galleries in addition to designer salons. Fashion boutiques and art and antiques galleries line rue Sherbrooke. Rue Crescent holds a tempting blend of antiques, fashions, and jewelry displayed beneath colorful awnings.

Plaza St-Hubert, a four-block stretch of rue St-Hubert a little out of the way, is a great place for bargain hunters. There are dozens of independent boutiques and end-of-the-line retailers and liquidation centers like Pennington's Dex and Le Château. You'll also find the biggest cluster of bridal shops in the city.

Rue Chabanel, in the city's north end, is the soul of Montréal's extensive garment industry. Every Saturday, from about 8:30 to 1, many of its manufacturers and importers open their doors to the general public. Well, they do if they feel like it. What results is part bazaar, part circus, and often all chaos—but friendly chaos.

When Montrealers say "Chabanel," they mean the eight-block stretch just west of boulevard St-Laurent. The factories and shops here are tiny—dozens of them are crammed into each building. The goods seem to get more stylish and more expensive the farther west you go. For really inexpensive leather goods, sportswear, children's togs, and linens, try the shops at 99 rue Chabanel; 555 rue Chabanel offers more-deluxe options. The manufacturers and importers at 555 have their work areas on the upper floors and have transformed the mezzanine into a glitzy mall with bargains in men's suits, winter coats, knit goods, and stylish leather jackets. A few places on Chabanel accept credit cards, but bring cash anyway. It's easier to bargain if you can flash bills, and if you pay cash, the price will often "include the tax."

Rue St-Denis, perhaps Montréal's trendiest area, has shops of all descriptions and some of the best restaurants in town. People-watching is a popular pastime as this is where the beautiful people go to see and be seen. Cutting-edge fashions can be found both in the shops and on the shoppers.

Vieux-Montréal may seem choked with garish souvenir shops, but shopping here can be worthwhile. Fashion boutiques and shoe stores with low to moderate prices line rues Notre-Dame and St-Jacques, from rue McGill to Place Jacques-Cartier. Rue St-Paul also has some interesting shops. During the warm-weather months, sidewalk cafés are everywhere, and so are street performers.

The fashionable place for antiquing is a formerly run-down five-block strip of **rue Notre-Dame Ouest** between rue Guy and avenue Atwater, a five-minute walk south from the Lionel-Groulx Métro station. Antiques stores have been popping up along **rue Amherst** between rues Ste-Catherine and Ontario (a five-minute walk west of the Beaudry Métro station). The area is shabbier than rue Notre-Dame, and a lot less expensive. Antiques hunters who want to spend more may want to head to **Westmount,** where shops cater to the tastes of the executives who live in the upscale suburb.

Department Stores

Les Ailes de la Mode. This shiny little department store is a sort of temple to the power of the clothing label. Its three floors carry a large number of those labels—Hugo Boss, Armani, Jax, Cerruti, Max Mara, Escada, Arnold Brant, Bugatti, Riviera—not to mention dozens of top lines of cosmetics, scents, jewelry, baby clothes, and housewares, plus Godiva chocolates. Despite the glitter, however, the store is hidden away at the back of a shopping mall of the same name, behind a distracting phalanx of high-priced boutiques. ⊠ *677 rue Ste-Catherine Ouest, Downtown* ☎ *514/282–5437.*

La Baie. The Bay is a descendant of the Hudson's Bay Company, the great 17th-century fur trading company that played a pivotal role in Canada's development. La Baie has been a department store since 1891. In addition to selling typical department-store goods, it's known for its duffel coats and signature Hudson's Bay blankets, with stripes of red, green, and white. ⊠ *585 rue Ste-Catherine Ouest, Downtown* ☎ *514/281–4422.*

Holt Renfrew. An exclusive shop where the specialty is furs and fashions, Holt Renfrew has supplied coats to four generations of British royalty. When Queen Elizabeth II got married in 1947, Holt gave her a priceless Labrador mink. The store carries the pricey line of furs by Newmont Fashion Group as well as the haute couture and ready-to-wear collections of Giorgio Armani, Calvin Klein, and Chanel. ⊠ *1300 rue Sherbrooke Ouest, Downtown* ☎ *514/842–5111.*

Ogilvy. Founded in 1865, Ogilvy still stocks traditional apparel by retailers such as Aquascutum and Jaeger. The store is divided into individual designer boutiques. A kilted piper regales shoppers daily at noon. ✉ *1307 rue Ste-Catherine Ouest, Downtown* ☎ *514/842–7711.*

Simons. This youth-oriented department store in elegant 19th-century digs specializes in high-quality clothes for men and women, including its own highly respected house label. Simons shares its address with a 12-screen Paramount theater, an IMAX theater, a bar, and a coffee shop. ✉ *977 rue Ste-Catherine Ouest, Downtown* ☎ *514/282–1840.*

Shopping Centers & Malls

Le Centre Eaton. Eaton Center has a youthful edge, with a huge Levi's store and some trendy sporting-goods stores. The five-story mall, the largest in the downtown core, with 175 boutiques and shops, is linked to the McGill Métro station. An instant tax refund service, for nonresidents, is on the 4th floor. ✉ *705 rue Ste-Catherine Ouest, Downtown* ☎ *514/288–3708.*

Complexe Desjardins. Splashing fountains and exotic plants create a sense of relaxation here. The roughly 80 stores range from budget-clothing outlets to the exclusive Jonathan Roche Monsieur for men's fashions. To get here, take the Métro to the Place des Arts and then follow the tunnels to the multitier atrium mall. ✉ *blvd. René-Lévesque at rue Jeanne Mance, Downtown* ☎ *514/845–4636.*

Le Complexe Les Ailes. The Les Ailes flagship store in this complex attached to Le Centre Eaton sells women's clothing and accessories; the other 57 retailers here include Tommy Hilfiger and Archambault, a music store. ✉ *677 rue Ste-Catherine Ouest, Downtown* ☎ *514/285–1080.*

Les Cours Mont-Royal. This elegant mall linked to the Peel and McGill Métro stations caters to expensive tastes, but even bargain hunters find it an intriguing spot for window shopping. The more than 80 shops include DKNY and Harry Rosen. Beware: the interior layout can be disorienting. ✉ *1455 rue Peel, Downtown* ☎ *514/842–7777.*

Le Faubourg Ste-Catherine. A vast indoor bazaar abutting the Couvent des Soeurs Grises, Le Faubourg includes clothing and crafts boutiques, but it's best known as a wonderful source of quality foods. The 3rd floor houses one of the downtown area's best food courts, with booths selling Greek, Moroccan, Lebanese, Italian, Indian, and Japanese food. The Chinese booth at the west end—Bai Taiwan—offers some unusual iced teas and other cold drinks. And unlike most food courts, this one is bright and airy, with lots of windows. ✉ *1616 rue Ste-Catherine Ouest, at rue Guy, Downtown* ☎ *514/939–3663.*

Marché Bonsecours. Inaugurated in the 1840s as the city's principal public market, this neoclassical building now houses boutiques that showcase Québecois, Canadian, and First Nation artwork, clothing, furniture, and designs. ✉ *350 rue St-Paul Est, Vieux-Montréal* ☎ *514/872–7730.*

Le Place Montréal Trust. This complex is a gateway to Montréal's vast Underground City. Its shops tend to specialize in high-end fashion. Indigo, one of the city's better bookstores, is also here. ✉ *1500 rue McGill College, at rue Ste-Catherine Ouest, Downtown* ☎ *514/843–8000.*

Place Ville-Marie. With its 42-story cruciform towers, Place Ville-Marie is where weatherproof indoor shopping came to Montréal in 1962. It was also the start of the underground shopping network that Montréal now enjoys. Stylish shoppers head to the 100-plus retail outlets for lunchtime sprees. When you're ready for a food break, consider the Mövenpick Marché restaurant, serving everything from salads and sandwiches to stir-frys and sushi; fresh juices, pastries, and wonderful coffees make it a good breakfast choice. ⊠ *Blvd. René-Lévesque and rue University, Downtown* ☎ *514/866–6666.*

Les Promenades de la Cathédrale. There are more than 50 shops at this complex directly beneath Christ Church Cathedral and connected to the McGill Métro station. Les Promenades includes Canada's largest Linen Chest outlet, with hundreds of bedspreads and duvets, plus aisles of china, crystal, linen, and silver. The Anglican Church's Diocesan Book Room sells an unusually good and ecumenical selection of books as well as religious objects. ⊠ *625 rue Ste-Catherine Ouest, Downtown* ☎ *514/286–8068.*

Square Westmount. This mall serves the mountainside suburb of Westmount, home of wealthy Montrealers, including businessmen and former prime ministers. So it's hardly surprising that the city's finest shops are here. With more than 50 boutiques as well as the exclusive Spa de Westmount, the prospects for self-indulgence are endless. To get here, take the Métro to the Atwater station and follow the tunnel. ⊠ *Rue Ste-Catherine Ouest and av. Greene, Westmount* ☎ *514/932–0211.*

Specialty Shops

Antiques

L'Antiquaire Joyal. Art deco furnishings and decorations have top billing at this modest little shop in the gay part of town. ⊠ *1751 rue Amherst, Village* ☎ *514/524–0057.*

Antiquité Landry. You'll find French and English furniture in pine, mahogany, walnut, and maple here. There's usually also a good selection of silver flatware and other accessories. ⊠ *1726 rue Notre-Dame Ouest, Village* ☎ *514/937–7040.*

Antiquités Curiosités. This shop carries well-priced Victorian-era tables and tallboys, as well as lamps and fixtures. The offerings are crammed into three rooms spread over two floors. ⊠ *1769 rue Amherst, Village* ☎ *514/525–8772.*

Antiquités Phyllis Friedman. In business since 1983, Phyllis Friedman specializes in 17th- to 19th-century English and European antiques. Offerings include English hunt tables, Empire nightstands, Anglo-Irish glass, ceramics, and crystal. ⊠ *1476 rue Sherbrooke Ouest, Square Mile* ☎ *514/935–1991* ⊕ *www.www.phyllisfriedman.com.*

Antiquités Pour La Table. As the name suggests, this store specializes in making your table look good, with an extensive selection of antique porcelain, crystal, and linens—all impeccably preserved and beautifully displayed. Don't bother coming here to replace missing or brozen pieces, though, since what's here are mostly complete sets. It also has a small selection of 18th- and 19th-century tables and chairs. ⊠ *902 rue Lenoir, Mile End* ☎ *514/989–8945.*

Cité Déco. Nostalgic for the 1950s? This is just the place to pick up a chrome-and-Arborite dining-room set and an RCA tube radio. It also has art deco furnishings and accessories from the 1930s and '40s. ⊠ *1761 rue Amherst, Village* ☎ *514/528–0659.*

Coach House. This cluttered little shop in the posh suburb of Westmount is packed with antique silverware, jewelry, glassware, crystal, and lamps. ⊠ *1325 av. Greene, Westmount* ☎ *514/937–6191.*

Galerie Tansu. The highlights here are 18th- and 19th-century porcelain and ceramic objects, furnishings from Japan and China, and Tibetan chests and carpets. ⊠ *1130 boul de Maisonneuve Ouest, Downtown* ☎ *514/ 846–1039.*

Héritage Antique Métropolitain. You can't turn your head without spotting another beautiful object among the clocks, lamps, and elegant English and French furniture sold here. ⊠ *1646 rue Notre-Dame Ouest, Mile End* ☎ *514/931–5517.*

Lapidarius. You'll find mostly watches, jewelry, and silverware at this Westmount shop. ⊠ *1312 av. Greene, Westmount* ☎ *514/935–2717 or 800/267–0373.*

Milord Antiques. Milord's two locations focus on 18th- and 19th-century art and European furniture. They also have a fine collection of porcelain and crystal. ⊠ *1870 rue Notre-Dame Ouest, Downtown* ☎ *514/ 933–2433* ⊠ *1434 rue Sherbrooke Ouest, Downtown* ☎ *514/286–2433.*

Rowntree. European country-style furniture and accessories fill this shop. ⊠ *780 av. Atwater, Downtown* ☎ *514/933–5030.*

Ruth Stalker. Ruth Stalker made her reputation finding and salvaging fine pieces of early-Canadian pine furniture, but she has also developed a good instinct for such folk art as exquisitely carved hunting decoys, weather vanes, and pottery. ⊠ *4447 rue Ste-Catherine Ouest, Westmount* ☎ *514/931–0822.*

Le Village Antiquaires. Several dealers share this space, including specialists in furniture, jewelry, books, and vintage clothing. Galerie du Louvre merits a special visit for its beautiful antique stained glass. ⊠ *1708 rue Notre-Dame Ouest, Mile End* ☎ *514/931–5121.*

Viva Gallery. Asian antique furniture and art take center stage at Viva, with a wide selection of carved tables, benches, and armoires. ⊠ *1970 rue Notre-Dame Ouest, Mile End* ☎ *514/932–3200.*

Art

Montréal brims with art galleries that present work by local luminaries as well as international artists. The downtown area has a wide choice; Vieux-Montréal is also rich in galleries, most of which specialize in Québecois and First Nations work.

Edifice Belago. In a nondescript building, Edifice Belago is in essence a mall of roughly 20 art galleries showing established and upcoming artists. Galerie René Blouin is one of the best galleries for contemporary art. Galerie Trois Points showcases the work of national and international contemporary artists. Both galleries are on the 5th floor. ⊠ *372 rue Ste-Catherine Ouest, Downtown* ☎ *514/393–9969 for Galerie René Blouin, 514/866–8008 for Galerie Trois Points.*

Galerie Art & Culture. Canadian landscapes from the 19th and 20th centuries are the specialty here. ⊠ *227 rue St-Paul Ouest, Vieux-Montréal* ☎ *514/843–5980.*

Galerie de Bellefeuille. This Westmount gallery has a knack for discovering important new talents. It represents many of Canada's top contemporary artists as well as some international ones. Its 5,000 square feet hold a good selection of sculptures, paintings and limited-edition prints. ⊠ *1367 av. Greene, Westmount* ☎ *514/933–4406.*

Galerie de Chariot. This gallery claims to have the largest collection of Inuit soapstone and ivory carvings in Canada. It also has a wide selection of drawings and beadwork, all of which is government authenticated. ⊠ *446 Place Jacques-Cartier, Vieux-Montréal* ☎ *514/875–6134.*

Galerie des Arts Relais des Époques. For modern and abstract works by contemporary Montréal painters, head to this gallery space. ⊠ *234 rue St-Paul Ouest, Vieux-Montréal* ☎ *514/844–2133.*

Galerie Elena Lee Verre. This is the city's leading dealer in glassworks. It exhibits both Canadian and international artists, some working strictly in glass, others incorporating metal, wood, and found materials. ⊠ *1460 rue Sherbrooke Ouest, Square Mile* ☎ *514/844–6009* ⊕ *www.galerieelenalee.com.*

Galerie Walter Klinkhoff. Brothers Alan and Eric Klinkhoff specialize in Canadian historical and contemporary art, but they also carry Victorian, Dutch, and French post-Impressionist works. ⊠ *1200 rue Sherbrooke Ouest, Square Mile* ☎ *514/288–7306.*

La Guilde Graphique. The Graphic Guild has an exceptional selection of original prints, engravings, and etchings. ⊠ *9 rue St-Paul Ouest, Vieux-Montréal* ☎ *514/844–3438.*

Books & Stationery

Bibliomania. It's possible to find some out-of-print gems among Bibliomania's extensive shelves of secondhand books. The store also sells engravings, postcards, and other printed collectibles. ⊠ *460 rue Ste-Catherine Ouest, Rm. 406, Downtown* ☎ *514/933–8156.*

Double Hook. This bookshop has been selling Canadian books—from fiction and poetry to children's literature, cookbooks, and business tomes—since 1974. ⊠ *1235A av. Greene, Westmount* ☎ *514/932–5093.*

L'Essence du Papier. With its selection of imported and handmade papers, the Essence of Paper is a reminder that letter-writing can be an art form. Here are pens suited to most tastes and budgets, as well as waxes and stamps with which to seal any romantic prose that you might be inspired to produce. There's also a wide selection of place cards, invitations, and journals. ⊠ *4160 rue St-Denis, Plateau Mont-Royal* ☎ *514/288–9691.*

Indigo. Indigo is mainly about books and magazines, but the chain has branched out into DVDs, cards, gifts, and housewares. This location also has a large children's section. ⊠ *1500 av. McGill College, Downtown* ☎ *514/281–5549.*

Paragraphe. Stubbornly independent until 2003 when it was bought out by Archambault, a Montréal chain of music stores, Paragraphe carries the usual selection of best sellers and thrillers, but also stocks Canadian works and histories. ⊠ *2220 av. McGill College, Square Mile* ☎ *514/ 845–5811.*

Renaud-Bray. With 23 branches in Québec and nearly half in Montréal, Renaud-Bray is the largest French-language book chain in Canada. Its shops stock translated best-sellers and thrillers as well as original works from Europe and Canada. The shops also carry a wide selection of magazines and stationery. ⊠ *1432 rue Ste-Catherine, Downtown* ☎ *514/876– 9119* ⊠ *3660 rue St-Denis, Plateau Mont-Royal* ☎ *514/288–0952.*

S. W. Welch. The old books here include books on religion and philosophy as well as mysteries and science fiction. ⊠ *3878 blvd. St-Laurent, Plateau Mont-Royal* ☎ *514/848–9358.*

The Word. Deep in the McGill University neighborhood, the Word is a timeless shop with sagging shelves that specializes in used books on art, philosophy, and literature. The owner here tallies his bills by hand. ⊠ *469 rue Milton, Downtown* ☎ *514/845–5640.*

Clothing

Aime Com Moi. Québecois designers create the exclusive women's clothing sold here. ⊠ *150 av. Mont-Royal Est, Plateau Mont-Royal* ☎ *514/ 982–0088.*

BCBG MAX AZRIA. Everything here fits right into Montréal's avant-garde attitude. Max Azria's super-stylish clothing, shoes, and handbags all make a statement. ⊠ *960 rue Ste-Catherine Ouest, Downtown* ☎ *514/398–9130.*

Chas. Johnson & Sons. The three expert kilt makers on hand here can cut any tartan to any size. The shop also rents Highland formal gear for all occasions and sells sporrans, *skean-dhus* (those knives worn at the top of the stocking in traditional Scottish dress), doublets, and day jackets, as well as a full line of classic British menswear. ⊠ *1184 Phillips Pl., Downtown* ☎ *514/878–1931.*

Club Monaco. The specialty here is urban attire—some of which might do in the office—for men and women. ⊠ *Les Cours Mont-Royal, 1455 rue Peel, Downtown* ☎ *514/499–0959.*

Diffusion Griff 3000. This is Anne de Shalla's showcase for leading Québecois fashion designers. ⊠ *350 rue St-Paul Est, Vieux-Montréal* ☎ *514/398–0761.*

Harricana. Yesterday's old fur coats and stoles are transformed into everything from car coats and ski jackets to baby wraps and cushion covers by the artisans of this Québec City–based company named for one of the province's great northern rivers. The fashions are available at dozens of shops, but the best place to see what's available is this combination *atelier* and boutique. ⊠ *3000 rue St-Antoine Ouest, Downtown* ☎ *877/894–9919* ⊕ *www.harricana.qc.ca.*

Jean Airoldi. The shop that bears the name of one of Québec's most talented clothing designers specializes in classic yet chic women's fashions. Made-to-measure is available. ⊠ *4455 rue St-Denis, Plateau Mont-Royal* ☎ *514/287–6524.*

Kanuk. The line of coats and sleeping bags designed by Kanuk could keep an arctic explorer warm. But the shop also sells elegant winter clothes that are meant to be layered. The company's owl trademark has become something of a status symbol among the shivering urban masses. Many retailers carry Kanuk coats, but you can also buy them at the display room over the factory here, along with sleeping bags, backpacks, and snow pants. ⊠ *485 rue Rachel Est, Plateau Mont-Royal* ☎ *514/527–4494.*

Mains Folles. You'll find tropical dresses, skirts, and blouses imported from Bali at this store. ⊠ *4427 rue St-Denis, Plateau Mont-Royal* ☎ *514/284–6854.*

Revenge. Nearly 40 Canadian and Québecois designers create Revenge's well-crafted original fashions for women. ⊠ *3852 rue St-Denis, Plateau Mont-Royal* ☎ *514/843–4379.*

Roots. Its quality materials and approachable, sometimes retro look have made Roots a fashion favorite. ⊠ *1035 rue Ste-Catherine Ouest, Downtown* ☎ *514/845–7995.*

Scandale. The cutting-edge fashions sold here are all originals created on-site by Québecois designer Georges Lévesque. In keeping with the name, the window displays are always lurid. ⊠ *3639 blvd. St-Laurent, Plateau Mont-Royal* ☎ *514/842–4707.*

Tilley Endurables. The famous, Canadian-designed Tilley hat is sold here, along with other easy-care travel wear. ⊠ *1050 av. Laurier Ouest, Outremont* ☎ *514/272–7791.*

Winners. This discount designer clothing store has turned shopping into a sport. And now that it carries housewares, leaving empty-handed is even more difficult. Suitably enough, its downtown outlet is on the lowest level of Place Montréal Trust. ⊠ *1500 av. McGill College, Downtown* ☎ *514/788–4949.*

CHILDREN'S **Oink Oink.** This piggy store carries fashions as well as toys and books for infants and children. It also stocks clothes for teenagers. It's fun to hear the staff answer the phone. ⊠ *1343 av. Greene, Westmount* ☎ *514/939–2634.*

FURS Montréal is one of the fur capitals of the world. Close to 90% of Canada's fur manufacturers are based in the city, as are many of their retail outlets. Many of the stores are clustered along rue Mayor and boulevard de Maisonneuve between rues de Bleury and Aylmer.

Alexandor. Nine blocks west of the main fur-trade area, Alexandor caters to downtown shoppers. ⊠ *2055 rue Peel, Downtown* ☎ *514/288–1119.*

Holt Renfrew. The fur showroom here is perhaps the most exclusive in the city, with prices to match. ⊠ *1300 rue Sherbrooke Ouest, Downtown* ☎ *514/842–5111.*

Marcel Jodoin Fourrures. This store carries a wide selection of nearly new (less than five years old) fur coats, jackets, and stoles, most of which go for less than the cost of an imitation. ⊠ *1228 rue St-Denis, Downtown* ☎ *514/288–1683.*

McComber Grosvenor. Two of Montréal's biggest fur merchants have merged to create this showroom filled with beautiful mink coats and jackets. ⊠ *402 blvd. de Maisonneuve Ouest, Downtown* ☎ *514/288–1255.*

LINGERIE **Collange.** Lacy goods of the designer variety are sold here. ⊠ *1 Westmount Sq., Westmount* ☎ *514/933–4634.*

Deuxième Peau. As its name suggests, Second Skin sells lingerie so fine you don't notice you're wearing it. While you're feeling brave and beautiful, kill two birds with one stone and try on a bathing suit. ⊠ *4457* *rue St-Denis, Plateau Mont-Royal* ☎ *514/842–0811.*

Lyla. Lyla carries seductively lacy lingerie. ✉ *400 av. Laurier Ouest, Outremont* ☎ *514/271–0763.*

VINTAGE **Boutique Encore.** In business for about 50 years, Boutique Encore has retained its popularity by maintaining a good selection of designer labels. Although best known for its nearly new women's fashions, it also includes the big names for men. ✉ *2165 rue Crescent, Downtown* ☎ *514/849–0092.*

Eva B. If your fantasy is being a flapper, or if you miss the 1960s, turn back the clock and perk up your wardrobe with an item from the vast collection sold here. ✉ *2013 blvd. St-Laurent, Downtown* ☎ *514/ 849–8246.*

Cigars

Casa del Habano. This cigar shop stocks the finest cigars Cuba produces. Note that U.S. law forbids Americans from bringing most Cuban products, including cigars, back into the country. ✉ *1434 rue Sherbrooke Ouest, Downtown* ☎ *514/849–0037.*

Davidoff. You'll find the best names in cigars here as well as a fine collection of smoking accessories and humidors. ✉ *1458 Sherbrooke Ouest, Downtown* ☎ *514/289–9118.*

H. Poupart. For more than 100 years, H. Poupart has been supplying Montrealers with the best cigars, cigarettes, chewing and pipe tobaccos, and snuff. The shop also stocks Waterman pens and Riedel glassware. ✉ *1474 rue Peel, Downtown* ☎ *514/842–5794.*

Fabrics

Créations Nicole Moisan. Miles and miles of lace are sold here, with thousands of patterns to choose from, all from Europe. Custom orders are available. ✉ *4324 rue St-Denis, Plateau Mont-Royal* ☎ *514/284–9506.*

Food

Charcuterie/Boucherie Hongroise. This family-owned and -operated store smokes and cures bacon and hams, and sells a wide selection of German, Polish, and Hungarian sausages. ✉ *3843 blvd. St-Laurent, Plateau Mont-Royal* ☎ *514/844–6734.*

Marché Atwater. The Atwater Market is one of the city's oldest public markets. It's a favorite with downtowners looking for fresh produce, specialty meat and sausages, fresh fish, and Québec cheese. The main produce market is outdoors under shelters. The restaurants and shops are inside a two-story complex that's well-suited to rainy-day browsing. The market's just off the Lachine Canal, so it's the ideal place for cyclists on the canal bicycle path to stop for lunch or to buy the makings of a picnic. ✉ *138 av. Atwater, Downtown* ☎ *514/937–7754* Ⓜ *Lionel-Groulx.*

Marché de Westmount. The shops at this indoor market sell pastries, cheeses, pâtés, fruits, cakes, and chocolates. You can assemble a picnic and eat it at one of the little tables scattered among the stalls. ✉ *1 Westmount Sq., Westmount* ☎ *No phone.*

Marché Jean-Talon. This is the biggest, best, and liveliest of the city's public markets. On weekends in summer and fall, crowds swarm the half-acre or so of outdoor produce stalls, looking for the fattest tomatoes, sweetest melons, and juiciest strawberries. Restaurants and shops on the periphery sell meat, fish, cheese, sausage, bread, pastries, and other delicacies. In spring, Jean-Talon is overrun with gardeners rushing to get the best plants and seeds. The market is in the north end of the city, but is easy to get to by Métro. ⊠ *7015 rue Casgrain, Little Italy* ☎ *514/ 277–1588* Ⓜ *Jean-Talon.*

Milano. One of the largest cheese selections in the city as well as fresh pasta of all kinds are the highlights of this market. An entire wall is devoted to olive oils and vinegars; there's also a butcher and a big produce section. ⊠ *6862 blvd. St-Laurent, Little Italy* ☎ *514/273–8558.*

Nino. On weekends this place gets hectic, as shoppers pack the narrow aisles scanning the shelves for spices, pickles, hams, and kitchen gadgets of all sorts. ⊠ *3667 blvd. St-Laurent, Plateau Mont-Royal* ☎ *514/ 844–7630.*

Gifts

Desmarais et Robitaille. The local clergy come here to buy vestments, chalices, altar candles, and other liturgical items, but Desmarais et Robitaille also stocks Québecois wood carvings, handicrafts, and religious articles for the laity. ⊠ *60 rue Notre-Dame Ouest, Vieux-Montréal* ☎ *514/845–3194.*

L'Empreinte Coopérative. Fine Québec handicrafts are sold here. ⊠ *272 rue St-Paul Est, Vieux-Montréal* ☎ *514/861–4427.*

Bella Pella. The soaps, shampoos, and body lotions are all handmade by area artisans, using organic ingredients such as olive oil, goats' milk, and cranberries. ⊠ *3933 rue St-Denis, Plateau Mont-Royal* ☎ *514/845–7328.*

Home Furnishings

Caban. A sister store of clothing retailer Club Monaco, Caban carries mainly laid-back yet stylish furnishings and home accessories, including crystal goblets, scented candles, leather sofas, and teak tables. It also carries bathwares, soaps, and linens. ⊠ *777 rue Ste-Catherine Ouest, Downtown* ☎ *514/844–9300.*

L'Institut de Design de Montréal. The Montreal Institute of Design has an amusingly innovative collection of kitchen brushes, buckets, CD-storage racks, clocks, bathroom equipment, and so forth. ⊠ *390 rue St-Paul Est, Vieux-Montréal* ☎ *514/866–2436.*

Jeunes d'Ici. Furniture and decorating accessories for children of all ages are sold here. ⊠ *134 av. Laurier Ouest, Outremont* ☎ *514/270–5512.*

Ma Provence. Thanks to the barrels of bulk lavender and the racks of bright yellow, blue, and purple fabrics, Ma Provence is a bright oasis on cold, wet days. Pottery condiment dispensers, olive oil, place mats, tablecloths, and oven mitts are among the offerings. ⊠ *3813A rue St-Denis, Plateau Mont-Royal* ☎ *514/840–9150.*

Ungava Factory Outlet. Canadian down comforters are sold at wholesale prices here. Custom orders are accepted. ⊠ *10 av. des Pins Ouest, Suite 112, Plateau Mont-Royal* ☎ *514/287–9276.*

Housewares

Ares Kitchen and Baking Supplies. You can probably find just about any kitchen gadget, as well as top-of-the-line equipment that would make a professional chef's flame burn brighter. It's a 30-minute drive from downtown. ✉ *2355 Trans-Canada Hwy., Pointe Claire* ☎ 514/695–5225.

Danesco. A manufacturer and importer of kitchen equipment and tableware, Danesco operates an outlet out of its head office, 45 minutes outside of downtown, with great deals on everything from pots and pans to cutlery and linen napkins. ✉ *18111 Trans-Canada Hwy., Kirkland* ☎ *514/694–0950.*

Faema. Coffee lovers come here for espresso machines and other paraphernalia, as well as the beans to make their favorite brew. Ice-cream machines are also available. ✉ *14 rue Jean-Talon Ouest, Little Italy* ☎ *514/276–2671.*

The Linen Chest. Inside is one of the largest selections of competitively priced china, crystal, and cutlery in the city—affectionately known as "The Great Wall of China." Down comforters and bedding are also a specialty. ✉ *625 rue Ste-Catherine Ouest, Downtown* ☎ 514/282–9525.

Zone. The collection of kitchen, table, and decorative items and gadgets here is eclectic, and prices are reasonable. ✉ *4246 rue St-Denis, Plateau Mont-Royal* ☎ *514/845–3530.*

Jewelry

Birks. Since 1879 Birks has been helping shoppers mark special occasions, whether engagements, weddings, or retirements. ✉ *1240 Phillips Sq., Downtown* ☎ *514/397–2511.*

Hemsleys Jewellers. In operation since 1870, Hemsleys is Canada's oldest jeweler. The family-run business takes pride in friendly service and reasonable prices. The selection and prices range wide, from small tokens to original creations. Private shopping is available. ✉ *660 rue Ste-Catherine Ouest, Downtown* ☎ *514/866–3706.*

Kaufmann de Suisse. Expert craftspeople create the fine jewelry sold here. ✉ *2195 rue Crescent, Downtown* ☎ *514/848–0595.*

Music

The Archambault chain has several Montréal outposts, including one at 500 rue Ste-Catherine Est.

Cheap Thrills. In addition to good new and secondhand CDs, Cheap Thrills has a large selection of secondhand books at bargain prices. ✉ *2044 Metcalfe, Downtown* ☎ *514/844–8988.*

HMV. This chain carries mainstream music and a limited number of imports. ✉ *1020 rue Ste-Catherine Ouest, Downtown* ☎ *514/875–0765.*

Steve's Music Store. A shabby warren of five storefronts, Steve's is jammed with just about everything you need to be a rock star, from instruments to sheet music. ✉ *51 rue St-Antoine Ouest, Downtown* ☎ *514/878–2216.*

Shoes

Browns. This local institution stocks fashion footwear, handbags, and accessories for men and women. As well as the store's own label, it stocks such well-known brands as Manolo Blahnik, Prada, Chanel, DKNY, Costume National, Dolce Gabana, Christian Dior, and Tods. ✉ *1191 rue Ste-Catherine Ouest, Downtown* ☎ *514/861–9346.*

Pegabo Shoes. This is a true Montréal success story. Aldo Bensadoun opened his first Pegabo store in 1972. His shoe empire now includes more than 600 stores across Canada, operating under the names Pegabo (there are several branches around Montréal), Simard et Voyer, Aldo, Globo, StoneRidge, and Transit. Pegabo, more high-end than the others, sells shoes for both men and women. ⊠ *770 rue Ste-Catherine Ouest, Downtown* ☎ *514/861–4324.*

Tony's Shoe Shop. Dedicated to the finely shod foot, Tony's places stylish imports beside elegantly sensible domestic footwear for men and women. ⊠ *1346 av. Greene, Westmount* ☎ *514/935–2993.*

Sporting Goods & Clothing

Boutique Classique Angler. Anglers can find everything they need for fly-fishing, from rods and reels to feathers for tying flies. Owner Peter Ferago gives great advice on where to fish. ⊠ *414 rue McGill, Downtown* ☎ *514/878–3474.*

Canadiens Boutique Centre Bell. Hockey sticks, posters, pucks, authentic jerseys, and other memorabilia—all bearing the emblem of the world's most storied hockey team—are for sale here. ⊠ *1250 rue de la Gauchetière, Downtown* ☎ *514/989–2836.*

Toys & Games

Cerf Volanterie. Claude Thibaudeau makes the sturdy, gloriously colored kites sold here. He signs the kites and guarantees them for three years. Visits are by appointment only. ⊠ *2019 Moreau, Hochelaga-Maisonneuve* ☎ *514/845–7613.*

Jouets Choo-Choo. This shop 20 minutes from downtown sells quality European toys and educational games. ⊠ *940 blvd. Ste-Jean, Pointe Claire* ☎ *514/697–7550.*

MONTRÉAL A TO Z

Updated by
Tracey Arial

To research prices, get advice from other travelers, and book travel arrangements, visit www.fodors.com.

AIRPORTS

Montréal–Trudeau International Airport (also known as Dorval), 22½ km (14 mi) west of the city, handles all passenger flights.

🚹 Airport Information **Aéroports de Montréal** ⊠ 1100 René-Lévesque Blvd. West, Suite 2100, Montréal ☎ 514/394-7200 ⊕ www.admtl.com. **Montréal–Pierre Elliott Trudeau International Airport** ⊠ 975 Romèo-Vachon blvd. N, Dorval ☎ 514/394-7377.

TRANSFERS A taxi from Trudeau International to downtown costs about C$31. All taxi companies must charge the same rate for travel between the airport and downtown.

L'Aerobus shuttles are a much cheaper alternative into town from the airport, with frequent service between Trudeau and the terminal next to the Gare Centrale, at 777 rue de la Gauchetière, downtown hotels (including Le Centre Sheraton, the Marriott, and Le Reine Elizabeth), and the central bus terminal. The shuttle to Trudeau runs about every half hour and costs C$12 (C$21.75 round-trip).

🚹 **L'Aerobus** ☎ 514/931-9002.

BUS TRAVEL TO & FROM MONTRÉAL

Greyhound Lines and its subsidiaries provide service to Montréal from various U.S. cities and to Toronto and other points west in Canada. Orléans Express provides service between Montreal and Sherbrooke, where SMT & Acadian Lines offer service to eastern Canada. All buses arrive at and depart from the city's downtown bus terminal, the Station Central d'Autobus Montréal, which connects with the Berri-UQAM Métro station. The staff at the station have schedule and fare information for all bus service from Montréal, including the independent companies that provide service to all Québec and some Ontario destinations.

🚌 Bus Information **Central Bus Station** ✉ 505 blvd. Maisonneuve Est ☎ 514/842-2281. **Greyhound Lines** ☎ 800/231-2222, 800/661-8747 in Canada ⊕ www.greyhound.ca. **Limocar** ☎ 450/681-3111, 866/700-8899 ⊕ www.limocar.ca. **Orléans Express** ☎ 514/395-4000 ⊕ www.orleansexpress.com. **Voyageur** ☎ 514/842-2281 ⊕ www.voyageur.com.

BUS TRAVEL WITHIN MONTRÉAL

Société de Transport de Montréal (STM) administers municipal buses as well as the Métro: the same tickets and transfers (free) are valid on either service. See Subway Travel for information on fares and transfers.

🚌 Bus Information **Société de Transport de Montréal (STM)** ☎ 514/288-6287 ⊕ www.stcum.qc.ca.

CAR RENTAL

🚗 Agencies **Avis** ☎ 800/879-2847 ✉ Trudeau International Airport ☎ 514/636-1902 ✉ 1225 rue Metcalfe, Downtown ☎ 514/866-2847 ✉ Voyageur Bus Terminal, de Maissonneuve between rues Berri and St. Hubert, Quartier Latin ☎ 514/288-2847. **Budget** ☎ 800/268-8900 ✉ Trudeau International Airport ☎ 514/636-0052 ✉ 150 rue Ste-Catherine Ouest ☎ 514/842-9931. **Discount** ☎ 514/286-1554 or 800/263-2355. **Enterprise** ☎ 800/562-2886 ✉ Trudeau International Airport ☎ 514/633-1433 ✉ 1005 rue Guy, Downtown ☎ 514/931-3722. **Hertz** ☎ 800/263-0600 ✉ Trudeau International Airport ☎ 514/636-9530 ✉ 1475 rue Aylmer, Downtown ☎ 514/842-8537. **National Car Rental** ☎ 514/636-9030 or 800/227-7368. **National Tilden** ☎ 514/878-2771 or 800/387-4747. **Thrifty** ✉ Trudeau International Airport ☎ 514/631-5567 ✉ 855 rue Ste-Catharine Est, Downtown ☎ 514/845-5954. **Via Route** ✉ 1255 rue Mackay, Plateau Mont-Royal ☎ 514/871-1166.

CAR TRAVEL

Montréal is accessible from the rest of Canada via the Trans-Canada Highway, which crosses the southern part of the island as Route 20, with Route 720 leading into downtown. Route 40 parallels Route 20 to the north; exits to downtown include St. Laurent and St. Denis. From New York, take I–87 north until it becomes Route 15 at the Canadian border; continue for another 47 km (29 mi) to the outskirts of Montréal. You can also follow U.S. I–89 north until it becomes two-lane Route 133, which eventually joins Route 10, an east-west highway that leads west across the Champlain Bridge and right into the downtown core. From I–91 through Massachusetts via New Hampshire and Vermont, you can take Route 55 to Route 10. Again, turn west to reach Montréal. At the border you must clear Canadian Customs, so be prepared with proof of citizenship (with photo I.D.) and your vehicle's ownership papers. On holidays and during the peak summer season, expect to wait a half hour or more at the major crossings.

In winter, remember that your car may not start on extra-cold mornings unless it has been kept in a heated garage.

Emergency Road Service ☎ 514/861-1313, 800/222-4357, *222 from mobile phone. **Touring Club de Montréal: AAA, CAA, RAC** ☎ 514/861-7111.

PARKING   The City of Montréal has a diligent tow-away and fine system for cars double-parked or stopped in no-stopping zones downtown during rush hours and business hours. A parking ticket costs between C$30 and C$100. If your car is towed after being illegally parked, it will cost an additional C$62 to C$88 to retrieve it. Be especially alert in winter: Montréal's street plowers are ruthless in dealing with parked cars in their way. If they don't tow them, they'll bury them. When parking in residential neighborhoods, beware of the alternate-side-of-the-street-parking rules.

RULES OF THE   In Québec the road signs are in French, but the important ones have
ROAD   pictograms. The no-stopping sign, for instance, is a red circle on a white background with a black octagon in the middle and a red line through it. Others are less clear, particularly those that emphasize positive action rather than prohibitions. Many of the signs for illegal turns, for example, use black arrows surrounded by a green circle to highlight permitted turns. Others, particularly parking signs, display a green circled *p* with either *2 hrs* to indicate that you can park for a maximum of two hours, or a list of time periods—using a 24-hour clock—to indicate permitted parking times. It's not unusual to have two or three road signs all together to indicate several different strictures. Keep in mind the following terms: *centreville* (downtown), *arrêt* (stop), *détenteurs de permis* (permit holders only), *gauche* (left), *droit* (right), *ouest* (west), and *est* (east).

The speed limit is posted in kilometers; on highways the limit is 100 kph (about 62 mph), and the use of radar-detection devices is prohibited. There are heavy penalties for driving while intoxicated, and drivers and front-seat passengers must wear over-the-shoulder seat belts. New York, Maine, and Ontario residents should take note: your traffic violations in the province of Québec are entered on driving records back home (and vice versa).

If you drive in the city, remember three things: Montréal law forbids you to turn right on a red light (though Québec allows the practice in the rest of the province), Montrealers are notorious jaywalkers, and the city has some potholes the size of craters.

DISCOUNTS & DEALS

The Montréal Museums Pass combines access to 30 museums over two consecutive days with a three-day public transit pass, all for C$39. The passes are available at museums or Centre Info-Touriste, at 1001 Square Dorchester.

Also available are various combination passes for the Jardin Botanique, Insectarium, Biodôme, and Tour Olympique. The C$27 "Get an Eyeful" Package, for instance, can be bought at any one of the attractions. It's good for one visit to each site over any 30-day period.

EMERGENCIES
The U.S. Consulate has a list of medical specialists in the Montréal area. There's a dental clinic on avenue Van Horne that's open 24 hours; Sunday appointments are for emergencies only.

Many pharmacies stay open until midnight, including Jean Coutu and Pharmaprix stores. Some are open around the clock, including the Pharmaprix on chemin de la Côte-des-Neiges.

🔢 **Dentists Dental clinic** ⊠ 3546 av. Van Horne, Côte-des-Neiges 🕾 514/342-4444. 🔢 **Emergency Services Ambulance, fire, police** 🕾 911. **Québec Poison Control Centre** 🕾 800/463-5060. **U.S. Consulate** 🕾 514/398-9695, 514/981-5059 for emergencies. 🔢 **Hospital Montréal General Hospital** ⊠ 1650 av. Cedar, Downtown 🕾 514/934-1934. 🔢 **Late-Night Pharmacies Jean Coutu** ⊠ 501 rue Mont-Royal Est, Quartier Latin 🕾 514/521-1058 ⊠ 5510 chemin de la Côte-des-Neiges, Côte-des-Neiges 🕾 514/344-8338. **Pharmaprix** ⊠ 1500 rue Ste-Catherine Ouest, Downtown 🕾 514/933-4744 ⊠ 5157 rue Sherbrooke Ouest, Notre-Dame-de-Grace 🕾 514/484-3531 ⊠ 901 rue Ste-Catherine Est, Village 🕾 514/842-4915 ⊠ 5122 chemin de la Côte-des-Neiges, Côte-des-Neiges 🕾 514/738-8464.

GAY & LESBIAN TRAVELERS
Montréal has one of the most visible gay communities in North America. Much of the scene centers on the Village. The French-language newspapers *RG* (🌐 www.rgmag.com) and *Fugues* (🌐 www.fugues.com), which has a limited English-language section, and the feminist/lesbian magazine *Gazelle* include events listings, articles on culture, and news. The gay and lesbian bilingual Web site 🌐 www.gaybek.com is another good resource.

LODGING
The room-reservation service of Hospitality Canada can help you find lodging in one of 80 hotels, motels, and B&Bs in the area. Tourisme Québec also operates a room-booking service.

🔢 **Toll-Free Numbers Hospitality Canada** 🕾 800/665-1528. **Tourisme Québec** 🕾 877/266-5687 🌐 www.bonjourquebec.com.

B&BS Bed and Breakfast à Montréal represents more than 50 homes in downtown and in the elegant neighborhoods of Westmount and Outremont. Downtown B&B Network represents 75 homes and apartments, mostly around the downtown core and along rue Sherbrooke, that have one or more rooms available for rent.

🔢 **Bed and Breakfast à Montréal** 🖉 Marian Kahn, 2033 St. Hubert, H2L 3Z6 🕾 514/738-9410 or 800/738-4338 🌐 www.bbmontreal.com. **Downtown B&B Network** 🖉 Bob Finkelstein, 3458 av. Laval, H2X 3C8 🕾 514/289-9749 or 800/267-5180 🌐 www.bbmontreal.qc.ca.

SIGHTSEEING TOURS
BOAT TOURS From May through October, Amphi Tour sells a unique one-hour tour of Vieux-Montréal and the Vieux-Port on both land and water in an amphibious bus. Bateau-Mouche runs four harbor excursions and an

evening supper cruise daily from May through October. The boats are reminiscent of the ones that cruise the canals of the Netherlands—wide-beamed and low-slung, with a glassed-in passenger deck. Boats leave from the Jacques Cartier Pier at the foot of Place Jacques-Cartier in the Vieux-Port.

Amphi Tour ☎ 514/849-5181 ⊕ www.amphibus.qc.ca. **Bateau-Mouche** ☎ 514/849-9952 or 800/361-9952 ⊕ www.bateau-mouche.com.

BUS TOURS Gray Line has nine different tours of Montréal from June through October and one tour during other months. It has pickup service at the major hotels and at Info-Touriste (1001 Square Dorchester).

Imperial Tours' double-decker buses follow a nine-stop circuit of the city. You can get off and on as often as you like and stay at each stop as long as you like. There's pickup service at major hotels.

Gray Line ☎ 514/934-1222. **Imperial Tours** ☎ 514/871-4733.

CALÈCHE RIDES Open horse-drawn carriages (fleece-lined in winter) leave from Place Jacques-Cartier, Square Dorchester, Place d'Armes, and rue de la Commune. A one- to two-hour ride costs about C$65, although slow days mean you have a better chance of bargaining.

WALKING TOURS You can walk through various historic, cultural or architecturally diverse areas of the city with a costumed guide, courtesy of Guidatour. Popular tours include Old Montréal, the red-light district, and the elite 19th-century neighborhood known as the *Golden Square Mile*.

Guidatour ✉ 477 rue St-François-Xavier Street, Suite 300, Old Montréal ☎ 514/844-4021 or 800/363-4021 ⊕ www.guidatour.qc.ca.

SUBWAY TRAVEL

The Métro, or subway, is clean, quiet (it runs on rubber wheels), and safe, and it's heated in winter and cooled in summer. As in any city, you should be alert and attentive to personal property such as purses and wallets. The Métro is connected to the more than 30 km (19 mi) of the Underground City.

Free maps are available at Métro ticket booths. Try to get the *Carte Réseau* (System Map); it's the most complete. Each Métro station connects with one or more bus routes, which cover the rest of the island, and transfers from Métro to buses are available from the dispenser just beyond the ticket booth inside the station. Bus-to-bus and bus-to-Métro transfers may be obtained from the bus driver.

Each of the 65 Métro stops has been individually designed and decorated. The largest of these is Berri-UQAM, a cross-shape station with many corridors for art. The most memorable pieces include a huge black granite bench; three Expo '67 murals depicting science, culture and recreation; a 25th-anniversary plaque and time capsule; a statue of Montréal heroine Mother Émilie Gamelin, and a vibrant red-and-blue stained-glass mural depicting three founders of Montréal.

The newer stations along the Blue Line are all worth a visit as well, particularly Outremont, with a glass-block design from 1988. Even Place d'Armes, one of the least visually remarkable stations in the system, includes a treasure; look for the small exhibit of archaeological artifacts depicting each of Montréal's four historical eras (Aboriginal, French, English, and multicultural).

Métro hours on the Orange, Green, and Yellow lines are weekdays 5:30 AM to 12:30 AM and weekends 5:30 AM to 12:30, 1, or 1:30 AM (it varies by line). The Blue Line runs daily 5:30 AM–12:15 PM. Trains run as often as every three minutes on the most crowded lines—Orange and Green— at rush hours.

Tickets and transfers are valid on buses and the subway. You should be able to get within a few blocks of anywhere in the city on one fare. Rates are C$2.50 for a single ticket, C$18 for a week-long pass, C$11 for six tickets, and C$59 for a monthly pass. Transfers are free. You can buy a day pass for C$8 or a three-day pass for C$16; they're available at some of the bigger hotels, at Berri-UQAM, and at some other down-town stations.

The Société de Transport de Montréal (STM) operates an automated line for information on bus and Métro schedules, but it's only in French. The STM Web site, however, is in French and English and is a particu-larly good resource, with excellent maps and route planners.
🚊 **Société de Transport de Montréal (STM)** ☎ 514/288-6287 ⊕ www.stcum.qc.ca.

TAXIS
Taxis in Montréal all run on the same rate: C$2.75 minimum and C$1.40 per km (½ mi). Taxis are usually easy to hail on the street, al-though finding one on a rainy night after the Métro has closed can be difficult. You can see if a taxi is available by checking its white or orange plastic rooftop light; if the panel is lit, the driver is ready to take passengers. You can also call a dispatcher to send a driver to pick you up at no extra cost (you'll usually have to wait about 15 minutes).
🚊 Taxi Companies **Atlas Taxi** ☎ 514/485-8585. **Champlain Taxi** ☎ 514/273-2435 or 514/271-1111. **Co-op Taxi** ☎ 514/725-9885. **Unitaxi** ☎ 514/482-3000.

TRAIN TRAVEL
Gare Centrale (Central Station), on rue de la Gauchetière between rues University and Mansfield (behind Le Reine Elizabeth), is the rail terminus for all trains from the United States and from other Canadian provinces. It's connected underground to the Bonaventure Métro station.

The Amtrak *Adirondack* leaves New York's Penn Station every morn-ing for the 10½-hour trip through upstate New York to Montréal. Am-trak also has bus connections with the *Vermonter* in St. Albans, Vermont. VIA Rail connects Montréal with all the major cities of Canada, including Québec City, Halifax, Ottawa, Toronto, Winnipeg, Edmonton, and Vancouver.
🚊 Train Lines **Amtrak** ☎ 800/872-7245 ⊕ www.amtrak.com. **VIA Rail** ☎ 514/989-2626, 888/842-7245 ⊕ www.viarail.ca.

TRANSPORTATION AROUND MONTRÉAL
Public transportation is easily the best and cheapest way to get around. Finding your way around Montréal by car is not difficult, since the streets

are laid out in a fairly straightforward grid and one-way streets are clearly marked. But parking isn't easy, and the narrow cobbled streets of Vieux-Montréal can be a trial. It's much easier to park near a Métro station and walk and use public transit.

TRAVEL AGENCIES

🔝 Agencies **American Express** ⊠ 1141 blvd. de Maisonneuve Ouest, Downtown ☎ 514/284-3300. **Canadian Automobile Club** ⊠ 1180 rue Drummond, Downtown ☎ 514/861-5111. **Vacances Tourbec** ⊠ 300 Sherbrooke Ouest, Downtown ☎ 514/842-1400. **Voyages Campus** ⊠ McGill University, 3480 rue McTavish, Downtown ☎ 514/398-0647.

VISITOR INFORMATION

Centre Info-Touriste, on Square Dorchester, has extensive tourist information on Montréal and the rest of the province of Québec, as well as a currency-exchange service and Internet café. It's open June through early September, daily 8:30–7:30, and early September through May, daily 9–6. The Vieux-Montréal branch is open from 9–7 between June and September and is often open daily from 9–5 during the winter, although it's sometimes closed during slow periods.

The Hochelaga-Maisonneuve tourist association can provide information on attractions and events in the colorful district around the Stade Olympique. Tourisme-Montréal has information on city attractions and events.

🔝 Tourist Information **Centre Info-Touriste** ⊠ 1255 rue Peel, Downtown ☎ 514/873-2015, 800/363-7777, or 877/266-5687 ⊠ 174 rue Notre-Dame Est, at pl. Jacques-Cartier, Vieux-Montréal. **Hochelaga-Maisonneuve** ☎ 514/256-4636 ⊕ www.tourismemaisonneuve.qc.ca. **Tourisme-Montréal** ☎ 514/844-5400 ⊕ www.tourism-montreal.org.

QUÉBEC CITY

2

Updated by
Mark Cardwell

NO TRIP TO FRENCH-SPEAKING Canada is complete without a visit to exuberant, romantic Québec City, founded by French explorer Samuel Champlain in 1608 and the oldest municipality in the province of Québec. In the 17th century the first French explorers, fur trappers, and missionaries came here to establish the colony of New France. It still resembles a French provincial town in many ways; its family-oriented residents have strong ties to their past. Roughly 96% of the Québec City region's population of more than 650,000 list French as their mother tongue.

French explorer Jacques Cartier was the first European to reach what the Algonquin people called Kebec, meaning "where the river narrows," in 1535. It was, however, Champlain who founded "New France" some 70 years later, when he decided to take advantage of the site's strategic position and build a fort on the banks of the St. Lawrence on a spot that is today called Place Royale. Fearing the site's vulnerability to attack, Champlain built another fort, the Château St-Louis, on the cliff above, not far from where the world-famous Château Frontenac now stands. Succeeding generations of colony administrators and high society followed Champlain up the steep hill.

During the early days of New France, the French and British fought often for control of the region. When an expedition led by Admiral Sir William Phipps arrived from England in 1690 and demanded the city's surrender, Comte de Frontenac, New France's most illustrious governor, defied him with the statement, "Tell your lord that I will reply with the mouth of my cannons." He did, and the British invasion failed.

The British, however, were persistent in their efforts to dislodge the French from North America. Their best allies may have been the French themselves. Preoccupied with scandals at the courts of Louis XV and Louis XVI, the French gave only grudging help to their possessions in the New World. Undaunted, the colonists of New France built forts and other military structures, such as a wooden palisade (defensive fence) that reinforced their position on top of the cliff. They couldn't do anything, however, about Britain's naval supremacy, which cut off the supply of men and supplies from France. After capturing all French forts east of Québec, including the supposedly impregnable fort of Louisbourg in Cape Breton, General James Wolfe led a British army to Québec City in the summer of 1759.

After a months-long siege that laid waste to much of the city, thousands of British soldiers scaled the heights along a narrow cow path on a moonless night. Surprised and alarmed to see British soldiers massed on a farmer's field so near the city, French General Louis-Joseph Montcalm rushed out to meet the British in what became known as the Battle of the Plains of Abraham. The French were routed in the violent 20-minute conflict, which claimed the lives of both Wolfe and Montcalm. The battle marked the death of New France and the birth of British Canada.

In many ways, British rule was a boon for Québec City. Thanks to more robust trade and large capital investments, the fishing, fur-trading, shipbuilding, and timber industries expanded rapidly. As the city's economic, social, religious, and political sectors developed and diversified, the quality of people's lives also greatly improved.

2

If you have 2 days

With only a couple of days, you should devote one day to Lower Town, which is the earliest site of French civilization in North America, and the second day to Upper Town. On Day 1, stroll the narrow streets of the Quartier Petit-Champlain, visiting the Maison Chevalier and browsing at the many handicraft stores. Moving on to Place Royale, head for the Église Notre-Dame-des-Victoires; in summer there's almost always entertainment in the square. On Day 2, view the St. Lawrence River from Terrasse Dufferin and visit the impressive buildings of Upper Town, where 17th- and 18th-century religious and educational institutions predominate.

If you have 4 days

A four-day trip allows you to wander farther afield, outside the walls of the Old City. On Day 3, watch the pomp and ceremony of the changing of the guard at the Citadelle, and then wander through and then have a picnic on the Plains of Abraham, site of the battle that ended France's colonial dreams in North America and marked the beginning of British rule in Canada. In the afternoon, tour the National Assembly. On Day 4, check out the Musée National des Beaux-Arts du Québec or the Musée de la Civilisation. Then check out the city from a different vantage point—aboard a horse-drawn *calèche* or from a walk atop the ramparts. In summer, do what the locals do—grab a seat on an outdoor *terrasse*, sip a cool drink, and watch the world go by.

If you have 6 days

Six days will give you time to experience some of Québec's scenic countryside. Follow the itinerary above for a four-day trip. On Day 5, you could spend more time exploring Vieux-Québec. Or you could take historic avenue Royale (Route 360) east to Montmorency Falls, which are 30 meters (100 feet) higher than Niagara Falls. From here, continue east along the avenue Royale through the centuries-old villages of the Cote de Beaupré, the breadbasket of colonial New France. Visit the colossal Basilique Ste-Anne-de-Beaupré in Sainte-Anne-de-Beaupré, then head to the Réserve Faunique du cap Tourmente, an internationally recognized wildlife reserve. If you're here during spring or fall, you may be able to get within a few feet of thousands of snow geese, which make the park their home as they travel to and from the Arctic. You may also see dozens of species of birds and other animals (including bears) while walking the park's well-maintained trails. If you're here in winter, consider spending the rest of Day 5 and all of Day 6 on the slopes of nearby Mont-Ste-Anne. You might also want to try Le Massif, Canada's highest ski mountain east of the Rockies, or Stoneham. You may even be up for climbing the ice-covered canyon wall next to the Montmorency Falls. In summer, spend Day 6 on a boat cruise on the St. Lawrence River, or instead go white-water rafting down the Jacques Cartier River.

Wary of new invasions from its former American colonies, the British also expanded the city's fortifications. They replaced the wooden palisades with a massive cut-stone wall and built a star-shape fortress. Both works are still prominent in the city's urban landscape.

The constitution of 1791 established Québec City as the capital of Lower Canada, a position it held until 1840, when the Act of Union united Upper and Lower Canada and made Montréal the capital. When Canada was created in 1867 by the Act of Confederation, which united four colonial provinces (Québec, Ontario, New Brunswick, and Nova Scotia), Québec City was named the province's capital city, a role it continues to play. Many Québecers also call the city, "la capitale Nationale," a reflection of the nationalist sentiments that have marked Québec society and politics for the past 40 years.

Beginning in the mid-19th century, the economic center of Canada shifted west to Montréal and Toronto. Today, government is Québec City's main business: about 27,000 full- or part-time civil-service employees work and live in the area. Office complexes continue to spring up outside the older part of town; modern malls, convention centers, and imposing hotels now cater to a business clientele. Québec City is also in the midst of a successful transformation into a technological hub. The city now has more than 100 research centers and one of the highest concentrations of research and development jobs in Canada.

EXPLORING QUÉBEC CITY

Located 250 km (155 mi) east of Montréal, Québec City was founded on a cliff overlooking a narrow point on the north shore of the St. Lawrence River, one of the most beautiful natural settings in North America.

The heart of the city is Vieux-Québec (Old Québec), which is divided between the Haute-Ville (Upper Town) and the Basse-Ville (Lower Town). Surrounded by walkable stone ramparts that once protected the city, Old Québec is today a small, dense, well-maintained neighborhood steeped in four centuries of French, English, and Canadian history and tradition. The city's finest 17th- and 18th-century buildings are here, as are its best parks and monuments. Because of its immaculate preservation as the only fortified city north of Mexico, Old Québec was designated a UNESCO World Heritage Site in 1985.

Numbers in the text correspond to numbers in the margin and on the Upper & Lower Towns (Haute-Ville, Basse-Ville), Outside the Walls, and Île d'Orléans & Côte de Beaupré maps.

Getting Your Bearings

By far the best way—and in some places, the only way—to explore Québec City is on foot. The best sights, restaurants, and hotels are within or near Old Québec, which takes up only 11 square km. The area is not flat, so walking takes a bit of effort, especially if you decide to walk to the Upper Town from the Lower Town. Helpful city maps are available at visitor-information offices, the best of which is on the public square in front of the Château Frontenac.

The city is made up of eight boroughs that were forcibly merged in 2002. Although the forced merging, and the possibility of de-merging in the near future, have caused some confusion in regards to street-name changes, such changes do not affect areas you're likely to visit.

Walking

Québec City is a wonderful place to explore on foot. Impressive vistas of the Laurentian Mountains and the St. Lawrence River are revealed on a walk along the city walls or a climb to the city's highest point, Cap Diamant, near the Citadelle. It's possible to spend days investigating the narrow cobblestone streets of Vieux-Québec, visiting historic sights, or browsing for local arts and crafts in the stores of Quartier Petit-Champlain. A stroll on the Promenade des Gouverneurs and the Plains of Abraham provides a view of the river as well as the Laurentians to the north and the Appalachians to the south.

Winter in Québec City

Québec City is the only major Canadian city guaranteed to be blanketed in snow in January and February, and in fact you're likely to find snow from mid-December to early April. The city is also at its most beautiful on those cold, clear mornings when the copper rooftops of centuries-old buildings in the Upper Town glisten with frost, and massive chunks of ice bob lazily in the frigid waters of the fast-flowing river below.

Rather than complain about the cold, the city's residents embrace the season by throwing the world's biggest outdoor snow party, the Québec Winter Carnival. The three-week-long bash starts in late January and includes such highlights as night parades and an international snow-sculpture contest. Many Québecois also take part in the many outdoor winter activities that the city and surrounding area have to offer, including ice skating, pick-up hockey, cross-country and downhill skiing, snowmobiling, ice-fishing, hiking, snowshoeing, tobogganing, and even dogsledding.

Québec City is, however, a confusing place for visitors to drive in—and not just those that don't speak French. Like many old cities built along rivers, Québec City has several streets that twist and turn. There are also many multi-point intersections, a vestige of the city's French roots. Fortunately, the street grids in both the Old City and in Upper Town neighborhoods developed after 1759 are laid out in practical British fashion: straight, clearly marked, and, like the St. Lawrence itself, running in a more or less east–west direction. A good system of city buses also runs through the region. Inside the walls of Upper Town, however, only buses carrying tourists are permitted, and only then for the time it takes to unload or pick up passengers. The best plan is to ditch the car and walk.

Upper Town

Like the Citadel, most of the many elegant homes that line the narrow streets in Upper Town are made of granite cut from nearby quarries in the 1800s. The stone walls, copper roofs, and heavy wooden doors on the government buildings and high-steepled churches in the area also reflect the Upper Town's place as the political, educational, and religious

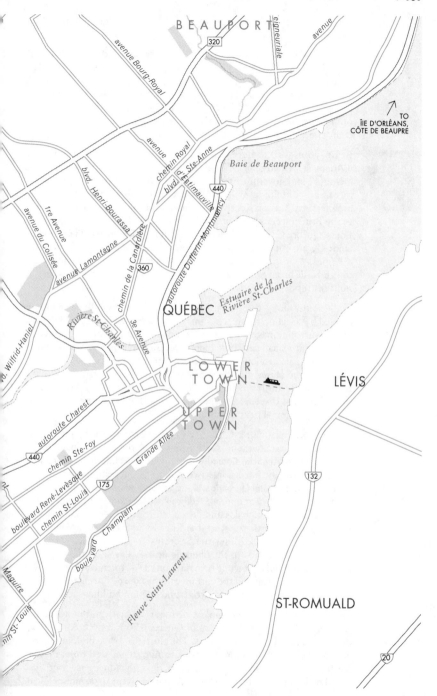

BEAUPORT

320

eigneuriale

avenue

avenue Bourg-Royal

avenue

chemin Royal

blvd. de Ste-Anne

blvd. Henri-Bourassa

blvd. Est mauville

440

Baie de Beauport

TO
ÎLE D'ORLÉANS,
CÔTE DE BEAUPRÉ

1re Avenue

avenue du Colisée

avenue Lamontagne

chemin de la Canardière

360

3e Avenue

autoroute Duffern Mont-Morency

QUÉBEC

*Estuaire de la
Rivière St-Charles*

d. Wilfrid-Haniel

Rivière St-Charles

LOWER
TOWN

LÉVIS

UPPER
TOWN

autoroute Charest

440

chemin Ste-Foy

Grande Allée

boulevard René-Lévèsque

175

chemin St-Louis

boulevard Champlain

Maguire

nin St-Louis

132

Fleuve Saint-Laurent

ST-ROMUALD

20

nerve-center of both the province and the country during much of the past four centuries.

No other place in Canada has so much history squeezed into such a small spot. The Upper Town was a barren, windswept cape when Champlain decided to build a fort here almost 400 years ago. Now, of course, it's a major tourist destination surrounded by cannon-studded stone ramparts. Home to many of the city's most famous sites, Upper Town also offers a dramatic view of the St. Lawrence River and the surrounding countryside.

a good walk

Begin your walk where rue St-Louis meets rue du Fort at **Place d'Armes** ❶ ▶, a large plaza brightened by artists and bordered by cafés, a church, and government buildings. To your right is the colony's former treasury building, **Maison Maillou** ❷, interesting for its 18th-century architecture. Maison Kent, where the terms of the surrender of Québec to the British were signed in 1759, is a little farther along, at 25 rue St-Louis. Québec City's most celebrated landmark, **Fairmont Le Château Frontenac** ❸, an impressive green-turreted hotel, stands south of Place d'Armes. As you head to the boardwalk behind the Frontenac, notice the glorious bronze statue of Samuel de Champlain, standing where he built his residence.

Walk south along the boardwalk called the **Terrasse Dufferin** ❹, enlivened by street performers in summer, for a panoramic view of the city and its surroundings. As you pass to the southern side of the Frontenac, you arrive at a small park called **Jardin des Gouverneurs** ❺. From the north side of the park, follow rue Haldimand, turn left on rue St-Louis, and walk past the **Musée d'Art Inuit Brousseau** ❻. Make a right and follow rue du Parloir until it intersects with tiny rue Donnacona. Here stands the **Couvent des Ursulines** ❼, a private school that houses a museum and has a lovely chapel next door.

Take rue Donnacona past No. 6, a house with a 12-foot-wide facade, said to be the narrowest in North America, to rue des Jardins and visit the **Holy Trinity Anglican Cathedral** ❽, a dignified church with precious objects on display. Next come two buildings interesting for their art-deco details: the **Hôtel Clarendon** ❾, on the corner of rue des Jardins and rue Ste-Anne, and, next door, the **Edifice Price** ❿. Continue along rue Ste-Anne up to rue St-Stanislas and take a left to reach **Morrin College** ⓫, a former prison that now houses the Literary and Historical Society of Québec library. Walk along rue St-Stanislas and turn left onto rue Dauphine, which leads to the **Chapelle des Jésuites** ⓬, at the corner of rues Dauphine and d'Auteuil. Turn right on rue d'Auteuil and head down the hill to rue St-Jean and the entrance to the **Parc de l'Artillerie** ⓭, a historic complex of military, industrial, and civilian buildings.

On your way out of the complex, turn left, away from the walls, and walk east along rue St-Jean, one of Québec City's most colorful thoroughfares; turn left on rue Collins. The cluster of stone buildings at the end of the street is the **Monastère des Augustines de l'Hôtel-Dieu de Québec** ⓮, which can be toured. Turn right (heading east) onto rue Charlevoix, then left on rue Hamel to rue des Remparts. **Maison Mont-**

calm ⑮, the famous general's former home, is to the right, on rue des Remparts between rues Hamel and St-Flavien.

Continue along rue des Remparts and then turn right on rue Ste-Famille. When you reach côte de la Fabrique, look for the iron entrance gates of the **Séminaire du Québec ⑯**. Head west across the courtyard to the **Musée de l'Amérique Française ⑰**; don't miss the seminary's ornate Chapelle Extérieure.

The historic **Basilique Notre-Dame-de-Québec ⑱**, which has an ornate interior, is nearby at the corner of rues Ste-Famille and de Buade. Turn left on rue de Buade, walk down the street and cross to the historical plaque on the wall next to the gift shop at 11 rue Buade. The plaque marks the spot where Champlain's funeral chapel is believed to have stood in 1636. (Where Champlain's body went after that is a mystery that has baffled historians and other sleuths.) Wander back 50 feet along rue Buade and turn left into Québec City's famous outdoor art gallery on **rue du Trésor ⑲**. At the end of the tourist-packed alley, turn left onto rue Ste-Anne and wind up your walk (and rest your feet) with a 30-minute recap of the six sieges of Québec City at the **Musée du Fort ⑳**.

TIMING   Plan on spending at least a day visiting the sights and museums in Upper Town. Lunchtime should find you around Parc de l'Artillerie and rue St-Jean, where the selection of restaurants is good. If you prefer a leisurely pace you could spread this walk out over two days, stopping to watch street performers and enjoying long lunches. May through October are the best months for walking; July and August are the busiest.

What to See

⑱ **Basilique Notre-Dame-de-Québec** (Our Lady of Québec Basilica). This basilica has the oldest parish in North America, dating from 1647. It's been rebuilt three times: in the early 1700s, when François de Montmorency Laval was the first bishop; in 1759, after cannons at Lévis fired on it during the siege of Québec; and in 1922, after a fire. The basilica's somber, ornate interior includes a canopy dais over the episcopal throne, a ceiling of painted clouds decorated with gold leaf, richly colored stained-glass windows, and a chancel lamp that was a gift of Louis XIV. The large and famous crypt was Québec City's first cemetery; more than 900 bodies are interred here, including 20 bishops and four governors of New France. Samuel de Champlain may be buried near the basilica: archaeologists have been searching for his tomb since 1950. ✉ *16 rue de Buade, Upper Town* ☎ *418/692–2533 church, 418/694–4000 show* ⊕ *www.patrimoine-religieux.com* ✉ *Basilica free, crypt C$1, sound-and-light show C$7.50* ◷ *Mid-Oct.–Apr., daily 7:30–4:30; May–mid-Oct., weekdays 7:30–3, weekends 7:30–6. Sound-and-light show May–mid-Oct., weekdays 3:30–8:30, weekends 6:30–8:30.*

⑫ **Chapelle des Jésuites** (Jesuits' Chapel). Built in 1820 from plans by architect François Baillairgé, the chapel, with its sculptures and paintings, is considered one of the monuments of Québec art of the period. Sculptor Pierre-Noël Levasseur created the mid-18th-century wooden statues of the Blessed Virgin and St. Joseph, which predate the chapel; the delicately carved high altar was designed by architect Eugène Taché. ✉ *20*

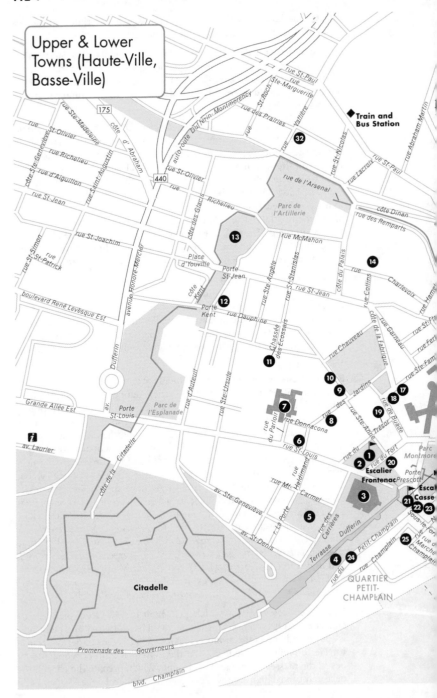

Upper & Lower
Towns (Haute-Ville,
Basse-Ville)

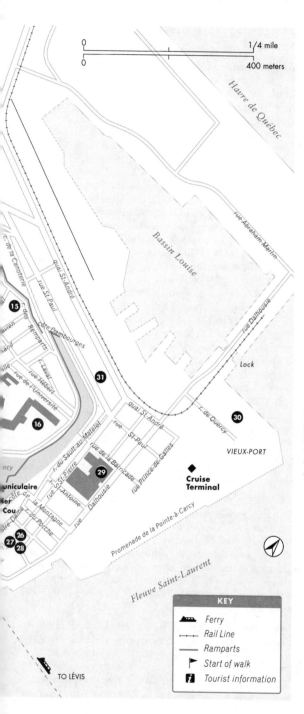

rue Dauphine, Upper Town ☎ *418/694–9616* 🎫 *Free* ☉ *Late June–Sept., weekdays 10–12:30; Oct.–late June, weekdays 11–1:30.*

➐ Couvent des Ursulines (Ursuline Convent). North America's oldest teaching institution for girls, still a private school, was founded in 1639 by French nun Marie de l'Incarnation and laywoman Madame de la Peltrie. The convent has many of its original walls intact, and houses a little chapel and a museum. The **Chapelle des Ursulines** (Ursuline Chapel; ✉ 10 rue Donnacona, Upper Town ☎ No phone) is where French general Louis-Joseph Montcalm was buried after he died in the 1759 battle that decided the fate of New France. In September 2001, Montcalm's remains were transferred to rest with those of his soldiers at the Hôpital Général de Québec's cemetery, at 260 boulevard Langelier. The exterior of the Ursuline Chapel was rebuilt in 1902, but the interior contains the original chapel, which took sculptor Pierre-Noël Levasseur from 1726 to 1736 to complete. The votive lamp was lit in 1717 and has never been extinguished. The chapel is open May through October, Tuesday through Saturday 10–11:30 and 1:30–4:30, Sunday 1:30–4:30. Admission is free. The **Musée des Ursulines** (✉ 12 rue Donnacona, Upper Town ☎ 418/694–0694) was once the residence of one of the convent's founders, Madame de la Peltrie. The museum provides an informative perspective on 120 years of the Ursulines' life under the French regime, from 1639 to 1759. It took an Ursuline nun nine years of training to attain the level of a professional embroiderer; the museum contains magnificent pieces of ornate embroidery, such as altar frontals with gold and silver threads intertwined with semiprecious jewels. Admission is C$5. May through September the museum is open Tuesday through Saturday 10–noon and 1–5, Sunday 1–5; in October, November, and February through April it's open Tuesday through Sunday 1–4:30. In the lobby of the museum is the **Centre Marie-de-l'Incarnation** (✉ 10 rue Donnacona, Upper Town ☎ 418/694–0413), a center with an exhibit and books for sale on the life of the Ursulines' first superior, who came from France and cofounded the convent. The center is open from May through October, Tuesday through Saturday 10–11:30, Sunday 1:30–4:30; February through April it's open Tuesday through Sunday 1:30–4:30. ✉ *18 rue Donnacona, Upper Town.*

➓ Edifice Price. Styled after the Empire State Building, the 15-story, art-deco structure was the city's first skyscraper. Built in 1929, it served as headquarters of the Price Brothers Company, a lumber firm founded by Sir William Price. Don't miss the interior: exquisite copper plaques depict scenes of the company's early pulp and paper activities, and the two maplewood elevators are '30s classics. The 16th and 17th floors of the building served as the official residence for Québec's premier in 2002–03. ✉ *65 rue Ste-Anne, Upper Town.*

★ **➌ Fairmont Le Château Frontenac.** Québec City's most celebrated landmark, this imposing green-turreted castle with a copper roof stands on the site of what was the administrative and military headquarters of New France. It owes its name to the Comte de Frontenac, governor of the French colony between 1672 and 1698. Considering the magnificence of the château's location overlooking the St. Lawrence River, you can see why Frontenac said, "For me, there is no site more beautiful nor more grandiose than that of Québec City." Samuel de Champlain, who founded Québec City in 1608, was responsible for Château St-Louis, the first structure to appear on the site of the Frontenac; it was built between 1620 and 1624 as a residence for colonial governors. In 1784 Château Haldimand was constructed here, but it was demolished in 1892 to make way for Château Frontenac, built as a hotel a year later. The Frontenac was considered remarkably luxurious at that time: guest rooms contained fireplaces, bathrooms, and marble fixtures, and a special commissioner purchased antiques for the establishment. The hotel was designed by New York architect Bruce Price, who also worked on Québec City's Gare du Palais (rail station) and other Canadian landmarks. The addition of a 20-story central tower in 1925 completed the Frontenac. It has accumulated a star-studded guest roster, including Queen Elizabeth and Ronald Reagan as well as Franklin Roosevelt and Winston Churchill, who met here in 1943 and 1944 for two wartime conferences. Guides dressed in 19th-century-style costumes conduct tours of the luxurious interior. ⊠ *1 rue des Carrières, Upper Town* ☎ *418/691–2166* ⊕ *www.fairmont.com* ⊞ *Tours C$7* ⊙ *Tours May–mid-Oct., daily 10–6; mid-Oct.–Apr., weekends noon–5 or on demand.*

★ ⑧ **Holy Trinity Anglican Cathedral.** Dating from 1804, this stone church was one of the first Anglican cathedrals built outside the British Isles. Its simple, dignified facade is reminiscent of London's St. Martin-in-the-Fields. The cathedral's land was given to the Recollet fathers (Franciscan monks from France) in 1681 by the king of France for a church and monastery. When Québec came under British rule, the Recollets made the church available to the Anglicans for services. Later, King George III of England ordered construction of the present cathedral, with an area set aside for members of the royal family. A portion of the north balcony still is reserved exclusively for the use of the reigning sovereign or her representative. The church houses precious objects donated by George III; wood for the oak benches was imported from the Royal Forest at Windsor. The cathedral's impressive rear organ has 3,058 pipes. On Sunday mornings the cathedral has traditional English bell ringing. ⊠ *31 rue des Jardins, Upper Town* ☎ *418/692–2193* ⊞ *Free* ⊙ *Mid-May–June, daily 9–6; July–Aug., daily 9–8; Sept.–early Oct., weekdays 10–4; Nov.–mid-May, services only; Sun. services year-round in English at 8:30 and 11 AM, in French at 9:30 AM.*

⑨ **Hôtel Clarendon.** One of the city's finest art-deco structures is also Québec's oldest hotel: the hotel dates from 1866, but it was reconstructed in its current style, with geometric patterns of stone and wrought iron decorating its interior, in 1930. ⊠ *57 rue Ste-Anne, at rue des Jardins, Upper Town* ☎ *418/692–2480.*

⑤ **Jardin des Gouverneurs** (Governors' Park). In this small park just south of the Château Frontenac stands the **Wolfe-Montcalm Monument**, a 50-foot-tall obelisk that is unique because it pays tribute to both a winning (English) and a losing (French) general. The monument recalls the 1759 battle on the Plains of Abraham, which ended French rule here. British general James Wolfe lived only long enough to hear of his victory;

French general Louis-Joseph Montcalm died shortly after Wolfe with the knowledge that the city was lost. During the French regime the public area served as a garden for the governors who lived in Château St-Louis. On the south side of the park is **avenue Ste-Geneviève,** lined with well-preserved Victorian houses dating from 1850 to 1900. Several have been converted to inns.

② **Maison Maillou.** The colony's former treasury building typifies the architecture of New France with its sharply slanted roof, dormer windows, concrete chimneys, shutters with iron hinges, and limestone walls. Built between 1736 and 1753, it stands at the end of rue du Trésor. Now housing the Québec City Chamber of Commerce, Maison Maillou is not open for tours. ⊠ *17 rue St-Louis, Upper Town.*

⑮ **Maison Montcalm.** Built in 1725, this was the home of French General Louis-Joseph Montcalm from 1758 until his death from wounds received in the Battle of the Plains of Abraham. A plaque dedicated to the general is on the right side of the house. A New England–style building, with 13 dormer windows on the 2nd floor, a sharply pitched roof, and arched stone vaults in the basement, the building is now given over to condominiums and is closed to the public. By looking at the upper-floor windows from the sidewalk across the street, however, it's easy to imagine a periwigged Montcalm examining the British invasion force on Orleans Island in the summer of 1759 through his telescope, or looking upriver in the vain hope of seeing supply ships coming from France. ⊠ *Rue des Remparts between rues Hamel and St-Flavien, Upper Town.*

⑭ **Monastère des Augustines de l'Hôtel-Dieu de Québec** (Augustine Monastery). Augustine nuns arrived from Dieppe, France, in 1639 with a mission to care for the sick in the new colony. They established the first hospital north of Mexico, the **Hôtel-Dieu,** the large building west of the monastery. Upon request the Augustines offer free guided tours of the 1800 **chapel** and the cellars used by the nuns as a shelter, beginning in 1695, during bombardments by the British. During World War II, the cellars hid national treasures that had been smuggled out of Poland for safekeeping. ⊠ *32 rue Charlevoix, Upper Town* ☎ *418/692–2492 for tours* ☜ *Free* ☉ *Tours by arrangement.*

⑪ **Morrin College.** Built between 1802–13, this stately graystone building was Québec City's first prison under British rule. Roughly 16 criminals were hanged publicly outside the building. (Two cell blocks, with a half-dozen cells in each, are still intact, but for now are closed to the public. The cells are part of a restoration project that will see the complex reopen as an English-language cultural center in 2006.)

When the jail closed in 1868, the building was converted into Morrin College, one of the city's first private schools, and the **Literary and Historical Society of Québec** moved in. Founded in 1824, this forerunner of Canada's National Archives still operates a public lending library and has a superb collection that includes some of the first books printed in North America. A 1779 wood statue of General James Wolfe overlooks the splendid wood-lined interior of the library from the wrap-around balcony on the 2nd floor. ⊠ *44 rue Chausée des Ecossais, Upper Town*

☎ *418/694–9147* ✉ *Free* ⊙ *Tues. and Thurs.–Fri. 9:30–4:30, Wed. 9:30–6:30, weekends 10–4.*

❻ Musée d'Art Inuit Brousseau. The first museum south of the Arctic Circle to be dedicated exclusively to Inuit art and culture includes some surviving examples of art from more than 200 years ago. The collection includes artifacts and many styles of works by Inuit artists, shaped from materials such as walrus tusks, bone, caribou antlers, soapstone, basalt, and serpentine. You can see from the art on view just how Inuit culture changed after contact with Europeans. ⊠ *39 rue St-Louis, Upper Town* ☎ *418/694–1828* ⊕ *www.artinuit.ca* ✉ *C\$6* ⊙ *Daily 9:30–5:30.*

⓱ Musée de l'Amérique Française. A former student residence of the Québec Seminary at Laval University houses this museum focusing on the history of the French in North America. You can view about 20 of the museum's 400 landscape and still-life paintings, some from as early as the 15th century, along with French colonial money and scientific instruments. The attached former chapel is used for exhibits, conferences, and cultural activities. ⊠ *2 côte de la Fabrique, Upper Town* ☎ *418/692–2843* ⊕ *www.mcq.org* ✉ *C\$4, free Tues. early Sept.–June 23* ⊙ *June 24–early Sept., daily 9:30–5; early Sept.–June 23, Tues.–Sun. 10–5.*

⓴ Musée du Fort. The museum's sole exhibit is a sound-and-light show that reenacts the area's important battles, including the battle of the Plains of Abraham and the 1775 attack by American generals Arnold and Montgomery. ⊠ *10 rue Ste-Anne, Upper Town* ☎ *418/692–1759* ✉ *C\$6.75* ⊙ *Feb.–Mar., Thurs.–Sun. 11–4; Apr.–June and Sept.–Oct., daily 10–5; July–Aug., daily 10–6; Nov.–Jan., by appointment.*

★ ⓭ Parc de l'Artillerie (Artillery Park). This national historic park showcases four buildings—all that remains of what was once a complex of up to 20 military, industrial, and civilian structures situated to guard the St. Charles River and the Old Port. The oldest buildings, dating to the early 1700s, served as headquarters for the French garrison. When they were overtaken by the British in 1759, they were used as barracks for British troops—30 years earlier than the first barracks used in England. In 1765, the Royal Artillery Regiment was stationed here, giving the fortress its name. From 1882 until 1964 the area served as an industrial complex, providing ammunition for the Canadian army. At the former **powder magazine,** which in 1903 was replaced by a shell foundry, a detailed model depicts the buildings, streets, and military structures of Québec City in 1808, as rendered by two surveyors in the Royal Engineers Corps. Sent to officials in Britain in 1813, the model was intended to prove the strategic importance of Québec in order to justify expansion of the city's fortifications. The **Dauphin Redoubt,** named in honor of the son of Louis XIV (the heir apparent), was constructed from 1712 to 1748. It served as a barracks for the French and then the English garrisons until 1784–85, when it became an officers' mess for the Royal Artillery Regiment. The **Officers' Quarters,** a dwelling for Royal Artillery officers until the British army's departure in 1871, illustrates military family life during the British regime. In July and August you may be able to sample bread baked in the outdoor oven and, in the afternoon, watch a French soldier reenactor demonstrate shooting with a flintlock musket. **Les Dames de Soie** (The Ladies of Silk; ☎ 418/692–

1516), in a former cannon warehouse, allows you to watch porcelain dolls being made and view an exhibit on the history of dolls. From late June to early September, it's open Monday through Saturday 10–6 and Sunday noon–5; the rest of the year it's open Monday through Saturday 11–5 and Sunday noon–4. Admission is free, and you can visit it separately from Artillery Park. ⊠ *2 rue d'Auteuil, Upper Town* ☎418/648–4205 ⊕*www. parkscanada.qc.ca* ⊠ *C$4, C$8 for guided tour* ⊙ *Apr., Wed.–Sun 10–5; May–mid-Oct., daily 10–5.*

▶ ❶ **Place d'Armes.** For centuries, this square atop a cliff has been used for parades and military events. Upper Town's most central location, the plaza is bordered by government buildings; at its west side stands the majestic **Ancien Palais de Justice** (Old Courthouse), a Renaissance-style building from 1887. The plaza is on land that was occupied by a church and convent of the Recollet missionaries (Franciscan monks), who in 1615 were the first order of priests to arrive in New France. The Gothic-style **fountain** at the center of Place d'Armes pays tribute to their arrival. ⊠ *Rues St-Louis and du Fort, Upper Town.*

❶❾ **Rue du Trésor.** (Treasure Road) The road that colonists took on their way to pay rent to the king's officials is now a narrow alley where colorful prints, paintings, and other kinds of artwork are on display. You won't necessarily find masterpieces, but this walkway is a good stop for a souvenir sketch or two—more than a few artists got their start selling their work here. In summer, activity on this street and nearby rue Ste-Anne, lined with eateries and boutiques, starts early in the morning and continues until late at night. Stores stay open, artists paint, and street musicians perform as long as there is an audience, even if it's 1 AM. At 8 rue du Trésor is the **Québec Experience** (☎418/694–4000), a multimedia sound-and-light show that traces Québec's history from the first explorers until modern days; the cost is C$7.50.

❶❻ **Séminaire du Québec.** Behind these gates lies a tranquil courtyard surrounded by austere stone buildings with rising steeples; these structures have housed classrooms and student residences since 1663. François de Montmorency Laval, the first bishop of New France, founded Québec Seminary to train priests in the new colony. In 1852 the seminary became Université Laval, the first Catholic university in North America. In 1946 the university moved to a larger campus in suburban Ste-Foy. Today, priests live on the premises, and Laval's architecture school occupies part of the building. The on-site ⇨ **Musée de l'Amérique Française** gives tours of the seminary grounds and the interior in summer. Tours start from the museum, located at 2 côte de la Fabrique. The small Second Empire–style **Chapelle Extérieure**, at the west entrance of the seminary, was built in 1888 after fire destroyed the 1750 original. Joseph-Ferdinand Peachy designed the chapel; its interior is patterned after that of the Église de la Trinité in Paris. ⊠ *1 côte de la Fabrique, Upper Town* ☎ *418/692–3981* ⊠ *C$4* ⊙ *Tours weekends mid-June–early Sept.; call for tour times.*

❹ **Terrasse Dufferin.** This wide boardwalk with an intricate wrought-iron guardrail has a panoramic view of the St. Lawrence River, the town of

Lévis on the opposite shore, Île d'Orléans, and the Laurentian Mountains. It was named for Lord Dufferin, governor of Canada between 1872 and 1878, who had this walkway constructed in 1878. The **Promenade des Gouverneurs** begins at the boardwalk's western end; the path skirts the cliff and leads up to Québec's highest point, Cap Diamant, and also to the Citadelle.

Lower Town

If there's a cradle of French civilization in North America, you're standing in it when you visit Lower Town. In 1608 Champlain chose this narrow, U-shape spit of land sandwiched between the frigid waters of the St. Lawrence River and the craggy heights of Cap Diamant as the site for his settlement. Champlain later abandoned the fortified "abitation" (residence) at the foot of Cap Diamant and relocated to the more easily defendable Upper Town.

However, the area continued to flourish as a bustling port and trading center for French merchants, fur traders, *coureurs de bois* (woodsmen), and France's Indian allies. It was also the base from which dozens of military campaigns and fact-finding missions were launched into the heart of an unknown continent. A bust of France's "Sun King," Louis XIV, was erected in the main square, Place du Marché, which was renamed Place Royale in 1686. Destroyed by British cannons that were set up on the opposite shore during the siege of 1759, the port and buildings were rebuilt by the British, and the area quickly regained its role as Canada's leading commercial and business center.

Lower Town went into an economic tailspin in the mid-1800s, becoming a slum whose narrow streets were lined with pawnshops, rough-and-tumble taverns, and smoky brothels that catered to sailors and lumberjacks. This lasted until the 1960s, when it received a multimillion-dollar facelift that remade it into a sanitized version of its 1700s self. Today, once-dilapidated houses and warehouses contain stylish boutiques, popular restaurants, and chic art and antique galleries. Bounded by the Dufferin-Montmorency Highway to the west, the St. Charles River to the north, the river to the east, and Petit Champlain shopping area to the south, the Lower Town is also home to approximately 850 people.

a good walk

Begin this walk on the northern end of rue du Petit-Champlain, at **Maison Louis-Jolliet** ㉑ ⮕ at the foot of the **Escalier Casse-Cou** ㉒. At the **Verrerie La Mailloche** ㉓ across the street, master glassblowers create contemporary works of art. Heading south on **rue du Petit-Champlain** ㉔, the city's oldest street, check out the cliff on the right that borders this narrow thoroughfare, where Upper Town is on the heights above. At the point where rue du Petit-Champlain intersects with boulevard Champlain, make a U-turn to head back north on rue Champlain. One block farther, at the corner of rue du Marché-Champlain, is **Maison Chevalier** ㉕, a stone house with a style typical of New France. Walk east to rue Notre-Dame, which leads directly to **Place Royale** ㉖. The interpretation center here has exhibits on life in the colony. The small 17th-century stone church on the south side of Place Royale is the **Église Notre-Dame-des-Victoires** ㉗, the oldest church in Québec.

On the east side of Place Royale, take rue de la Place, which leads to an open square, **Place de Paris** ㉘. Head north on rue Dalhousie until you come to the **Musée de la Civilisation** ㉙, devoted to Québecois culture. Walk east toward the river to the **Vieux-Port de Québec** ㉚, at one time the busiest port on the continent. The breezes from the St. Lawrence provide a cool reprieve on a hot summer day, and you can browse through the farmers' market here. You are now in the ideal spot to explore Québec City's **antiques district** ㉛.

In summer, walk 10 minutes west along rue St-Paul, past the train station, built in 1915 in the style of the castles in France's Loire Valley. Turn left on rue Vallière to **L'Ilot des Palais** ㉜, an archaeological museum with the remnants of the first two palaces of the French colonial *intendants* (administrators).

TIMING This is a good day of sightseeing. A morning stroll takes you to two of the city's most famous squares, Place Royale and Place de Paris. You can see the city from the Lévis ferry, if you wish, or pause for lunch before touring the Musée de la Civilisation and the antiques district. Note that L'Ilot des Palais is open only in summer.

What to See

㉛ **Antiques district.** Antiques shops cluster around rues St-Pierre and St-Paul. Rue St-Paul was once part of a business district packed with warehouses, stores, and businesses. After World War I, shipping and commercial activities plummeted; low rents attracted antiques dealers. Today numerous cafés, restaurants, and art galleries have made this area one of the town's more fashionable sections.

㉗ **Église Notre-Dame-des-Victoires** (Our Lady of Victory Church). The oldest church in Québec stands on the site of Samuel de Champlain's first residence, which also served as a fort and trading post. The church was built in 1688 and has been restored twice. Its name comes from two French victories against the British: one in 1690 against Admiral William Phipps and another in 1711 against Sir Hovendon Walker. The interior contains copies of paintings by European masters such as Van Dyck, Rubens, and Boyermans; its altar is shaped like a fort. A scale model suspended from the ceiling represents *Le Brezé,* the boat that transported French soldiers to New France in 1664. The side chapel is dedicated to Ste-Geneviève, the patron saint of Paris. ⊠ *Pl. Royale, Lower Town* ☎ *418/692–1650* ⊠ *Free* ⊗ *Mid-May–mid-Oct., daily 9–5; mid-Oct.–mid-May, daily 10–4; closed to visitors during mass (Sun. at 10:30 and noon), marriages, and funerals.*

㉒ **Escalier Casse-Cou.** The steepness of the city's first iron stairway, an ambitious 1893 design by city architect and engineer Charles Baillairgé, is ample evidence of how it got its name: Breakneck Steps. The 170 steps were built on the site of the original 17th-century stairway that linked the Upper Town and Lower Town. There are shops and restaurants at various levels.

③② L'Îlot des Palais (The Palace Block). More than 300 years of history are laid bare at this archaeological museum on the site of the first two palaces of New France's colonial intendants. The first palace, built as a brewery by Jean Talon in 1669, was turned into the intendant's residence in 1685 and destroyed by fire in 1713. In 1716 a second palace was built facing the first. It was later turned into a modern brewery, but the basement vaults that remain house an archaeology exhibit and a multimedia display. ⊠ *8 rue Vallière, Lower Town* ☎ *418/691–6092* 🎟 *C$3* ☉ *June 24–early Sept., daily 10–5.*

②⑤ Maison Chevalier. This old stone house was built in 1752 for shipowner Jean-Baptiste Chevalier. The house's classic French style is one rich aspect of the urban architecture of New France. The fire walls, chimneys, vaulted cellars, and original wood beams and stone fireplaces are noteworthy. ⊠ *50 rue du Marché-Champlain, Lower Town* ☎ *418/643–2158* 🎟 *Free* ☉ *May–June 23, Tues.–Sun. 10–5; June 24–Oct. 21, daily 9:30–5; Oct. 22–Apr., weekends 10–5.*

▶ ②① Maison Louis-Jolliet. The first settlers of New France used this 1683 house as a base for further westward explorations. Today it's the lower station of the funicular. A monument commemorating French explorer Louis Jolliet's 1672 discovery of the Mississippi River stands in the park next to the house. The ⇨ **Escalier Casse-Cou** is at the north side of the house. ⊠ *16 rue du Petit-Champlain, Lower Town.*

★ ☾ ②⑨ Musée de la Civilisation (Museum of Civilization). Wedged between narrow streets at the foot of the cliff, this spacious museum with a striking limestone-and-glass facade was artfully designed by architect Moshe Safdie to blend into the landscape. Its campanile echoes the shape of the city's church steeples. Some of the museum's innovative exhibits tell the story of how Québec's first settlers lived and how they survived such harsh winters. Others illustrate the extent to which the Roman Catholic Church affected people's lives, and explain the evolution of Québec nationalism. The *Nous, les Premières Nations* (*Encounter with the First Nations*) exhibit looks at the 11 aboriginal nations that inhabit Québec. Several of the shows, with their imaginative use of artwork, video screens, computers, and sound, appeal to both adults and children. The museum's interactive approach also extends to exhibits of an international nature: from April 2005 until March 2006, the museum will present *God, Tsars and the Revolution,* which covers Russia's history from the 9th century to the Russian Revolution. Other exhibits in 2005 will include an examination of the commercial and artistic uses of light since the discovery of electricity, and a tribute to the men and women who have changed Québec since the time of New France. ⊠ *85 rue Dalhousie, Lower Town* ☎ *418/643–2158* ⊕ *www.mcq.org* 🎟 *C$8, free Tuesdays Nov.–Apr.* ☉ *May–Labor Day, daily 9:30–6:30; early Sept.–Apr., Tues.–Sun. 10–5.*

②⑧ Place de Paris. An often-ridiculed black-and-white geometric sculpture, *Dialogue avec l'Histoire* (*Dialogue with History*) dominates this square. A 1987 gift from France, the sculpture is on the site where the first French settlers landed. ⊠ *Rue Dalhousie, Lower Town.*

<table>
<tr><td>

need a break?

</td><td>

Beer has been brewed in Québec since the early 1600s, and **L'Inox** (✉ 37 quai St-André, Lower Town ☎ 418/692–2877) carries on the tradition with a combination brewpub and museum. Cherry-red columns and a stainless-steel bar contrast with exposed stone and brick walls, blending the old with the new. A large, sunny terrace is open in summer. L'Inox serves many of its own beers, as well as other beverages, alcoholic and not. Food is limited to plates of Québec cheeses or European-style hot dogs served in drilled-out baguettes. Tours of the brewery are available for groups of eight or more.

</td></tr>
<tr><td>

off the beaten path

</td><td>

QUÉBEC–LÉVIS FERRY – En route to the opposite shore of the St. Lawrence River on this ferry, you get a striking view of the Québec City skyline, with the Château Frontenac and the Québec Seminary high atop the cliff. The view is even more impressive at night. Ferries generally run every half hour from 6 AM until 6 PM, and then hourly until 2 AM; there are additional ferries from April through November. From late June to August you can combine a Québec–Lévis ferry ride with a bus tour of Lévis, getting off at such sights as the star-shape Fort No. 1, one of three built by the British between 1865 and 1872 to defend Québec. The combined round-trip ferry and shuttle operates daily 10–5 and costs C$6. ✉ *Rue Dalhousie, 1 block south of Place de Paris* ☎ *418/644–3704* ⊕ *www.traversiers.gouv.qc.ca* 🗓 *June–Sept. C$2.50, Oct.–May C$2.*

</td></tr>
</table>

★ ☺ ❷ **Place Royale.** Once the homes of wealthy merchants, houses with steep Normandy-style roofs, dormer windows, and several chimneys encircle this cobblestone square. Until 1686 the area was called Place du Marché, but its name changed when a bust of Louis XIV was placed at its center. During the late 1600s and early 1700s, when Place Royale was continually under threat of British attack, the colonists moved progressively higher to safer quarters atop the cliff in Upper Town. After the French colony fell to British rule in 1759, Place Royale flourished again with shipbuilding, logging, fishing, and fur trading. The Fresque des Québecois, a 4,665-square-foot trompe-l'oeil mural depicting 400 years of Québec's history, is to the east of the square, at the corner of rue Notre-Dame and côte de la Montagne. An information center, the **Centre d'Interprétation de Place Royale** (✉ 27 rue Notre-Dame, Lower Town ☎ 418/646–3167) includes exhibits, a multimedia show, and a Discovery Hall with a replica of a 19th-century home, where children can try on period costumes. Admission is C$4, but it's free on Tuesday from early September to June 23. It's open daily 9:30–5 from June 24 to early September; the rest of the year it's open Tuesday through Sunday 10–5.

❷ **Rue du Petit-Champlain.** The oldest street in the city was once the main street of a harbor village, with trading posts and the homes of rich merchants. Today it has pleasant boutiques and cafés. Natural-fiber weaving, Inuit carvings, hand-painted silks, and enameled copper crafts are some of the local specialties that are good buys here.

☺ ❷ **Verrerie La Mailloche.** The glassblowing techniques used in this workshop, boutique, and museum are as old as ancient Egypt, but the results are contemporary. In the workshop, master glassblower Jean Vallières and his assistants can answer your questions as they turn 1,092°C (2,000°F) molten glass into works of art. Examples of Vallières's work have been presented by the Canadian government to visiting dignitaries such as Queen Elizabeth and Ronald Reagan. ✉ *58 rue Sous-le-Fort, Lower Town* ☎ *418/694–0445* ⊕ *www.lamailloche.com* ✉ *Free* ☉ *Mid-June–mid-Oct., daily 9–10; Nov.–mid-June daily 9:30–5:30.*

㉚ Vieux-Port de Québec (Old Port of Québec). The old harbor dates from the 17th century, when ships brought supplies and settlers to the new colony. At one time this port was among the busiest on the continent: between 1797 and 1897, Québec shipyards turned out more than 2,500 ships, many of which passed the 1,000-ton mark. The port saw a rapid decline after steel and steam replaced wood and the channel to Montréal was deepened to allow larger boats to reach a good port upstream. Today this historic 72-acre area encompasses several parks. You can stroll along the riverside promenade, where merchant and cruise ships dock. At the port's northern end, where the St. Charles meets the St. Lawrence, a lock protects the marina in the Louise Basin from the generous Atlantic tides that reach even this far up the St. Lawrence. In the northwest section of the port, the **Old Port of Québec Interpretation Center** (✉ 100 quai St-André, Lower Town ☎ 418/648–3300) presents the history of the port in relation to the lumber trade and shipbuilding. Admission to the center is C$3; it's open daily May to Labor Day 10–5, early September to early October 1–5, and by reservation only from mid-October through April. From June 22 through August 31, guides in 19th-century costume conduct walking tours of the port (C$8). At the **Marché du Vieux-Port** (Old Port Market), at the port's northwestern tip, farmers sell fresh produce and cheese, as well as handicrafts. The market, near quai St-André, is open daily 8–8 in summer. Some stalls stay open in winter, 9–4.

The Fortifications

Declared a Canadian historical monument in 1957, the 4.6-km-long wall (3-mi-long) is the heart of a defensive belt that circles the Old City. The wall began as a series of earthworks and wooden palisades built by French military engineers to protect the Upper Town from an inland attack following the siege of the city by Admiral Phips in 1690. Two of the city's three sides have the natural protection of the 90-meter-high facade of Cap Diamant, so the cape itself was studded with cannon batteries overlooking the river.

Over the next century, the French used tremendous time, energy, and money to shore up and strengthen the city's fortifications. One of the most sumptuous additions was the Dauphine Redoubt. Built in 1712, it is the only one of 11 such buildings that remain, and is fully restored and open to the public. After the fall of New France, the British were equally concerned about strengthening the city's defenses. They set to work building an earth-and-wood citadel atop Cap Diamant. During the Napoleonic Wars, they added four medieval-looking Martello towers to the fortifications. Of the three that remain, two are open to the public. They also slowly replaced the wooden palisades that surrounded the city with a massive cut-stone wall. Other buildings, added later, include the Officers' Quarters (1818) and an iron foundry. Both have been restored and are open to the public.

The crowning touch came after the War of 1812, with the construction of the cut-stone, star-shape citadel. An irregular pentagon with two cannon-lined sides facing the river below, the structure earned Québec City its 19th-century nickname "North America's Gibraltar." When the citadel was finished, the city's fortifications took up one-quarter of the entire city's surface. For its part, almost half of Upper Town was owned by the British military, which garrisoned more than 2,000 troops within the city's walls. American naturalist Henry David Thoreau was so struck with the fortress atmosphere of Québec City during a visit in 1850 that he wrote, "A fortified town is like a man cased in the heavy armor of antiquity with a horse-load of broadswords and small arms slung to him, endeavouring to go about his business."

Time, treaties, and technology have lessened Québec City's military importance. Now a modern metropolis that has long outgrown the confines of the Old City's walls, Québec City is an exceptional opportunity to see Canada's military history up close in the form of its fortifications and battlements.

a good walk

Start close to Porte St-Louis (St-Louis Gate) at the Parc de l'Esplanade, part of the **Fortifications of Québec National Historic Site** ❶ ☞ and the site of a former military parade ground. From here you can tour the walls of the Old City. From the powder magazine in the park, head south on côte de la Citadelle, which leads directly to **La Citadelle** ❷, a historic fortified base. Retrace your steps on côte de la Citadelle to **Grande Allée** ❸. Once you pass through the Porte St-Louis, turn left on avenue Georges VI and walk past the concrete building to the **Parc des Champs-de-Bataille** ❹. Head up the hill to Cap Diamant. From the observation point here you can get a spectacular view of the St. Lawrence River and the cliff that British general James Wolfe and his troops scaled to win the 1759 battle that decided the fate of New France. The exact point where Wolfe's forces made the ascent is just to the west of the plains at Gilmour Hill. Retrace your steps down the hill and turn left along avenue Georges VI.

Look left as you walk west along avenue Georges VI to see the **Plains of Abraham** ❺, site of the famous battle. The neatly tended garden **Parc Jeanne d'Arc** ❻ is a little farther along, on the right. To the left, toward the south end of the park, stands **Tour Martello No. 1** ❼, a stone defensive tower. Continue along avenue Georges VI past where it turns into avenue de Bernières. The Tour Martello No. 2 is to the right, up avenue Taché. Continue west along avenue de Bernières to avenue Wolfe-Montcalm, where you come to the tall **Wolfe Monument** ❽, which marks the place where the British general died.

Turn left on avenue Wolfe-Montcalm to visit the **Musée National des Beaux-Arts du Québec** ❾. Attached to the museum, the **Centre d'Interprétation**

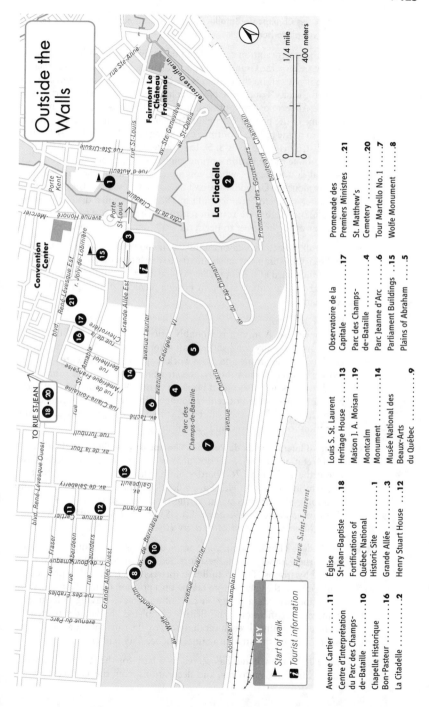

Outside the Walls

Avenue Cartier **11**
Centre d'Interprétation
du Parc des Champs-
de-Bataille **10**
Chapelle Historique
Bon-Pasteur **16**
La Citadelle **2**

Église
St-Jean-Baptiste **18**
Fortifications of
Québec National
Historic Site **1**
Grande Allée **3**
Henry Stuart House ... **12**

Louis S. St. Laurent
Heritage House **13**
Maison J. A. Moisan ... **19**
Montcalm
Monument **14**
Musée National des
Beaux-Arts
du Québec **9**

Observatoire de la
Capitale **17**
Parc des Champs-
de-Bataille **4**
Parc Jeanne d'Arc **6**
Parliament Buildings ... **15**
Plains of Abraham **5**

Promenade des
Premiers Ministres ... **21**
St. Matthew's
Cemetery **20**
Tour Martello No. 1 ... **7**
Wolfe Monument **8**

KEY
➤ *Start of walk*
🛈 *Tourist information*

du Parc des Champs-de-Bataille ⑩ has a multimedia show on the battles that took place here.

From the interpretation center, head north on avenue Wolfe-Montcalm, turning right on the Grande Allée and walking a block to **avenue Cartier** ⑪. Across the street, on the corner, is the **Henry Stuart House** ⑫, which once marked the city's outskirts. Near the intersection of avenue Cartier and Grande Allée, take note of the simple white house with green trim, once the home of the painter Cornelius Krieghoff. It remains a private house, not open to the public. Continue east along Grande Allée to 201 Grande Allée Est. This is the **Louis S. St. Laurent Heritage House** ⑬, once the residence of one of the nation's prime ministers. Continue east to Cours du Général-de Montcalm, where you arrive at the **Montcalm Monument** ⑭. Farther along the Grande Allée, past the bars and restaurants, is the Manège Militaire, a turreted armory built in 1888 that is still a drill hall for the Royal 22nd Regiment. You can return on Grande Allée to your starting point or cross the street to begin the walk outside the walls.

TIMING   This walk takes a half day, or a full day if you begin by walking the walls of the city. In summer you should try to catch the colorful 10 AM changing of the guard at the Citadelle. For lunch, try one of the many restaurants around avenue Cartier, or bring a picnic and eat on the Plains of Abraham.

What to See

⑪ **Avenue Cartier.** A mix of reasonably priced restaurants and bars, groceries and specialty food shops, hair salons, and similar stores, Cartier is a favorite lunchtime and after-work stop for many downtown office workers. After business hours, the street hums with locals running errands or soaking in sun (and beer) on patios. When darkness falls, the avenue's patrons get noticeably younger. The attraction? A half-dozen nightclubs and pubs that offer everything from cigars and quiet conversation to Latin music and ear-splitting dance tunes.

⑩ **Centre d'Interprétation du Parc des Champs-de-Bataille** (Battlefields Park Interpretation Center). A section of an old jail houses a multimedia show about the 1759 and 1760 battles on the Plains of Abraham. Also here are exhibits on Battlefields Park's development into a historic site and examples of uniforms worn at the time. ⊠ *Montcalm* ☎ *418/648–5641* ⊕ *www.ccbn-nbc.gc.ca* 🖃 *C$5* ☉ *Mid-May–mid-Oct., daily 10–5:30; mid-Oct.–mid-May, daily 10–5.*

★ ❷ **La Citadelle** (The Citadel). Built at the city's highest point, on Cap Diamant, the Citadel is the largest fortified base in North America still occupied by troops. The 25-building fortress was intended to protect the port, prevent the enemy from taking up a position on the Plains of Abraham, and provide a refuge in case of an attack. Having inherited incomplete fortifications, the British completed the Citadel to protect themselves against French retaliations. By the time the Citadel was finished in 1832, the attacks against Québec City had ended.

Since 1920 the Citadel has served as a base for the Royal 22nd Regiment. Firearms, uniforms, and decorations from the 17th century are displayed in the **Royal 22nd Regiment Museum,** in the former powder magazine, built in 1750. If weather permits, you can watch the Changing of the Guard, a ceremony in which troops parade before the Citadel in red coats and black fur hats. Note that you must join a guided tour to visit the Citadel and the museum. ⊠ *1 côte de la Citadelle, Upper Town* ☎ *418/694–2815* ⊕ *www.lacitadelle.qc.ca* ☒ *C$6* ⊙ *Apr.–mid-May, daily 10–4; mid-May–June, daily 9–5; July–Labor Day, daily 9–6; Sept., daily 9–4; Oct., daily 10–3; Nov.–Mar., groups only (reservations required). Changing of the guard June 24–Labor Day, daily at 10 AM. Retreat ceremony July–Aug., Fri.–Sun. at 7 PM.*

▶ ❶ **Fortifications of Québec National Historic Site.** In the early 19th century, this was a clear space surrounded by a picket fence and poplar trees. What's here now is the **Poudrière de l'Esplanade** (⊠ 100 rue St-Louis, Upper Town ☎ 418/648–7016 ⊕ www.parkscanada.gc.ca), the powder magazine that the British constructed in 1820, and an interpretation center with a multimedia video and a model depicting the evolution of the wall surrounding Vieux-Québec. There's a C$3 charge to enter the site, which is open 10–5 daily from mid-May to October 6. The French began building ramparts along the city's cliffs as early as 1690 to protect themselves from British invaders. However, the colonists had trouble convincing the French government to take the threat of invasion seriously, and when the British invaded in 1759 the walls were still incomplete. The British, despite attacks by the Americans during the American Revolution and the War of 1812, took a century to finish them. From June to October, the park can also be the starting point for walking the city's 4½ km (3 mi) of walls. There are two guided tours (C$10 each). One starts at the interpretation center and the other begins at Terrasse Dufferin.

❸ **Grande Allée.** One of the city's oldest streets, Grande Allée was the route people took from outlying areas to sell their furs in town. In the 19th century, the wealthy built neo-Gothic and Queen Anne–style mansions here; they now house trendy cafés, clubs, and restaurants. The street actually has four names: inside the city walls it's rue St-Louis; outside the walls, Grande Allée; farther west, chemin St-Louis; and farther still, boulevard Laurier.

off the
beaten
path

GROSSE ÎLE NATIONAL PARK – For thousands of immigrants from Europe in the 1800s, the first glimpse of North America was the hastily erected quarantine station at Grosse Île—Canada's equivalent of Ellis Island. During the time Grosse Île operated (1832–1937), 4.3 million immigrants passed through the port of Québec. For far too many passengers on plague-racked ships, particularly the Irish fleeing the potato famine, Grosse Île became a final resting place. Several buildings have been restored to tell the story of the tragic period of Irish immigration. It's necessary to take a boat tour or ferry to visit the park, and you should reserve in advance. **Croisières Le Coudrier** (☎ 888/600–5554 ⊕ www.croisierescoudrier.qc.ca) has tours that depart from Québec City's Old Port for Grosse Île. Tours cost C$49, which includes admission to the island. **Croisières Lachance** (☎ 888/476–7734 ⊕ www.croisiereslachance.ca) runs a ferry that departs from Berthier sur Mer to Grosse Île for C$37, which includes admission. From Québec City, head south on the Pont Pierre-Laporte (Pierre Laporte Bridge) and follow Autoroute 20 east for about an hour to Berthier-sur-Mer. Follow the signs to the marina. ☎ 418/248–8888 or 800/463–6769 ⊕ www.pc.gc.ca ☑ C$37–C$49, boat tour or ferry included ⊙ May–Oct., daily 9–6.

⑫ **Henry Stuart House.** If you want to get a firsthand look at how the well-to-do English residents of Québec City lived in a bygone era, this is the place. Built in 1849 by the wife of wealthy businessman William Henry, the Regency-style cottage was bought in 1918 by the sisters Adèle and Mary Stuart. Active in such philanthropic organizations as the Red Cross and the Historical and Literary Society, the sisters were pillars of Québec City's English-speaking community. The sisters also maintained an English-style garden behind the house. Soon after Adéle's death in 1987 at the age of 98, the home was classified a historic site for its immaculate physical condition and the museum-like quality of its furnishings, almost all of them Victorian. Guided tours of the house and garden start on the hour, and include a cup of tea. ⊠ 82 Grande Allée Ouest, Montcalm ☎ 418/647–4347 ☑ C$5 ⊙ June 24–Labor Day, daily 11–4; early Sept.–June 23, Sun. 1–5.

> **need a break?** Halles Petit-Cartier (⊠ 1191 av. Cartier, Montcalm ☎ 418/688–1630), a food mall near the Henry Stuart House, has restaurants and shops that sell cheeses, pastries, breads, vegetables, and candies.

⑬ **Louis S. St. Laurent Heritage House.** A costumed maid or chauffeur greets you when you visit this elegant Grande Allée house, the former home of Louis S. St. Laurent, prime minister of Canada from 1948 to 1957. Within the house, period furnishings and multimedia touches tell St. Laurent's story and illustrate the lifestyle of upper-crust families in 1950s Québec City. ⊠ 201 Grande Allée Est, Montcalm ☎ 418/648–4071 ☑ C$4 ⊙ Mid-June–Aug., daily 10–5:30; Sept.–mid-June, Wed.–Sun. 10–5:30.

⑭ **Montcalm Monument.** France and Canada jointly erected this monument honoring Louis-Joseph Montcalm, the French general who gained his fame by winning four major battles in North America. His most famous battle, however, was the one he lost, when the British conquered New France on September 13, 1759. Montcalm was north of Québec City at Beauport when he learned that the British attack was imminent. He quickly assembled his troops to meet the enemy and was wounded in battle in the leg and stomach. Montcalm was carried into the walled city, where he died the next morning. The monument depicts the standing figure of Montcalm, with an angel over his shoulder. ⊠ Pl. Montcalm, Montcalm.

★ ⑨ **Musée National des Beaux-Arts du Québec** (National Museum of Fine Arts of Québec). A neoclassical Beaux Arts showcase, the museum has more than 22,000 traditional and contemporary pieces of Québec art. The portraits by artists well known in the area, such as Jean-Paul Riopelle (1923–2002), Jean-Paul Lemieux (1904–1990), and Horatio Walker

(1858–1938), are particularly notable. The museum's dignified building in Parc des Champs-de-Bataille was designed by Wilfrid Lacroix and erected in 1933 to commemorate the 300th anniversary of the founding of Québec. Incorporated within is part of an abandoned prison dating from 1867. A hallway of cells, with the iron bars and courtyard still intact, has been preserved as part of a permanent exhibition on the prison's history. ⊠ *1 av. Wolfe-Montcalm, Montcalm* ☎ *418/643–2150* ⊕ *www.mdq.org* 🏛 *Free; C$10 for special exhibits* ☉ *Sept.–May, Tues. and Thurs.–Sun. 10–5, Wed. 10–9; June–Aug., Thurs.–Tues. 10–6, Wed. 10–9.*

❹ **Parc des Champs-de-Bataille** (Battlefields Park). These 250 acres of gently rolling slopes have unparalleled views of the St. Lawrence River. Within the park and west of the Citadel are the ⇨ **Plains of Abraham.**

❻ **Parc Jeanne d'Arc.** An equestrian statue of Joan of Arc is the focus of this park, which is bright with colorful flowers in summer. A symbol of military courage and of France herself, the statue stands in tribute to the heroes of 1759 near the place where New France was lost to the British. The park also commemorates the Canadian national anthem, "O Canada"; it was played here for the first time on June 24, 1880. ⊠ *avs. Laurier and Taché, Montcalm.*

❺ **Plains of Abraham.** This park, named after the river pilot Abraham Martin, is the site of the famous 1759 battle that decided New France's fate. People cross-country ski here in winter and in-line skate in summer. In summer a bus driven by a guide portraying Abraham Martin provides an entertaining tour—with commentary in French and English—around the park. At the **Discovery Pavilion,** the multimedia display "Canada Odyssey" depicts 400 years of Canada's history and has a 2nd floor with computer games, videos, and displays focusing on the biological and scientific history of the area. ⊠ *Discovery Pavilion, 835 av. Wilfrid Laurier, Montcalm* ☎ *418/648–4071 for Discovery Pavilion and bus-tour information* 🏛 *Discovery Pavilion C$6.50, bus tour C$3.50* ☉ *Discovery Pavilion mid-June–mid-Oct., daily 10–5:30; mid-Oct.–mid-June, daily 10–5. Tours June 12–Sept. 1, daily 10–5:30; June 1–11 and Sept. 3–mid-Oct., weekends 10–5:30.*

FodorśChoice
★

❼ **Tour Martello No. 1** (Martello Tower No. 1). Of the 16 Martello towers in Canada, four were built in Québec City, because the British government feared an invasion after the American Revolution. Tour Martello No. 1, which exhibits the history of the four structures, was built between 1802 and 1810. **Tour Martello No. 2,** at avenues Taché and Laurier, hosts Council of War, a three-hour weekend mystery dinner show with a theme that draws on the War of 1812. Tour No. 3, which guarded westward entry to the city, was demolished in 1904. Tour No. 4, on rue Lavigueur overlooking the St. Charles River, is not open to the public. ⊠ *South end of Parc Jeanne d'Arc, Montcalm* ☎ *418/648–4071 for information on towers, 418/649–6157 for Tour No. 2 mystery dinner show* 🏛 *C$4* ☉ *Mid-June–Aug., daily 10–5:30; early June, Sept., and Oct., weekends 10–5:30.*

❽ **Wolfe Monument.** This tall monument marks the place where the British general James Wolfe died in 1759. Wolfe landed his troops about 3 km

(2 mi) from the city's walls; 4,500 English soldiers scaled the cliff and began fighting on the Plains of Abraham. Wolfe was mortally wounded in battle and was carried behind the lines to this spot. ⊠ *Rue de Bernières and av. Wolfe-Montcalm, Montcalm.*

Outside the Walls

Although Québec City's economy is slowly diversifying, the fortunes of it and the provincial government remain inseparable. One of the city's trendiest neighborhoods is down the hill on rue St-Jean.

a good walk

Head to avenue Honoré-Mercier and Grande Allée for the **Parliament Buildings** ⑮ ▶, home of the National Assembly, headquarters of the provincial government. As you leave the legislature, turn right and then right again onto Grande Allée. The modern concrete building across the street once held the offices of Québec's premier. Now it houses the Treasury Board, which controls the government's purse strings. As you walk west along Grande Allée, look to the right for a statue of former Québec premier Maurice Duplessis, who ruled the province with an iron fist from 1936 to 1939 and from 1944 to 1959. At the corner of Grande Allée and des Parlementaires is the Parc de la Francophonie, dedicated to French-speaking countries around the world. Turn right on rue de la Chevrotière and walk past rue St-Amable. The **Chapelle Historique Bon-Pasteur** ⑯, a church surrounded by office buildings, is on the west side of the street. The entrance to Edifice Marie-Guyart is across the street; its observation tower, **Observatoire de la Capitale** ⑰, provides a spectacular view.

Turn left on boulevard René-Lévesque Est and walk two blocks past the Parc de l'Amérique-Française, dedicated to places in North America with French-speaking populations. At the corner, the modern concrete building is the Grande Théâtre de Québec, a performing-arts center. Turn right at rue Claire-Fontaine, cross the street, and walk down the hill to rue St-Jean, where the **Église St-Jean-Baptiste** ⑱ dominates the neighborhood. Turn right and stroll down rue St-Jean past trendy shops in century-old buildings to **Maison J. A. Moisan** ⑲, which claims to be the oldest grocery store in North America. Farther down the street you arrive at **St. Matthew's Cemetery** ⑳, the city's oldest remaining graveyard. Cut through the cemetery to rue St-Simon, walk up the hill, cross the street, and turn right on boulevard René-Lévesque. In summer you can end your walk by crossing the street and strolling along the raised **Promenade des Premiers Ministres** ㉑, which tells the stories of Québec's premiers. On the right, at the corner of des Parlementaires, is the Honoré Mercier building, which houses the offices of Québec's premier. Past the National Assembly, at the end of the promenade, is a statue of the late premier René Lévesque, considered the father of Québec's independence movement.

TIMING This walk should take a half day. From March through June and from October through December, try to set aside some time to listen to the debates or Question Period in the National Assembly at the Parliament Buildings. For lunch, you can dine among decision-makers at the legislature's Le Parlementaire restaurant or in one of the many interesting and affordable restaurants along rue St-Jean.

What to See

⓰ **Chapelle Historique Bon-Pasteur** (Historic Chapel of the Good Pastor). Charles Baillargé designed this slender church with a steep sloping roof in 1868. Within the ornate baroque-style interior are carved-wood designs elaborately highlighted in gold leaf. The chapel houses 32 religious paintings created by the nuns of the community from 1868 to 1910. In addition to the regular weekday hours below, the chapel is also open Sunday between 10 and 1, before and after a musical artists' mass, which begins at 10:45; call ahead on a weekday if you want to visit during this time. ⊠ *1080 rue de la Chevrotière, Montcalm* ☏ *418/641–1069* ▧ *Free* ⊙ *Weekdays 8:30–4.*

★ ⓲ **Église St-Jean-Baptiste** (St. John the Baptist Church). Architect Joseph-Ferdinand Peachy's crowning glory, this church was inspired by the facade of the Église de la Trinité in Paris and rivals the Our Lady of Québec Basilica in beauty and size. The first church on the site, built in 1847, burned in the 1881 fire that destroyed much of the neighborhood. Seven varieties of Italian marble were used in the soaring columns, statues, and pulpit of the present church, which dates from 1884. Its 36 stained-glass windows consist of 30 sections each, and the organ, like the church, is classified as a historic monument. From October 1 to June 23 and outside regular opening hours, knock at the **presbytery** at 490 rue St-Jean to see the church. ⊠ *410 rue St-Jean, St. Jean Baptiste* ☏ *418/525–7188* ⊙ *June 24–Sept., weekdays 10–4:30, Sun. 9–4.*

off the beaten path

ICE HOTEL – At this hotel—the first of its kind in North America—constructed completely of ice and snow, you can tour the art galleries of ice sculptures, get married in the chapel, lounge in the hot tub, have a drink at the bar made of ice, dance in the ice club, then nestle into a sleeping bag on a bed lined with deerskin. The hotel is open from mid-January to March 31. A night's stay, a four-course supper, breakfast, and a welcome cocktail, costs around C$230 per person. ⊠ *Duchesnay Ecotourism Station, 143 route Duchesnay, Ste-Catherine-de-la-Jacques-Cartier, (about 20 mins west of Québec City)* ☏ *418/875–4522 or 877/505–0423* ⊕ *www.icehotel-canada.com.*

☾ **Jardin Zoologique du Québec** (Québec Zoological Gardens). This zoo is especially scenic because of the DuBerger River, which traverses the grounds. Opened in 1931 as an experimental farm that raised and displayed fur-bearing animals, it was reopened in 2003 after a major overhaul. Gone is the zoo's traditional collection of animals, and in its place are 380 species, almost half of which are birds. The new zoo gives the animals more natural living environments and the visitor better places to watch the animals. You can walk among lemurs in the African Garden, or stroll among flamingos in the Parrot Garden. At one fabulous twice-daily show, birds of prey swoop over visitors in the outdoor amphitheater. A huge climate-controlled greenhouse shelters Asian birds along with tree kangaroos and bearded dragons. ⊠ *9300 rue de la Faune, Charlesbourg* ☏ *418/622–0312* ⊕ *www.jardinzoologique.ca* ▧ *C$15* ⊙ *Daily 10–5.*

⑲ Maison J. A. Moisan. Founded in 1871 by Jean-Alfred Moisan, this store claims the title of the oldest grocery store in North America. The original display cases, woodwork, and tin ceilings preserve the old-time feel. The store's many products include difficult-to-find delicacies from other regions of Québec. ☒ *699 rue St-Jean, St. Jean Baptiste* ☎ *418/522–0685* ⊕ *www.jamoisan.com* ⊘ *Sept.–June 8:30–9; July and Aug., 8:30–10.*

need a break?   **La Piazzeta** (☒ 707 rue St-Jean, St. Jean Baptiste ☎ 418/529–7489), with its delicious thin-crust square pizzas, is just one of the many good and affordable restaurants along the stretch of rue St-Jean near Maison J. A. Moisan.

⑰ Observatoire de la Capitale. This observation gallery is atop Edifice Marie-Guyart, Québec City's tallest office building. The gray, modern concrete tower, 31 stories tall, has by far the best view of the city and the surrounding area. ☒ *1037 rue de la Chevrotière, Montcalm* ☎ *418/644–9841* ☜ *C$5* ⊘ *Late June–mid-Oct., daily 10–5; mid-Oct.–late June, Tues.–Sun. 10–5.*

☺ Parc Aquarium du Québec. Like the zoo, Quebec City's aquarium reopened in 2003 after a great deal of work. Next to the Québec Bridge on the heights that overlook the St. Lawrence River and about 10 km (6 mi) from the city center, the 16-acre site contains 3,500 specimens drawn from as near as the river's estuary and as far as the Arctic. The aquarium's centerpiece is a massive three-level aquatic gallery of fresh- and saltwater animals and plants. It is the only aquarium in North America with examples of all five species of cold-water seals. Other mammals on display include polar bears and a walrus. ☒ *1675 av. des Hôtels, Ste-Foy* ☎ *418/659–5264* ⊕ *www.parcaquarium.ca* ☜ *C$15* ⊘ *Daily 10–5.*

★ ☞ ⑮ Parliament Buildings. Erected between 1877 and 1884, these structures are the seat of the Assemblée Nationale (the National Assembly) of 125 provincial representatives. Québec architect Eugène-Étienne Taché designed the stately buildings in the late-17th-century Renaissance style of Louis XIV, with four wings set in a square around an interior court. On the front of the Parliament, statues pay tribute to important figures of Québec history: Cartier, Champlain, Frontenac, Wolfe, and Montcalm. A 30-minute tour (in English, French, or Spanish) takes in the President's Gallery, the Parlementaire restaurant, the Legislative Council Chamber, and the National Assembly Chamber, which is blue, white, and gold. ☒ *Av. Honoré-Mercier and Grande Allée, Door 3, Montcalm* ☎ *418/643–7239* ⊕ *www.assnat.qc.ca* ☜ *Free* ⊘ *Guided tours weekdays 9–4:30; late June–early Sept. also open weekends 10–4:30.*

㉑ Promenade des Premiers Ministres. This walk has a series of panels that tell the story (in French) of the premiers who have led the province and their contributions to its development. Because of strong winds, the panels are taken down in winter. ☒ *Parallel to blvd. René-Lévesque Est between rue de la Chevrotière and the Parliament Buildings, Montcalm* ⊘ *Closed in winter, usually Nov.–Feb.*

LOOKING DOWN ON QUÉBEC

FOR A BIRD'S-EYE VIEW OF THE WHOLE CITY, go to the Observatoire de la Capitale, the observation deck on the 31st floor of the Marie-Guyart Building, a five-minute walk from the National Assembly. At 210 meters (750 feet) above sea level, the glassed-in deck is the highest perch in Quéebc City, a place for superb views of the copper roofs and architectural gems of the Upper Town, which is at your feet, to the east. Looking south, you can peek inside the Citadelle, the still-active military garrison built by the British to thwart 19th-century American expansionists, and even stare at the Appalachian Mountains (and the Maine border) on the distant horizon.

To the near west, watch the lunchtime throngs of people on the Grande-Allée, Québec City's café-lined version of the Champs d'Élysée, or admire the elm-lined splendor of Québec's most chic residential avenues. To the north, you can see the suburbs of Beauport and Charlesbourg, which are hemmed in by the Laurentians, one of the Earth's oldest mountain chains. Looking northeast, look for the historic villages of the Cote-de-Beaupré, the ski trails at Mont-Ste-Anne, and Île d'Orléans, which is chock-full of pick-your-own fruit farms, sugar camps, and New France history and architecture. Looking down, you'll see the St. Charles River, part of Lower Town, and all of both the Faubourg and St. Jean Baptiste, two lively neighborhoods where downtown residents shop and eat, and gays and lesbians party.

If you're afraid of heights, or want a more horizontal perspective than the Observatory can provide, head to the Terrasse Dufferin in Upper Town. Starting next to the Château Frontenac, the terrace stretches almost a half-mile to the Plains of Abraham, passing under the imposing stone walls of the Citadelle. From the terrace you can get a commanding view of both the St. Lawrence and the countryside to the south, east, and north. Directly below is Quartier Petit-Champlain. Accessible from the terrace by a series of perilously steep staircases or via funicular, the tiny neighborhood is home to Place Royale and rue Petit Champlain, a narrow street full of souvenir stores that's often jammed with tourists. On the St. Lawrence, ferries glide back and forth, and cruise ships and Great Lakes freighters put in at the harbor below.

To get a better appreciation of the split-level landscape of the Old City, take the Lower Town ferry to Lévis on the south shore of the St. Lawrence, directly opposite Québec City. From Lévis you can get an unparalleled view of both Old Québec and the city's modern skyline—it will soon become clear why the most famous paintings of Québec City have been done from here.

⑳ St. Matthew's Cemetery. The burial place of many of the earliest English settlers in Canada was established in 1771 and is the oldest cemetery remaining in Québec City. Also buried here is Robert Wood, the disavowed half-brother of Queen Victoria. Closed in 1860, the cemetery has been turned into a park. Next door is **St. Matthew's Anglican Church,** now a public library. It has a book listing most of the original tombstone inscriptions, including those on tombstones removed to make way for the city's modern convention center. ✉ *755 rue St-Jean, St. Jean Baptiste* ☎ *No phone.*

WHERE TO EAT

Most restaurants here have a selection of dishes available à la carte, but more creative specialties are often found on the table d'hôte, a two- to four-course meal chosen daily by the chef. This can also be an economical way to order a full meal. At dinner many restaurants will offer a *menu dégustation* (tasting menu), a five- to seven-course dinner of the chef's finest creations. In French-speaking Québec City, an *entrée,* as the name suggests, is an entry into a meal, or an appetizer. It is followed by a *plat principal,* the main dish. Lunch generally costs about 30% less than dinner, and many of the same dishes are available. Lunch is usually served 11:30 to 2:30, dinner 6:30 until about 11. Tip at least 15% of the bill.

Reservations are necessary for most restaurants during peak season, May through September, as well as on holidays and during Winter Carnival, in January and/or February.

WHAT IT COSTS In Canadian dollars				
	$$$$	**$$$**	**$$**	**$**	**¢**
AT DINNER	over C$30	C$20–C$30	C$12–C$20	C$8–C$12	under C$8

Prices are per person for a main course.

Upper Town

Cafés

★ ✕ **Casse-Crêpe Breton.** Crepes in generous proportions are served in this busy café-style restaurant. From a menu of more than 20 fillings, pick your own chocolate or fruit combinations; design a larger meal with cheese, ham, and vegetables; or sip a bowl of Viennese coffee topped with whipped cream. Many tables surround three round griddles at which you watch your creations being made. Crepes made with two to five fillings cost less than C$7. This place is popular with tourists and locals alike, and there can be lines to get in at peak hours and seasons. ✉ *1136 rue St-Jean, Upper Town* ☎ *418/692–0438* ⌚ *Reservations not accepted* ▭ *No credit cards.*

¢–$$ ✕ **Rôtisserie Ste-Angèle.** A 1780 building tucked away on a quiet street off busy rue St-Jean houses this two-story café with stone floors. In summer you can eat in the secluded garden, where birds flutter among the trees. The specialty is chicken, but the inexpensive dishes also include

ON THE MENU IN QUÉBEC CITY

Québec's finest restaurants, found both inside and outside the city's walls, serve contemporary fare, often with Asian or Italian as well as French and Québecois influences. There are still fine French restaurants, though, and you can sample French-Canadian cuisine composed of robust, uncomplicated dishes that make use of the region's bounty of foods, including fowl and wild game (quail, caribou, venison), maple syrup, and various berries and nuts. Other specialties include creton (pâtés), tourtière (meat pie), and tarte au sucre (maple-syrup pie).

sandwiches, tasty ribs, pasta, and pizza. ⊠ *32 rue Ste-Angèle, Upper Town* 🕾 *418/694–3339* ☱ *AE, D, DC, MC, V.*

¢–$ ✕ **Brulerie Tatum.** Piles of coffee beans and an old coffee grinder in the window signal this lively café's specialty, and the smell of coffee roasting permeates the brightly colored main floor and mezzanine. Along with more than 50 different types of coffee are 30 kinds of tea. Brulerie is a favorite with students and shoppers, who come for their daily fix as well as for soup, sandwiches, salads, and desserts. It's also popular at breakfast for its omelets, crepes, and such dishes as egg in phyllo pastry with hollandaise sauce and potatoes and fruit. ⊠ *1084 rue St-Jean, Upper Town* 🕾 *418/692–3900* ☱ *AE, D, MC, V.*

¢ ✕ **Le Temporel.** At this small, crowded, smoky café, city dwellers of all sorts—struggling writers, marginal musicians, street-smart bohemians, bureaucrats, businessmen, and busy moms and dads—enjoy the city's best coffee, not to mention its best *croque monsieurs* (open-face French-bread sandwiches with ham, tomato, and broiled cheese), chili, and soups. Good, modestly priced beer and wine are also served. Some patrons start their day here with croissants and coffee at 7 AM, and are still here when the place closes at 1:30 AM (an hour later on Friday and Saturday). If you want to meet someone glad to explain why so many Quebeckers want to separate from the rest of Canada, this is the place. ⊠ *25 rue Couillard, Upper Town* 🕾 *418/694–1813* ⌦ *Reservations not accepted* ☱ *V.*

Canadian

$$–$$$$ ✕ **Aux Anciens Canadiens.** This establishment is named for a 19th-century book by Philippe-Aubert de Gaspé, who once resided here. The house, dating from 1675, has servers in period costume and five dining rooms with different themes. For example, the *vaisselier* (dish room) is bright and cheerful, with colorful antique dishes and a fireplace. People come for the authentic French-Canadian cooking; hearty specialties include duck in a maple glaze, Lac St-Jean meat pie, and maple-syrup pie with

fresh cream. One of the best deals is a three-course meal for C$14.75, served from noon until 5:45. ⊠ *34 rue St-Louis, Upper Town* ☎ *418/ 692–1627* ⊟ *AE, DC, MC, V.*

Chinese

$–$$ ✕ **L'Elysée Mandarin.** A 19th-century home has been transformed into an elegant Chinese mandarin's garden where you can sip jasmine tea to the strains of soothing Asian music. Owner David Tsui uses rosewood and imported stones from China to emulate his native Yanchao, a city near Shanghai known for training great chefs. Among the restaurant's Szechuan specialties are beef fillets with orange flavoring and crispy chicken in ginger sauce. The crispy duck with five spices is also delicious. ⊠ *65 rue d'Auteuil, Upper Town* ☎ *418/692–0909* ⊟ *AE, DC, MC, V.*

Continental

$$$–$$$$ ✕ **Le Continental.** If Québec City had a dining hall of fame, Le Continental would be there among the best. Since 1956, the Sgobba family has been serving very good traditional dishes. Deep-blue walls, mahogany paneling, and crisp white tablecloths create a stately air, and house specialties such as orange duckling and filet mignon are flambéed right at your table. ⊠ *26 rue St-Louis, Upper Town* ☎ *418/694–9995* ⊟ *AE, D, DC, MC, V.*

French

$$$–$$$$ ✕ **À la Bastille Chez Bahüaud.** Whether you dine surrounded by modern
Fodor'sChoice art inside the old stone house or, in summer, shaded by trees in one of
★ the Old City's rare gardens, you'll be eating some of the best food in the city. Chef Patrick Schmidt's innovative dishes include loin of lamb accompanied by *gremolata* (chopped lemon zest, parsley, and garlic) and cheese polenta, and spicy shrimp in a lemon-grapefruit sauce. Be sure to try one of the delicious desserts, like the *tentation au chocolat noir et blanc*—a dark-chocolate cup filled with white-chocolate fondant. ⊠ *47 av. Ste-Geneviève, Upper Town* ☎ *418/692–2544* ⊛ *Reservations essential* ⊟ *AE, D, DC, MC, V* ☾ *Closed Mon. No lunch Oct.–May.*

$$$–$$$$ ✕ **Le Saint-Amour.** Light spills in through an airy atrium at one of the city's most romantic restaurants. The acclaimed chef and co-owner Jean-Luc Boulay entices diners with such creations as caribou steak grilled with a wild-berry and peppercorn sauce, and filet mignon with port wine and local blue cheese. Sauces are generally light, with no flour or butter. Desserts are inspired; try the white-chocolate flower bud accompanied by a maple cream cup, white-wine ice cream, and vanilla sauce. The C$80 menu has nine courses; the C$42 table d'hôte has four. More than 800 wines are available. ⊠ *48 rue Ste-Ursule, Upper Town* ☎ *418/ 694–0667* ⊛ *Reservations essential* ⊟ *AE, DC, MC, V.*

$–$$$ ✕ **Les Frères de la Côte.** With its central location, Mediterranean influence, and reasonable prices, this busy bistro is a favorite among politicians and the journalists who cover them. The menu, inspired by the south of France, changes constantly, but osso buco and a tender leg of lamb are among the regular choices. If you sit near the back, you can watch the chefs at work. This kitchen is often among those open the latest. ⊠ *1190 rue St-Jean, Upper Town* ☎ *418/692–5445* ⊟ *AE, D, MC, V.*

Italian

$-$$$ ✗ **Portofino Bistro Italiano.** By joining two 18th-century houses, owner James Monti has created an Italian restaurant with a bistro flavor. The room is distinctive: burnt-sienna walls, soccer flags hanging from the ceiling, a wood pizza oven set behind a semicircular bar, and deep-blue tablecloths and chairs. Don't miss the thin-crust pizza and its accompaniment of oils flavored with pepper and oregano. The *pennini al'arrabiata*—tubular pasta with a spicy tomato sauce—is also good. Save room for the homemade tiramisu. From 3 PM–7 PM the restaurant serves a beer and pizza meal for less than C$11. ✉ *54 rue Couillard, Upper Town* ☎ *418/692–8888* ▤ *AE, D, DC, MC, V.*

Lower Town

Café

$-$$ ✗ **Le Cochon Dingue.** The café fare at this cheerful chain, whose name translates into the Crazy Pig, includes delicious mussels, *steak frites* (steak with french fries), thick soups, and apple pie with maple cream. At the boulevard Champlain location, sidewalk tables and indoor dining rooms artfully blend the chic and the antique; black-and-white checkerboard floors contrast with ancient stone walls. ✉ *46 blvd. Champlain, Lower Town* ☎ *418/692–2013* ✉ *6 rue Cul-de-Sac, Lower Town* ☎ *418/694–0303* ▤ *AE, DC, MC, V.*

Canadian

¢-$ ✗ **Le Buffet de L'Antiquaire.** Hearty home cooking, generous portions, and rock-bottom prices have made this no-frills, diner-style eatery a Lower Town institution. As the name suggests, it's in the heart of the antiques district. In summer it has a small sidewalk terrace where you can sit and watch the shoppers stroll by. It's also a good place to sample traditional Québecois dishes such as tourtière. Desserts, such as the triple-layer orange cake, are homemade and delicious. ✉ *95 rue St-Paul, Lower Town* ☎ *418/692–2661* ▤ *AE, MC, V.*

Contemporary

$$$-$$$$ ✗ **Laurie Raphaël.** One of the city's top dining spots, this restaurant is known
Fodor'sChoice for eclectic recipes that mix classic French cuisine with flavors from else-
★ where. Among chef Daniel Vézina's creations are duck foie gras with cranberry juice and port, and an Australian rack of lamb with a shallot sauce, blue potatoes from Charlevoix, and goat cheese. There's a C$79 seven-course menu dégustation, with wines to complement each course available by the glass. The outside terrace looks tempting, but this is a busy corner with heavy traffic. ✉ *117 rue Dalhousie, Lower Town* ☎ *418/692–4555* ▤ *AE, D, DC, MC, V* ☉ *Closed Sun.–Mon. and Jan. 1–15.*

French

$$$-$$$$ ✗ **L'Initiale.** Sophistication and gracious service place L'Initiale in good
Fodor'sChoice standing to rival great tables the world over. The simple lines and light
★ colors are modern, and widely spaced tables favor intimate dining. Chef Yvan Lebrun roasts many of the meats on the menu over a spit: this produces a unique taste, particularly with lamb. The constantly changing menu follows the whims of the chef and the season. Try the *escalope de*

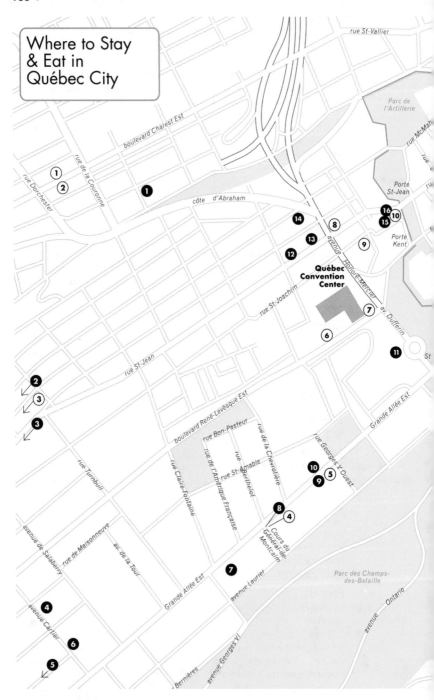

Where to Stay
& Eat in
Québec City

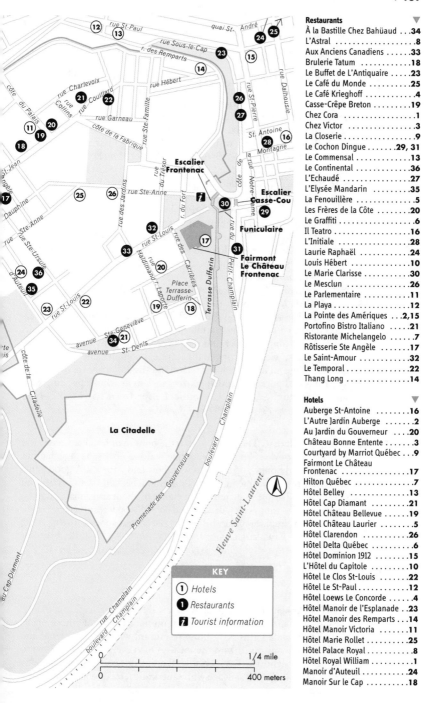

Restaurants ▼

À la Bastille Chez Bahüaud . . . **34**
L'Astral **8**
Aux Anciens Canadiens . . . **33**
Brulerie Tatum **18**
Le Buffet de L'Antiquaire **23**
Le Café du Monde **25**
Le Café Krieghoff **4**
Casse-Crêpe Breton **19**
Chez Cora **1**
Chez Victor **3**
La Closerie **9**
Le Cochon Dingue **29, 31**
Le Commensal **13**
Le Continental **36**
L'Echaudé **27**
L'Elysée Mandarin **35**
La Fenouillère **5**
Les Frères de la Côte **20**
Le Graffiti **6**
Il Teatro **16**
L'Initiale **28**
Laurie Raphaël **24**
Louis Hébert **10**
Le Marie Clarisse **30**
Le Mesclun **26**
Le Parlementaire **11**
La Playa **12**
La Pointe des Amériques . . . **2,15**
Portofino Bistro Italiano **21**
Ristorante Michelangelo **7**
Rôtisserie Ste Angèle **17**
Le Saint-Amour **32**
Le Temporal **22**
Thang Long **14**

Hotels ▼

Auberge St-Antoine **16**
L'Autre Jardin Auberge **2**
Au Jardin du Gouverneur **20**
Château Bonne Entente **3**
Courtyard by Marriot Québec . . . **9**
Fairmont Le Château
Frontenac **17**
Hilton Québec **7**
Hôtel Belley **13**
Hôtel Cap Diamant **21**
Hôtel Château Bellevue **19**
Hôtel Château Laurier **5**
Hôtel Clarendon **26**
Hôtel Delta Québec **6**
Hôtel Dominion 1912 . . . . **15**
L'Hôtel du Capitole **10**
Hôtel Le Clos St-Louis **22**
Hôtel Le St-Paul **12**
Hôtel Loews Le Concorde **4**
Hôtel Manoir de l'Esplanade . . **23**
Hôtel Manoir des Remparts . . . **14**
Hôtel Manoir Victoria **11**
Hôtel Marie Rollet **25**
Hôtel Palace Royal **8**
Hôtel Royal William **1**
Manoir d'Auteuil **24**
Manoir Sur le Cap **18**

(scallop of) foie gras or the lamb. There's also a C$76 eight-course menu dégustation. For dessert, many small treats are arranged attractively on a single plate. ⊠ *54 rue St-Pierre, Lower Town* ☎ *418/694–1818* ▭ *AE, DC, MC, V.*

$$–$$$$ ✕ **L'Echaudé.** A chic beige-and-green bistro, L'Echaudé attracts a mix of business people and tourists because of its location between the financial and antiques districts. Lunch offerings include duck confit with french fries and fresh salad. Highlights of the three-course brunch are eggs Benedict and tantalizing desserts. The decor is modern, with hardwood floors, a mirrored wall, and a stainless-steel bar where you can dine atop a high stool. ⊠ *73 Sault-au-Matelot, Lower Town* ☎ *418/ 692–1299* ▭ *AE, DC, MC, V* ☺ *No Sun. brunch mid-Oct.–mid-May.*

$$–$$$ ✕ **Le Mesclun.** When Frédéric Casadei and Cendrine Bailly vacationed in Québec City in 2000, they fell so much in love with the city that they moved here. Now they combine their love of the city with their love of Provençal cuisine in this sunny restaurant, tucked away on a side street in Lower Town. Trained at Thonons-les-Bains, the oldest hotel school in France, Casadei specializes in such dishes as duck in peppercorn sauce, daube (stew) Provençal, bouillabaisse, and crème brûlée with vanilla. ⊠ *93 Sault-au-Matelot, Lower Town* ☎ *418/692–0600* ▭ *AE, MC, V* ☺ *Closed Sun.–Mon. Nov.–May; lunch served Mon.–Tues.*

★ $$ ✕ **Le Café du Monde.** Next to the cruise terminal in the Old Port, this restaurant has a view to equal its food. The outdoor terrace in front overlooks the St. Lawrence River, while the side *verrière* (glass atrium) looks onto l'Agora amphitheater and the old stone Customs House. Etched-glass dividers, wicker chairs, and palm trees complement the Parisian-bistro-style menu, which includes such classics as duck confit accompanied by garlic-fried potatoes, and appetizers such as artichoke pudding with smoked salmon. ⊠ *84 rue Dalhousie, Lower Town* ☎ *418/692–4455* ⌂ *Reservations essential* ▭ *AE, DC, MC, V.*

Seafood

$$–$$$$ ✕ **Le Marie Clarisse.** This restaurant at the bottom of Escalier Casse-Cou near Place Royale is known for unique seafood dishes, such as halibut with nuts and honey and scallops with port and paprika. A good game dish is usually on the menu, such as a deer and beef duo with berries and sweet garlic. The menu du jour has a choice of about seven main courses; dinner includes soup, salad, dessert, and coffee. Wood-beam ceilings, stone walls, and a fireplace make this one of the coziest spots in town. ⊠ *12 rue du Petit-Champlain, Lower Town* ☎ *418/692–0857* ⌂ *Reservations essential* ▭ *AE, DC, MC, V* ☺ *No lunch weekends Oct.–Apr.*

Outside the Walls

Café

¢ ✕ **Le Café Krieghoff.** Modeled after a typical Paris bistro café and named for a Canadian painter who lived just up the street (and whose prints hang on the walls), this busy, noisy restaurant with patios in front and back is a popular place with the locals. Open every day from 7 AM to midnight, Krieghoff serves specialties that include coffee, croissants, "la Toulouse" (big French sausage with sauerkraut), steak with french fries, spinach pie, *boudin* (pig-blood sausage), and "la Bavette" (a French-style minute steak). ✉ *1089 rue Cartier, Montcalm* ☎ *418/522–3711* ▭ *DC, MC, V.*

Contemporary

$$$–$$$$ ✕ **L'Astral.** A spectacular view of Québec City is the chief attraction at this revolving restaurant atop the Hôtel Loews Le Concorde. Chef Jean-Claude Crouzet makes use of local products—fillet of pork from the Beauce region in soy and orange sauce with pearl barley, braised-celeriac stew, and fried leeks, for example, or Barbarie duck with honey and Szechuan pepper, turnip confit, and red cabbage with apples. L'Astral offers a three-course table d'hôte and a C$40 nightly buffet, but no à la carte menu. ✉ *1225 Cours du Général-de Montcalm , Montcalm* ☎ *418/647–2222* ▭ *AE, D, DC, MC, V.*

★ $–$$ ✕ **Le Parlementaire.** Despite its magnificent Beaux Arts interior and its reasonable prices, the National Assembly's restaurant remains one of the best-kept secrets in town. Chef Réal Therrien prepares contemporary cuisine with products from Québec's various regions. In summer, for example, the three-course lunch menu includes everything from mini-fondues made with Charlevoix cheese to ravioli made from lobster caught in the Gaspé. Other dishes might include pork from the Beauce region, trout from the Magdalen Islands, and candied-duck salad. The restaurant's typical hours are 8–11 for breakfast and 11:30–2 for lunch. Opening hours may change when the National Assembly is in session in the fall and spring, and the restaurant sometimes opens for supper during late-evening debates. Call ahead. ✉ *Av. Honoré-Mercier and Grande Allée Est, Door 3, Montcalm* ☎ *418/643–6640* ▭ *AE, MC, V* ☉ *Closed weekends June 24–Labor Day; closed Sat.–Mon. Labor Day–June 23; usually no dinner.*

Eclectic

$–$$ ✕ **La Playa.** The more than 90 different martinis and a brick-walled courtyard terrace that's heated in spring and fall make this restaurant on rue St-Jean a popular choice. A West Coast influence is evident in the cuisine and in the design. Pasta can be combined with any of 28 sauces, including the Bangkok, with shrimp, chicken, peanuts, and coconut sauce, or the Île d'Orléans, with smoked duck and goat cheese. ✉ *780 rue St-Jean, St. Jean Baptiste* ☎ *418/522–3989* ▭ *AE, DC, MC, V* ☉ *Closed Mon. Nov.–Apr.*

★ ¢–$ ✕ **Chez Cora.** Spectacular breakfasts with mounds of fresh fruit are the specialty at this sunny chain restaurant. Whimsy is everywhere, from the plastic chicken decorations to the inventive dishes, often named after customers and family members who inspired them. Try the Eggs Ben et Dictine, which has smoked salmon, or the Gargantua—two eggs, sausage, ham, pancakes, *cretons* (pâtés), and baked beans. Kids love the Banana Surprise, a banana wrapped in a pancake with chocolate or peanut butter and honey. The restaurant also serves light lunch fare, such as salads and sandwiches. ✉ *545 rue de l'Église, St. Roch* ☎ *418/524–3232* ▭ *AE, DC, MC, V* ☉ *No dinner.*

Fast Food

¢–$ ✕ **Chez Victor.** It's no ordinary burger joint: this cozy café with brick and stone walls attracts an arty crowd to rue St-Jean. Lettuce, tomatoes, onions, mushrooms, pickles, hot mustard, mayonnaise, and a choice of cheeses (mozzarella, Swiss, blue, goat, and cream) top the hearty burgers. French fries are served with a dollop of mayonnaise and poppy seeds. Salads, sandwiches, and a daily dessert are also available. ✉ *145 rue St-Jean, St. Jean Baptiste* ☎ *418/529–7702* ▭ *MC, V.*

French

★ $$$ ✕ **La Fenouillère.** Although this restaurant is connected to a standard chain hotel, inside there's an elegant, spacious dining room with a view of the Pierre Laporte Bridge. Chefs Yvon Godbout and Bernard St. Pierre serve a constantly rotating table d'hôte, going out of their way to use seasonal products. The house specialty is salmon, but lamb is also popular among the restaurant's regulars. ✉ *Hotel Best Western Aristocrate, 3100 chemin St-Louis, Ste-Foy* ☎ *418/653–3886* ▭ *AE, DC, MC, V.*

$$$ ✕ **Louis Hébert.** With its fine French cuisine and convenient location on the bustling Grande Allée, this restaurant has long been popular with many of Québec's top decision-makers. Dining areas range from the very public summer terrace to discreet second-floor meeting rooms, a solarium with bamboo chairs, and a cozy dining room with exposed stone walls and warm wood accents. In winter, chef Hervé Toussaint's roast lamb in a nut crust with Stilton and port is a favorite. In summer, seafood dishes such as lobster and fresh pasta with a lobster sauce and asparagus are popular. ✉ *668 Grande Allée Est, Montcalm* ☎ *418/525–7812* ▭ *AE, D, DC, MC, V* ☉ *No lunch weekends Oct.–Apr.*

$$–$$$ ✕ **La Closerie.** In 2003 acclaimed chef-owner Jacques LePluart returned from France to relaunch two restaurants, both named La Closerie, in the Hôtel Château Laurier. In the spacious, more elegant Grande Table dining room, rich sauces enhance such dishes as *magret de canard aux cerises séchées* (duck breast with dried-cherry sauce). A casserole of scallops and lobster roe comes with crunchy vegetables in rice vinegar. For dessert, try the delicious white-chocolate mille-feuille with fresh cherries. The kitchen also supplies the slightly less expensive French bistro, which has dining on the ✉ *1220 pl. Georges V Ouest, Montcalm* ☎ *418/523–9975* ▭ *AE, DC, MC, V.*

$$–$$$ ✕ **Le Graffiti.** Housed in an upscale food mall, this French restaurant with tiny lights roped around the ceiling is a good alternative to Vieux-Québec dining. Large windows look out onto avenue Cartier. The seasonal menu lists such dishes as deer flank with oyster mushrooms in red wine sauce, and veal medallions with apples in a calvados sauce. The table d'hôte is priced at between C$21.50 and C$31.75 per person. ✉ *1191 av. Cartier, Montcalm* ☎ *418/529–4949* ▭ *AE, DC, MC, V* ☉ *No lunch Sat.*

Italian

$$$–$$$$ ✕ **Ristorante Michelangelo.** Don't be put off by the funeral-home appearance of this first-class restaurant. One of only a handful of eateries outside Italy recognized as a genuine Italian restaurant by the Italian government, Michelangelo's has a menu with many succulent meat, pasta, and seafood dishes. Among the house's specialties are *côte de veau* (veal cut-

lets), *escalopes de veau* (veal scallops), and homemade pasta. The restaurant also has the city's largest wine cellar, with some 18,000 bottles. There's also an impressive dessert table. ✉ *3111 Chemin Saint-Louis, Sainte Foy* ☎ *418/651–6262* ☐ *AE, DC, MC, V* ☉ *Closed Sun.; no lunch Sat.*

$$-$$$$ ✕ **Il Teatro.** Celebrities show up regularly at this upscale Italian restaurant just outside the St. Jean gate. The person sitting at the next table may be singing on stage at the adjacent Capitole theater after dinner, or be in town to promote his or her latest record, film, or play. The drama is enhanced by royal-blue curtains and cherry-red chairs. Pastas are made on-site. Try the spaghetti with scampi or the osso buco *d'agnello alle erbe* (braised lamb shanks with herbs). ✉ *972 rue St-Jean, Carré d'Youville* ☎ *418/694–9996* ⬥ *Reservations essential* ☐ *AE, DC, MC, V.*

Pan-Asian

$-$$ ✕ **Thang Long.** Low prices and some of the best Asian food in the city ensure this restaurant's popularity. The simple menu of Vietnamese, Chinese, Thai, and Japanese dishes has a few surprises. *Chakis,* for example, is a tasty fried appetizer of four wrappers filled with shrimp, onions, and sugared potatoes. Thang Long doesn't serve any alcohol, but you can bring your own (SAQ, the government liquor store, is two blocks up the hill on rue St-Jean). Chinese lanterns and dark-blue walls and tablecloths decorate this tiny spot. ✉ *869 Côte d'Abraham, St. Jean Baptiste* ☎ *418/524–0572* ⬥ *Reservations essential* ☐ *MC, V* ⬚ *BYOB* ☉ *No lunch weekends.*

Pizza

$-$$$ ✕ **La Pointe des Amériques.** Adventurous pizza lovers should explore the fare at this bistro. Some pizza combos (like alligator, smoked Gouda, Cajun sauce, and hot peppers) are strange. But don't worry—there are more than 27 different pizzas as well as meat and pasta dishes, soups, salads, and Southwestern cuisine. The original brick walls of the century-old building just outside the St-Jean Gate contrast boldly with modern mirrors and artsy wrought-iron lighting. Connected to the downtown restaurant is the Biloxi Bar, which has the same menu. ✉ *964 rue St-Jean, Carré d'Youville* ☎ *418/694–1199* ✉ *2815 blvd. Laurier, Ste-Foy* ☎ *418/658–2583* ☐ *AE, DC, MC, V.*

Vegetarian

$ ✕ **Le Commensal.** At this upscale cafeteria, you serve yourself from an outstanding informal vegetarian buffet and then grab a table in the vast dining room, where brick walls and green plants add a touch of class. Plates are weighed to determine the price. Hot and cold dishes, all health conscious in some way, include stir-fry tofu and ratatouille with couscous. ✉ *860 rue St-Jean, St. Jean Baptiste* ☎ *418/647–3733* ☐ *AE, DC, MC, V* ⬚ *BYOB.*

WHERE TO STAY

More than 35 hotels are within Québec City's walls, and there is also an abundance of family-run bed-and-breakfasts. Landmark hotels are as prominent as the city's most historic sights; modern high-rises outside the ramparts have spectacular views of the old city. Another choice is to immerse yourself in the city's historic charm by staying in an old-fashioned inn, where no two rooms are alike.

Be sure to make a reservation if you visit during peak season (May through September) or during the Winter Carnival, in January and/or February.

Prices

During especially busy times, hotel rates usually rise 30%. From November through April, many lodgings offer weekend discounts and other promotions.

WHAT IT COSTS In Canadian dollars				
	$$$$	$$$	$$	$	¢
FOR 2 PEOPLE	over C$250	C$175–C$250	C$125–C$175	C$75–C$125	under C$75

Prices are for a standard double room in high season; they exclude 7.5% provincial sales tax, 7% goods-and-services tax (GST), and a C$2.30 city tax.

Upper Town

$$–$$$$ ▦ **Fairmont Le Château Frontenac.** Towering above the St. Lawrence River, the Château Frontenac is a Québec City landmark. Its public rooms—from the intimate piano bar to the 700-seat ballroom reminiscent of the Hall of Mirrors at Versailles—are all opulent. Rooms are elegantly furnished, but some are small; some have views of the river. At Le Champlain, classic French cuisine is served by waitstaff in traditional French costumes. This hotel is a tourist attraction in its own right, so the lobby can be quite busy. Reserve well in advance, especially for late June to mid-October. ⊠ *1 rue des Carrières, Upper Town, G1R 4P5* ☎ *418/692–3861 or 800/441–1414* 🖷 *418/692–1751* ⊕ *www.fairmont. com* 🛏 *585 rooms, 33 suites* ♨ *2 restaurants, snack bar, room service, in-room data ports, some in-room hot tubs, minibars, cable TV with movies and video games, indoor pool, wading pool, health club, hair salon, spa, piano bar, shops, babysitting, dry cleaning, laundry service, concierge, concierge floors, Internet, business services, convention center, parking (fee), some pets allowed* ▤ *AE, D, DC, MC, V* ⑩ *EP.*

$$–$$$$ ▦ **Hôtel Manoir Victoria.** A discreet, old-fashioned entrance leads you into this European-style hotel with a good fitness center. Victorian- and Regency-style furnishings decorate the large, wood-paneled foyer. Standard hotel furnishings fill the rooms, but three rooms and three suites have whirlpool baths and electric fireplaces. ⊠ *44 côte du Palais, Upper Town, G1R 4H8* ☎ *418/692–1030 or 800/463–6283* 🖷 *418/692–3822* ⊕ *www. manoir-victoria.com* 🛏 *142 rooms, 3 suites* ♨ *2 restaurants, room service, in-room data ports, some in-room hot tubs, minibars, cable TV with movies and video games, indoor pool, health club, hair salon, massage, sauna, babysitting, dry cleaning, concierge, Internet, meeting rooms, parking (fee), no-smoking rooms* ▤ *AE, D, DC, MC, V* ⑩ *EP.*

$$$ ▦ **Hôtel Le Clos St-Louis.** Winding staircases and crystal chandeliers add to the Victorian elegance of this central inn made up of two 1845-era houses. All of the rooms have antiques or reproductions; some have romantic four-poster or sleigh beds; eight have decorative fireplaces. If you stay on the main floor you can avoid having to climb the steep stairs. ✉ *69 rue St-Louis, Upper Town, G1R 3Z2* ☎ *418/694–1311 or 800/ 461–1311* 🖷 *418/694–9411* ⊕ *www.clossaintlouis.com* ➦ *16 rooms, 2 suites* ♿ *In-room data ports, some in-room hot tubs, cable TV, parking (fee); no a/c in some rooms, no phones in some rooms, no TV in some rooms, no smoking* ▭ *AE, MC, V* ⦿ *CP.*

$$–$$$ ⌖ **Hôtel Château Bellevue.** Behind the Château Frontenac, this 1898 hotel has comfortable accommodations at reasonable prices in a good location. Guest rooms are modern, with standard hotel furnishings; many have a view of the St. Lawrence River. The rooms vary considerably in size (many are a bit cramped), and package deals are available. ✉ *16 rue de la Porte, Upper Town, G1R 4M9* ☎ *418/692–2573 or 800/463– 2617* 🖷 *418/692–4876* ⊕ *www.old-quebec.com/bellevue* ➦ *58 rooms* ♿ *In-room data ports, cable TV, dry cleaning, meeting room, free parking* ▭ *AE, D, DC, MC, V* ⦿ *EP.*

$$–$$$ ⌖ **Hôtel Clarendon.** Built in 1866, the Clarendon is the oldest operating hotel in Québec City, and now it's been refurbished in art-deco and art-nouveau styles, most notably in the public areas. Some guest rooms have period touches, and some are more modern. Half the rooms have excellent views of Old Québec; the others overlook a courtyard. ✉ *57 rue Ste-Anne, Upper Town, G1R 3X4* ☎ *418/692–2480 or 888/554–6001* 🖷 *418/692–4652* ⊕ *www.hotelclarendon.com* ➦ *138 rooms, 5 suites* ♿ *Restaurant, café, room service, in-room data ports, some in-room hot tubs, cable TV with movies and video games, massage, spa, bar, meeting rooms, parking (fee)* ▭ *AE, D, DC, MC, V* ⦿ *EP.*

★ $$ ⌖ **Hôtel Cap Diamant.** An eclectic collection of vintage furniture and ecclesiastical accents—stained glass from a church, a confessional door, even the odd angel—complement the decorative marble fireplaces, stone walls, and hardwood floors at this hotel made up of two adjacent 1826 houses. In the morning you can bring coffee, orange juice, and muffins to your room or dine in a sunroom that overlooks one of the Old City's few gardens. Stairs to third-floor rooms are a bit steep, but there is a baggage lift. ✉ *39 av. Ste-Geneviève, Upper Town, G1R 4B3* ☎ *418/ 694–0313* 🖷 *418/694–1187* ⊕ *www.hcapdiamant.qc.ca* ➦ *12 rooms* ♿ *Refrigerators, cable TV, dry cleaning, laundry service, Internet; no room phones, no smoking* ▭ *MC, V* ⦿ *CP.*

$–$$ ⌖ **Hôtel Marie Rollet.** In the heart of Vieux-Québec, this intimate little inn built in 1876 by the Ursuline Order has warm woodwork and antique charm to match its surroundings. It's one of the few hotels in the Old City to have two rooms with working fireplaces. Some bathrooms are so tiny, the sink is in the bedroom. Steep stairs lead to a rooftop terrace with a garden view. ✉ *81 rue Ste-Anne, Upper Town, G1R 3X4* ☎ *418/ 694–9271 or 800/275–0338* ⊕ *www.hotelmarierollet.com* ➦ *10 rooms* ♿ *Cable TV, parking (fee); no room phones, no smoking* ▭ *MC, V* ⦿ *EP.*

$–$$ ⌖ **Manoir d'Auteuil.** One of the more lavish manors in town, this lodging was originally a private house. A major renovation in the 1950s reinstated many of its art-deco and art-nouveau details. An ornate sculpted iron banister wraps up through four floors (note that there is no elevator), and guest rooms blend modern design with the art-deco structure. Each room is different; one was once a chapel, and two have a tiny staircase leading to their bathrooms. Two rooms have showers with seven showerheads. Rooms on the fourth floor are smaller, but are less expensive and come with great views of the Parliament Buildings. ⊠ *49 rue d'Auteuil, Upper Town, G1R 4C2* ☎ *418/694–1173* 🖷 *418/694– 0081* ⊕ *www.quebecweb.com/dauteuil* ⇆ *16 rooms* ♨ *In-room data ports, cable TV, babysitting, dry cleaning, laundry service, parking (fee); no smoking* ⊟ *AE, D, DC, MC, V* ¶⊙¶ *CP.*

$–$$ ▦ **Manoir Sur le Cap.** No two rooms are alike in this elegant 19th-century inn with beautiful views of Governors' Park and the St. Lawrence River. Built in 1837 as a private home, it was severely damaged in 1849 by a major fire in the neighborhood. It was rebuilt the same year by George Mellis Douglas, the medical superintendent at Grosse Île. Rooms are light and airy, with antiques and hardwood floors. Some have brass beds, brick walls, or small balconies. Note that some bathrooms have only showers and no tubs, and that one room is in the basement. There's also no elevator. ⊠ *9 av. Ste-Geneviève, Upper Town, G1R 4A7* ☎ *418/694– 1987 or 866/694–1987* 🖷 *418/627–7405* ⊕ *www.manoir-sur-le-cap.com* ⇆ *11 rooms, 3 suites, 1 apartment* ♨ *2 restaurants, fans, some in-room data ports, some microwaves, some refrigerators, cable TV, babysitting; no a/c in some rooms, no phones in some rooms, no smoking* ⊟ *AE, MC, V* ¶⊙¶ *EP.*

$ ▦ **Au Jardin du Gouverneur.** This cream-color stone house with windows trimmed in dark blue is an inexpensive, unpretentious hotel behind the Château Frontenac. Light-wood furnishings and two double beds fill most of the rooms. The stairs are steep leading up to the fourth floor, where many rooms have sinks in the corner and only a shower. ⊠ *16 rue Mont-Carmel, Upper Town, G1R 4A3* ☎ *418/692–1704* 🖷 *418/692–1713* ⊕ *www.quebecweb.com/hjg* ⇆ *16 rooms, 1 suite* ♨ *Cable TV; no room phones, no smoking* ⊟ *AE, MC, V* ¶⊙¶ *CP.*

$ ▦ **Hôtel Manoir de L'Esplanade.** Four 1845 stone houses at the corner of rues d'Auteuil and St-Louis conceal one of the city's best deals: a charming, inexpensive hotel with well-appointed rooms. Rooms have either rich dark-wood furniture or more modern light-wood furniture, and colors and fabrics vary as well. Some rooms have exposed brick walls, a fireplace, and a glass chandelier. The front rooms, facing St. Louis gate, are the most spacious. Those on the 4th floor (no elevator) are right under the eaves. ⊠ *83 rue d'Auteuil, Upper Town, G1R 4C3* ☎ *418/694–0834* 🖷 *418/692–0456* ⇆ *36 rooms* ♨ *Some refrigerators, cable TV, dry cleaning, laundry service; no smoking* ⊟ *AE, MC, V* ¶⊙¶ *EP.*

$ ▦ **Hôtel Manoir des Remparts.** A home away from home every May for Mississippi State University students studying French, this hotel has homey furnishings, basic but cheery rooms, and inexpensive rates that also attract many Europeans. The two 1830 houses forming this hotel are opposite the wall enclosing Upper Town, only a short walk from Lower Town. Rooms at the front have a view of the port. On the fourth floor, 10 rooms contain sinks and share bathrooms and a TV. ⊠ *3½ rue des Remparts, Upper Town, G1R 3R4* ☎ *418/692–1125* 🖷 *418/692–1125* ✉ *manoirdesremparts@canada.com* ⇆ *34 rooms, 24 with bath* ♨ *Some fans, some kitchenettes, some refrigerators, cable TV, Internet, no-smoking rooms; no a/c in some rooms, no room phones, no TV in some rooms* ⊟ *AE, DC, MC, V* ¶⊙¶ *CP.*

Lower Town

$$$$ 🏨 **Auberge St-Antoine.** On the site of a 19th-century maritime warehouse, this charming hotel incorporates the historic stone walls of the old building along with artifacts dating to the 1600s, many of which are encased in glass displays in the public areas and guest rooms. Antiques and contemporary pieces fill the bedrooms, some of which have fireplaces, hot tubs, large terraces, or river views. Many have themes, such as the Captaine, decorated as a ship captain's quarters, or the Sorbet Room, in yellow, pink, and green. The buffet-style Continental breakfast (not included in the room rate) is extensive. ⊠ *10 rue St-Antoine, Lower Town, G1K 4C9* 🕿 *418/692–2211 or 888/692–2211* 🖷 *418/ 692–1177* ⊕ *www.saint-antoine.com* 🛏 *83 rooms, 12 suites* 🍴 *Restaurant, room service, in-room data ports, some in-room hot tubs, cable TV, lounge, babysitting, dry cleaning, laundry service, concierge, convention center, meeting rooms, parking (fee), no-smoking rooms* ☰ *AE, DC, MC, V* ⊙ *EP.*

$$$–$$$$
Fodor'sChoice
★
🏨 **Hotel Dominion 1912.** Sophistication and attention to the smallest detail prevail in the modern rooms of this boutique hotel—from the custom-designed swing-out night tables to the white goose-down duvets and custom umbrellas. The hotel, which was built in 1912 as a warehouse, has rooms on higher floors with views of either the St. Lawrence River or the Old City. ⊠ *126 rue St-Pierre, Lower Town, G1K 4A8* 🕿 *418/ 692–2224 or 888/833–5253* 🖷 *418/692–4403* ⊕ *www.hoteldominion. com* 🛏 *60 rooms* 🍴 *In-room data ports, minibars, cable TV, babysitting, dry cleaning, concierge, Internet, business services, meeting rooms, parking (fee)* ☰ *AE, DC, MC, V* ⊙ *CP.*

$$ 🏨 **Hôtel Le Saint-Paul.** Perched at the edge of the antiques district, this basic hotel converted from a 19th-century office building is near art galleries and the train station. Rooms have hunter-green carpeting and bedspreads with a Renaissance motif of characters in period dress. Some rooms have exposed brick walls. ⊠ *229 rue St-Paul, Lower Town, G1K 3W3* 🕿 *418/694–4414 or 888/794–4414* 🖷 *418/694–0889* ⊕ *www.lesaintpaul.qc.ca* 🛏 *23 rooms, 3 suites* 🍴 *Restaurant, room service, in-room data ports, some in-room hot tubs, some refrigerators, cable TV, dry cleaning, laundry service, meeting rooms, no-smoking rooms* ☰ *AE, DC, MC, V* ⊙ *EP.*

$–$$ 🏨 **Hôtel Belley.** Modern artwork by local artists is everywhere in this modest little hotel up the stairs above Belley Tavern, a stone's throw from the train station and the antiques district. Built as a private home around 1842, the building has housed various taverns since 1868. The current hotel opened in 1987. Rooms are simple, with exposed brick walls and beamed ceilings. Bathrooms have showers but no tubs. Downstairs, the old-fashioned tin ceilings and modern furniture attract a café crowd. Five apartments are also available in a separate building. ⊠ *249 rue St-Paul, Lower Town, G1K 3W5* 🕿 *418/692–1694 or 888/692–1694* 🖷 *418/692–1696* ⊕ *www.oricom.ca/belley* 🛏 *8 rooms, 5 apartments* 🍴 *Restaurant, in-room data ports, cable TV, dry cleaning, laundry service, parking (fee)* ☰ *AE, D, MC, V* ⊙ *EP.*

Outside the Walls

$$$–$$$$ ☒ **Hôtel Palace Royal.** A soaring indoor atrium with balconies over-looking a tropical garden, swimming pool, and hot tub lends a sense of drama to this luxury hotel. Its eclectic design makes use of everything from Asian styles to art deco. Elegant rooms with antique gold accents have views of either the Old City or the atrium. Views of the river can be had from rooms on the seventh floor and up. ☒ *775 av. Honoré-Mercier, Carré d'Youville, G1R 6A5* ☎ *418/694–2000 or 800/567–5276* 🖷 *418/380–2553* ⊕ *www.jaro.qc.ca* ↩ *69 rooms, 165 suites* ☆ *Restaurant, room service, in-room data ports, refrigerators, cable TV with movies, indoor pool, health club, bar, babysitting, meeting rooms, parking (fee)* ▤ *AE, D, DC, MC, V* ⦿I *EP.*

$$–$$$$ ☒ **Hilton Québec.** Just opposite the National Assembly, the spacious Hilton rises from the shadow of Parliament Hill. The lobby, which can be busy at times, has a bar and an open-air restaurant. The standard, modern rooms have tall windows; those on upper floors have fine views of Vieux-Québec. The hotel is connected to the convention center and a mall, Place Québec, which has 10 shops and a food court. If you stay on an executive floor, you get a free Continental breakfast and an open bar from 5 PM to 10:30 PM. ☒ *1100 blvd. René-Lévesque Est, Montcalm, G1K 7K7* ☎ *418/647–2411, 800/447–2411 within Canada* 🖷 *418/647–6488* ⊕ *www.hiltonquebec.com* ↩ *531 rooms, 42 suites* ☆ *Restaurant, room service, in-room data ports, minibars, cable TV with movies and video games, indoor-outdoor pool, health club, massage, sauna, bar, shops, babysitting, dry cleaning, laundry service, concierge, business services, meeting rooms, parking (fee), some pets allowed, no-smoking floors* ▤ *AE, D, DC, MC, V* ⦿I *EP.*

$$–$$$$ ☒ **Hôtel Château Laurier.** Brown leather sofas and easy chairs and wrought-iron and wood chandeliers fill the spacious lobby of this for-mer private house. All rooms have sleigh beds with bedspreads in green, beige, or blue. Rooms in the newer section are a bit larger; deluxe rooms have fireplaces and double whirlpool baths. Some rooms look out on the Plains of Abraham, but most have a view of the National Assembly and the Upper Town. Nearby, the busy Grande Allée is crowded with popular restaurants and trendy bars. ☒ *1220 pl. Georges V Ouest, Montcalm, G1R 5B8* ☎ *418/522–8108 or 800/463–4453* 🖷 *418/524–8768* ⊕ *www.oldquebec.com/laurier* ↩ *151 rooms, 3 suites* ☆ *2 restaurants, room service, in-room data ports, some in-room hot tubs, cable TV, massage, bar, babysitting, dry cleaning, business ser-vices, meeting rooms, free parking, no-smoking floors* ▤ *AE, D, DC, MC, V* ⦿I *EP.*

$$–$$$$ ☒ **Hôtel Delta Québec.** This large establishment opposite the Parliament Buildings has standard and business-class rooms (the latter come with Continental breakfast and nightly appetizers and drinks). The hotel oc-cupies the first 12 floors of a tall office complex; views of Vieux-Québec are limited to the higher floors. The heated outdoor pool is open year-round. ☒ *690 blvd. René-Lévesque Est, Montcalm, G1R 5A8* ☎ *418/647–1717, 888/884–7777, or 800/333–3333* 🖷 *418/647–2146* ⊕ *www.deltahotels.com* ↩ *371 rooms, 6 suites* ☆ *Restaurant, room service, in-room data ports, minibars, cable TV with movies and video games, out-*

door pool, health club, sauna, bar, dry cleaning, laundry service, Internet, meeting rooms, parking (fee), some pets allowed (fee) ⊟ *AE, D, DC, MC, V* ⫟ *EP.*

★ **$$–$$$$** ▦ **Hôtel Loews Le Concorde.** When Le Concorde was built in 1974, the 29-story concrete structure aroused controversy because it supplanted 19th-century Victorian homes. But the hotel's excellent location—on Grande Allée, dotted with cafés, restaurants, and bars—has ensured its longevity. Celebrity guests have ranged from the Rolling Stones to President George W. Bush. Rooms are larger than average, with good views of Battlefields Park and the St. Lawrence River. Nearly all rooms combine modern and traditional furnishings. ⊠ *1225 Cours du Général-de Montcalm, Montcalm, G1R 4W6* ☎ *418/647–2222 or 800/463–5256* ⊟ *418/647–4710* ⊕ *www.loewshotels.com* ⤳ *388 rooms, 16 suites* ⚭ *2 restaurants, room service, in-room data ports, minibars, cable TV with movies, pool, health club, sauna, bar, babysitting, laundry service, concierge, business services, convention center, parking (fee), some pets allowed* ⊟ *AE, D, DC, MC, V* ⫟ *EP.*

$$$ ▦ **L'Hôtel du Capitole.** This turn-of-the-20th-century structure just outside the St-Jean Gate is a fancy hotel, an Italian bistro, and a 1920s cabaret-style dinner theater (the Théâtre Capitole) all rolled into one. The showbiz theme, with stars on the doors, has attracted Québec celebrities, including Céline Dion. Art-deco furnishings fill the small, simple rooms. Painted ceilings have a blue-and-white sky motif, and white down-filled comforters dress the beds. ⊠ *972 rue St-Jean, Carré d'Youville, G1R 1R5* ☎ *418/694–4040 or 800/363–4040* ⊟ *418/694–1916* ⊕ *www.lecapitole.com* ⤳ *39 rooms, 1 suite* ⚭ *Restaurant, room service, in-room data ports, some in-room hot tubs, minibars, cable TV, in-room VCRs, bar, 2 theaters, babysitting, dry cleaning, laundry service, business services, meeting room, parking (fee)* ⊟ *AE, DC, MC, V* ⫟ *EP.*

$$–$$$ ▦ **Courtyard by Marriott Québec.** This former office building exudes a quiet elegance with stained-glass windows, two fireplaces, and a tiny wood-lined corner bar in the lobby. At the restaurant in back, you can dine around the open kitchen or on the mezzanine. Free Danish and croissants are set out in the lobby in the morning; they're replaced by cookies in the afternoon. Wood furniture fills the modern rooms, most of which are decorated in blue and beige. The least expensive standard rooms face an office building. The best views are from rooms at the front overlooking Place d'Youville. The washing machine and dryer are a rarity in downtown Québec hotels. ⊠ *850 pl. d'Youville, Carré d'Youville, G1R 3P6* ☎ *418/694–4004 or 866/694–4004* ⊟ *418/694–4005* ⊕ *www.marriott-quebec.com* ⤳ *102 rooms, 9 suites* ⚭ *Restaurant, room service, in-room data ports, cable TV with movies, exercise equipment, hot tub, piano bar, dry cleaning, laundry facilities, business services, meeting rooms, parking (fee), no-smoking floors* ⊟ *AE, D, DC, MC, V* ⫟ *EP.*

$$ ▦ **Hôtel Royal William.** Like its namesake, the first Canadian steamship to cross the Atlantic (in 1833), the Royal William brings the spirit of technology and innovation to this hotel, designed with the business traveler in mind. Rooms have two phone lines, a fax connection, plus a high-speed Internet port. The meeting rooms on each floor have Internet connections, and several are equipped for video conferencing. Throughout, the style is art deco with a modern twist. Five minutes from Vieux-

Québec, the hotel is in the St. Roch district, popular with young artists, academics, and techies. ⊠ *360 blvd. Charest Est, St. Roch, G1K 3H4* ☎ *418/521–4488 or 888/541–0405* 🖷 *418/521–6868* ⊕ *www. royalwilliam.com* ⤧ *36 rooms, 8 suites* ⚇ *Restaurant, in-room data ports, in-room safes, some in-room hot tubs, minibars, gym, library, babysitting, dry cleaning, Internet, meeting rooms, parking (fee), no-smoking floors* ▤ *AE, D, DC, MC, V* ¶◎¶ *EP.*

★ **$–$$$** 🏨 **Château Bonne Entente.** In a grassy residential parkland with a pond inhabited by swans and ducks, this English-style country inn is off the beaten path but worth the trip. In keeping with the hotel's English roots, tea and cookies are served every afternoon near the fireplace in the wood-panel tearoom. Some rooms have art-deco furnishings; others are upscale country, with white duvets, dormer ceilings, and claw-foot bathtubs. In the newer wing, some rooms have multijet showers, and two suites have fireplaces. Two family suites have colorful bunk beds for kids. The hotel is 20 minutes from downtown, with free shuttle service June through mid-September. ⊠ *3400 chemin Ste-Foy, Ste-Foy, G1X 1S6* ☎ *418/653–5221 or 800/463–4390* 🖷 *418/653–3098* ⊕ *www. chateaubonneentente.com* ⤧ *123 rooms, 17 suites* ⚇ *2 restaurants, in-room data ports, in-room safes, cable TV with movies, 1 tennis court, outdoor pool, gym, health club, outdoor hot tub, sauna, spa, badminton, volleyball, ice-skating, bar, recreation room, babysitting, playground, dry cleaning, laundry service, concierge, Internet, business services, convention center, meeting rooms, airport shuttle (summer), free parking, no-smoking rooms* ▤ *AE, DC, MC, V* ¶◎¶ *EP.*

$–$$
Fodor'sChoice
★

🏨 **L'Autre Jardin Auberge.** Across the street from the Royal William, this modern, pleasant inn is owned and operated by a non-profit organization. In the heart of the burgeoning Saint-Roch district in downtown Québec, the inn is geared towards the academics, high-tech entrepreneurs, and others who visit the many new office and administrative buildings that surround it. The inn, which has a friendly, helpful staff, has three floors of comfortable rooms and suites with cable TV and Internet access. Some rooms have therapeutic baths. There's also a meeting room. The breakfast buffet, which includes a variety of breads, fresh croissants, and local cheeses, is served in a dining room in the basement. In keeping with its owner's aims, there's also a "fair-trade" shop selling artisanal foods and other items from developing countries. ⊠ *365 blvd. Charest Est, St. Roch, G1K 3H4* ☎ *418/523–1790 or 877/747–0447* 🖷 *418/523–9735* ⊕ *www.autrejardin.com* ⤧ *24 rooms, 3 suites* ⚇ *Cable TV, in-room hot tubs, shop, Internet, meeting room, parking (fee), no-smoking floors* ▤ *AE, D, DC, MC, V* ¶◎¶ *CP.*

NIGHTLIFE & THE ARTS

Québec City has a good variety of cultural institutions for a town of its size, from its renowned symphony orchestra to several small theater companies. The arts scene changes with the seasons. From September through May, a steady repertory of concerts, plays, and performances is presented in theaters and halls. In summer, indoor theaters close, making room for outdoor stages. For arts and entertainment listings in English, consult the *Québec Chronicle-Telegraph* (⊕ www.qctonline.com), published on Wednesday. The French-language daily newspaper *Le Soleil* (⊕ www.cyberpresse.ca) has listings on a page called "Agenda." *Voir* (⊕ www.voir.ca), a French-language weekly devoted to arts listings and reviews, appears on the street every Thursday.

Tickets for most shows are sold at **Billetech** (✉ Bibliothèque Gabrielle-Roy, 350 rue St-Joseph Est, St. Roch ☎ 418/691–7400 ✉ Colisée Pepsi, Parc de l'Expocité, 250 blvd. Wilfrid-Hamel, Limoilou ☎ 418/691–7211 ✉ Comptoir postal Le Soleil, pl. Laurier, 2nd floor, Ste-Foy ☎ 418/656–6095 ✉ Grand Théâtre de Québec, 269 blvd. René-Lévesque Est, Montcalm ☎ 418/643–8131 or 877/643–8131 ✉ Palais Montcalm, 995 pl. d'Youville, Carré d'Youville ☎ 418/670–9011 ✉ Salle Albert-Rousseau, 2410 chemin Ste-Foy, Ste-Foy ☎ 418/659–6710 ✉ Théâtre Capitole, 972 rue St-Jean, Carré d'Youville ☎ 418/694–4444 ⊕ www.billetech.com). Hours vary.

The Arts

The **Grande Théâtre de Québec** (✉ 269 blvd. René-Lévesque Est, Montcalm ☎ 418/643–8111) is Québec City's main theater, with two stages for concerts, plays, dance performances, and touring companies of all sorts. A three-wall mural by Québec sculptor Jordi Bonet depicts Death, Life, and Liberty. Bonet wrote "La Liberté" on one wall to bring attention to the Québecois struggle for freedom and cultural distinction.

Dance

Dancers appear at the Bibliothèque Gabrielle-Roy, Salle Albert-Rousseau, and Palais Montcalm theaters. **Grand Théâtre de Québec** (✉ 269 blvd. René-Lévesque Est, Montcalm ☎ 418/643–8131) presents a dance series with Canadian and international companies.

Film

Most theaters screen French films and American films dubbed into French. A few show films VOA—"Version Originale Anglaise"—without dubbing in French. **Cineplex Odeon Ste-Foy** (✉ 1200 blvd. Duplessis, Ste-Foy ☎ 418/871–1550) almost always shows some films in English. **Cinéma Star Cité** (✉ 1150 blvd. Duplessis, Ste-Foy ☎ 418/874–0066) is a megaplex that usually shows English films. **Le Clap** (✉ 2360 chemin Ste-Foy, Ste-Foy ☎ 418/650–2527) has a repertoire of foreign, offbeat, and art films. The **IMAX Theatre** (✉ Galeries de la Capitale, 5401 blvd. des Galeries, Lebourgneuf ☎ 418/627–4629, 418/627–4688, or 800/643–4629) has extra-large-screen movies—educational fare on scientific, historical, and adventure topics—and translation headsets.

Music

The **Bibliothèque Gabrielle-Roy** (✉ 350 rue St-Joseph Est, St. Roch ☎ 418/691–7400) hosts children's concerts in its **Joseph Lavergne Auditorium;** tickets must be bought in advance. Popular music concerts are often booked at the **Colisée Pepsi** (✉ Parc de l'Expocité, 250 blvd. Wilfrid-Hamel, Limoilou ☎ 418/691–7211).

Maison de la Chanson (✉ Théâtre Petit Champlain, 68 rue du Petit-Champlain, Lower Town ☎ 418/692–4744) is a fine spot to hear contemporary Francophone music.

The renowned **Orchestre Symphonique de Québec** (Québec Symphony Orchestra; ✉ 269 blvd. René-Lévesque Est, Montcalm ☎ 418/643–8131) is Canada's oldest. It performs at Louis-Frechette Hall in the Grand Théâtre de Québec.

For classical concerts at the **Salle de l'Institut Canadien** (✉ 42 Chaussée des Ecossais, Upper Town ☎ 418/691–7411), buy tickets in advance at the Palais Montcalm.

MUSIC FESTIVALS An annual highlight in mid-July is the **Festival d'Eté International de Québec** (Québec City Summer Festival; ☎ 418/523–4540 ⊕ www.infofestival.com), an 11-day music festival with more than 400 shows and concerts (most of them free), from classical music to Francophone song and street performers. Events are held in more than 10 locations, including outdoor stages and public squares.

The streets of the Lower Town are transported back in time during the five-day **Fêtes de la Nouvelle France** (New France Festival; ☎ 418/694–3311 ⊕ www.nouvellefrance.qc.ca) in early August. Events, ranging from an old-time farmers' market to games, music, demonstrations, and spontaneous skits, are held throughout the Old City, and everywhere you'll see people in period costume.

During the **Québec City International Festival of Military Bands** (☎ 418/694–5757), held in mid-August, the streets of Old Québec resound with military airs. Bands from several countries participate in the four-day festival, which includes a gala parade. Shows—most of them free—are held in Vieux-Québec or just outside the walls.

Theater
Most theater productions are in French. The theaters listed below schedule shows from September to April.

Grand Théâtre de Québec (✉ 269 blvd. René-Lévesque Est, Montcalm ☎ 418/643–8131) offers classic and contemporary plays staged by the leading local company, le **Théâtre du Trident** (☎ 418/643–5873). **Palais Montcalm** (✉ 995 pl. d'Youville, Carré d'Youville ☎ 418/670–9011), a municipal theater outside St-Jean Gate, presents a broad range of productions.

A diverse repertoire, from classic to comedy, is staged at **Salle Albert-Rousseau** (✉ 2410 chemin Ste-Foy, Ste-Foy ☎ 418/659–6710). **Théâtre Le Capitole** (✉ 972 rue St-Jean, Carré d'Youville ☎ 418/694–4444), a restored cabaret-style theater, schedules pop music and musical comedy shows. **Théâtre Périscope** (✉ 2 rue Crémazie Est, Montcalm ☎ 418/529–2183), a multipurpose theater, hosts about 125 shows a year, including performances for children.

In summer, **open-air concerts** are presented at Place d'Youville (just outside St-Jean Gate) and on the Plains of Abraham.

Nightlife

Québec City nightlife centers on the clubs and cafés of rue St-Jean, avenue Cartier, and Grande Allée. In winter, evening activity grows livelier as the week nears its end, beginning on Wednesday. As warmer temperatures set in, the café-terrace crowd emerges, and bars are active seven days a week. Most bars and clubs stay open until 3 AM.

Bars & Lounges

One of the city's most romantic spots is the Château Frontenac's **Bar St-Laurent** (⊠ 1 rue des Carrières, Upper Town ☎ 418/692–3861), with soft lights, a panoramic view of the St. Lawrence, and a fireplace. The nightclub **Chez Maurice** (⊠ 575 Grande Allée Est, 2nd floor, Montcalm ☎ 418/647–2000) is named after the former prime minister Maurice Duplessis. The crowd is young, the atmosphere racy, provocative, and sexually charged. **Cosmos Café** (⊠ 575 Grande Allée Est, Montcalm ☎ 418/640–0606) is a lively club and restaurant. **L'Inox** (⊠ 37 quai St-André, Lower Town ☎ 418/692–2877), a popular Lower Town brew pub, serves beers brewed on-site. Some of them, like Transat and Viking, were developed to mark special events. Inside are billiard tables; outside there's a summer terrace.

Le Pub Saint-Alexandre (⊠ 1087 rue St-Jean, Upper Town ☎ 418/694–0015), a popular English-style pub, serves 40 kinds of single-malt scotch and 200 kinds of beer, 20 of which are on tap. Perched on the cliff just above the St. Roch district, **Les Salons d'Edgar** (⊠ 263 rue St. Vallier Est, St. Roch ☎ 418/523–7811) attracts those in their thirties with its eclectic music—everything from salsa beats and tango to jazz and techno. It's closed in July and August. The brick walls and wine cellar–like atmosphere help make **Les Voutes de Napoleon** (⊠ 680 Grande Allée Est, Montcalm ☎ 418/640–9388) a popular place to listen to Québecois music and taste beer from local microbreweries.

Dance Clubs

There's a little bit of everything—from rock bands to loud disco—at **Chez Dagobert** (⊠ 600 Grande Allée Est, Montcalm ☎ 418/522–0393), a large, popular club. Electronic music and a trendy vibe have made **Le Sonar** (⊠ 1147 av. Cartier, Montcalm ☎ 418/640–7333) one of the hottest dance clubs in town. Patrons at the second-story **Vogue** (⊠ 1170 rue d'Artigny, Montcalm ☎ 418/529–9973) move to techno and pop beats.

Folk, Jazz & Blues

French-Canadian and Québecois folk songs fill **Chez Son Père** (⊠ 24 rue St-Stanislas, Upper Town ☎ 418/692–5308), a smoky pub on the second floor of an old building in the Latin Quarter. Singers perform nightly. The first jazz bar in Québec City when it opened in the mid-1980s, **L'Emprise at Hôtel Clarendon** (⊠ 57 rue Ste-Anne, Upper Town ☎ 418/692–2480) is the preferred spot for the music's many fans. The art-deco style sets the mood for Jazz Age rhythms.

SPORTS & THE OUTDOORS

Scenic rivers and nearby mountains (no more than 30 minutes away by car) make Québec City a great place for the sporting life. For information about sports and fitness, contact **Québec City Tourist Information** (✉ 835 av. Laurier, Montcalm G1R 2L3 ☎ 418/649–2608 ⊕ www.quebecregion. com/e). The **Québec City Bureau of Culture, Recreation and Community Life** (✉ 275 rue de l'Eglise, 4ᵉ, St. Roch G1K 6G7 ☎ 418/641–6224 ⊕ www. ville.quebec.cq.ca) has information about municipal facilities.

Sprawling along the cliffs from the Citadel to just past the Musée National des Beaux-Arts, the 250-acre **Parc des Champs-de-Bataille** (Battlefields Park) has panoramic views of the St. Lawrence River and trails for running, biking, in-line skating, and cross-country skiing, plus walking paths, volleyball courts, and open fields. Bordering the St. Charles River, **Cartier-Brébeuf National Historic Site** (✉ 175 rue de l'Espinay, Limoilou ⊕ www.ccbn.nbc.gc.ca) is popular with runners, hikers, cyclists, and cross-country skiers.

Tickets for sporting events can be bought at **Colisée Pepsi** (✉ Parc de l'-Expocité, 250 blvd. Wilfrid-Hamel, Limoilou ☎ 418/691–7211). You can order tickets for many events through **Billetech** (⊕ www.billetech. com).

Baseball

The **Capitales de Québec** (✉ Stade Municipal, 100 rue du Cardinal Maurice-Roy, St. Roch ☎ 418/521–2255 or 877/521–2244), part of the Northern League, play Single A professional baseball from May 24 through September in an old-fashioned ballpark built in 1938.

Biking

There are 64 km (40 mi) of fairly flat, well-maintained bike paths on Québec City's side of the St. Lawrence River, and an equal amount on the south shore. Detailed route maps are available through tourism offices. The best and most scenic of the bike paths is the one that follows the old railway bed in Lévis. Take the Québec–Lévis Ferry to reach the marvelous views along this 10-km-long (6 mi-long) trail. By 2005 it will be part of the province-wide Route Verte, a government-funded, 4,000-km-long circuit of long-distance bicycle paths and road routes.

Bike paths along hills cross **Parc des Champs-de-Bataille** (Battlefields Park), which encompasses the Plains of Abraham, at the south side of the city. Ambitious cyclists appreciate the 22-km-long (14-mi-long) **Corridor des Cheminots**, which runs from Limoilou near Vieux-Québec to the town of Shannon. Paths along the **Côte de Beaupré**, beginning at the confluence of the St. Charles and St. Lawrence rivers, are especially scenic. They begin northeast of the city at rue de la Verandrye and boulevard Montmorency or rue Abraham-Martin and Pont Samson (Samson Bridge) and continue 10 km (6 mi) along the coast to Montmorency Falls. **Mont Ste-Anne,** site of the 1998 world mountain-biking championship and races for the annual World Cup, has 150 km (93 mi) of mountain-bike trails, 14 downhill runs, a gondola, and an extreme-mountain-biking park.

From late March to late October you can rent bicycles, including helmets and locks, for C$23 a day, or C$19 for four hours, at **Vélo Passe-Sport** (⌧ 22 côte du Palais, Upper Town ☎ 450/641–8356), which also gives guided bike tours of the area.

Boating

Manoir St-Castin (⌧ 99 chemin du Tour du Lac, Lac Beauport ☎ 418/841–4949), at Lac Beauport, has canoes, kayaks, and pedal boats. Follow Route 73 north of the city to Lac Beauport and then take Exit 157 to boulevard du Lac. Just west of Québec City, on the St. Lawrence River, canoes, pedal boats, and small sailboats can be rented at **Parc Nautique du Cap-Rouge** (⌧ 4155 chemin de la Plage Jacques Cartier, Cap-Rouge ☎ 418/641–6148).

Dogsledding

Aventures Nord-Bec (⌧ 665 rue St-Aimé, St-Lambert de Lévis ☎ 418/889–8001), 30 minutes from the bridges south of the city, can teach you how to mush in the forest. A half-day spent here, which includes initiation, dogsledding, and a snack, costs C$85 per person for a minimum of two people. Overnight camping trips are also available.

Fishing

Permits are needed for fishing in Québec. Most sporting-goods stores and all Wal-Mart and Canadian Tire stores sell permits. A one-day fishing permit for a non-resident is C$10.25; a three-day permit is C$22.75; seven-day is C$35; season is C$52 (includes all sports fish except Atlantic salmon). The **Société de la Faune et les Parcs** (⌧ 675 blvd. René-Lévesque Est, Montcalm ☎ 418/521–3830 ⊕ www.fapaq.gouv.qc.ca) publishes a pamphlet on fishing regulations which is available at ministry offices and wherever permits are sold. **Latulippe** (⌧ 637 rue St-Vallier Ouest, St. Roch ☎ 418/529–0024) sells permits and also stocks a large amount of hunting and fishing equipment.

Réserve Faunique des Laurentides (☎ 418/528–6868, 800/665–6527 fishing reservations ⊕ www.sepaq.com), a wildlife reserve with good lakes for fishing, is approximately 48 km (30 mi) north of Québec City via Route 73. Reserve a boat 48 hours in advance by phone.

Québec Outfitters Federation (☎ 418/877–5191) represents 400 hunting and fishing outfitters across Québec province.

Gesitfaune (☎418/848–5424 ⊕www.gestifaune.com), is a corporate fishing outfitter with three properties, two of them within easy driving distance of Québec City. From May to September, the company's nature guides organize trout-fishing trips that include food and lodging in private wilderness retreats. Trips, organized from September to May, cost from C$300 to C$500 per day. Reservations are required.

Golf

The Québec City region has 18 golf courses, and most are open to the public. Reservations are essential in summer. The 18-hole, par-72 course at **Club de Golf de Cap-Rouge** (⌧ 4600 rue St-Felix, Cap-Rouge ☎ 418/653–9381), 25 minutes by car from Vieux-Québec, is one of the closest courses to Québec City. Eighteen holes are C$70. **Club de Golf de Mont**

Tourbillon (✉ 55 montée du Golf, Lac Beauport ☎ 418/849–4418), a par-70, 18-hole course, is 20 minutes from the city by car via Route 73 North (Lac Beauport exit). Eighteen holes are C$45. **Le Saint-Ferréol** (✉ 1700 boulevard les Neiges, St-Ferréol-les-Neiges ☎ 418/827–3778), a half-hour drive north of Québec City, has one of the better 18-hole, par-72 courses (C$39) in the region.

Harness Racing
There's horse racing at **Hippodrome de Québec** (✉ Parc de l'Expocité, 250 blvd. Wilfrid-Hamel, Limoilou ☎ 418/524–5283).

Health & Fitness Clubs
One of the city's most popular health clubs is **Club Entrain** (✉ Place de la Cité , 2600 blvd. Laurier, Ste-Foy ☎ 418/658–7771). Facilities, available for a daily fee of C$11.50, include a weight room with Nautilus, a sauna, a whirlpool, and squash courts. **Hilton Québec** (✉ 1100 blvd. René-Lévesque Est, Montcalm ☎ 418/525–9909) has a health club—with weights, exercise machines, a sauna, and a year-round heated outdoor pool—available to nonguests for a C$10 fee. At the **YWCA** (✉ 855 av. Holland, St. Sacrement ☎ 418/683–2155), pool facilities cost C$3.50 for nonmembers.

Hiking & Jogging
Along with Battlefields Park, **Bois-de-Coulonge Park** (✉ 1215 chemin St-Louis, Sillery ☎ 418/528–0773) is one of the most popular places for jogging. **Cartier-Brébeuf National Historic Site** (✉ 175 rue de l'Espinay, Limoilou ☎ 418/648–4038), north of the Old City along the banks of the St. Charles River, is connected to about 13 km (8 mi) of hiking and biking trails. This historic site also has a small museum and a reconstruction of a Native American longhouse. For mountainous terrain, head 19 km (12 mi) north on Route 73 to the suburb of **Lac Beauport.**

Horseback Riding
Excursions et Mechoui Jacques Cartier (✉ 978 av. Jacques-Cartier Nord, Tewkesbury ☎ 418/848–7238), also known for rafting, offers summer and winter horseback riding. A summer excursion that includes an hour of instruction and three hours of riding costs C$45.

Ice-Skating
The ice-skating season is usually December through March. Try the **Patinoire de la Terrasse** (☎ 418/692–2955), adjacent to the Château Frontenac and open November through April, daily 11–11; it costs C$5 to skate with skate rental included, and C$2 to skate if you have your own. **Place d'Youville,** outside St-Jean Gate, has an outdoor rink that's open November through April, from 8 AM–10 PM. Skate rental is C$4, and skating itself is free. Nighttime skating is an option at **Village Vacances Valcartier** (✉ 1860 blvd. Valcartier, St-Gabriel-de-Valcartier, ☎ 418/844–2200), although closing times vary.

Outfitters
Outdoor enthusiasts flock to **Latulippe** (✉ 637 rue St-Vallier Ouest, St. Roch ☎ 418/529–0024) for its wide selection of clothing and equipment for such open-air pursuits as hiking, camping, snowmobiling, and fishing.

Rafting

The Jacques Cartier River, about 48 km (30 mi) northwest of Québec City, has good rafting. **Excursions et Mechoui Jacques Cartier** (✉ 978 av. Jacques-Cartier Nord, Tewkesbury ☎ 418/848–7238) runs rafting trips on the river from May through October. Tours originate from Tewkesbury, a half-hour drive from Québec City. A half-day tour costs less than C$45; wet suits are C$18. In winter, you can slide on inner tubes for about C$22 a day.

Village Vacances Valcartier (✉ 1860 blvd. Valcartier, St-Gabriel-de-Valcartier ☎ 418/844–2200) runs rafting excursions on the Jacques Cartier River from May through September. A three-hour excursion costs C$44, plus C$20 to rent a wet suit. Also available are hydro-speeding—running the rapids on surfboards—and quieter family river tours.

Skiing

Brochures about ski centers in Québec are available from the **Québec Tourism and Convention Bureau** (☎ 877/266–5687 ⊕ www.bonjourquebec.com). The **Hiver Express** (☎ 418/525–5191) winter shuttle is a taxi service that runs between major hotels in Vieux-Québec and ski centers. It leaves hotels in Vieux-Québec at 8 and 10 AM for the ski hills and returns at 2:30 and 4:30 PM. The cost is C$23; reserve and pay in advance at hotels. One of the two biggest, most challenging hills in the region is **Mont-Ste-Anne** (☎ 418/827–4561 ⊕ www.mont-sainte-anne.com), 40 minutes east of Québec City on the Cote-de-Beaupré. It features 60-plus slopes of groomed downhill runs, a snowboard park, the longest system of brightly lit night-ski runs in Canada, and more than 300 km (180 mi) of groomed cross-country ski trails. **Le Massif** (☎ 877/536-2774 ⊕ www.lemassif.com), 20 minutes east of Mont-Sainte-Anne in Charlevoix and owned by Cirque du Soleil co-founder Michel Gauthier, is the highest skiing mountain in Eastern Canada. If you want to stay closer to the city, try **Stoneham** (☎ 418/848–2411 ⊕ www.stoneham.ca). Twenty minutes north of Old Québec, it features some two dozen good, mostly intermediate and beginner trails, not to mention the area's best après-ski action.

CROSS-COUNTRY   Thirty-seven ski centers in the Québec area have 2,000 km (1,240 mi) of groomed trails and heated shelters between them; for information, contact the **Regroupement des Stations de Ski de Fond** (☎ 418/653–5875 ⊕ www.rssfrq.qc.ca). **Parc des Champs-de-Bataille** (Battlefields Park), which you can reach from Place Montcalm, has scenic, marked cross-country skiing trails.

Le Centre de Randonnée à Skis de Duchesnay (✉ 143 rue de Duchesnay, St-Catherine-de-Jacques-Cartier ☎ 418/875–2711), north of Québec City, has 150 km (93 mi) of marked trails. **Mont-Ste-Anne** (☎ 418/827–4561), 40 km (25 mi) northeast of Québec City, may be the best cross-country ski center in Canada, if not North America. The training ground for Olympic-level athletes from across the continent, Mont-Sainte-Anne has 27 trails: 224 km (139 mi) for classic skiing and 135 km (84 mi) for skating stride. **Lac Beauport**, 19 km (12 mi) north of the city, has more than 20 marked trails (150 km, or 93 mi); contact **Les Sentiers du Moulin** (✉ 99 chemin du Moulin, Lac Beauport ☎ 418/849–9652).

DOWNHILL   Three downhill ski resorts, all with night skiing, are within a 30-minute drive of Québec City. **Mont-Ste-Anne** (✉ 2000 blvd. Beaupré, Beaupré ☎ 418/827–4561, 800/463–1568 for lodging) is one of the largest resorts in eastern Canada, with a vertical drop of 2,050 feet, 56 downhill trails, a half-pipe for snowboarders, a terrain park, and 13 lifts, including a gondola. There are 25 trails and a vertical drop of 734 feet at the relatively small **Le Relais** (✉ 1084 blvd. du Lac, Lac Beauport ☎ 418/849–1851), where you can buy lift tickets by the hour. **Station Touristique Stoneham** (✉ 1420 av. du Hibou, Stoneham ☎ 418/848–2411), with a vertical drop of 1,380 feet, is known for its long, easy slopes. It has 32 downhill runs and 10 lifts, plus three terrain parks and one super-half-pipe.

Snow Slides

At the **Glissades de la Terrasse** (☎ 418/692–2955), a wooden toboggan, takes you down a 700-foot snow slide that's adjacent to the Château Frontenac. The cost is C$2 per ride per adult and C$1.25 for children under six.

Use inner tubes or carpets on any of 42 snow slides at **Village Vacances Valcartier** (✉ 1860 blvd. Valcartier, St-Gabriel-de-Valcartier ☎ 418/844–2200 ⊕ www.valcartier.com), or join 6 to 12 others for a snowraft ride down one of three groomed trails. You can also take a dizzying ride on the Tornado, a giant inner tube that seats eight and spins down the slopes. Rafting and sliding cost C$23 per day, C$25 with skating. Trails open daily at 10 AM; closing times vary.

Snowmobiling

Québec is the birthplace of the snowmobile, and with 32,000 km (19,840 mi) of trails, it's one of the best places in the world for the sport. Two major trails, the 2,000-km (1250-mi)Trans-Québec Snowmobile Trail and the 1,300-km (806-mi) Fur Traders Tour, run just north of Québec City. Trail maps are available at tourist offices. Snowmobiles can be rented near Mont Ste-Anne, a half-hour drive north of the city, at **Centre de Location de Motoneiges du Québec** (✉ 15 blvd. du Beaupré, Beaupré ☎ 418/827–8478), starting at C$40 an hour or C$100 a day, plus taxes, insurance, and gas. **SM Sport** (✉ 113 blvd. Valcartier, Loretteville ☎ 418/842–2703) will pick you up from several downtown hotels at prices starting at C$20 per person. Snowmobile rentals begin at C$45 per hour, or C$135 per day, plus tax, C$15 insurance, and the cost of gas.

Tennis & Racquet Sports

At **Montcalm Tennis Club** (✉ 901 blvd. Champlain, Sillery ☎ 418/687–1250), southwest of Québec City, four indoor and seven outdoor courts are open weekdays from 7 AM and weekends from 8 AM to midnight. **Tennisport** (✉ 6280 blvd. Hamel, Ancienne Lorette ☎ 418/872–0111) has nine indoor tennis courts, two squash courts, one racquetball court, and eight badminton courts. It's 20 minutes from downtown Québec City.

Water Parks

Village Vacances Valcartier (✉ 1860 blvd. Valcartier, St-Gabriel-de-Valcartier ☎ 418/844–2200) has the largest water park in Canada with 25 water slides, a wave pool, a half-mile tropical-river adventure called the Amazon, and a 100-foot accelerating water slide, on which bathers reach a speed of up to 80 kph (50 mph). The park's newest attraction is a winding indoor river in a medieval setting. Admission is C$25 a day for those at least 52 inches tall, C$17 for those under 52 inches.

Winter Carnival
One winter highlight is the **Carnaval de Québec** (⌂ 290 rue Joly, GIL 1N8 ☎ 418/626–3716 ⊕ www.carnaval.qc.ca). The whirl of activities over three weekends in January and/or February includes night parades, a snow-sculpture competition, and a canoe race across the St. Lawrence River. You can participate in or watch just about every snow activity imaginable, from dogsledding to ice climbing.

SHOPPING

On the fashionable streets of Old Québec, shopping has a European tinge. The boutiques and specialty shops clustered along narrow streets such as rue du Petit-Champlain, and rues de Buade and St-Jean in the Latin Quarter, are like trips back in time.

Prices in Québec City tend to be on a par with those in Montréal and other North American cities. The city's main attractions for shoppers have been antiques, furs, and works by local artisans rather than good prices, but the exchange rate for the U.S. dollar and sales-tax rebates available to international visitors make shopping particularly tempting. Sales are usually advertised in both of Québec City's daily French-language newspapers, *Le Soleil* and *Le Journal de Québec.*

Stores are generally open Monday through Wednesday 9:30–5:30, Thursday and Friday until 9, Saturday until 5, and Sunday noon–5. In summer, most shops have later evening hours.

Department Stores

Most large department stores can be found in the malls of suburban Ste-Foy.

La Baie. The Bay is Québec's version of the Canadian Hudson's Bay Company conglomerate, founded in 1670 by Montréal trappers Pierre Radisson and Médard Chouart des Groseilliers. La Baie carries clothing for the entire family, as well as household wares. ⊠ *Pl. Laurier, Ste-Foy* ☎ *418/627–5959.*

Holt Renfrew. One of the country's more expensive stores, Holt Renfrew carries furs in winter, perfume, and tailored designer collections for men and women. ⊠ *Pl. Ste-Foy, Ste-Foy* ☎ *418/656–6783.*

Simons. An old Québec City store, Simons used to be the city's only source for fine British woolens and tweeds. Now the store also carries designer clothing, linens, and other household items. ⊠ *20 côte de la Fabrique, Upper Town* ☎ *418/692–3630* ⊠ *Pl. Ste-Foy, Ste-Foy* ☎ *418/692–3630.*

Shopping Malls

☺ **Galeries de la Capitale.** An indoor amusement park with a roller coaster and an IMAX theater attracts families to this 250-store mall. It's about a 20-minute drive from Vieux-Québec. ⊠ *5401 blvd. des Galeries, Lebourgneuf* ☎ *418/627–5800.*

Place de la Cité. There are more than 150 boutiques, services, and restaurants at this shopping center. ⊠ *2600 blvd. Laurier, Ste-Foy* ☎ *418/657–6920.*

Place Laurier. With 350 stores, this massive mall is your best bet for one-stop shopping. ⊠ *2700 blvd. Laurier, Ste-Foy* ☎ *418/651–5000.*

Place Ste-Foy. Designer labels and upscale clothing are easy to find at the 190 stores here. ⊠ *2450 blvd. Laurier, Ste-Foy* ☎ *418/653–4184.*

Quartier Petit-Champlain. A pedestrian mall in Lower Town, surrounded by rues Champlain and du Marché-Champlain, Quartier Petit-Champlain has some 50 boutiques, local businesses, and restaurants. This popular district is the best area for native Québec wood sculptures, weavings, ceramics, and jewelry. ☎ *418/692–2613.*

Specialty Stores

Antiques

Québec City's antiques district centers on rues St-Paul and St-Pierre, across from the Old Port. French-Canadian, Victorian, and art-deco furniture, along with clocks, silverware, and porcelain, are some of the rare collectibles found here. Authentic Québec pine furniture, characterized by simple forms and lines, is rare—and costly.

Les Antiquités du Matelot. Engravings, maps, prints of Québec and Canada, and white ironstone are the specialties here. ⊠ *137 rue St-Paul, Lower Town* ☎ *418/694–9585.*

Antiquités Marcel Bolduc. This is the largest antiques store on rue St-Paul. Wares include furniture, household items, old paintings, and knick-knacks. ⊠ *74 rue St-Paul, Lower Town* ☎ *418/694–9558.*

Argus Livres Anciens. Antique books, most of them in French, are what draws people to this store. ⊠ *160 rue St-Paul, Lower Town* ☎ *418/694–2122.*

Boutique Aux Mémoires Antiquités. Here you'll find a good selection of Victorian and Edwardian pieces, plus silver, porcelain, curiosities, paintings, and bronzes. ⊠ *105 rue St-Paul, Lower Town* ☎ *418/692–2180.*

Gérard Bourguet Antiquaire. You're not likely to find any bargains here, but this shop has a very good selection of authentic 18th- and 19th-century Québec pine furniture. ⊠ *97 rue St-Paul, Lower Town* ☎ *418/694–0896.*

L'Héritage Antiquité. This is probably the best place in the antiques district to find good Québecois furniture, clocks, oil lamps, porcelain, and ceramics. ⊠ *110 rue St-Paul, Lower Town* ☎ *418/692–1681.*

Art

On Upper Town's Rue du Trésor, local artists display their sketches, paintings, and etchings. It's a good source for less expensive artwork as well as pieces by promising young artists. Good portrayals of Québec City and the region are plentiful.

Aux Multiples Collections. Inuit art and antique wood collectibles are sold here. ✉ *69 rue Ste-Anne, Upper Town* ☎ *418/692–1230.*

Galerie Brousseau et Brousseau. This gallery showcases fine Inuit art in its store and adjacent museum (admission C$6). ✉ *39 rue St-Louis, Upper Town* ☎ *418/694–1828.*

Galerie Madeleine Lacerte. Head to this gallery for contemporary art and sculpture. ✉ *1 côte Dinan, Lower Town* ☎ *418/692–1566.*

Books

English-language books are difficult to find in Québec City.

Librairie du Nouveau Monde. This bookshop stocks titles in French and some in English. ✉ *103 rue St-Pierre, Lower Town* ☎ *418/694–9475.*

Librairie Smith. In the Place Laurier mall, this store sells both English and French books. ✉ *2700 blvd. Laurier, Ste-Foy* ☎ *418/653–8683.*

La Maison Anglaise. The English House, in the Place de la Cité mall, only carries English-language titles and specializes in fiction. ✉ *2600 blvd. Laurier, Ste-Foy* ☎ *418/654–9523.*

Ceramics

Pauline Pelletier. Ms. Pelletier specializes in porcelain, with an emphasis on comical golden porcelain cats. ✉ *38 rue du Petit-Champlain, Lower Town* ☎ *418/692–4871.*

Pot-en-Ciel. An eclectic assortment of unique ceramics and tablewares is sold here. ✉ *27 rue du Petit-Champlain, Lower Town* ☎ *418/692–1743.*

Clothing

Le Blanc Mouton. The White Sheep, in Quartier Petit-Champlain, specializes in unique, locally designed creations for women, including accessories and handcrafted jewelry. ✉ *51 Sous le Fort, Lower Town* ☎ *418/692–2880.*

François Côté Collection. This chic boutique sells fashions for men. ✉ *1200 Germain des Prés, Ste-Foy* ☎ *418/657–1760.*

Louis Laflamme. A large selection of stylish men's clothes is available here. ✉ *1192 rue St-Jean, Upper Town* ☎ *418/692–3774.*

La Maison Darlington. Head here for well-made woolens, dresses, and other items for men, women, and children by fine names in couture. ✉ *7 rue de Buade, Upper Town* ☎ *418/692–2268.*

Crafts

Regard d'Ici. Crafts by Québec artisans sold at this shop include jewelry, clothing, leather goods, and decorative items. ✉ *Pl. Québec, 880 autoroute Dufferin-Montmorency, Upper Town* ☎ *418/522–0360.*

Les Trois Colombes Inc. Handmade items, including clothing made from handwoven fabric, native and Inuit carvings, furs, and ceramics, are available here. ✉ *46 rue St-Louis, Upper Town* ☎ *418/694–1114.*

Food

Choco-Musée Érico. Food becomes a work of art at this store, where chocolatier Éric Normand crafts whatever you like out of chocolate within a few days. ✉ *634 rue St-Jean, St. Jean Baptiste* ☎ *418/524–2122.*

Fur

The fur trade has been an important industry here for centuries. Québec City is a good place to purchase high-quality furs at fairly reasonable prices.

J. B. Laliberté. This department store carries furs. ⊠ *595 rue St-Joseph Est, St. Roch* ☎ *418/525–4841.*

Gifts

Collection Lazuli. This store carries unusual art objects and jewelry from around the world. ⊠ *774 rue St-Jean, St. Jean Baptiste* ☎ *418/525–6528* ⊠ *Place de la Cité, 2600 blvd. Laurier, Ste-Foy* ☎ *418/652–3732.*

Jewelry

Joaillier Louis Perrier. Louis Perrier sells Québec-made gold and silver jewelry. ⊠ *48 rue du Petit-Champlain, Lower Town* ☎ *418/692–4633.*
Zimmermann. Exclusive handmade jewelry can be found at this Upper Town shop. ⊠ *46 côte de la Fabrique, Upper Town* ☎ *418/692–2672.*

SIDE TRIPS FROM QUÉBEC CITY

Several easy excursions show you another side of the province and provide more insight into its past. The spectacular Montmorency Falls can be seen on a day trip. A drive around Île d'Orléans, east of the city, is an easy way to experience rural Québec. The farms, markets, and churches here evoke the island's long history. The island can be toured in an energetic day, though rural inns make it tempting to extend a visit.

Côte de Beaupré & Montmorency Falls

As legend has it, when explorer Jacques Cartier first caught sight of the north shore of the St. Lawrence River in 1535, he exclaimed, *"Quel beau pré!"* ("What a lovely meadow!"), because the area was the first inviting piece of land he had spotted since leaving France. Today the Côte de Beaupré (Beaupré Coast), first settled by French farmers, stretches 40 km (25 mi) east from Québec City to the famous pilgrimage site of Ste-Anne-de-Beaupré. Historic Route 360, or avenue Royal, winds its way from Beauport to St-Joachim, east of Ste-Anne-de-Beaupré. The impressive Montmorency Falls lie midway between Québec City and Ste-Anne-de-Beaupré.

Montmorency Falls

❶ *10 km (6 mi) east of Québec City.*

The Montmorency River was named for Charles de Montmorency, viceroy of New France in the 1620s and explorer Samuel Champlain's immediate commander. The river cascading over a cliff into the St. Lawrence River is one of the most beautiful sights in the province—and at 27 stories high, the falls are 50% higher than Niagara Falls. A cable car runs to the top of the falls in **Parc de la Chute-Montmorency** (Montmorency Falls Park) from late April to early November. During very cold weather, the falls' heavy spray freezes and forms a giant loaf-shape ice cone known to Québecois as the Pain du Sucre (Sugarloaf); this phe-

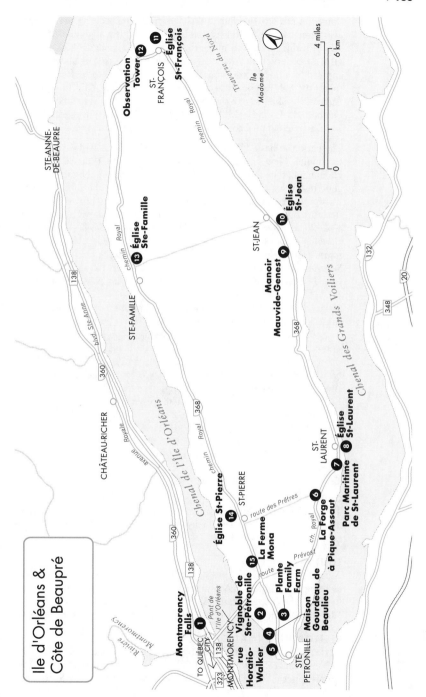

nomenon attracts sledders and sliders from Québec City. Ice climbers also come to scale the falls; from late December through mid-March, a school trains novices to make the ascent. In warmer months you can visit an observation tower in the river's gorge that is continuously sprayed by a fine drizzle from water pounding onto the cliff rocks. The top of the falls can be observed from avenue Royale. Mid-July to early August, the skies above the falls light up with **Les Grands Feux Loto-Québec** (☎ 418/523–3389 or 888/934–3473 ⊕ www.lesgrandsfeux. com), an international competition of fireworks performances set to music.

The park also has a historic side. The British general Wolfe, on his way to conquer New France, camped here in 1759. In 1780 Sir Frederick Haldimand, then the governor of Canada, built a summer home—now a good restaurant called Manoir Montmorency—atop the cliff. Prince Edward, Queen Victoria's father, rented this villa from 1791 to 1794. The structure burned down, however, and what stands today is a re-creation. ✉ 2490 av. Royale, Beauport ☎ 418/663–3330, 418/647–4422 for ice-climbing school ⊕ www.chutemontmorency.qc.ca ⌗ Cable car C$7.50 round-trip, parking C$8 ☉ Cable car Jan. 31–Apr. 9, weekends 9–4 (to Sugarloaf slide); Apr. 10–June 13 and Aug. 24–Oct. 18, daily 8:30–6:45; June 14–Aug. 23, daily 8:30 AM–9 PM; Dec. 26–Jan. 5, daily 9–4.

off the beaten path

MUSÉE DE L'ABEILLE – Things are buzzing at this Economuseum (part of an organization of museums focusing on traditional trades) devoted to bees and honey. A giant glassed-in hive with a tube leading outdoors allows you to take a close look at life inside a beehive. On the bee safari, guides take a hive apart, explaining how it works and how bees behave, before taking you indoors to taste honey wines. You can also taste honey made by bees that have fed on different kinds of flowers, from clover to blueberry. The museum is a 10-minute drive east of Montmorency Falls. ✉ 8862 blvd. Ste-Anne, Château-Richer ☎ 418/824–4411 or 877/499–4411 ⊕ www.musee-abeille.qc.ca ⌗ Museum free, bee safari C$3 ☉ Museum June 24–Oct., daily 9–6; Nov.–June 23, daily 9–5. Bee safari June 24–Labor Day.

Côte de Beaupré & Montmorency Falls A to Z

CAR TRAVEL

To reach Montmorency Falls, take Route 440 (Autoroute Dufferin–Montmorency) east from Québec City approximately 9½ km (6 mi) to the exit for Montmorency Falls.

TOURS

Autocar Dupont-Gray Line leads afternoon excursions along the Côte de Beaupré, with stops at Montmorency Falls and the Ste-Anne-de-Beaupré basilica. The cost is about C$38 plus tax per person.

🚌 **Autocar Dupont-Gray Line** ☎ 418/649-9226 ⊕ www.orleansexpress.com/grayline.

VISITOR INFORMATION

At the Beaupré Coast Interpretation Center, in a former convent, guides in New France costumes explain displays on the history of the region. Admission is C$4. The center is open from late June to late September, daily 10–5. During the rest of the year, the center is open by reservation only. Québec City Tourist Information has a bureau in Beauport, in Montmorency Falls Park. It's open June 3 to mid-October, daily 9–5. ⏹ Tourist Information **Beaupré Coast Interpretation Center** ✉ 7976 av. Royale, Château-Richer ☎ 418/824–3677. **Québec City Tourist Information** ✉ Montmorency Falls Park, Beauport ☎ 418/641–6649 ✉ 4300 blvd. Ste-Anne/Rte. 138, Québec City ☎ No phone.

Île d'Orléans

The Algonquins called it Minigo, the "Bewitched Place," and over the years the island's tranquil rural beauty has inspired poets and painters. Île d'Orléans is only 15 minutes by car from downtown Québec City, but a visit here is one of the best ways to get a feel for traditional life in rural Québec. Centuries-old homes and some of the oldest churches in the region dot the road that rings the island. Île d'Orléans is at its best in summer, when the boughs of trees in lush orchards bend under the weight of apples, plums, or pears, and the fields burst with strawberries and raspberries. Roadside stands sell woven articles, maple syrup, baked goods, jams, fruits, and vegetables. You can also pick your own produce at about two dozen farms. The island, immortalized by one of its most famous residents, the poet and songwriter Félix Leclerc (1914–88), is still fertile ground for artists and artisans.

The island was discovered at about the same time as the future site of Québec City, in 1535. Explorer Jacques Cartier noticed an abundance of vines and called it the Island of Bacchus, after the Greek god of wine. (Today, native vines are being crossbred with European varieties at Ste-Pétronille's fledgling vineyard.) In 1536 Cartier renamed the island in honor of the duke of Orléans, son of the French king François I. Its fertile soil and abundant fishing made it so attractive to settlers that at one time there were more people living here than in Québec City.

About 8 km (5 mi) wide and 34 km (21 mi) long, Île d'Orléans is made up of six small villages that have sought over the years to retain their identities. The bridge to the mainland was built in 1935, and in 1970 the island was declared a historic area to protect it from most sorts of development.

Ste-Pétronille
17 km (10½ mi) northeast of Québec City.

The lovely village of Ste-Pétronille, the first to be settled on Île d'Orléans, is west of the bridge to the island. Founded in 1648, the community was chosen in 1759 by British general James Wolfe for his headquarters. With 40,000 soldiers and a hundred ships, the English bombarded French-occupied Québec City and Côte de Beaupré.

In the late 19th century, the English population of Québec developed Ste-Pétronille into a resort village. This area is considered to be the island's most beautiful, not only because of its spectacular views of Montmorency Falls and Québec City, but also for its Regency-style English villas and exquisitely tended gardens.

❷ At the **Vignoble de Ste-Pétronille,** hardy native Québec vines have been crossbred with three types of European grapes to produce a surprisingly good dry white wine as well as a red and a rosé. A guided tour of the vineyard includes a tasting. ⌧ *1A chemin du Bout de l'Île* ☎ *418/828–9554* ⌨ *Guided tour C$2.50* ⊙ *Late Apr.–May and mid-Oct.–mid-Nov., weekends 11–5; June–mid-Oct., daily 10–6.*

❸ At **Plante family farm** (⌧ 20 chemin du Bout de l'Île ☎ 418/828–9603) you can pick apples and strawberries (in season) or buy fresh fruits, vegetables, and apple cider.

❹ The island's first home, the **Maison Gourdeau de Beaulieu** (⌧ 137 chemin du Bout de l'Île) was built in 1648 for Jacques Gourdeau de Beaulieu, the first seigneur (a landholder who distributed lots to tenant farmers) of Ste-Pétronille. Remodeled over the years, this white house with blue shutters now incorporates both French and Québecois styles. Its thick walls and dormer windows are characteristic of Breton architecture, but its sloping, bell-shape roof, designed to protect buildings from large amounts of snow, is typically Québecois. The house is not open to the public.

❺ The tiny street called **rue Horatio-Walker,** off chemin Royal, was named after the early-19th-century painter known for his landscapes of the island. Walker lived on this street from 1904 until his death in 1938. At Nos. 11 and 13 rue Horatio-Walker are his home and workshop, but they are both closed to the public.

WHERE TO STAY & EAT
$$–$$$

✕⊡ **La Goéliche.** This English-style country manor, rebuilt in 1996–97 following a fire, is steps away from the St. Lawrence River. Antiques decorate the small but elegant rooms, which all have river views. Classic French cuisine ($$$–$$$$, table d'hôte only in the evening, reservations essential) includes veal fillet with Armagnac and dried cranberries accompanied by scampi-and-mushroom risotto, and chicken breast stuffed with game in red-wine sauce. The romantic dining room overlooks the river; an enclosed terrace is open year-round. ⌧ *22 chemin du Quai, G0A 4C0* ☎ *418/828–2248 or 888/511–2248* ⌨ *418/828–2745* ⊕ *www.goeliche.ca* ⤳ *12 rooms, 1 suite, 2 apartments* ⌂ *Restaurant, fans, some in-room hot tubs, some minibars, some cable TV, pool, babysitting, dry cleaning, Internet, meeting rooms, free parking, no-smoking rooms; no a/c, no room TVs* ⊟ *AE, DC, MC, V* ⍾ *BP.*

SHOPPING

Chocolaterie de l'Île d'Orléans. (⌧ 150 chemin du Bout de l'Île ☎ 418/828–2250) combines Belgian chocolate with local ingredients to create handmade treats—chocolates filled with maple butter, for example, or *framboisette,* made from raspberries. In summer try the homemade ice creams and sherbets.

St-Laurent de l'Île d'Orléans
9 km (5½ mi) east of Ste-Pétronille.

Founded in 1679, St-Laurent is one of the island's maritime villages. Until as late as 1935, residents here used boats as their main means of transportation. ❻ **La Forge à Pique-Assaut** belongs to the talented and local artisan Guy Bel, who has done ironwork restoration for Québec City. He was born in Lyon, France, and studied there at the École des Beaux Arts. You can watch him and his team at work; his stylish candlesticks, chandeliers, fireplace tools, and other ironwork are for sale. ✉ *2200 chemin Royal* ☎ *418/828–9300* ⊕ *www.forge-pique-assaut.com* ⊙ *June–mid-Oct., daily 9–5; mid-Oct.–June, weekdays 9–noon and 1:30–5.*

7 The **Parc Maritime de St-Laurent**, at a former boatyard, is where craftspeople specializing in boatbuilding practiced their trade. Now you can picnic here and visit the Chalouperie Godbout (Godbout Longboat), which holds a collection of tools used during the golden era of boatbuilding. ✉ *120 chemin de la Chalouperie* ☎ *418/828–9672* 🎟 *C$3* ⊙ *June 24–Labor Day, daily 10–5; early Sept.–early Oct., weekends 10–4 and by reservation; mid-May–mid-June by reservation.*

8 The tall, inspiring **Église St-Laurent**, which stands next to the village marina on chemin Royal, was built in 1860 on the site of an 18th-century church that had to be torn down. One of the church's procession chapels is a miniature stone reproduction of the original. ✉ *1532 chemin Royal* ☎ *418/828–2551* 🎟 *Free, guided tour of religious art C$1* ⊙ *Late June–early Sept., daily 9–5.*

WHERE TO STAY ✕ **Moulin de St-Laurent.** You can dine inside or outside at the foot of the
& EAT   waterfall of this restaurant, converted from an early-18th-century stone
$$–$$$ mill. Scrumptious snacks, such as quiche, bagels, and salads, are available at the café. Evening dishes include salmon wrapped in pastry with spinach and goat cheese, served with orange-peppercorn sauce. ✉ *754 chemin Royal* ☎ *418/829–3888 or 888/629–3888* 🍴 *AE, DC, MC, V* ⊙ *Closed mid-Oct.–May.*

★ **$$** ✕🖼 **Le Canard Huppé.** As the inn's name—The Crested Duck—suggests, its contemporary cuisine ($$–$$$$) usually includes at least one dish with duck, perhaps the rendition with clover honey, fresh thyme, and wild garlic. Chef Maïka Courval uses local produce—for example, duck from a neighbor's farm slowly cooked with balsamic and clover-honey dressing, or grain-fed chicken stuffed with truffles. Upstairs, each of the inn's rooms has unusual antiques and original paintings by area artists. Deluxe rooms, in a separate building with a pool, have fireplaces, whirlpool tubs, and river views. ✉ *2198 chemin Royal, G0A 3Z0* ☎ *418/828–2292 or 800/838–2292* 🖷 *418/828–0966* ⊕ *www.canard-huppe.com* 🛏 *15 rooms, 1 suite* 🍴 *Restaurant, fans, refrigerators, cable TV in some rooms, pool, meeting room, free parking, no-smoking rooms; no a/c in some rooms, no room phones* 🍽 *AE, DC, MC, V* ¹⊙ *CP* ⊙ *No dinner Nov.–Apr.*

St-Jean
12 km (7 mi) northeast of St-Laurent.

The village of St-Jean used to be occupied by river pilots and navigators. At sea most of the time, the sailors didn't need the large homes and plots of land that the farmers did. Often richer than farmers, they displayed their affluence by building their houses with bricks brought back from Scotland as ballast. Most of St-Jean's small, homogeneous row houses were built between 1840 and 1860.

9 St-Jean's beautiful Normandy-style manor, **Manoir Mauvide-Genest,** was built in 1734 for Jean Mauvide, surgeon to Louis XV, and his wife, Marie-Anne Genest. The most notable thing about this house, which still has its original thick walls, ceiling beams, and fireplaces, is the degree to which it has held up over the years. The house serves as an interpretation center of New France's seigneurial regime, with 18th-century furniture, a multimedia presentation, and tours with guides dressed in 18th-century costumes. ⊠ *1451 chemin Royal* ☎ *418/829–2630* 🖃 *C$5* 🕔 *May–Nov., daily 10–5.*

10 At the eastern end of the village is **Église St-Jean,** a massive granite structure built in 1749, with large red doors and a towering steeple. The church resembles a ship; it's big and round and appears to be sitting right on the river. Paintings of the patron saints of seamen line the interior walls. The church's cemetery is also intriguing, especially if you can read French. Back in the 1700s, piloting the St. Lawrence was a dangerous profession; the cemetery tombstones recall the many lives lost in these harsh waters. ⊠ *2001 chemin Royal* ☎ *418/828–2551* 🖃 *Free* 🕔 *Late June–early Sept., daily 10–5.*

St-François
12 km (7 mi) northeast of St-Jean.

Sprawling open fields separate 17th-century farmhouses in St-François, the island's least toured and most rustic village. This community at the eastern tip of the island was settled mainly by farmers. St-François is the perfect place to visit one of the island's *cabanes à sucre* (maple-sugaring shacks), found along chemin Royal. Stop at a hut for a tasting tour; sap is gathered from the maple groves and boiled until it turns to syrup. When it's poured on ice, it tastes like toffee. The maple syrup season is from late March through April.

11 **Église St-François,** built in 1734, is one of eight extant provincial churches dating from the French regime. At the time the English seized Québec City in 1759, General James Wolfe knew St-François to be a strategic point along the St. Lawrence. Consequently, he stationed British troops here and used the church as a military hospital. In 1988 a car crash set the church on fire, and most of the interior treasures were lost. A separate children's cemetery stands as a silent witness to the difficult life of early residents. ⊠ *341 chemin Royal* ☎ *419/828–2551* 🖃 *Free* 🕔 *Late June–early Sept., daily 10–5.*

12 A picnic area with a wooden **observation tower** is well situated for viewing the majestic St. Lawrence. In spring and fall, wild Canada geese can be seen here. The area is about 2 km (1 mi) north of Église St-François on chemin Royal.

Ste-Famille
14 km (9 mi) west of St-François.

The village of Ste-Famille, founded in 1661, has exquisite scenery, including abundant apple orchards and strawberry fields with views of Côte de Beaupré and Mont Ste-Anne in the distance. But it also has plenty of historic charm, with the area's highest concentration of stone houses dating from the French regime.

⑬ The impressive **Église Ste-Famille**, constructed in 1749, is the only church in Québec province to have three bell towers at its front. The ceiling was redone in the mid-19th century with elaborate designs in wood and gold. The church also holds a famous painting, *L'Enfant Jésus Voyant la Croix (Baby Jesus Looking at the Cross)*. It was done in 1670 by Frère Luc (Father Luc), sent from France to decorate churches in the area. ✉ *3915 chemin Royal* ☎ *418/828–2656* 💲 *Free* ⊙ *Late June–early Sept., daily 11–5.*

St-Pierre
14 km (9 mi) southwest of St-Famille.

St-Pierre, established in 1679, is set on a plateau that has the island's most fertile land. The town has long been the center of traditional farming industries. The best products grown here are potatoes, asparagus, and corn. In 2002 the Espace Félix Leclerc—an exhibit by day and a *boîte à chansons* (combination of a coffee house and bar with live performances) by night—was opened to honor the late singer and songwriter who made St-Pierre his home. If you continue west on chemin Royal, just ahead is the bridge to the mainland and Route 440.

⑭ **Église St-Pierre**, the oldest church on the island, dates from 1717. It's no longer used for worship, but it was restored during the 1960s and is open to visitors. Many original components are still intact, such as benches with compartments below where hot bricks and stones were placed to keep people warm in winter. Félix Leclerc, the first Québecois singer to make a mark in Europe, is buried in the cemetery nearby. ✉ *1249 chemin Royal* ☎ *418/828–9824* 💲 *Free* ⊙ *May–June and Aug.–Oct., daily 10–5; July, daily 9–6.*

⑮ **La Ferme Monna** has won international awards for its crème de cassis de l'Île d'Orléans, a liqueur made from black currants. The farm offers free samples of the strong, sweet cassis or one of its black-currant wines; the tour explains how they are made. In summer you can sample foods made with cassis on a terrace overlooking the river. ✉ *723 chemin Royal* ☎ *418/828–1057* 💲 *Free; guided tours C$4* ⊙ *Mid-June–Sept., daily 10–6; Mar.–mid-June and Oct.–Dec., weekends 10–5.*

SHOPPING The only remaining commercial fisherman on the island smokes his fish and sells it from **Poissonnerie Jos Paquet** (✉ 2705 chemin Royal ☎ 418/828–2760), a tiny shack. You can sample surprisingly tasty smoked eel as well as smoked trout and salmon. Also on sale are fresh and smoked walleyed pike and sturgeon, all from the St. Lawrence River. It's open March through January, daily 8:30–6.

Île d'Orléans A to Z

CAR TRAVEL
From Québec City, take Route 440 (Autoroute Dufferin–Montmorency) northeast. After a drive of about 10 km (6 mi) take the Pont de l'Île d'Orléans (a bridge) to the island. The main road, chemin Royal (Route 368),

circles the island, extending 67 km (42 mi) through the island's six villages; the route turns into chemin du Bout de l'Île in Ste-Pétronille.

Parking can sometimes be a problem, but you can leave your car in each town's church parking lot and explore each village on foot.

EMERGENCIES
Centre Médical Prévost is the principal medical clinic on the island.
🔲 Hospital **Centre Médical Prévost** ✉ 1015 Rte. Prévost, St-Pierre ☎ 418/828-2213.

LODGING
Reservations are necessary at the island's 40 B&Bs, which charge about C$55–C$125 per night for a double-occupancy room. The Chamber of Commerce runs a referral service.
🔲 Reservation Service **Chamber of Commerce** ☎ 418/828-9411 ⊕ www.iledorleans.com.

TOURS
The island's Chamber of Commerce rents a cassette tape or compact disc for C$10 a day with an interesting 108-minute tour of the island by car; it's available at the tourist kiosk in St-Pierre, just past the bridge.

Québec City tour companies, including Autocar Dupont-Gray Line, run bus tours of the western tip of the island, combined with sightseeing along the Côte de Beaupré.
🔲 **Autocar Dupont-Gray Line** ☎ 418/649-9226 ⊕ www.orleansexpress.com/grayline.

VISITOR INFORMATION
Any of the offices of the Québec City Region Tourism and Convention Bureau can provide information on island tours and accommodations. The island's Chamber of Commerce operates a tourist-information kiosk just over the bridge at the first stoplight, at the west corner of côte du Pont and chemin Royal in St-Pierre. Look for the question mark.
🔲 Tourist Information **Chamber of Commerce** ✉ 490 côte du Pont, St-Pierre ☎ 418/828-9411 or 866/941-9411 ⊕ www.iledorleans.com.

QUÉBEC CITY A TO Z

To research prices, get advice from other travelers, and book travel arrangements, visit www.fodors.com.

AIR TRAVEL
Canada's national airline, Air Canada, offers direct flights daily to Québec City from Toronto, Halifax, and Ottawa. Discount carriers Jazz (an Air Canada subsidiary) and Québecair have, respectively, 15 and 3 daily flights to Québec City from Montréal. Another discount carrier, JetsGo, has two flights a day from Toronto. Two U.S. carriers also offer direct flights to Québec City: Continental has one from Newark; Northwest has two from Detroit.

AIRPORTS

Jean Lesage International Airport is about 19 km (12 mi) northwest of downtown.

🛈 **Jean Lesage International Airport** ✉ 500 rue Principale, Ste-Foy ☎ 418/640–2600 ⊕ www.aeroportdequebec.com.

TRANSFERS   If you're driving from the airport into town, take Route 540 (Autoroute Duplessis) to Route 175 (boulevard Laurier), which becomes Grande Allée and leads right to Vieux-Québec. The ride takes about 30 minutes and may be slightly longer (45 minutes or so) during rush hours (7:30–8:30 AM into town and 4–5:30 PM leaving town).

Private limo service is expensive, starting at C$55 for the ride from the airport into Québec City. Try Groupe Limousine A-1. Taxis are available immediately outside the airport exit near the baggage-claim area. A ride into the city costs about C$24.50. Two local taxi firms are Taxi Coop de Québec, the largest company in the city, and Taxi Québec.

🛈 **Groupe Limousine A-1** ✉ 361 rue des Commissaires Est, St. Roch ☎ 418/523–5059. **Taxi Coop de Québec** ✉ 496 2ᵉ av., Limoilou ☎ 418/525–5191. **Taxi Québec** ✉ 975 8ᵉ av., Limoilou ☎ 418/522–2001.

BOAT & FERRY TRAVEL

Les Dauphins du Saint-Laurent provides hydrofoil service along the St. Lawrence River between Montréal and Québec City. The trip takes 4½ hours. Boats depart Montréal daily at 7:30 AM, and 2 or 3 PM mid-June through August; at 7:30 AM mid-May through mid-June; and at 9 AM September to mid-October. Boats depart Québec City daily at 7:30 AM, and 2 or 3 PM mid-June through August; at 3 PM mid-May through June; and at 9 AM September to mid-October. Tickets cost C$69 one-way, C$109 round-trip; it's C$5 extra to bring a bike. Tickets can be bought at the docks, but to ensure a seat you should order your ticket in advance by phone. In Québec City, the hydrofoil docks at Quay 19, near the corner of rues Dalhousie and André in the Old Port; in Montréal, the hydrofoil docks at the foot of Place Jacques Cartier at the Old Port.

The Québec–Lévis ferry crosses the St. Lawrence River to the town of Lévis and gives you a magnificent panorama of Old Québec. Although the crossing takes 15 minutes, waiting time can increase the trip to an hour. The cost is C$2.50 June through September, and C$2 October through May. The first ferry from Québec City leaves daily at 6:30 AM from the pier at rue Dalhousie, opposite Place Royale. Crossings run every half hour from 7:30 AM until 6:30 PM, then hourly until 2:30 AM. From April through November, the ferry adds extra service every 10 to 20 minutes during rush hours (7–10 AM and 3–6:45 PM). Schedules can change, so be sure to check the ferry Web site or call ahead.

🛈 Boat & Ferry Information **Les Dauphins du Saint-Laurent** ☎ Montréal 514/288–4499, Québec City 418/694–2476, toll-free 877/648–4499 ⊕ www.dauphins.ca. **Québec–Lévis ferry** ☎ Québec City 418/644–3704, Lévis 418/837–2408 (bilingual service 8:30 to 4:30 daily) ⊕ www.traversiers.gouv.qc.ca.

BUS TRAVEL TO & FROM QUÉBEC CITY

Orléans Express provides daily service between Montréal and Québec City. The trip takes three hours.

Buses from Montréal to Québec City depart daily on the hour from 6 AM to 8 PM, with additional departures at 12:15 AM, 4:50 AM, 7:45 AM, 3:30 PM, 9:30 PM, and 10:30 PM. Buses from Québec City to Montréal depart daily on the half hour from 5:30 AM to 11:30 PM, and also at 6:45 AM, 9:45 AM, 4 PM, 5:15 PM, and 6:15 PM. A one-way ticket costs about C$45; a round-trip ticket costs C$68, so long as you return within 10 days and do not travel on Friday or certain days during holiday periods. Otherwise, the price is double the one-way fare. Tickets can be purchased only at terminals.

🚍 Bus Line **Orléans Express** ☎ 418/525-3000.

🚍 Terminals **Québec City Terminal** ✉ 3020 rue Abraham Martin, Lower Town ☎ 418/525-3000. **Ste-Foy Terminal** ✉ 3001 chemin Quatre Bourgeois, Ste-Foy ☎ 418/650-0087. **Voyageur Terminal** ✉ 505 blvd. de Maisonneuve Est, Downtown, Montréal ☎ 514/842-2281.

BUS TRAVEL WITHIN QUÉBEC CITY

The city's transit system, the Réseau de Transport de la Capitale, runs buses approximately every 10 minutes on up to once an hour, stopping at major points around town.

The cost is C$2.45, and you must have exact change. For a discount on your fare, buy bus tickets at magazine shops and some grocery stores for C$1.95 (C$5.50 for a day pass, which can be used by two people on the weekend). The terminals are in Lower Town at Place Jacques-Cartier and outside St-Jean Gate at Place d'Youville in Upper Town. Timetables are available at some visitor information offices and at Place Jacques Cartier.

🚍 **Réseau de Transport de la Capitale** ☎ 418/627-2511 ⊕ www.stcuq.qc.ca.

BUSINESS HOURS

In winter, many attractions and shops change their hours, so it's a good idea to call ahead. Most banks are open Monday through Wednesday 10–3 and close later on Thursday and Friday. Museum hours are typically 10–5, with longer evening hours in summer. Most are closed on Monday.

CAR RENTAL

🚗 Agencies **Budget** ✉ 29 côte du Palais, Upper Town ☎ 418/692-3660 or 800/363-8111. **Hertz Canada** ✉ Jean Lesage International Airport ☎ 418/871-1571 🚗 44 côte du Palais, Upper Town ☎ 418/694-1224, 800/263-0600 in English, 800/263-0678 in French. **National** ✉ Jean Lesage International Airport ☎ 418/871-1224 🚗 295 rue St-Paul, Lower Town ☎ 418/694-1727.

CAR TRAVEL

A car is necessary only if you plan to visit outlying areas. Automated seasonal information about the roads in the region is available November through April by calling the number below.

Montréal and Québec City are linked by Autoroute 20 on the south shore of the St. Lawrence River and by Autoroute 40 on the north shore. On both highways, the ride between the two cities is about 240 km (149 mi) and takes about three hours. U.S. I–87 in New York, U.S. I–89 in Vermont, and U.S. I–91 in New Hampshire connect with Autoroute 20, as does Highway 401 from Toronto.

Driving northeast from Montréal on Autoroute 20, follow signs for Pont Pierre-Laporte (Pierre Laporte Bridge) as you approach Québec City. After you've crossed the bridge, turn right onto boulevard Laurier (Route 175), which becomes the Grande Allée leading into Québec City.

Keep in mind that street signs are in French. It's useful to know the following terms: *gauche* (left), *droit* (right), *ouest* (west), and *est* (east).
🚩 **Automated seasonal information** ☎ 418/684-2363.

PARKING The narrow streets of the old city leave few two-hour metered parking spaces available. However, several parking garages at central locations charge about C$12 a day on weekdays or C$6 for 12 hours on weekends. Main garages are at Hôtel de Ville (City Hall), Place d'Youville, Edifice Marie-Guyart, Place Québec, Château Frontenac, rue St-Paul, and the Old Port.

EMERGENCIES
Centre Hospitalier Universitaire de Québec is the city's largest institution and incorporates the teaching hospitals the Pavillon CHUL in Ste-Foy and the Pavillon Hôtel-Dieu, the main hospital in Vieux-Québec.

If you don't have a major emergency but require medical assistance, you can walk into the Centre Hospitalier Jeffery Hale. The city's only English-speaking hospital and mainly a long-term-care facility, it's open 24 hours. For an English-speaking doctor or dentist, call the Holland Centre referral service weekdays 8:30–4:30.

Dr. Pierre Auger operates his dental practice on weekdays; both he and his receptionist speak English. Call for an appointment.

Pharmacie Brunet, north of Québec City in the Charlesbourg district, is open 8 AM–midnight. Most outlets of the big pharmacy chains in the region (including Jean Coutu, Racine, Brunet, and Uniprix) are open every day and offer free delivery.
🚩 Doctors & Dentists **Centre Hospitalier Jeffery Hale** ✉ 1250 chemin Ste-Foy, St. Sacrement ☎ 418/684-2252. **Dr. Pierre Auger** ✉ 1330 av. Maguire, Room 204, Sillery ☎ 418/527-2516. **Holland Centre** ☎ 418/683-9274.
🚩 Emergency Services **Distress Center** ☎ 418/686-2433. **Fire** ☎ 418/691-6292 or 911. **Police** ☎ 418/691-6151 or 911. **Poison Center** ☎ 418/656-8090. **Provincial police** ☎ 418/310-4141.
🚩 Hospitals **Centre Hospitalier Universitaire de Québec, Pavillon CHUL** ✉ 2705 blvd. Laurier, Ste-Foy ☎ 418/656-4141, 418/654-2114 for emergencies. **Centre Hospitalier Universitaire de Québec, Pavillon Hôtel-Dieu** ✉ 11 côte du Palais, Upper Town ☎ 418/691-5151, 418/691-5042 for emergencies.
🚩 Late-Night Pharmacy **Pharmacie Brunet** ✉ Les Galeries Charlesbourg, 4250 1ʳᵉ av., Charlesbourg ☎ 418/623-1571.

LODGING

B&BS Québec City has many hostels and B&Bs, which increasingly are known as Couette & Cafés ("small beds and coffees." To guarantee a room during peak season, reserve in advance. Québec City Tourist Information has B&B listings.

🛈 Reservation Service **Québec City Tourist Information** ✉ 835 av. Laurier, Montcalm G1R 2L3 ☎ 418/649-2608.

MONEY MATTERS

ATMs, or *guichets automatiques,* are widely available throughout Québec City. ATMs accept many types of bank cards and are generally linked to international banking networks such as Cirrus.

BANKS From May through September, Caisse Populaire Desjardins de Québec is open weekends 9–6, in addition to weekday hours.

🛈 **Caisse Populaire Desjardins de Québec** ✉ 19 rue des Jardins, Upper Town ☎ 418/522-6806.

CURRENCY Echange de Devises Montréal is open September to mid-June, daily
EXCHANGE 9–5, and mid-June to early September, daily 8:30–7:30.

🛈 Exchange Service **Echange de Devises Montréal** ✉ 12 rue Ste-Anne, Upper Town ☎ 418/694-1014.

SIGHTSEEING TOURS

Tours can include Montmorency Falls, whale-watching, and Ste-Anne-de-Beaupré in addition to sights in Québec City. Combination city and harbor-cruise tours are also available. Québec City tours operate year-round; excursions to outlying areas may operate only in summer.

BOAT TOURS Croisières AML has day and evening cruises on the St. Lawrence River aboard the MV *Louis-Jolliet.* The 1½- to 3-hour cruises run from May through mid-October and start at C$24.95 plus tax. Croisières Dufour runs 2½-hour evening cruises to view the fireworks (Les Grands Feux) at Montmorency Falls and day-long cruises to Tadoussac for whale-watching. The latter trip starts at C$139 and includes breakfast and dinner.

Other possibilities, starting at $79 on the same cruise, include disembarking with your bike for the day at Île aux Coudres, or getting off at Pointe-aux-Pic to spend the day rambling around La Malbaie or gambling at the casino at the Manoir Richelieu, in the Charlevoix. Day cruises depart at 7:30 AM and return between 6-7 PM mid-June through Labor Day, Tuesday through Sunday.

🛈 **Croisières AML** ✉ Pier Chouinard, 10 rue Dalhousie, beside the Québec–Lévis ferry terminal, Lower Town ☎ 418/692-1159. **Groupe Dufour Croisières** ✉ Bassin Louise, Wharf 19, at rues Dalhousie and St-André, Lower Town ☎ 418-692-0222 or 800/463-5250.

BUS TOURS Autocar Dupont-Gray Line bus tours of Québec City depart across the square from the Château Laurier Hotel (1230 pl. Georges V); you can purchase tickets at most major hotels. The company also runs guided tours in a minibus or trolley, as well as tours of Côte de Beaupré and Île d'Orléans, and for whale-watching. Tours run year-round and cost

C$26–C$85. Call for a reservation and the company will pick you up at your hotel.

🚗 **Autocar Dupont-Gray Line** ☎ 418/649-9226 or 888/558-7668.

CALÈCHE TOURS You can hire a calèche, a horse-drawn carriage, at Place d'Armes near the Château Frontenac, at the St. Louis gate, or on rue d'Auteuil between the St-Louis and Kent gates. Balades en Calèche et Diligence, La Belle Epoque, and Les Calèches du Vieux-Québec are three calèche companies. If you call ahead, some companies can also pick you up at your hotel. Some drivers talk about Québec's history and others don't; if you want a storyteller, ask for one in advance. The cost is about C$60 including all taxes for a 45-minute tour of Vieux-Québec.

🚗 **Balades en Calèche et Diligence** ☎ 418/624-3062. **La Belle Epoque** ☎ 418/687-6653. **Les Calèches du Vieux-Québec** ☎ 418/683-9222.

WALKING TOURS Adlard Tours leads walking tours of the old city through the narrow streets that buses cannot enter. The C$17 cost includes a refreshment break; tours are available in many languages. Tours leave from 12 rue Ste-Anne.

Ghost Tours of Québec gives ghoulish 90-minute evening tours of Québec City murders, executions, and ghost-sightings. Costumed actors lead the C$17.50 tours, in English or French, from May through October. Le Promenade des Écrivains (Writers' Walk) takes you through the Old City with a guide that stops to read passages about Québec City from the works of famous writers that include Melville, Thoreau, Camus, Ferron, and others. The two-hour tours cost C$15 and are given Wednesday and Saturday. La Compagnie des six associés gives several historical theme-driven walking tours year-round. Starting at C$12, a tour-ending drink is included. The themes cover such timeless topics as "Killers and Beggars," "Ghost Crimes," and "Lust and Drunkenness." You can also discover Old Québec on your own with one of several self-guided walking tour books. The best, *Vieux-Québec* is by Jean-Marie Lebel, and available only in French.

🚗 **Adlard Tours** ✉ 13 rue Ste-Famille, Upper Town ☎ 418/692-2358. **Ghost Tours of Québec** ✉ 41½ rue d'Auteuil, Upper Town ☎ 418/692-9770 ⊕ www.ghosttoursofquebec. com. **Le Promenade des Écrivains** ✉ 1588 av. Bergemont, Upper Town ☎ 418/264-2772. **La Compagnie des six associés** ✉ 381 des Franciscains, Upper Town ☎ 418/692-3033 ⊕ www.sixassocies.com.

TAXIS & LIMOUSINES

Taxis are stationed in front of major hotels and the Hôtel de Ville (City Hall), along rue des Jardins, and at Place d'Youville outside St-Jean Gate. You're charged an initial C$2.50, plus C$1.20 for each kilometer (½ mi). For radio-dispatched cars, try Taxi Coop de Québec or Taxi Québec.

Groupe Limousine A-1 has 24-hour limousine service.

🚗 **Groupe Limousine A-1** ✉ 361 rue des Commissaires Est, St. Roch ☎ 418/523-5059. **Taxi Coop de Québec** ☎ 418/525-5191. **Taxi Québec** ☎ 418/522-2001.

TRAIN TRAVEL

VIA Rail, Canada's passenger rail service, has service between Montréal and Québec City. The train arrives at the 19th-century Gare du Palais in Lower Town. Trains from Montréal to Québec City and from Québec City to Montréal run four times daily on weekdays, three times daily on weekends. The trip takes less than three hours, with a stop in Ste-Foy. Tickets can be purchased in advance at any VIA Rail office, travel agent, at the station before departure, or online. The basic one-way fare, including taxes, is C$65.56.

First-class service costs C$124.23 each way and includes early boarding, seat selection, and a three-course meal with wine. One of the best deals, subject to availability, is the round-trip ticket bought 10 days in advance for C$85.12.

🚆 **Train Information** **Gare du Palais** ✉ 450 rue de la Gare du Palais, Lower Town ☎ No phone. **VIA Rail** ☎ 418/692-3940, 800/561-3949 in the U.S., 800/361-5390 within Canada ⊕ www.viarail.ca.

TRANSPORTATION AROUND QUÉBEC CITY

A car isn't necessary unless you plan to explore beyond Québec City. Walking is the best way to see the city. Vieux-Québec measures 11 square km (about 4 square mi), and most historic sites, hotels, and restaurants are within the walls or a short distance outside. City maps are available at visitor information offices.

TRAVEL AGENCIES

🚆 **Agencies** **American Express** ✉ Place Laurier, 2700 blvd. Laurier, Ste-Foy ☎ 418/658-8820. **Voyages Claire Champoux** ✉ 1050 blvd. René-Lévesque, Suite 411, Montcalm ☎ 418/522-5234.

VISITOR INFORMATION

The Québec City Region Tourism and Convention Bureau's visitor information centers in Montcalm and Ste-Foy are open June 24 to early September, daily 8:30–7:30; early September to mid-October, daily 8:30–6:30; and mid-October through June 23, Monday through Thursday and Saturday 9–5, Friday 9–6, and Sunday 10–4. A mobile information service operates between mid-June and September 7 (look for the mopeds marked with a big question mark.

The Québec government tourism department, Tourisme Québec, has a center open daily 9–6 from September 3 through March and daily 8:30–7:30 from April through September 2.

🚆 Tourist Information **Québec City Tourist Information** ✉ 835 av. Laurier, Montcalm G1R 2L3 ☎ 418/649-2608 ⊕ www.quebecregion.com. **Ste-Foy information center** ✉ 3300 av. des Hôtels, Ste-Foy G1W 5A8 ☎ 418/651-2891. **Tourisme Québec** ✉ 12 rue Ste-Anne, Place d'Armes, Upper Town ☎ 877/266-5687 ⊕ www.bonjourquebec.com.

PROVINCE OF QUÉBEC

THE LAURENTIANS, THE EASTERN TOWNSHIPS, CHARLEVOIX & THE GASPÉ PENINSULA

3

DINE ON DELICIOUS *CONFIT DU CANARD*
At the Auberge Knowlton ⇨*p.206*

FLEE THE BUSTLE BY ESCAPING
to the posh Manoir Hovey ⇨*p.212*

SHIP OFF TO L'ÎLE BONAVENTURE
to commune with its vast colony
of marine birds ⇨*p.227*

DELIGHT IN THE LOCAL BOUNTY
Over a six-course meal at Aux Berges
de l'Aurore ⇨*p.216*

MAKE A PILGRIMAGE
To Basilique Ste-Anne-de-Beaupré ⇨*p.199*

SNAP ON YOUR SKIS AND HIT THE TRAILS
On the slopes of Mont-Tremblant ⇨*p.199*

GET READY FOR A SPRINGTIME FEAST
In the region's many sugar shacks ⇨*p.181*

QUÉBEC IS SET APART FROM THE OTHER PROVINCES OF CANADA by its strong French heritage, a matter not only of language but of customs, religion, and political structure. The province covers a vast area—almost one-sixth of Canada's total—although the upper three-quarters is only sparsely inhabited. Outside Montréal and Québec City, serenity and natural beauty abound in the province's innumerable lakes, streams, and rivers; in its farmlands and villages; in its great mountains and deep forests; and in its rugged coastline along the Gulf of St. Lawrence. During the long winters, but skiing, snowmobiling, and other activities lure both residents and visitors outdoors.

The first European to arrive in Québec was French explorer Jacques Cartier, in 1534; another Frenchman, Samuel de Champlain, arrived in 1603 to build French settlements in the region, and Jesuit missionaries followed. In 1663 Louis XIV of France proclaimed the area "New France." As a crown colony, the land was allotted to French aristocrats and administrators in large grants called *seigneuries.* Tenants, known as *habitants,* settled on the farms belonging to those who received the grants, the *seigneurs.* The Roman Catholic Church took on an importance that went beyond religion. Priests and nuns acted as doctors, educators, and arbiters among the habitants, and as liaisons between French-speaking fur traders and English-speaking merchants. After the British conquest of 1759, a church priority in Québec became *survivance*: the survival of the French people and their culture.

Québec's threats to secede from the Canadian union are part of this longstanding tradition of independence. Although the British won control of Canada in the French and Indian War in 1763, Parliament passed the Québec Act in 1774. The act ensured the continuation of French civil law in Québec and left provincial authority in the hands of the Catholic Church. In general the law preserved the traditional French-Canadian way of life. Tensions between French- and English-speaking Canada continued throughout the 20th century, however, and in 1974 the province proclaimed French its sole official language, in much the same way that the provinces of Manitoba and Alberta took steps earlier in the century to make English their sole official language.

Québec is part of the Canadian union and a signatory to its original constitution, but it hasn't accepted the changes made in that document during the 1980s. Two attempts to get Québec to sign the revised constitution in the 1990s failed. In 2003 after years of rule by the Parti Québécois (which favored separation from Canada), a Liberal provincial government was elected, and it may address the issue.

The ability to speak French can make a visit to the province more pleasant—many locals, at least in rural areas, don't speak English. If you don't speak French, arm yourself with a phrase book or at least a knowledge of some basic phrases. It's also worth your while to sample the regional Québecois cuisine—this is a place where food is taken seriously.

3

If you have
2 days

If you have only a couple of days for a visit, you need to concentrate on one area, and the Laurentians, outside Montréal, are a good choice. This resort area has recreational options (depending on the season) that include golf, hiking, and great skiing. Pick a resort town to stay in, whether it's 🖼 **St-Sauveur-des-Monts** ④ 🏃, 🖼 **Ste-Adèle** ⑥, or 🖼 **Mont-Tremblant** ⑩ near the vast **Parc du Mont-Tremblant,** and use that as a base to visit some of the surrounding towns. There's good eating and shopping here.

If your starting point is Québec City, you could take two days to explore the towns of Charlevoix east of the city, with an overnight in the elegant resort town 🖼 **La Malbaie** ㉕.

If you have
5 days

You can combine a taste of the Eastern Townships with a two-day visit to the Laurentians. Get a feel for the Laurentians by staying overnight in 🖼 **St-Sauveur-des-Monts** ④ 🏃 or 🖼 **Ste-Adèle** ⑥ 🏃 and exploring surrounding towns such as **St-Jérôme** ③ and **Morin Heights** ⑤. Then head back south of Montréal to the Townships, which extend to the east along the border with New England. Overnight in 🖼 **Granby** ⑪ or 🖼 **Bromont** ⑫: Granby has a zoo and Bromont is known for golf and its water park. The next day, you can shop in pretty **Knowlton** ⑭ (look for signs to Lac Brome) and explore regional history in such towns as **Valcourt** ⑮. Spend a night or two in the appealing resort town of 🖼 **Magog** ⑱, along Lac Memphrémagog, or the quieter 🖼 **North Hatley** ⑲, on Lac Massawippi. You'll have good dining in either. Save a day for something outdoors, whether it's golfing, skiing, biking on former railroad lines, or hiking.

If you have
10–12 days

A longer visit can show you a number of regions in Québec, but you must do some driving between them. You can spend a few days in either the Laurentians or the Eastern Townships before heading east to Québec City and historic Charlevoix, the heart of what was New France, along the St. Lawrence River. The drive from Montréal or Sherbrooke to Québec City is more than 240 km (149 mi); 33 km (20 mi) to the east lies **Ste-Anne-de-Beaupré** ㉒, with its famous basilica. Colonial-era homes and farmhouses dot several Charlevoix villages; some are still homes, and others are now theaters, museums, or restaurants. Spend time in 🖼 **Baie St-Paul** ㉓ and 🖼 **La Malbaie** ㉕, or just drive lovely roads such as Route 362. In season (around July through September) you can whale-watch in **Tadoussac** ㉖. To get to the Gaspé Peninsula, you have to cross the St. Lawrence River. An hour-long ferry ride from St-Siméon, between La Malbaie and Tadoussac, takes you to Rivière-du-Loup. From there it's a day to get to 🖼 **Carleton** ㉗ on the Gaspé's southern shore. The peninsula offers one of the most scenic drives in North America; you can stop in 🖼 **Percé** ㉘ and spend a day visiting **l'Île Bonaventure,** which has a fascinating bird colony.

Exploring Québec

Two major recreational areas attract stressed-out urban-dwellers and anyone else who wants to relax: the Laurentians and the Eastern Townships. The Laurentians resort area, which begins 60 km (37 mi) north of Montréal, has fine ski hills and thousands of miles of wilderness. The Eastern Townships, which start 80 km (50 mi) in a southern corner of the province, have ski slopes, lakes, and provincial parks as well as some important cultural attractions.

Charlevoix is often called the Switzerland of Québec due to its terrain of mountains, valleys, streams, and waterfalls. Charming villages line the north shore of the St. Lawrence River for about 200 km (124 mi)— from Ste-Anne-de-Beaupré, east of Québec City, to the Saguenay River. The knobby Gaspé Peninsula is where the St. Lawrence River meets the Gulf of St. Lawrence. This isolated peninsula, which begins about 200 km (124 mi) east of Québec City, has a wild beauty all its own: mountains and cliffs tower above its beaches. The drive around the Gaspé is 848 km (526 mi).

Numbers in the text correspond to numbers in the margin and on the Laurentians (les Laurentides), Eastern Townships (les Cantons de l'Est), and Montérégie, Charlevoix & Gaspé Peninsula (Gaspésie) maps.

About the Hotels & Restaurants

In the countryside, a number of inns, including some in the Eastern Townships, provide food that can compete with any served in the cities for quality and creativity. Whether you choose a mixed-game pie such as *cipaille* or a sweet–salty dish like ham with maple syrup, you won't soon forget your meals here. Cooking in the province tends to be hearty: cassoulet, *tourtières* (meat pies), onion soup, and apple pie head up menus. Maple syrup, much of it produced locally, is a mainstay of Québecois dishes. Cloves, nutmeg, cinnamon, and pepper—spices used by the first settlers—haven't gone out of style.

The Eastern Townships are one of Québec's foremost regions for good food, and chefs at the finer Laurentian inns have attracted an international following. Early reservations are essential. Many restaurants are closed Monday, but Tuesday isn't too soon to book weekend tables at the best provincial restaurants.

More casual fare, such as a croissant and an espresso, or *poutine*—a heaped plate of *frites* (french fries) smothered with gravy and melted cheese curds—is available from sidewalk cafés and fast-food restaurants.

Accommodations in the province range from resort hotels and elegant Relais & Châteaux properties in the Laurentians and Eastern Townships to simple motels and *auberges* (inns) in the heart of the Gaspé. Many inns operate on the Modified American Plan—especially in high season (winter in the Laurentians and other ski areas, summer elsewhere), which means that two meals, usually breakfast and dinner, are included in the cost of a night's stay. Be sure to ask what's included, and expect prices to be lower off-season. Some inns require a minimum two-night stay; always ask.

3

Fishing

More than 20 outfitters (some of whom are also innkeepers) work in the northern Laurentians area, where provincial parks and game sanctuaries abound. Pike, walleye, and lake and speckled trout are plentiful. Open year-round in most cases, the lodging facilities range from luxurious, first-class resorts to log cabins. As well as supplying trained guides, all provide services and equipment to allow both neophytes and experts the best possible fishing in addition to boating, swimming, river rafting, wind-surfing, ice fishing, cross-country skiing, or hiking.

Rafting

The Rivière Rouge in the Laurentians rates among the best rivers for rafting in North America. Just an hour's drive north of Montréal, the Rouge cuts across the rugged Laurentians through canyons and alongside beaches. April through October you can experience what travers-ing the region must have meant in the days of the voyageurs, though today's trip is much safer and more comfortable.

Skiing

The Laurentians are well known internationally as a downhill destination, from St-Sauveur to majestic Mont-Tremblant. Night skiing is available on some slopes. Cross-country skiing is popular throughout the area from December to the beginning of April, especially at Val David, Val Morin, and Estérel. Each has a cross-country ski center and at least a dozen groomed trails. The East-ern Townships have more than 1,000 km (620 mi) of cross-country trails; the area is also popular as a downhill ski center, with ski hills on four mountains that dwarf anything the Laurentians have to offer, with the exception of Mont-Tremblant. Charlevoix has three main ski areas, with excellent facilities for both downhill and cross-country skiers.

Lift ticket prices vary by resort, and the cost is often included in hotel pack-ages. Expect to pay about C$40 per day. Road names near ski areas are sel-dom labeled (they're up the mountain, where else?) but the signage is extremely good, with ski symbols and distances clearly marked.

Sugar Shacks

In late March and early April the combination of sunny days and cold nights causes the sap to run in the maple trees. *Cabanes à sucre* (sugar shacks) go into operation, boiling the sap collected from the trees in buckets (at some places, complicated tubing and vats now do the job). The many commercial enterprises scattered over the area host "sugaring offs" and tours of the process, including tapping the maple trees, boiling the sap in vats, and *tire sur la neige*—pouring hot syrup over cold snow to give it a taffy con-sistency just right for "pulling" and eating. A number of cabanes serve hearty meals of ham, baked beans, and pancakes, all drowned in maple syrup.

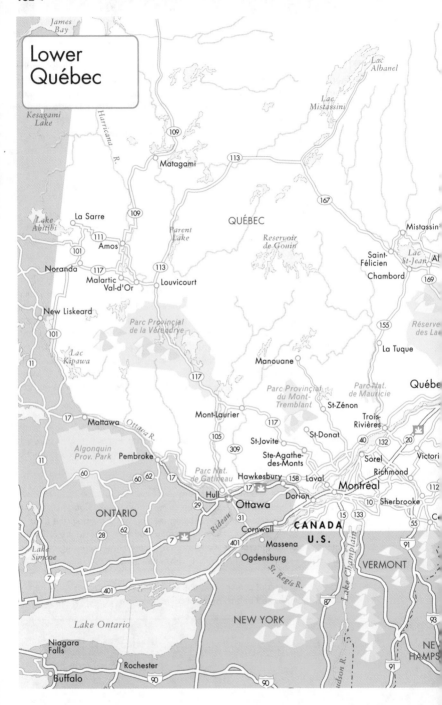

Lower Québec

James Bay

Lac Albanel

Kesagami Lake

Lac Mistassini

109

113

Matagami

167

Harricana R.

QUÉBEC

Mistassin

Lake Abitibi

La Sarre

109

Parent Lake

Reservoir de Gouin

Saint-Félicien

Lac St-Jean

Al

111

Amos

101

113

Chambord

169

Noranda

117

Malartic

Val-d'Or

Louvicourt

155

Réserve des Lac

New Liskeard

101

Parc Provincial de la Vérendrye

La Tuque

Lac Kipawa

11

117

Manouane

Québe

Parc Provincial du Mont-Tremblant

St-Zénon

Parc Nat. de Mauricie

17

Mattawa

Ottawa R.

Mont-Laurier

117

Trois-Rivières

105

St-Donat

40

132

20

Algonquin Prov. Park

Pembroke

309

St-Jovite

Victori

11

60

60

62

Parc Nat. de Gatineau

Ste-Agathe-des-Monts

Sorel

Richmond

Hawkesbury

158

Laval

112

Hull

17

Montréal

Dorion

10

Sherbrooke

ONTARIO

29

Ottawa

C

62

41

31

15

133

55

28

Cornwall

CANADA

7

401

Massena

U.S.

91

Lake Simcoe

Ogdensburg

VERMONT

7

St. Regis R.

401

Lake Champlain

Lake Ontario

NEW YORK

87

93

Niagara Falls

Hudson R.

NEW HAMPS

Rochester

91

Buffalo

90

90

	$$$$	**$$$**	**$$**	**$**	**¢**
	WHAT IT COSTS In Canadian dollars				
RESTAURANTS	over C$30	C$20–C$30	C$12–C$20	C$8–C$12	under C$8
HOTELS	over C$250	C$175–C$250	C$125–C$175	C$75–C$125	under C$75

Restaurant prices are for a main course at dinner (or at the most expensive meal served). Hotel prices are for two people in a standard double room in high season, excluding 7% GST and 7.5% provincial tax.

Timing

The Laurentians are a big skiing destination in winter but the other seasons all have their own charms: you can drive up from Montréal for the fall foliage; to hike, bike, or play golf; or to engage in spring skiing—and still get back to the city before dark. The only slow periods are early November, when there isn't much to do, and June, when the area has plenty but do but is also plagued by blackflies, which are biting gnats. Control programs have improved the situation somewhat.

The Eastern Townships are best in fall, when the foliage is at its peak; the region borders Vermont and has the same dramatic colors. It's possible to visit wineries at this time, but you should call ahead, since harvest is a busy time. Charlevoix is lovely in fall, but winter is particularly magical—although the steep and narrow roads aren't great. In summer, the special, silvery light, born of the mountains and the proximity of the sea, attracts many painters.

Summer is really the only time to tour the Gaspé. Some attractions have already closed by Labor Day (the first Monday in September), and few hotels are open in winter. The weather can be harsh, too, and driving the coast road can be difficult.

THE LAURENTIANS

Updated by
Mary Ann
Simpkins

The Laurentians (les Laurentides) are divided into two major regions: the Lower Laurentians (les Basses Laurentides) and the Upper Laurentians (les Hautes Laurentides). But don't be fooled by the designations; they don't signify great driving distances. Avid skiers might call Montréal a bedroom community for the Laurentians, which start just 60 km (37 mi) to the north. These rocky hills are relatively low, but many are eminently skiable, with a few peaks above 2,500 feet. Mont-Tremblant, at 3,150 feet, is the highest.

The P'tit Train du Nord—the former railroad line that is now a 200-km (124-mi) "linear park" used by cyclists, hikers, skiers, and snowmobilers—made it possible to transport settlers and cargo easily to the Upper Laurentians. It also opened the area up to skiing by the early 1900s. Before long, trainloads of skiers replaced settlers and cargo as the railway's major trade. At first a winter weekend getaway for Montrealers who stayed at boardinghouses and fledgling resorts, the Upper Laurentians soon began attracting international visitors.

Ski lodges and private family cottages for wealthy city dwellers were accessible only by train until the 1930s, when Route 117 was built. Today there is an uneasy peace between the longtime cottagers, who want to restrict development, and resort entrepreneurs, who want to expand. At the moment, commercial interests seem to be prevailing. A number of large hotels have added indoor pools and spa facilities, and efficient highways have brought the country even closer to the city—45 minutes to St-Sauveur, 1½–2 hours to Mont-Tremblant.

The Lower Laurentians start almost immediately outside Montréal and are rich in historic and architectural interest. Towns such as St-Eustache and Oka are home to the manors, mills, churches, and public buildings seigneurs built for themselves and their habitants.

The resort area truly begins at St-Sauveur-des-Monts (Exit 60 on Autoroute 15) and extends as far north as Mont-Tremblant. Beyond, the region turns into a wilderness of lakes and forests best visited with an outfitter. Guides that offer fishing trips are concentrated around Parc du Mont-Tremblant. To the first-time visitor, the hilly areas around St-Sauveur, Ste-Adèle, Morin Heights, Val Morin, and Val David up to Ste-Agathe-des-Monts form a pleasant hodgepodge of villages, hotels, and inns that seem to blend one into another.

Oka

❶ *40 km (25 mi) west of Montréal.*

To promote Christianity among the local Native Americans, the Catholic order of priests, the Sulpicians, erected the **Calvaire d'Oka** (⊠ Rte. 344, opposite the entrance to Parc d'Oka ☎ No phone). Representing the Stations of the Cross, the Oka Calvary and its seven chapels were built between 1740 and 1742. Three chapels are still maintained, and every September 14 since 1870 Québecois pilgrims have congregated here to participate in the half-hour ceremony that proceeds on foot to the calvary's summit. A sense of the divine is enhanced by the magnificent view of Lac des Deux-Montagnes.

The **Abbaye Cistercienne d'Oka** is one of the oldest North American abbeys. In 1887 the Sulpicians donated about 865 acres of their property near the Oka Calvary to the Trappist monks, who had arrived in 1880 from Bellefontaine Abbey in France. Within a decade they had built their monastery and transformed this land. Trappists established the Oka School of Agriculture, which operated until 1960. The monks became famous for their creamy Oka cheese; it's now produced commercially, but the monks still oversee the operations. (The abbey store sells Oka cheese and products from other Québec monasteries, such as chocolate, cheese, and cider.) The monastery is notable for its prayer retreat. ⊠ *1600 chemin d'Oka* ☎ *450/479–8361* ⊕ *www.abbayeoka.com* ⬚ *Free* ☉ *Chapel Mon.–Sat. 4 AM–8 PM; gardens and shop Mon. 10–noon and 12:30–4:30, Tues.–Fri. 9:30–noon and 12:30–4:30, Sat. 9:30–4.*

Parc d'Oka, surrounded by low hills, has a lake fringed by a sandy beach with picnic areas and hiking and biking trails. This is a good place

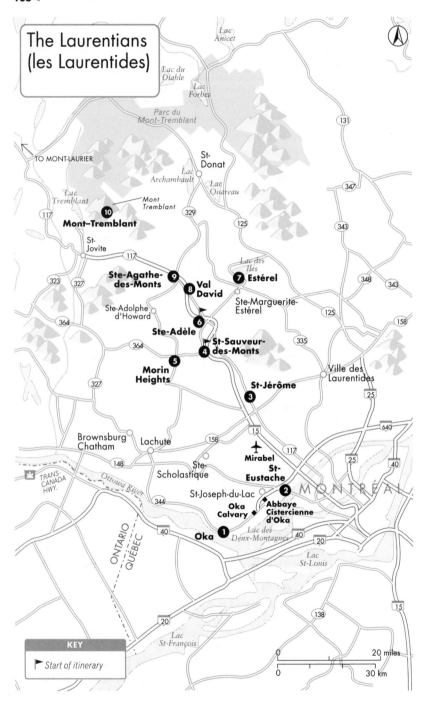

The Laurentians (les Laurentides)

Lac Anicet

Lac du Diable

Lac Forbes

Parc du Mont-Tremblant

131

TO MONT-LAURIER

St-Donat

Lac Archambault

Lac Ouareau

347

Lac Tremblant

Mont Tremblant

329

125

343

117

10

Mont–Tremblant

St-Jovite

117

Lac des Îles

Ste-Marguerite-Estérel

348

343

323 327

Ste-Agathe-des-Monts **9**

8 **Val David**

7 **Estérel**

125

158

Ste-Adolphe d'Howard

364

6

Ste-Adèle

335

St-Sauveur-des-Monts

Ville des Laurentides

364

5

4

Morin Heights

St-Jérôme

25

327

3

15

640

Brownsburg Chatham

Lachute

158

117

25

40

148

Ste-Scholastique

Mirabel

St-Eustache

M O N T R É A L

344

St-Joseph-du-Lac

2

ONTARIO QUÉBEC

40

Oka Calvary

Abbaye Cistercienne d'Oka

TRANS-CANADA HWY.

Ottawa River

Oka **1**

Lac des Deux-Montagnes

40

20

Lac St-Louis

20

138

15

Lac St-François

KEY

► Start of itinerary

0 ——— 20 miles
0 ——— 30 km

for kayaking, canoeing, fishing, and, in winter, snowshoeing and cross-country skiing. There are nearly 900 camp sites here. ⊠ *2020 chemin Oka* ☎ *450/479–8365, 800/665–6527 activities* ⊕ *www.sepaq.com* ▨ *C$3.50 plus C$5 per car* ☉ *Daily 8* AM–10 PM.

A quick detour on the ferry (C$7 one-way) across Lac des Deux Montagnes brings you to **Hudson,** a small town with old homes housing art galleries, boutiques, and Christmas shops. In winter, there's an ice bridge: basically a plowed path across a well-frozen lake. Taking such a bridge is a singular experience.

So many apple orchards produce cider around Saint-Joseph-du-Lac, about a ten-minute drive from Oka, that there's a Route des *Vergers.* This "Orchard Route" lists 39 growers selling all types of cider: dry, sweet, white, and red. Many of the growers have tastings and tours. There's also a winery on the route: La Roche des Brises, whose whites and reds include the port-like *L'été Indien* (Indian Summer). You can tour the vineyard, taste the wines for C$5, and dine in an adjacent restaurant. Across the road and overlooking some of the grape vines is a charming five-room bed-and-breakfast with a spa, the **Auberge Roches des Brises** ⊠ *2007 rue Principale, St-Joseph-du-Lac* ☎ *450/472–2722, 450/472–3477, 450/ 472–8756* ⊕ *www.rochesdesbrises.com* ☉ *Closed Jan.–mid-Feb.*

Where to Stay

$$$ ☷ **Hotel du Lac Carling.** The modern but classically furnished hotel is near Lachute (about 40 km, or 25 mi, northwest of Oka) and on the doorstep to 5,000 acres of wilderness. In addition to a large sports center, 20 km (12 mi) of cross-country ski trails, and an excellent par-72 golf course, there's also an impressive restaurant. The menu includes good salmon appetizers smoked by the chef and a main course of lamb. The hotel's rooms are furnished with oil paintings, and antiques line the corridors. The standard rooms are among the largest in the province. Loft suites, with kitchenettes and fireplaces, are entered from the upper floor. ⊠ *2255 Rte. 327 Nord, Brownsburg-Chatham, J0V 1A0* ☎ *450/533– 9211 or 800/661–9211* ⊟ *450/533–4495* ⊕ *www.laccarling.com* ▭ *88 rooms, 9 suites* ♿ *Restaurant, room service, some fans, in-room data ports, in-room safes, some in-room hot tubs, some kitchenettes, mini-bars, cable TV with movies, 18-hole golf course, 2 tennis courts, pro shop, pool, lake, gym, hot tub, sauna, spa, beach, dock, boating, fishing, mountain bikes, racquetball, squash, volleyball, cross-country skiing, ice-skating, two bars, babysitting, children's programs (ages 3–18), laundry service, meeting rooms, some pets allowed, no-smoking rooms* ▤ *AE, DC, MC, V* ⦿⦿ *BP.*

St-Eustache

❷ *25 km (16 mi) northeast of Oka, 15 km (9 mi) north of Montréal.*

One of the most important and tragic battles in Canadian history was fought here during the 1837 Rebellion. After the British conquest of 1759, French Canadians were confined to preexisting territories, and the new townships were allotted exclusively to the English. Adding to this insult was the government's decision to tax all products imported from

England, which made them prohibitively expensive. The result? In 1834 the French Canadian Patriot party defeated the British party locally. Lower Canada, as it was then known, became a hotbed of tension between the French and English.

Rumors of rebellion were rife, and in December 1837, some 2,000 English soldiers led by General Colborne were sent in to surround St-Eustache and put down the "army" of North Shore patriots. Jean-Olivier Chénier and his 200 men took refuge in the local church, which Colborne's cannons bombed. Chénier and 80 of his followers were killed during the battle, and more than 100 of the town's buildings were looted and burned by Colborne's soldiers.

Traces of shots fired by the English army cannons are visible on the facade of **Église St-Eustache** (St-Eustache Church), at 123 rue St-Louis. The Montréal Symphony Orchestra makes all its recordings here: the acoustics are superb. The church doors are locked except during services.

The oldest structure in St-Eustache is the **Moulin Légaré,** a flour mill that dates to 1762. Designated a National Historic Site, it's the oldest working water-operated mill in North America. About 40 tons a year of wheat and buckwheat are ground on the premises and sold here. Guides show how the mill operates. ⊠ *236 rue St-Eustache* ☎ *450/974–5400* 🖃 *C$3* ⊙ *May–Oct., daily 9–5; Oct.–May, weekdays 9–5.*

The **Musée de Saint-Eustache et de ses Patriotes,** inside a handsome 1903 manor house, includes an exhibit about the 1837 Rebellion. ⊠ *Manoir Globensky, 235 rue St-Eustache* ☎ *450/974–5170* ⊕ *www.tourisme-st-eustache.com* 🖃 *C$3* ⊙ *Tues.–Sun. 10–5.*

St-Jérôme

❸ *25 km (16 mi) north of St-Eustache, 48 km (30 mi) north of Montréal.*

Founded in 1834, St-Jérôme is a thriving economic center and cultural hub. The town first gained prominence in 1868, when Curé Antoine Labelle became pastor of this parish on the shores of the Rivière du Nord. Curé Labelle devoted himself to opening up northern Québec to French Canadians. Between 1868 and 1890, he founded 20 parish towns—an impressive achievement given the harsh conditions of this vast wilderness. But his most important legacy was the famous P'tit Train du Nord railroad line, which he persuaded the government to build in order to open St-Jérôme to travel and trade.

Le P'tit Train du Nord, immortalized by singer Félix Leclerc, spurred settlement into what was then virgin wilderness. In the 1920s and 1930s, it also boosted the just-emerging tourist industry. "Snow trains" carried Montrealers into the hinterland to enjoy what was then a trendy new sport. By the beginning of the 1940s, some 10,000 skiers were heading north every weekend—nothing compared with today's numbers, of course, but a record at the time.

The Le P'tit Train du Nord no longer exists, but in 1996 the track was transformed into the 200-km (124-mi) **Linear Park** (Parc Linéaire). From the moment it opened, the park proved hugely popular. By the end of 1997, it had already attracted more than 1 million visitors. The well-sign-posted trail starts at the former railway station (1 place de la Gare) in St-Jérôme and is used mostly by cyclists (walkers use it at their peril, be-cause the bikers hurtle by quickly). The path runs all the way to Mont-Laurier in the north. It's flanked by distance markers, so that cyclists can track their progress, or ride just parts of the trail; some of the old rail-way stations and historic landmarks along the route have been converted into places where *velo-touristes* (bike tourists) can stop for a snack. In winter, the trail is taken over by cross-country skiers and snowmobilers.

St-Jérôme's **promenade,** a boardwalk stretching 4 km (2½ mi), follows the Rivière du Nord from the rue de Martigny bridge to the rue St-Joseph bridge. Descriptive plaques en route highlight episodes of the Battle of 1837, a French–Canadian uprising.

Musée d'art contemporain des Laurentides, in the old courthouse, has changing exhibits of contemporary art. Most of the artists whose work is included are from Québec. ⊠ *185 rue du Palais* ☎ *450/432–7171* ⊠ *Free* ☉ *Sun. and Tues.–Fri. noon–5, Sat. 9–5.*

Parc Régional de la Rivière-du-Nord was created as a nature retreat. Trails through the regional park lead to the spectacular **Wilson Falls.** The **Pavil-lon Marie-Victorin** has summer weekend displays and workshops devoted to nature, culture, and history. You can hike, bike, cross-country ski, snow-shoe, or snow-slide here. ⊠ *1051 blvd. International* ☎ *450/431–1676* ⊠ *C$4* ☉ *Sept. 2–late May, daily 9–5; late May–Sept. 1, daily 9–7.*

Sports & the Outdoors

Parachutisme Para-Vision (⊠ 881 rue Lamontagne, St-Jérôme ☎450/438–0855 or 866/323–4443 ⊕ www.paradrenaline.ca), a parachuting school with a flying center that's 15 minutes from the middle of St-Jérôme, caters to novice and seasoned jumpers alike. Courses (C$245–C$285 per per-son) are limited to those ages 16 and up.

St-Sauveur-des-Monts

▶ ❹ *25 km (16 mi) north of St-Jérôme, 63 km (39 mi) north of Montréal.*

The town of St-Sauveur encompasses St-Sauveur-des-Monts, a focal point for area resorts. A sleepy Laurentian hamlet in the 1980s, St-Sauveur-des-Monts now attracts visitors on weekends. Rue Principale, the main street, has dozens of restaurants serving everything from lamb bro-chettes to spicy Thai fare. The narrow strip is so choked with cars and tourists in summer that it's called Crescent Street of the North, after the action-filled street in Montréal. Despite all this development, St-Sauveur-des-Monts has maintained some of its rural character.

Skiing and other snow sports are the main things to do in winter. Mont-St-Sauveur, Mont-Avila, Mont-Gabriel, and Mont-Olympia all have special season passes and programs, and some ski-center passes can be used at more than one center in the region. Blue signs on Route 117 and Autoroute 15 indicate where the ski hills are.

The **Mont-St-Sauveur Water Park,** on the town's outskirts, keeps children occupied with slides, a giant wave pool, a wading pool, and snack bars. The rafting river attracts an older, braver crowd; the nine-minute ride follows the natural contours of steep hills. On the tandem slides, plumes of water flow through figure-eight tubes. ⊠ *350 rue St-Denis* ☎ *450/227–4671 or 800/363–2426* ⊕ *www.mssi.ca* ☎ *Full day C$29, after 3* PM *C$23, after 5* PM *C$16* ☉ *Early June–mid-June and late Aug.–early Sept., daily 10–5; mid-June–mid-Aug., daily 10–7.*

Where to Stay & Eat

$–$$$ ✕ **Le Bifthèque.** French-Canadians flock to this local institution for perfectly aged steaks and other hearty fare. This branch of the chain, in the heart of St-Sauveur, also serves lamb loin with Dijon mustard and trout stuffed with crab and shrimp. The list of wines is long. Children have their own menu. Pick up steaks to go at the meat counter if you're staying where you can grill your own. ⊠ *86 rue de la Gare* ☎ *450/227–2442* ▤ *AE, MC, V* ☉ *No lunch Mon–Thurs.*

$–$$$$ ✕▦ **Relais St-Denis.** A traditional sloping Québecois roof and dormer windows cap this traditional inn, where every guest room has a fireplace. Junior suites have whirlpool baths. La Reine Victoria ($$$$), one of two restaurants in the inn, serves multicourse meals with an emphasis on regional cuisine. It caters to a business-breakfast crowd during the week. ⊠ *61 rue St-Denis, J0R 1R4* ☎ *450/227–4766 or 888/997–4766* ⊟ *450/227–8504* ⊕ *www.relaisst-denis.com* ⟿ *22 rooms, 22 suites* ⟐ *2 restaurants, in-room data ports, some in-room hot tubs, refrigerators, cable TV, pool, outdoor hot tub, massage, bar, meeting rooms, some pets allowed, no smoking floors* ▤ *AE, D, MC, V.*

Sports & the Outdoors

La Vallée de Saint-Sauveur is the collective name for the ski area north of St-Sauveur-des-Monts. The area is especially well known for its night skiing. **Mont St-Sauveur** (⊠ 350 rue St-Denis, St-Sauveur ☎ 450/227–4671, 514/871–0101, or 800/363–2426 ⊕ www.mssi.ca) has 9 trails each for beginning and intermediate-level skiers, 15 for experts, and 5 trails that are extremely difficult; eight lifts, and a vertical drop of 700 feet. Next to the Mont St-Sauveur ski resort and sharing an owner is **Mont Avila** (⊠ 500 chemin Avila, Piedmont ☎ 450/227–4671 or 514/871–0101 ⊕ www.mssi. ca), with eleven trails (two rated for beginners, three at an intermediate level, and the rest for experts), three lifts, and a 615-foot vertical drop. **Station de Ski Mont-Habitant** (⊠ 12 blvd. des Skieurs, St-Sauveur-des-Monts ☎ 866/887–2637 or 450/227–2637 ⊕ www.monthabitant.com) has 14 trails (three rated beginner, four expert, and the remainder, intermediate), three lifts, and a vertical drop of 600 feet.

Shopping

At **Factoreries St-Sauveur** (⊠ 100 rue Guindon, Autoroute 15, Exit 60 ☎ 450/227–1074), Canadian, American, and European manufacturers sell goods, from designer clothing to household items, at reduced prices. The factory-outlet mall has more than 25 stores and sells labels such as Guess, Tommy Hilfiger, and Polo Ralph Lauren. Fashion boutiques and gift shops, adorned with bright awnings and flowers, line **rue Principale.**

Morin Heights

❺ *10 km (6 mi) west of St-Sauveur-des-Monts, 73 km (45 mi) northwest of Montréal.*

The town's British architecture and population reflect its settlers' heritage; most residents here speak English. Although Morin Heights has escaped the overdevelopment of neighboring St-Sauveur, there are still many restaurants, bookstores, boutiques, and craft shops to explore.

In summer, windsurfing, swimming, and canoeing on the area's two lakes—Claude and Lafontaine—are popular. You can also head for the region's golf courses (including the 18 holes at Mont-Gabriel) and the campgrounds at Val David and the two lakes, which have beaches. In fall and winter, come for the foliage and the alpine and Nordic skiing.

Where to Stay & Eat

$ ⬚ **L'Ombrelle B&B.** Nearly ringed by a pine forest, this stately New England–style house opened as a B&B in 2003. Down comforters cover brass queen-size beds in the country-style decorated rooms. A main attraction is the three-course breakfast, which sometimes includes homemade raspberry cake. You can eat in your room or at the dining table framed by windows overlooking the garden. Relax by the outdoor pool or, in the winter, by the fireplace in the lounge. ✉ *160 de Christieville, J0R 1H0* ☎*450/226–2334 or 514/592–2840* 🖷*450/226–8027* ⊕*www. lombrelle.com* ⇨ *3 rooms* ⚘ *Some fans, some in-room hot-tubs, cable TV, pool, hiking, lounge, babysitting, Internet; no room phones, no smoking* ▭ *MC, V* ⊚❘ *BP.*

$$–$$$$ ✕ **Le Petit Prince.** Many locals adore this restaurant in a tiny blue-shingled wood house on a side-road near Highway 364 which runs through Morin Heights. Lace curtains on the windows and wood walls accent the bistro-style cuisine. Scallops in Pernod sauce and grilled rib steak are some of the dishes on the menu. ✉ *139 St-Adolphe Rd.* ☎ *450/226–6887* ▭ *AE, MC, V* ⊘ *Closed Mon.–Tues. No lunch.*

Sports & the Outdoors

The vertical drop at **Ski Morin Heights** (✉ 231 rue Bennett ☎ 450/227–2020 ⊕ www.mssi.ca), near Exit 60 of Autoroute 15 North, is 656 feet. The 23 trails include 8 for beginners, 7 each for intermediate and expert levels, and 1 glade run. The 44,000-square-foot chalet houses eateries, a pub, a day-care center, and equipment rental, but the center doesn't have lodging.

Ste-Adèle

▶ ❻ *12 km (7 mi) north of Morin Heights, 85 km (53 mi) north of Montréal.*

With a permanent population of more than 10,000, Ste-Adèle is the largest community in the lower part of the Laurentians. A number of government offices and facilities for local residents are here: cinemas, shopping malls, and summer theater (in French). Of interest to visitors are the sports shops, boutiques, restaurants, and family-oriented amusements.

At ☺ **Au Pays des Merveilles,** fairy-tale characters such as Snow White, Little Red Riding Hood, and Alice in Wonderland wander the grounds, playing games with children. Small fry may also enjoy the petting zoo, amusement rides, wading pool, and puppet theater. A ride called Le Petit Train des Merveilles (the Marvelous Little Train) is a nod to the historic train that launched the tourism industry in the Laurentians. There are 39 activities, enough to occupy those aged 2 to 9 for about half a day. Check the Web site for discount coupons. ✉ *3795 rue de la Savane* ☎ *450/229–3141* ⊕ *www.paysmerveilles.com* 🎟 *C$15* ⊙ *Early June–late-June and late Aug.–early Sept., weekends 10–6; late June–late August, daily 10–6.*

☺ The Laurentians region has more than its share of water parks; Ste-Adèle started the trend with **Super Splash Sainte-Adèle.** On hot, humid weekends, Montrealers with families fill the water park, which has water slides, a wading pool, a wave pool, and miniature golf. ✉ *1791 blvd. Sainte-Adèle* ☎ *450/229–2909* ⊕ *www.supersplash.qc.ca* 🎟 *C$10–C$17* ⊙ *Mid-June–late Aug., daily 10–7.*

Where to Stay & Eat

$$$–$$$$ ✕ **La Clef des Champs.** The French food served at this romantic restaurant tucked amid trees is all quite good. Game dishes, such as medallions of roasted ostrich in a port-infused sauce, grilled venison, or caribou in red-currant marinade, are specialties. Good dessert choices include *gâteaux aux deux chocolats* (two-chocolate cake) and crème brûlée. A C$60 table d'hôte is available Saturdays. ✉ *875 chemin Ste-Marguerite* ☎ *450/229–2857* ▭ *AE, DC, MC, V* ⊙ *Closed 3 wks in Apr. and Mon. Oct.–late June. No lunch.*

$$$–$$$$ ✕▥ **L'Eau à la Bouche.** Superb service, stunning rooms awash with color,
FodorśChoice   and a terrace with a flower garden are highlights of this charming inn.
★   Guest rooms, some with fireplaces, are decorated in styles that include Victorian, safari, and Inuit. Skiing is literally at your door, since the inn faces Le Chantecler's slopes. The restaurant here ($$$$) interprets nouvelle cuisine with regional ingredients. The menu changes with the seasons, but it has included foie gras with apple-cider sauce, breast of Barbary duck, and red wine–marinated venison. Owner-chef Anne Desjardins is a well-known and highly regarded Québecois personality. ✉ *3003 blvd. Ste-Adèle, J8B 2N6* ☎ *450/229–2991 or 888/828–2991* 🖷 *450/229–7573* ⊕ *www.leaualabouche.com* 📞 *23 rooms, 2 suites* ♨ *Restaurant, some fans, in-room data ports, some in-room hot tubs, cable TV with movies, pool, massage, bar, babysitting, dry cleaning, laundry service; no smoking* ▭ *AE, DC, MC, V.*

$–$$ ✕▥ **Hôtel Mont-Gabriel.** Built by Josephine Hartford Bryce, whose grandfather founded the A&P grocery chain, the hotel started as a log structure with about a dozen rooms. The simple structure has evolved into a 1,200-acre resort where you can relax in a contemporary room with a valley view or commune with nature in a rustic-style cabin with a fireplace. In winter, you can ski out from many rooms. The French cuisine is good, with entrées such as salmon with braised leeks, and pork with ginger and orange. ✉ *1699 chemin du Mont Gabriel (Autoroute 15, Exit 64), J8B 1A5* ☎ *450/229–3547 or 800/668–5253* 🖷 *450/229–7034*

⊕ *www.montgabriel.com* ⇗ *126 rooms, 3 suites, 2 chalets* ⟁ *Restaurant, snack bar, room service, some fans, in-room data ports, some in-room hot tubs, some refrigerators, room TVs with movies and video games, driving range, 18-hole golf course, putting green, 6 tennis courts, pro shop, 2 pools (1 indoor), gym, sauna, spa, basketball, boccie, hiking, shuffleboard, volleyball, cross-country skiing, downhill skiing, ski shop, ski storage, sports bar, babysitting, business services, meeting rooms, no-smoking rooms* ⊟ *AE, DC, MC, V* ⦿ *EP.*

$–$$$ 🖼 **Le Chantecler.** This Montrealer favorite is beside Lac Ste-Adèle and at the base of a mountain with 25 downhill ski runs; trails begin almost at the hotel entrance. The rooms and chalets, furnished with Canadian pine, have a rustic appeal. Given all the activities here, which include snowshoeing with a trapper as well as cycling races, Le Chantecler is for people looking for an energetic holiday. ⊠ *1474 chemin Chantecler, J0B 1A2* ☎ *450/229–3555 or 888/916–1616* 🖷 *450/229–5593* ⊕ *www.lechantecler.com* ⇗ *185 rooms, 28 suites, 7 chalets* ⟁ *Restaurant, room service, in-room data ports, some in-room hot tubs, some kitchenettes, minibars, cable TV with movies, 9-hole golf course, 6 tennis courts, indoor pool, lake, gym, hair salon, sauna, spa, beach, dock, boating, bicycles, boccie, hiking, horseback riding, horseshoes, shuffleboard, squash, volleyball, cross-country skiing, downhill skiing, ski shop, bar, video game room, shop, babysitting, children's programs, dry cleaning, laundry service, concierge, business services, no-smoking rooms; no a/c in some rooms* ⊟ *AE, D, DC, MC, V* ⦿ *EP.*

$–$$$ 🖼 **Auberge & Spa Beaux Rêves.** Rooms at this rustic Québecois retreat along a river bank give you plenty of space in which to spread out. The fieldstone building has hardwood floors; furnishings are spare, but many of the suites have fireplaces. The outdoor hot tub and Finnish sauna are used all year. The restaurant's homey dishes include chicken in wine sauce and leg of rabbit marinated in mushroom sauce. A table d'hôte of five courses is available for dinner. ⊠ *2310 blvd. Ste-Adèle, J8B 2N5* ☎ *450/229–9226 or 800/279–7679* 🖷 *450/229–2999* ⊕ *www.beauxreves.com* ⇗ *7 rooms, 6 suites* ⟁ *Restaurant, some in-room hot tubs, outdoor hot tub, massage, sauna, spa, meeting rooms; no a/c in some rooms, no room phones, no room TVs, no smoking* ⊟ *MC, V* ⦿ *CP.*

Sports & the Outdoors

GOLF The par-72, 18-hole **Club de Golf Chantecler** (⊠ 2520 chemin du Club ☎ 450/229–3742 ⊕ www.golflachute.com/chantecler) is off Exit 67 of Autoroute 15. Greens fees range from C$29 on weekdays to C$35 on weekends.

SKIING **Ski Chantecler** (⊠ 1474 rue Chantecler, Mont-Chantecler ☎ 450/229–3555) has six lifts, 25 runs, and a vertical drop of 663 feet, in addition to 50 km (31 mi) of cross-country trails. **Ski Mont-Gabriel** (⊠ 350 rue St-Denis, Monté Mont-Gabriel ☎ 450/227–1100 or 800/363–2426 ⊕ www.skimontgabriel.com), 19 km (12 mi) northeast of Ste-Adèle, has seven lifts and 18 superb downhill trails, which are primarily for intermediate and advanced skiers. The vertical drop is 656 feet.

Estérel

❼ *15 km (9 mi) north of Ste-Adèle, 100 km (62 mi) north of Montréal.*

The permanent population of Estérel is just over 2,400, but visitors to Estérel Resort and Convention Centre, a hotel off Route 370, at Exit 69 near Ste-Marguerite Station, swell the total population throughout the year. Founded in in the 1920s on the shores of Lac Dupuis, the 5,000-acre estate was named Estérel by Baron Louis Empain because it evoked memories of his native village in Provence. In 1959 Fridolin Simard bought the property and Hôtel l'Estérel soon became a household word for Québecois in search of a first-class resort.

Where to Stay & Eat

★ **$$$–$$$$** ✕ **Bistro à Champlain.** Its astonishing selection of wines—some 2,000—put this bistro on the map. You can tour the cellars, where some 35,000 bottles (at last count) had prices from C$28 to C$25,000. The restaurant is in a former general store built in 1864; paintings by Jean-Paul Riopelle adorn the walls. The C$79 *menu dégustation* (tasting menu) includes a different wine with each of several courses. Fillet of Angus beef in red wine, foie gras, and roast duckling with dried figs and port are typical dishes. Next to the 150-seat dining room is a lounge for cigar-smokers. Both Cuban and Davidoff cigars are available. ✉ *75 chemin Masson, Ste-Marguerite-Estérel* ☎ *450/228–4988 or 450/228-4949* ⊕ *www.bistroachamplain.com* ▭ *AE, DC, MC, V* ☽ *Restaurant closed Sun. early Sept.–late June. No lunch.*

$$–$$$ ⬚ **Estérel Resort and Convention Centre.** Dogsledding and an ice-skating disco are two of the more unusual options at this resort, where buses shuttle guests to nearby downhill ski sites. Comfortable air-conditioned rooms have a view of either the lake or the beautiful flower gardens. On weekdays the resort tends to attract groups and conventioneers. Following the lead of the airlines, it offers "name your price" deals on rooms, available only online. Only table d'hôte meals are available at dinner. ✉ *39 blvd. Fridolin Simard, J0T 1E0* ☎ *450/228–2571 or 888/378–3735* 🖷 *450/228–4977* ⊕ *www.esterel.com* ⇥ *121 rooms, 3 suites* ♨ *Restaurant, room service, in-room data ports, room TVs with movies, driving range, 18-hole golf course, pro shop, tennis court, indoor pool, gym, hair salon, hot tub, spa, beach, dock, windsurfing, boating, bicycles, billiards, hiking, racquetball, volleyball, cross-country skiing, ice-skating, ski shop, ski storage, sleigh rides, snowmobiling, sports bar, babysitting, dry cleaning, laundry service, meeting rooms, no-smoking rooms* ▭ *AE, DC, MC, V* ⑩ *BP.*

Val David

❽ *18 km (11 mi) west of Estérel, 82 km (51 mi) north of Montréal.*

Besides being a center for arts and crafts, Val David is a destination for mountain-climbers, hikers, and campers. Children know Val David because of the **Village du Père Noël** (Santa Claus Village). At Santa Claus's summer residence, kids can sit on his knee and speak to him in French or English. The grounds contain bumper boats, a petting zoo (with goats, sheep, horses, and colorful birds), games, and a large outdoor pool. There is a snack bar, but visitors are encouraged to bring their own food (there are numerous picnic tables). ⊠ *987 rue Morin* ☎ *819/322–2146 or 800/287–6635* ⊕ *www.noel.qc.ca* ☞ *C$10* ☉ *Early June–early Sept., daily 10–6; also open Dec., call for hrs.*

Where to Stay & Eat

¢–$$ ✕ **Au Petit Poucet.** At this beloved Laurentians institution (in business since 1945), you can savor hearty traditional fare such as meatball ragout, the restaurant's own maple-smoked ham, *cipaille* (a stew of game meats and chicken), pigs' knuckles with meatballs, pickled beets, pea soup, baked beans, and ham casserole. The dinner buffet served on the weekend has an even wider selection of high-calorie items. Maple syrup pie is the perfect sweet (but not cloying) ending. ⊠ *1030 Rte. 117* ☎ *819/322–2146 or 888/334–2246* ⊕ *www.aupetitpoucet.com* ☐ *MC, V.*

★ $$$$ ✕☐ **Hôtel La Sapinière.** This homey, dark-brown wood-frame hotel, built in 1936, overlooks a lake surrounded by fir trees (*sapins* in French). Rooms, with country-style furnishings and pastel floral accents, come with such luxurious extras as thick terry bathrobes, and some rooms have romantic four-poster beds and fireplaces. You can relax in front of a blazing fire in one of several lounges. The property is renowned for its French nouvelle cuisine: salmon smoked on the premises comes with black-olive tapenade, and bison is cooked in a red-wine sauce with shiitake mushrooms. For dessert, try the mascarpone cheese mousse with berries and a spicy fruit terrine: it's just one of the pastry chef's striking creations. ⊠ *1244 chemin de la Sapinière, J0T 2N0* ☎ *819/322–2020 or 800/567–6635* ☐ *819/322–6510* ⊕ *www.sapiniere.com* ☞ *44 rooms, 25 suites* ☖ *Restaurant, room service, in-room data ports, some refrigerators, cable TV, driving range, putting green, 2 tennis courts, pool, lake, gym, hair salon, outdoor hot tub, massage, dock, boating, mountain bikes, billiard, boccie, croquet, hiking, Ping-Pong, cross-country skiing, ice-skating, bar, recreation room, babysitting, dry cleaning, business services, meeting rooms, no-smoking rooms* ☐ *AE, DC, MC, V* ⚏ *MAP.*

$–$$ ☐ **Auberge Edelweiss.** From the outside, where it stands on the edge of a forest near Val David, this small inn with a white stucco exterior and carved wood balconies resembles a Swiss chalet. Adding to the charm are two deer in the backyard. Inside, it's cozy and romantic; each room has a balcony, and most have hot tubs. The restaurant draws nonguests to its highly rated dinners ($$–$$$$), which include such dishes as Belgium ragout cooked in beer and breast of duck with verbena tea sauce. ⊠ *3050 Chemin Doncaster, J0T 2N0* ☎ *819/322-7800 or 866/355-7800* ☐ *819/322-1550* ⊕ *www.ar-edelweiss.com* ☞ *11 rooms, 2 suites* ☖ *Restaurant, some fans, cable TV, outdoor pool, outdoor hot tub, massage, bicycles, hiking, bar, meeting room; no room phones, no smoking* ☐ *AE, MC, V* ☉ *Restaurant closed Mon. and Tues.* ⚏ *BP.*

Sports & the Outdoors

Mont-Alta (⊠2114 Rte. 117 ☎819/322–3206) has 22 downhill ski runs—about 40% of them for advanced skiers—and one lift. The vertical drop is 587 feet. **Station de Ski Vallée-Bleue** (⊠ 1418 chemin Vallée-Bleue ☎ 866/322-3427 or 819/322-3427 ⊕ www.vallee-bleue.com), with a vertical drop of 365 feet, has 17 runs, and is geared toward intermediate and expert skiers. There are three lifts.

Shopping

Many of the artists who live in town open their studios to the public. **Atelier Bernard Chaudron, Inc.** (⊠ 2449 chemin de l'Île ☎ 819/322–3944 or 888/322–3944) sells hand-forged, lead-free pewter objets d'art such as oil lamps, plus hammered-silver beer mugs, pitchers, and candleholders, as well as some crystal. **La Verdure** (⊠ 1310 Dion ☎ 819/322–7813) has everything from wood walking-sticks to duck decoys and gold, platinum, and silver jewelry made by the owner, Paul Simard. One of the most interesting events in Val David is **1001 Pots** (⊠ L'Atelier du Potier, 2435 rue de l'Église ☎ 819/322–6868 ⊕ www.1001pots.com), which showcases the Japanese-style pottery of Kinya Ishikawa—as well as pieces by some 110 other ceramicists. The exhibition takes place from mid-July through mid-August. Ishikawa's studio also displays work by his wife, Marie-Andrée Benoît, who makes fish-shape bowls with a texture derived from pressing canvas on the clay.

Ste-Agathe-des-Monts

❾ *5 km (3 mi) north of Val David, 96 km (60 mi) northwest of Montréal.*

The wide, sandy beaches of Lac des Sables are the most surprising feature of Ste-Agathe-des-Monts, a tourist town best known for its ski hills. Water activities include canoeing, kayaking, swimming, and fishing. Ste-Agathe is also a stopover point on the Linear Park, the bike trail between St-Jérôme and Mont-Laurier.

Where to Stay & Eat

$$–$$$ ⊞ **Auberge Watel.** A steep driveway leads up to this white-painted, distinguished hotel overlooking Lac Des Sables. Inside, the lounge and restaurant are decorated in a casual country style. Some rooms have a double-size Jacuzzi, fireplace, and a balcony with a superb view of the lake. You have a choice of either a basic motel-style room or a larger room with pine or wicker furnishings. ⊠ *250 rue Saint-Venant, J8C 2Z7* ☎ *819/326-7016 or 800/363-6478* 🖷 *819/326-7556* ⊕ *www.watel.ca* ⤳ *25 ⚭ Restaurant, fans, some in-room data ports, cable TV, pool, hot tub, sauna, beach, dock, boating, fishing, cross-country skiing, ice-skating, snowmobiling, lounge, no-smoking floors* ⊟ *AE, MC, V* ⦿ *MAP.*

¢ 🜂 **Au Parc des Campeurs.** In the woods near a lively resort area, this spacious campground has activities for all age groups, from sport competitions to outings for the kids. There's a sandy beach where you can rent canoes and kayaks and launch your boat from the city's marina. Reservations are recommended. ⚭ *Flush toilets, pit toilets, full hookups, partial hookups, dump station, drinking water, guest laundry, showers, fire pits, picnic tables, food service, electricity, public telephone, general store, swimming (lake)* ⤳ *482 tent sites, 67 RV sites* ⊠ *Tour du Lac and Rte. 329,, K8C 1M9* ☎ *819/324–0482 or 800/561-7360* 🖷 *819/324-2307* ⊕ *www.parcdescampeurs.com* ⬚ *Tent site with water $26, Tent site with water and electricity $29, RV site $34* ⊟ *MC, V* ⦿ *Mid-May–Sept.*

Sports & the Outdoors

Sailing is the favorite summer sport around here, especially during the **24 Heures de la Voile,** a weekend sailing competition that takes place in mid-July. The sightseeing boats *Alouette V and VI* (⊠ Municipal Dock, rue Principale ☏ 819/326–3656 or 866/326–3656 ⊕ www. croisierealouette.com) offer guided, 50-minute tours of Lac des Sables. They leave the dock at least four times a day from mid-May to mid-October.

Mont-Tremblant

★ ❿ *25 km (16 mi) north of Ste-Agathe-des-Monts, 100 km (62 mi) north of Montréal.*

Mont-Tremblant, at more than 3,000 feet, is the highest peak in the Laurentians and a major draw for skiers. It's also the name of a nearby village. The resort area at the foot of the mountain (called simply Tremblant; ⊕ www.tremblant.com), is spread around 14-km-long (9-mi-long) Lac Tremblant. *Ski* magazine consistently rates it among the top ski resorts in eastern North America, and the area encompasses several golf courses, so it's not surprising that Tremblant has become the most fashionable vacation venue in Québec for sporty types.

The hub of the resort is a pedestrian-only village that looks a bit like a displaced Québec City. The buildings, constructed in the style of New France, with dormer windows and steep roofs, hold pubs, restaurants, boutiques, sports shops, a movie theater, and lodging that includes self-catering condominiums as well as hotels. An indoor water-recreation complex includes pools, water slides, and whirlpool baths. If you don't have a car with you in Tremblant, you can still dine in Saint-Jovite or hotels outside the resort by taking by taking the bus, C$1 one-way.

The mountain, and the hundreds of square miles of wilderness beyond, constitute the **Parc National du Mont-Tremblant** (☏ 819/688–2281 ⊕ www. sepaq.com). Created in 1894, the park was the home of the Algonquins, who called this area Manitonga Soutana, meaning "mountain of the spirits." Today it's a vast wildlife sanctuary of more than 400 lakes and rivers holding nearly 200 species of birds and animals, including moose, deer, bear, and beaver. In winter its trails are used by cross-country skiers, snowshoers, and snowmobilers. Camping and canoeing are the main summer activities. Entrance to the park costs $3.50 for adults; the main entry point is through the town of St-Donat, about 45 minutes north of Mont-Tremblant, via routes 329 and 125.

Where to Stay & Eat

$$$–$$$$ ✕ **Restaurant Le Cheval de Jade.** "The Jade Horse" specializes in French haute cuisine. The elegant dining room has lace curtains in the windows and white linens and ivory china on the tables. The food is the real thing—local ingredients and organic produce are used to create classic French fare such as rack of lamb, bouillabaisse, and shrimp flambéed with black pepper sauce and green tea. ⊠ *688 rue de Saint-Jovite, Saint-Jovite* ☏ *819/425–5233* ⊕ *www.chevaldejade.com* ⟡ *Reservations essential* ▭ *AE, DC, V* ⊙ *Closed Wed. mid-Oct. to mid-June. No lunch.*

$$–$$$ ✕ **Auberge du Coq de Montagne.** This restaurant on Lac Moore, and five minutes from the ski slopes, has garnered much praise for its Italian cuisine ($$$), which draws a local crowd. Menu offerings include tried-and-tested favorites such as veal marsala and veal *fiorentina* (cooked with spinach and cheese). The chef also makes great pasta. ⊠ *2151 chemin du Village* ☎ *819/425–3380 or 800/895–3380* ⏵ *Reservations essential* ▭ *AE, MC,V.*

★ **$$$$**   ✕▦ **Fairmont Tremblant.** The sporty but classy centerpiece of the Tremblant resort area takes its cues from the historic railroad "castles" scattered throughout Canada. This contemporary hotel has wood paneling, copper and wrought-iron details, stained glass, and stone fireplaces. If you stay on the Gold floor, expect a free breakfast, evening appetizers, free Internet access, and minimalist rooms. Skiers can zoom off the mountain right into the ground-level deli, near the full-service spa. Elaborate themed buffets are the draw at the Windigo restaurant. ⌂ *Box 100, 3045 chemin de la Chapelle, J8E 1B1* ☎ *819/681–7000 or 800/441–1414* ⎙ *819/681–7099* ⊕ *www.fairmont.com* ⇥ *252 rooms, 62 suites* ⏶ *Restaurant, café, room service, some kitchens, in-room data ports, room TVs with movies and video games, 2 pools (1 indoors), gym, outdoor hot tub, sauna, spa, steam room, downhill skiing, ski shop, ski storage, bar, lobby lounge, video game room, shops, babysitting, laundry services, concierge, business services, convention center, meeting rooms, no-smoking floors* ▭ *AE, DC, MC, V* ⧉ *BP.*

$$$$ ✕▦ **Hotel Club Tremblant.** Built as a family house in the early 1900s, this building has been a rooming house, brothel, and private club. Now a European-owned hotel, it's just down the lakeside road from the ski station at Mont-Tremblant. The original log-cabin lodge is furnished in a colonial style, with wooden staircases and huge stone fireplaces. Rustic but comfortable, it has excellent facilities. The French restaurant ($$$–$$$$) is outstanding; the Saturday-night buffet includes a wide selection of seafood. Both the main lodge and the split-level condominium complex (with fireplaces, private balconies or patios, kitchenettes, and split-level design), up the hill from the lodge, have magnificent views of Mont-Tremblant. A complementary shuttle takes you to the ski hills. ⊠ *121 rue Cuttle, J0T 1Z0* ☎ *819/425–2731 or 800/567–8341* ⎙ *819/425–5617* ⊕ *www.clubtremblant.com* ⇥ *122 suites* ⏶ *Restaurant, café, some fans, some in-room hot tubs, in-room data ports, some kitchenettes, cable TV, tennis court, indoor-outdoor pool, gym, hair salon, sauna, spa, beach, 3 docks, boating, parasailing, waterskiing, fishing, billiards, boccie, croquet, Ping-Pong, volleyball, cross-country skiing, ski shop, ski storage, bar, dance club, babysitting, children's programs (ages 4–16), 2 playgrounds, concierge, business services, convention center, meeting rooms, no-smoking rooms; no a/c in some rooms* ▭ *AE, DC, MC, V* ⧉ *MAP.*

$$$$ ✕▦ **Westin Resort–Tremblant.** The Westin, part of the Tremblant resort town and a short walk from the ski slopes, is plush and polished. Some rooms have fireplaces; most have balconies, and all have kitchenettes. The pathway to the heated saltwater pool and hot tub is kept warm itself, enabling you to use the tub and pool all winter long. At the chic U restaurant ($$$), you can sample sushi in its many forms as well as entrées such as seared filet mignon in teriyaki sauce. Many menu items employ tofu. ⊠ *100 chemin Kandahar, J8E 1E2* ☎ *819/681–8000, 866/687–9330 in U.S.* 🖷 *819/681–8001* ⊕ *www.westin.com* ➥ *55 rooms, 71 suites △ Restaurant, room service, in-room data ports, kitchenettes, some microwaves, room TVs with movies and video games, pool, gym, outdoor hot tub, sauna, spa, babysitting, dry cleaning, concierge, Internet, business services, meeting rooms, no-smoking rooms* ▭ *AE, D, DC, MC, V* ⦿| *EP.*

$$$$ 🏨 **Quintessence.** This stone-and-wood all-suites hotel, which opened in 2003, bills itself as the first boutique property in Mont-Tremblant. The quiet, chic Quintessence is on three acres along the shore of Lac Tremblant and near the ski slopes. Each suite has a king-size bed, a balcony or patio with lake views, a wood-burning fireplace, a stereo, and a bathroom with a heated marble floor and Jacuzzi. Service, including a ski shuttle and a concierge who can provide firewood, is an emphasis here. ⊠ *3004 chemin de la Chapelle, J8E 1E1* ☎ *819/425–3400 or 866/425–3400* 🖷 *819/425–3480* ⊕ *hotelquintessence.com* ➥ *30 suites, 1 cabin △ Restaurant, room service, in-room data ports, in-room safes, in-room hot tubs, minibars, cable TV with movies, in-room VCRs, pool, lake, gym, outdoor hot tub, sauna, spa, steam room, ice-skating, ski storage, bar, wine bar, library, babysitting, dry cleaning, laundry service, concierge, Internet, business services, meeting room, some pets allowed; no smoking* ⦿| *CP.*

$–$$$ 🏨 **Le Grand Lodge.** This Scandinavian-style, log cabin hotel is on 13½ acres on Lac Ouimet. Accommodations, from studios to two-bedroom suites, are spacious, with kitchenettes, stone fireplaces, and balconies that overlook the water. The indoor–outdoor café, which serves light dishes, also looks out on the lake. The more formal Chez Borivage, which has a good wine cellar, specializes in French cuisine. Although the resort attracts a sizable number of business travelers here for conferences, it caters to families as well, with day-care facilities, a game room for teens, and activities that include summer bonfires on the beach and making taffy on the snow. ⊠ *2396 rue Labelle, J8E 1T8* ☎ *819/425–2734 or 800/567–6763* 🖷 *819/425–9725* ⊕ *www.legrandlodge.com* ➥ *11 rooms, 101 suites △ Restaurant, café, in-room data ports, kitchenettes, room TVs with video games, 4 tennis courts, indoor pool, lake, gym, sauna, spa, steam room, boating, bicycles, badminton, billiards, Ping-Pong, shuffleboard, volleyball, cross-country skiing, ice-skating, ski shop, ski storage, bar, lounge, recreation room, video game room, shop, babysitting, 2 playgrounds, dry cleaning, laundry service, concierge, business services, meeting rooms, no-smoking rooms* ▭ *AE, D, DC, MC, V* ⦿| *EP.*

Sports & the Outdoors

With a 2,131-foot vertical drop, **Mont-Tremblant** (☎ 819/425–8711 or 819/681–3000 ⊕ www.tremblant.ca) has 94 downhill trails, 13 lifts, and 110 km (68 mi) of cross-country trails. Downhill beginners favor the 6-km (4-mi) Nansen trail; experts often choose the McCulloch, Taschereau, and Kandahar trails on the south side and the Duncan and Expo runs on the mountain's north side. The speedy Duncan Express is a quadruple chairlift; there's also a heated, high-speed gondola.

On the other side of the mountain is the **Versant Soleil** (sunny slope). The area has a vertical drop of 2,132 feet and 15 runs (including glade skiing) served by a high-speed quad chair that's capable of moving 2,250 people to the summit every hour. Sixty percent of the trails are for advanced skiers and half are classified for expert skiers only. The remainder are for skiers who consider themselves intermediate.

THE EASTERN TOWNSHIPS

Updated by
Chris Barry

The Eastern Townships (also known as les Cantons de l'Est, and formerly as l'Estrie) refers to the area in the southwest corner of the province of Québec—bordering Vermont, New Hampshire, and Maine. Its northern Appalachian hills, rolling down to placid lakeshores, were first home to the Abenaki people, long before "summer people" built their cottages and horse farms. The Abenaki are gone, but the names they gave to the region's lakes remain: Memphrémagog, Massawippi, Mégantic.

The Townships, as locals call them, were populated by Empire Loyalists fleeing first the Revolutionary War and, later, the newly created United States of America. They wanted to continue living under the English king in British North America. It's not surprising that the covered bridges, village greens, white church steeples, and country inns are reminiscent of New England. The Loyalists were followed, around 1820, by the first wave of Irish immigrants (ironically, Catholics fleeing their country's union with Protestant England). Some 20 years later the potato famine sent more Irish pioneers to the Townships.

The area became more Francophone after 1850 as French Canadians moved in to work on the railroad and in the lumber industry. During the late 19th century, English families from Montréal and Americans from the border states began summering at cottages along the lakes. During Prohibition the area attracted even more cottagers from the United States. Lac Massawippi became a favorite summer resort of wealthy families, whose homes have since been converted into inns and B&Bs.

Today the summer houses fill up with equal parts French and English visitors, though the year-round residents are primarily French. The locals are proud of their multiethnic heritage. They boast of "Loyalist tours" and Victorian gingerbread homes, and in the next breath direct visitors to the snowmobile museum in Valcourt, where in 1937 Joseph-Armand Bombardier built the first *moto-neige* (snowmobile) in his garage. (Bombardier's other inventions became the basis for one of Canada's biggest industries, that of supplying New York City and Mexico City with subway cars; the Bombardier company is Canada's biggest manufacturer.)

Since the 1980s, the Townships have developed from a series of quiet farm communities and wood-frame summer homes to a thriving all-season resort area. In winter, skiers flock to six downhill centers and more than 1,000 km (622 mi) of cross-country trails. Still less crowded and commercialized than the Laurentians, the area has ski hills on four mountains that dwarf anything the Laurentians have to offer, with the exception of Mont-Tremblant. And compared to Vermont, ski-pass rates are still a bargain. Owl's Head, Mont-Orford, and Mont-Sutton have interchangeable lift tickets.

By early spring, the sugar shacks are busy with the new maple syrup. In summer, boating, swimming, sailing, golfing, rollerblading, hiking, and bicycling take over. And every fall the inns are booked solid with visitors eager to take in the brilliant foliage.

The fall is also a good time to visit the wineries (although most are open all year). Because of its mild microclimate, the Townships area has become one of the fastest-developing wine regions in Canada, with a dozen of the more than 30 wineries in Québec province. The wines don't quite measure up to the standards of Ontario's Niagara Peninsula or British Columbia's Okanagan Valley—at least not yet—but the vintners produce some good hearty reds and sparkling whites that go well with the regional cuisine. Wine makers are also making some inroads with ice wine, a sweet dessert wine made, as the name suggests, from frozen grapes, which have a very high sugar content. A wine route, the Route des Vins (look for road signs embellished with a bunch of grapes), links the major wineries.

Granby

⑪ *80 km (50 mi) east of Montréal.*

Granby, the western gateway to the Eastern Townships, is home to a notable zoo. It also hosts a number of annual festivals: among them are the Festival of Mascots and Cartoon Characters, a great favorite with youngsters and families, and the Granby International, an antique-car competition held at the Granby Autodrome. Both of these are held in July. The Festival International de la Chanson, a songfest of budding composers and performers that has launched several of Québec's current megastars, is a nine-day event in mid-September. It's held in Granby's small but elegant Palace Theatre, one of several notable historic structures on rue Principale (Main Street).

★ ♡ The **Jardin Zoologique de Granby** (Granby Zoo), one of the biggest attractions in the area, houses some 1,000 animals representing 225 species in a naturally landscaped setting. The Afrika pavilion, with its gorillas, lions, and birds, is a favorite with youngsters; they also love the camel rides and Amazoo, an aquatic park with turbulent wave pools and rides. At certain times of day, keepers demonstrate the acrobatic skills of the birds of prey as well as the clever tricks of the elephants, who perform for the public like old circus pros. The complex includes amusement rides and souvenir shops, as well as a playground and picnic area. ⊠ *525 rue St-Hubert* ☎ *450/372–9113 or 877/472–6299* ⊕ *www.zoogranby.ca* ▣ *C$23.45* ☉ *Mid-May–early Sept., daily 10–7; late Sept., weekends 10–6.*

Sports & the Outdoors

Biking is big here. The quiet back roads lend themselves to exploring the region on two wheels, as does the network of off-road trails. There

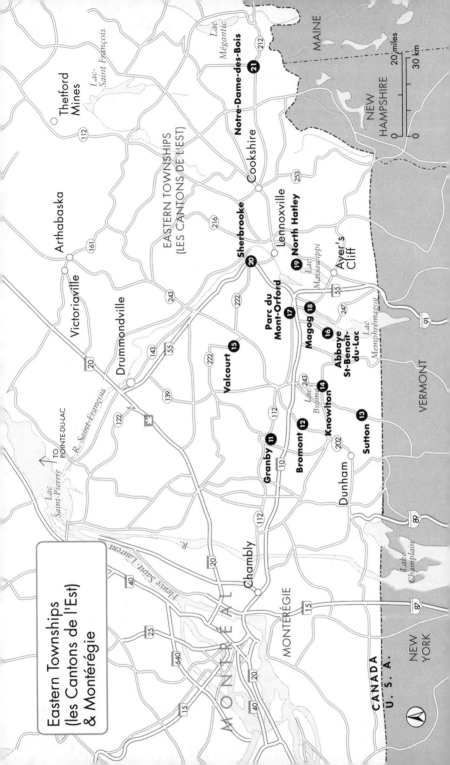

Eastern Townships
(les Cantons de l'Est)
& Montérégie

CANADA
U. S. A.

MONTRÉAL

MONTÉRÉGIE

EASTERN TOWNSHIPS
(LES CANTONS DE L'EST)

MAINE

NEW
HAMPSHIRE

VERMONT

NEW
YORK

Thetford
Mines

Arthabaska

Victoriaville

Drummondville

Chambly

Granby **11**

Bromont **12**

Knowlton **14**

Sutton **13**

Valcourt **15**

Dunham

Abbaye
St-Benoît-
du-Lac **16**

Magog **18**

Parc du
Mont-Orford **17**

North Hatley **19**

Ayer's
Cliff

Lennoxville

Sherbrooke **20**

Cookshire

Notre-Dame-des-Bois **21**

Lac-
Saint-Pierre

Lac
Saint-François

Lac-
Saint-François

Lac
Mégantic

Lac
Massawippi

Lac
Memphrémagog

Lac
Brome

Lake
Champlain

Fleuve Saint-Laurent

R. Saint-François

TO
POINTE-DU-LAC

20 miles

30 km

are 450 km (279 mi) of bike-friendly trails, some linked to **La Route Verte** (The Green Route), a province-wide network that is being expanded by leaps and bounds. For details and a map, contact Vélo Québec (☎ 514/ 521–8356 or 800/567–8356 ⊕ www.routeverte.com). One of the most popular (and flattest) bike and in-line skating trails is the 21-km (13- mi) paved **l'Estriade,** which links Granby to Waterloo. The **Montéré- giade** bike trail between Granby and Farnham is 21 km (13 mi) long.

Mountain biking is also popular in the Townships. The mountain-bik- ing season kicks off in late May with the **Canada Cup** (☎ 450/534–2453 ⊕ www.bromontbiking.com), a 6-km (4-mi) race. Competitions for se- rious mountain bikers are held in summer, culminating in early Septem- ber's **Masters World Cup** (☎ 450/534–2453 ⊕ www.bromontbiking. com), which attracts competitors from around the world.

Bromont

⑫ *78 km (48 mi) east of Montréal.*

The boating, camping, golf, horseback riding, swimming, tennis, bik- ing, canoeing, fishing, hiking, cross-country and downhill skiing, and snowshoeing available here make this a place for all seasons. Bromont has the only night skiing in the Eastern Townships—and there's even a slope-side disco, Le Bromontais. The town also has more than 100 km (62 mi) of maintained trails for mountain bikers. Once an Olympic eques- trian site, Bromont hosts the **International Bromont Equestrian Competi- tion** (☎ 450/534–0787 ⊕ www.internationalbromont.org) every June.

Bromont Aquatic Park is a water park with over 23 rides and games, in- cluding the Corkscrew and the Elephant's Trunk (where kids shoot out of a model of an elephant's head). Slides are divided into four degrees of difficulty, from easy to extreme (recommended for adults and older chil- dren only). Admission includes a chairlift ride to the top of the ski hill. September through late October it's open only for mountain biking. ✉ *Autoroute 10, Exit 78* ☎ *450/534–2200* ⊕ *www.skibromont.com* 🎫 *C$28* ⊙ *Late May–Aug., daily 10–6:30; Sept.–mid Oct., daily 10–5.*

Safari Aventure Loowak. The brainchild of butterfly collector Serge Poirier, this park sprawls over 500 acres of wooded land 10 km (6 mi) northeast of Bromont. It's a sort of Indiana Jones–theme guided tour in which you head off into the bush to hunt for treasure and to look for downed planes. It's a great hit with little ones, but parents get caught up in the fantasy, too. Reservations are recommended. ✉ *475 Horizon Blvd. (off Exit 88 of Autoroute 10), Waterloo* ☎ *450/539–0501* ⊕ *www. safariloowak.qc.ca* 🎫 *C$10 and up per person (4 people minimum).*

> **off the beaten path**
>
> **DUNHAM –** Almost a dozen wineries along the Route des Vins (Wine Route) in and around the town of Dunham, about 20 km (12 mi) south of Bromont on Route 202, offer tastings and tours. Call for business hours, which can be erratic, especially in the autumn, when harvesting is underway. **Vignoble Domaine Côtes d'Ardoise** (✉ 879 Rte. 202, Dunham ☎ 450/295–2020) was one of the first wineries to set up shop in the area, back in 1980. Before walking through the

vineyard at **Vignoble de l'Orpailleur** (✉ 1086 Rte. 202, Dunham ☏ 450/295–2763 ⊕ www.orpailleur.ca.), stop by the ecomuseum to learn everything you ever wanted to know about the production of wine, from the growing of the grapes right up to the bottling process. There's also a gift shop and patio restaurant. **Vignoble Les Trois Clochers** (✉ 341 chemin Bruce, or Rte. 202, Dunham ☏ 450/295–2034) produces a dry, fruity white from Seyval grapes as well as several other white wines.

Where to Stay

$$–$$$ 🏨 **Hôtel Château Bromont.** Massages, "electropuncture," algae wraps, and aromatherapy are just a few of the services at this European-style resort. It also includes a large, Turkish-style *hammam* (steam room). Rooms are large and comfortable, with contemporary furniture. Sunny Mediterranean colors dress the atrium walls, and center-facing rooms have balconies and window boxes. Greenery and patio furniture surround the swimming pool in the middle of the atrium. The restaurant Les Quatres Canards serves regional cuisine, much of which features duck. The dining room has a panoramic view. ✉ *90 rue Stanstead, J2L 1K6* ☏ *450/534–3433 or 800/304–3433* 🖷 *450/534–0514* ⊕ *www.chateaubromont.com* ↪ *164 rooms, 8 suites ⚓ 2 restaurants, some in-room hot tubs, cable TV with movies and video games, 2 pools (1 indoor), hot tub, sauna, spa, badminton, racquetball, squash, volleyball, bar, babysitting, Internet, meeting rooms, no-smoking rooms* 🖃 *AE, D, DC, MC, V* 🍽 *EP, MAP.*

$–$$$ 🏨 **Hôtel Le Menhir.** Set among the rolling hills of the Townships and with great views of the local countryside from every room, this modern hotel is well priced, considering all the amenities available. The indoor pool, sauna, and whirlpool, along with its proximity to some of the best ski hills in the area, make it a great choice for a winter getaway. ✉ *125 Boulevard Bromont, J2L 2K7* ☏ *418/266–2165, 877/778–8977, 800/461–3790* 🖷 *450/534–1933* ⊕ *www.hotellemenhir.com* ↪ *41 rooms ⚓ Some in-room hot tubs, indoor pool, hot tub, bar, meeting room, no-smoking rooms* 🖃 *AE, MC, V.*

Sports & the Outdoors

The **Royal Bromont** (✉ 400 chemin Compton ☏ 450/534–4653 or 888/281–0017 ⊕ www.royalbromont.com) is an 18-hole, par-72, bent-grass course. Greens fees are C$38–C$60 plus $29 to rent a cart.

Station de Ski Bromont (✉ 150 rue Champlain ☏ 450/534–2200 ⊕ www.skibromont.com), with 46 trails for downhill skiing (20 of which are lighted for night skiing), was the site of the 1986 World Cup Slalom. The vertical drop is 1,336 feet, and there are three lifts. Hiking and mountain biking are popular here in summer and early fall.

Shopping

Shopping for bargains at yard sales and flea markets is a popular weekend activity in the Townships; the **Bromont Five-Star Flea Market** is the largest—its gigantic sign on Autoroute 10 is hard to miss. More than 1,000 vendors sell their wares—everything from T-shirts to household gadgets—

each Saturday and Sunday from May to the end of October, and shoppers come from Montréal as well as Vermont, just over the border.

Sutton

🔞 *106 km (66 mi) southeast of Montréal.*

Sutton is a sporty community with crafts shops, welcoming eateries, and bars (La Paimpolaise is a favorite among skiers). Surrounded by mountains, the town is best explored on foot; a circuit of 12 heritage sites makes an interesting self-guided walk past the boutiques and the houses built by Loyalists. For a route map with a description of each building and its history, go to the tourist office. It's inside the City Hall building at 11B Rue Principal.

Where to Stay

$–$$ ⊞ **Au Diable Vert.** This inn is in one of the most beautiful areas of the province, deep in the heart of the Appalachian Mountains and overlooking the waters of the Missisquoi River. The interior of this farmhouse from the early 1900s is tastefully decorated with antiques. Set on 200 acres, Au Diable Vert hosts a wide variety of outdoor activities, including hiking, guided moonlight kayak excursions along the Missisquoi, and horseback riding lessons. ⊠ *169 Chemin Staines, J0E 2K0* ☎ *450/538-5639, 888/779-9090* 🖷 *450/538-2059* ⊕ *www.audiablevert.qc.ca* ➥ *4 rooms (1 with bath), 1 apartment, 2 cabins, 30 campsites* ↺ *Hiking.*

$ ⊞ **Auberge la Paimpolaise.** The alpine-style auberge on Mont-Sutton is 50 feet from the ski trails. It's nothing fancy, but the location is hard to beat. Rooms are simple and comfortable, with a woodsy appeal. Weekend ski packages are available. ⊠ *615 rue Maple, J0E 2K0* ☎ *450/538-3213 or 800/263-3213* 🖷 *450/538-3970* ⊕ *www.paimpolaise.com* ➥ *27 rooms, 2 suites* ↺ *Dining room, cable TV, meeting rooms, some pets allowed (fee); no a/c, no phones in some rooms, no smoking* ⊟ *AE, DC, MC, V* ⦿ *BP.*

Sports & the Outdoors

GOLF   You need a reservation to golf at **Les Rochers Bleus** (⊠ 550 Rte. 139 ☎450/538-2324 ⊕ www.lesrochersbleus.com), a par-72, 18-hole course. Its narrow fairways, surrounded by mountains, can be a challenge. Greens fees are C$29–C$39 plus an additional C$29 to rent a motorized cart.

HIKING   **Au Diable Vert** (⊠ 160 chemin Staines, Glen Sutton ☎ 450/538-5639 or 888/779-9090 ⊕ www.audiablevert.qc.ca) is a 200-acre mountainside site with hiking trails that look out over spectacular scenery. (Glen Sutton, 15 minutes from the village of Sutton, is between the Appalachians and Vermont's Green Mountains; the Missisquoi River runs through the middle.)

SKIING   **Mont-Sutton** (⊠ Rte. 139 S, Autoroute 10, Exit 68 ☎ 450/538-2339 ⊕ www.montsutton.com) has 53 downhill trails, a vertical drop of 1,518 feet, and nine lifts. This ski area, one of the region's largest, attracts a die-hard crowd of mostly Anglophone skiers and snowboarders from Québec. Trails plunge and meander through pine, maple, and birch trees.

Shopping

Rumeur Affamée (⊠ 15 rue Principal N ☎ 450/538–1888) carries over 130 kinds of cheese—60 of them produced locally—along with local and imported meats, fresh bread, and spectacular desserts. Be sure to sample their famous maple syrup pie, a tasty treat unique to the region. **Monica** (⊠ 22 rue Principal S ☎ 450/538–8333) is where to go to pick up souvenirs. Available items include T-shirts, shot glasses, and small toys. **Arts Sutton** (⊠ 7 rue Academy ☎ 450/538–2563) is one of the town's long-established art galleries. **Galerie Farfelu** (⊠ 12 Rue Principal N ☎ 450/538–5959) is a cooperatively run gallery selling works by local artisans. It's open from 11–5 Thursday to Sunday.

Knowlton (Lac Brome)

⑭ *101 km (63 mi) southeast of Montréal.*

Knowlton is a good stop for antiques, clothes, and gifts. The village is full of high-quality boutiques, art galleries, and interesting little restaurants that have taken residence in renovated clapboard buildings painted every shade of the rainbow. The town also has several factory outlets. Along the shore of Lac Brome, Knowlton is also known for its distinctive Lake Brome ducks, which are found on local menus and celebrated in a food event over several weeks during late September and early October. You can pick up a self-guided walking-tour map at the reception area of Auberge Knowlton.

Where to Stay & Eat

$ ✕▢ **Auberge Knowlton.** The 12-room inn, at the main intersection in FodorsChoice Knowlton, has been a local landmark since 1849, when it was a stage- ★ coach stop. The inn attracts businesspeople, as well as vacationers and locals who like coming to the old, familiar hotel for special occasions. On-site bistro Le Relais ($$–$$$) serves local wines and cheeses and has a wide range of duck dishes, including warm duck salad served with gizzards. Confit du canard is made with a leg of duck, roasted slowly in the oven and then stored in its own fat for several days before being reheated. The result is tender and tasty. ⊠ *286 chemin Knowlton, J0E 1V0* ☎ *450/242–6886* 🖷 *450/242–1055* ⊕ *www.cclacbrome.qc.ca/ak* ☞ *12 rooms* ⚫ *Restaurant, fans, in-room data ports, cable TV, Internet, meeting rooms, some pets allowed, no-smoking rooms; no a/c in some rooms* ⊟ *AE, MC, V* ▯◎▯ *EP.*

Nightlife & the Arts

Arts Knowlton (⊠ 9 Mount Echo Rd. ☎ 450/242–2270 or 450/242–1395 ⊕ www.cclacbrome.qc.ca/tlb) stages plays, musicals, and productions of classic Broadway and West End hits. It hosts professional and amateur English-language productions, but also has dabbled in bilingual productions and some new Canadian works. The 175-seat, air-conditioned theater is behind the Knowlton Pub.

Sports & the Outdoors

Not far from Knowlton is **Golf Inverness** (⊠ 511 chemin Bondville/Rte. 215 ☎ 450/242–1595 or 800/468–1595 ⊕ www.golfinverness.ca.), an

18-hole, par-71 course with an elegant 1915 clubhouse. Greens fees are C$30–C$42 plus an additional C$28 to rent a gas-powered cart.

Many Montréal families come for the downhill skiing and snowboarding at **Parc du Mont-Glen** (⊠ off Rte. 243 ☎ 450/243–6142 or 877/243–6142 ⊕ www.glen.qc.ca). The mountain is less challenging than the other "biggies" in the region, such as Owl's Head or Mont Orford, but the area has 32 trails, four lifts, and a vertical drop of 1,099 feet. Tubing, cross-country skiing, and snowshoeing are also available. For hiking you have 40 km (25 mi) of trails; swimming and camping are among the warm-weather options.

Shopping

Hurricane Grace (⊠ 285 chemin Knowlton ☎ 450/243–0164) carries designer clothing for women and children. You can find handmade jewelry by Québec artisans at **Jules Perrier-Joaillier** (⊠ 264 chemin Knowlton ☎ 450/243–6444), at the same address as a Woolrich store. **L. L. Brome Factory Outlet** (⊠ 61 rue Lakeside ☎ 450/243–0123) carries well-made sportswear and casual clothing. **RoCoCo** (⊠ 299 chemin Knowlton ☎ 450/243–6948), a women's clothing boutique, is owned by U.S.-born Anita Laurent, a former model. Drawing on her many contacts in the fashion world, she buys samples directly from manufacturers and sells her stylish, elegant suits and pants at a fraction of the price charged by large retail stores.

Big and small kids visit **Township Toy Trains** (⊠ 5 chemin du Mont-Echo ☎ 450/243–1881) to check out its stock of trains and dollhouse miniatures. **Station Knowlton** (⊠ 7 chemin du Mont Echo ☎ 450/242–5862), inside an old wrought-iron workshop, carries locally made gift items, including its own line of homemade soaps and bath salts. The comfortable café here attracts a mix of tourists and locals.

Valcourt

⓯ *158 km (98 mi) east of Montréal.*

Valcourt is the birthplace of the inventor of the snowmobile, and the sport is understandably popular in the Eastern Townships, with more than 2,000 km (1,240 mi) of paths cutting through the woods and meadows. In February Valcourt hosts the **Grand Prix Ski-doo de Valcourt** (☎ 450/532–3443 or 866/532–7543 ⊕ www.grandprixvalcourt.com), a three-day event with competitions, concerts, and family-oriented festivities.

The **Musée Joseph-Armand Bombardier** displays innovator Bombardier's many inventions, including the snowmobile. The museum is partly a showcase for Bombardier's products, including the Ski-Doo snowmobiles, but it also documents the history of snow transportation, with interesting facts about winter weather, a topic of import in this corner of the world. As you walk around, you can compare yesteryear's simple modes of snow transportation—loggers working with horses in the woods, Lapps harnessing their reindeer, and so on—shown on photographic backdrops, with today's sleek vehicles. ⊠ *1001 av. Joseph-Armand Bombardier*

☎ 450/532–5300 ⊕ *www.museebombardier.com.* ✉ C$5 ⊙ *May–Aug., daily 10–5; Sept.–Apr., Tues.–Sun. 10–5.*

Abbaye St-Benoît-du-Lac

★ ⑯ *132 km (82 mi) southeast of Montréal.*

The abbey's slender bell tower juts up above the trees like a fairy-tale castle. Built by the Benedictines in 1912 on a wooded peninsula on Lac Memphrémagog, the abbey is home to some 60 monks who sell apples and sparkling apple wine from their orchards as well as cheeses: Ermite (which means "hermit"), St-Benoît, and ricotta. Gregorian prayers are sung daily, and some masses are open to the public; call for the schedule. Dress modestly if you plan to attend vespers or other rituals, and avoid shorts. If you wish to experience a few days of retreat, reserve well in advance (a contribution of C$40 per night, which includes meals, is suggested). To get to the abbey from Magog, take Route 112 and follow the signs for the side road (Rural Route 2, or rue des Pères) to the abbey. ✉ *R.R. 2, St-Benoît-du-Lac* ☎ *819/843–4080* ⊕ *www.st-benoit-du-lac.com* ⊙ *Store open Mon.–Sat. 9–10:45 and 11:45–4:30 (between services).*

Parc du Mont-Orford

⑰ *115 km (72 mi) east of Montréal.*

Part of the township of Orford, the **Parc du Mont-Orford** (✉ 3321 chemin du Parc ☎ 819/843–6548 or 800/567–2772) is in use year-round, whether for skiing, snowshoeing, camping, or hiking.

Since 1951 thousands of students have come to the **Orford Arts Centre** (✉ 3165 chemin du Parc ☎ 819/843–8595, 800/567–6155 in Canada May–Aug. ⊕ www.arts-orford.org) to study and perform classical music in summer. The annual summertime celebration of music and art, Festival Orford, brings classical-music, jazz, and chamber-orchestra concerts to Parc du Mont-Orford.

Where to Stay

$$–$$$$ 🏠 **Auberge Estrimont.** An attractive complex built of cedar, Auberge Estrimont is close to ski hills, riding stables, and golf courses. All rooms have fireplaces and private balconies. The restaurant serves regional specialties: its table d'hôte menu, priced at C$30 per person, includes such dishes as venison sausage, game hen with garlic and orange sauce, and salmon-and-scallop roulade (the mixture is rolled up like a jelly roll). ✉ *44 av. de l'Auberge, Rte. 141 N, J1X 6J3* ☎ *819/843–1616 or 800/ 567–7320* 🖷 *819/843–4909* ⊕ *www.estrimont.qc.ca* ⇗ *76 rooms, 7 suites* ⚷ *Restaurant, some in-room hot tubs, some microwaves, cable TV, 2 tennis courts, 2 pools (1 indoor), gym, hot tub, sauna, spa, badminton, racquetball, squash, bar, babysitting, Internet, meeting rooms, no-smoking rooms* 🖃 *AE, DC, MC, V.*

Sports & the Outdoors

Mont-Orford Ski Area (✉ Rte. 141 ☎ 819/843–6548 or 800/567–2772 ⊕ www.orford.com), at the center of Parc du Mont-Orford, has plenty of challenges for alpine and cross-country skiers, from novices to veterans. It has 54 runs, a vertical drop of 1,782 feet, and eight lifts, as well as 56 km (35 mi) of cross-country trails, an 18-hole, par-72 golf course, and a day-care center. Gondola rides to the top of Mont Orford are offered year-round at a cost of C$9.75 per person.

Magog

🔞 *118 km (74 mi) east of Montréal.*

This bustling town is at the northern tip of Lac Memphrémagog, a large body of water that reaches into northern Vermont. Its sandy beaches are a draw, and it's also a good place for boating, bird-watching, sailboarding, horseback riding, dogsledding, rollerblading, golfing, and snowmobiling. You might even see Memphré, the lake's sea dragon, on one of the many lake cruises—there have been more than 100 sightings of one kind or another since 1816.

The streets downtown are lined with century-old homes that have been converted into boutiques, stores, and a variety of restaurants—including Japanese and Vietnamese restaurants, fast-food outlets, bistros serving Italian and French dishes, and many others.

If the weather's right for it, you can stroll or picnic in the Linear Park—when there's snow, it's perfect for skating or cross-country skiing. A trail for cyclists, walkers, and cross-country skiers hugs the lake, then parallels Route 112 before turning into an off-road recreational trail that leads into the Parc du Mont-Orford, 13½ km (8 mi) from town.

Magog is the site of one of the largest wineries in the province, **Le Cep d'Argent** (✉ 1257 chemin de la Rivière 🕾 819/864–4441 or 877/864–4441 ⊕ www.cepdargent.com). The sparkling white wine is particularly good, and the dessert wine, which is similar to a port and flavored with a little maple syrup, goes well with the local cheese. The winery plays a leading role in the annual wine festival that's held in Magog (late August and early September) and has guided visits, a boutique, and tastings.

off the beaten path

SUCRERIE DES NORMAND – One of the oldest, most traditional maple-syrup operations in the Eastern Townships is in Eastman, about 15 km (9 mi) west of Magog. Run by third-generation-farmer Richard Normand, the farm is spread over 250 acres of wooded land and includes 10,000 maple trees. You can tour the property in a horse-drawn wagon and watch the "sugaring off" process—from the tapping of trees to the rendering down of the sweet liquid into syrup and sugar. After the tour, Richard and his wife, Marlene (she designs the menus), serve traditional Québecois food in a wood cabin, to the sounds of harmonica and spoons. ✉ *426 George Bonnalie, Eastman* 🕾 *450/297–2659* ⊕ *www.acbm.qc.ca/sucrerie.*

Where to Stay & Eat

★ $$$$ ✕🖹 **Ripplecove Inn.** The accommodations, service, and food at the Ripplecove, 11 km (7 mi) south of Magog, are excellent. Bedrooms are elegant, furnished with antiques; colorful walls nicely set off the artwork.

Some rooms and suites have lake views. The chef assembles Eastern Townships menus that might consist of pheasant with wild-mushroom sauce, braised leg of rabbit, panfried local trout with a white wine–and–watercress emulsion, and crème brûlée with a crust of local maple syrup—for C$52 a person. ⊠ *700 rue Ripplecove, C.P. 246, Ayer's Cliff J0B 1C0* ☎ *819/838–4296 or 800/668–4296* 🖷 *819/838–5541* 🌐 *www.ripplecove.com* 🛏 *28 rooms, 5 suites, 3 cottages* ⟐ *Restaurant, some in-room hot tubs, cable TV, pool, beach, windsurfing, boating, cross-country skiing, Internet, meeting room, no-smoking rooms; no TV in some rooms* ▤ *AE, MC, V* ⦿I *MAP.*

$$ ✕⌂ **Auberge l'Étoile Sur-le-Lac.** The rooms at this popular inn on Magog's waterfront are modern and have fresh furnishings; some have water views or whirlpools and fireplaces. Large windows overlooking mountain-ringed Lac Memphrémagog make the restaurant bright and airy. In summer you can eat outside and take in the smells and sounds, as well as the beautiful view. Specialties include wild game and Swiss fondue. ⊠ *1150 rue Principale Ouest* ☎ *819/843–6521 or 800/567–2727* 🌐 *www.etoile-sur-le-lac.com* 🛏 *51 rooms, 2 suites* ⟐ *Restaurant, in-room data ports, cable TV, spa, boating, bicycles, hiking, ice-skating, meeting rooms, no-smoking rooms* ▤ *AE, DC, MC, V.*

★ **$$** ⌂ **Spa Eastman.** The oldest spa in Québec has evolved from a simple health center into a bucolic haven for anyone seeking rest and therapeutic treatments, including lifestyle and weight-management counseling. Surrounded by 350 acres of rolling, wooded land 15 km (9 mi) west of Magog, the spa itself is an elegant, simple structure that brings to mind the calm of a Japanese garden. Some bedrooms have fireplaces, large balconies, and views of Mont-Orford. Vegetarian dishes, prepared with organic ingredients and produce from the chef's garden, predominate in the dining room, which is filled with light during the day. Fish, rabbit, and chicken courses accompanied by interesting herbs and sauces are also served from time to time. ⊠ *895 chemin des Diligences, Eastman J0E 1P0* ☎ *450/297–3009 or 800/665–5272* 🖷 *450/297–3370* 🌐 *www.spa-eastman.com* 🛏 *44 rooms* ⟐ *Dining room, pool, spa, cross-country skiing, meeting rooms; no a/c in some rooms, no room TVs, no kids* ▤ *AE, MC, V* ⦿I *MAP.*

Nightlife & the Arts

NIGHTLIFE Magog is lively after dark, with many bars, cafés, bistros, and restaurants. A patio bar at **Auberge Orford** (⊠ 20 rue Merry Sud ☎ 819/843–9361) overlooks the Magog River (you can moor your boat alongside it). Sometimes there's live entertainment, but when musicians aren't around to keep them at bay, flocks of ducks line up alongside the café to beg crumbs from patrons' plates—an entertaining sight in itself. **Café St-Michel** (⊠ 503 rue Principale Ouest ☎ 819/868–1062), in a century-old building, is a chic pub outfitted in shades of charcoal and ebony that serves Tex-Mex food, pasta, and local beers. Its patio bar, which is noisy because it's at Magog's main intersection, is a great spot to watch the world go by. *Chansonniers* (singers) belt out popular hits for a full house on weekends—and every night but Monday during summer. **Le Chat du Mouliner** (⊠ 101 rue du Moulin ☎ 819/868–5678) is a hot spot in a former factory on the waterfront. The jazz club and restaurant has exposed-brick walls with climbing vines, and a concrete dance floor with a grand piano in the center. The owner, Jean-Jacques Dubuc, who plays a mean saxophone, brings in headline acts from Montréal to augment performances by local musicians. Huge windows allow for panoramic views of Lac Memphrémagog. **La Grosse Pomme** (⊠ 270 rue Principale Ouest ☎ 819/843–9365) is a multilevel entertainment complex with video screens, dance floors, and restaurant service. **La Memphré** (⊠ 12 rue Merry Sud ☎ 819/843–3405), a pub named after the monster said to lurk in Lake Memphrémagog, dates to the 1800s, when it belonged to Magog's first mayor. Now a microbrewery, it serves Swiss-cheese fondue, sausages with sauerkraut, and panini (pressed sandwiches)—good accompaniments for a cold one.

THE ARTS   **Le Vieux Clocher de Magog** (⊠ 64 rue Merry Nord ☎ 819/847–0470 ⊕ www.vieuxclocher.com) is one of two former churches converted into theaters by local impresario Bernard Caza. (The other is in Sherbrooke.) It headlines well-known comedians and singers. Most performances are in French.

Sports & the Outdoors

GOLF   **Golf Owl's Head** (⊠ 181 chemin du Mont Owl's Head, Mansonville ☎ 450/292–3666 or 800/363–3342 ⊕ www.owlshead.com), close to the Vermont border, has some spectacular views. Laid out with undulating fairways, bent-grass greens, and 64 sand bunkers, the 6,705-yard, 18-hole course (par 72), designed by Graham Cooke, is surrounded by mountain scenery. The clubhouse, a stunning timber-and-fieldstone structure with five fireplaces and 45-foot-high ceilings, is a favorite watering hole for locals and visitors alike. Greens fees are C$41–C$50; motorized cart rental costs C$30.

Manoir des Sables golf course (⊠ 90 av. des Jardins, Magog-Orford ☎ 819/847–4299 or 800/567–3514 ⊕ www.hotel.manoirdessables.com) is a 6,120-yard, 18-hole, par-71 course built on a sandy base. Lessons with Marc Viens, the resident pro, start at C$35. Greens fees start at C$21.

Orford Le Golf (⊠ 3074 chemin du Parc ☎ 819/843–5688 ⊕ www.mt-orford.com) is a venerable course—it was laid out in 1939. The 18-hole, par-70, 6,287-yard course winds around forested land; from many of the greens you can see the peak of Mont-Orford. Greens fees are C$14–C$34.

SKIING   **Owl's Head Ski Area** (⊠ Rte. 243 S; Autoroute 10, Exit 106 ☎ 450/292–3342 or 800/363–3342 ⊕ www.owlshead.com), on the Knowlton side of Lake Memphrémagog, is great for skiers seeking sparser crowds. It has eight lifts, a 1,782-foot vertical drop, and 43 trails, including a 4-km (2½-mi) intermediate run, the longest such run in the Eastern Townships.

North Hatley

(19) *134 km (83 mi) east of Montréal.*

North Hatley, the small resort town on the tip of Lac Massawippi, has a theater and excellent inns and restaurants. Set among hills and farms, it was discovered by rich vacationers in the early 1900s and has been drawing people ever since.

Where to Stay & Eat

$–$$$ ✕ **Pilsen Pub.** Québec's first microbrewery no longer brews beer on-site, but Massawippi pale and brown ales and a vast selection of microbrews and imports are on tap here. Good pub food—pasta, homemade soups, burgers, and the like—is served in the upstairs restaurant and in the tavern, both of which overlook the water. It can get busy at lunch, so try to get here by noon. ⊠ *55 rue Principale* ☎ *819/842–2971* ▤ *AE, MC, V.*

★ **$$$$** ✕▣ **Auberge Hatley.** As befits a member of the fancy Relais & Châteaux chain, the service at this intimate and elegant country inn is consistently good. Some rooms in the 1903 country manor have whirlpool baths and fireplaces. Chef Alain Labrie specializes in regional dishes, and the menu changes seasonally: the rich foie gras, piglet, and venison are recommended. Herbs and vegetables, grown in the inn's greenhouse, turn up in many dishes. You can dine in a corner of the kitchen, at the "chef's table," on weekends and watch the behind-the-scenes goings-on. The wine cellar stocks 13,000 bottles and 1,300 brands; a cellar tour (for guests only, although exceptions are sometimes made) is given daily in the late afternoon. ⊠ *325 chemin Virgin, C.P. 330, J0B 2C0* ☎ *819/842–2451 or 800/336–2451* ▤ *819/842–2907* ⊕ *www.aubergehatley. com* ➫ *25 rooms* ⟐ *Restaurant, some in-room hot tubs, cable TV, pool, massage, boating, bicycles, hiking, Internet, meeting rooms* ▤ *AE, MC, V* ⵗ *MAP.*

★ **$$$$** ✕▣ **Manoir Hovey.** Overlooking Lac Massawippi, this retreat feels like a private estate, with many of the activities included in room rates. Built in 1900, the manor was modeled after George Washington's Mount Vernon. Rooms have a mix of antiques and more-modern wood furniture, richly printed fabrics, and lace trimmings; many have fireplaces and private balconies overlooking the lake. The restaurant serves exquisite Continental and French cuisine; try the goat cheese–and–endive tatin, fruit with cheese from the Benedictine Abbey, or sautéed venison loin with mushroom stuffing. There's also a light menu. If you get the post-lunch munchies, try the posh English-style afternoon tea. Not only are you served homebaked scones, clotted cream, and jam, but you also have a choice of more than 40 teas and infusions. ⊠ *575 chemin Hovey, J0B 2C0* ☎ *819/842–2421 or 800/661–2421* ▤ *819/842–2248* ⊕ *www. manoirhovey.com* ➫ *40 rooms, 3 suites, 1 4-bedroom cottage* ⟐ *Restaurant, cable TV, tennis court, pool, massage, beach, mountain bikes, cross-country skiing, ice-skating, 2 bars, library, Internet, meeting rooms, no-smoking rooms* ▤ *AE, DC, MC, V* ⵗ *MAP.*

$ ✕▣ **Auberge Le Saint-Amant.** Rooms at this B&B, a 19th-century home on a hill overlooking Lac Massawippi, are hung with plants and fur-

nished with antiques. Jean-Claude, the chef-owner, whips up sophisti-
cated fare at reasonable prices: venison with blackberries, rabbit terrine,
sorrel-flavored salmon, sweetbreads in raspberry-vinegar sauce, and
rack of lamb with cedar jelly. A four-course "health menu"—miso soup,
salad, a tofu dish, and dessert—is C$30. ⊠ *3 chemin Côte Minton, J0B
2C0* ☎ *819/842–1211* ⌨ *3 rooms* ⌂ *Restaurant, pool, Internet, meeting rooms; no a/c in some rooms, no room TVs* ▤ *MC, V* ⦿ *MAP.*

Nightlife & the Arts

The **Piggery** (⊠ 215 chemin Simard, off Rte. 108 ☎ 819/842–2431
⊕ www.piggery.com), a theater that was once a pig barn, reigns supreme
in the Townships' cultural life. The venue, which has an on-site restaurant, often presents new plays by Canadian writers and experiments with
bilingual productions. The season runs July through mid-September.

L'Association du Festival du Lac Massawippi (☎ 819/823–7810) presents
an annual antiques and show in July. The association also sponsors classical-music concerts at the Église Ste-Elizabeth in North Hatley on Sun-
days from late April through June and presents lively Sunday-afternoon
band concerts at Dreamland Park from June through August.

Sherbrooke

20 *130 km (81 mi) east of Montréal.*

The region's unofficial capital and largest city, Sherbrooke was founded
by Loyalists in the 1790s. This town didn't get its current name, however, until 1818, when it was named for Canadian governor general Sir
John Coape Sherbrooke.

On the corner of rues Dufferin and Frontenac is a realistic mural illus-
trating storefronts and businesses from Sherbrooke's past. Close up
you notice whimsical little details—a bulldog blocking the path of a Fos-
sMobile (Canada's first gas-powered automobile, designed by local inventor George Foote Foss); a woman, hair in rollers, yelling at a dog
from a balcony; a policeman trying to coax the animal to move out of
the way.

Sherbrooke has a number of art galleries and museums, including the
Musée des Beaux-Arts de Sherbrooke. This fine-arts museum has a permanent exhibit on the history of art in the region from 1800 to the present.
⊠ *241 rue Dufferin* ☎ *819/821–2115* ⊕ *www.mba.ville.sherbrooke.
qc.ca* ⌨ *C$6* ⊙ *Tues. and Thurs.–Sun. 11–5, Wed. 11–9.*

The **Musée de la Nature et des Sciences** is in what used to be the Julius
Kayser & Co. factory, once famous for the silk stockings it made. The
elegant building, which has granite floors and marble stairs, makes
good use of its lofty space. State-of-the-art light and sound effects (the
buzzing of mosquitoes may be *too* lifelike) and hands-on displays en-
hance the exhibits. ⊠ *225 rue Frontenac* ☎ *819/564–3200* ⊕ *www.mnes.
qc.ca* ⌨ *C$7.50* ⊙ *Tues.–Sun. 10–5.*

The **Sherbrooke Tourist Information Center** (⊠ 2964 King St. W ☎ 819/
821–1919) conducts animated tours, mainly in French, led by costumed

actors representing figures from Sherbooke's past. The history-focused tours, which run on weekends from mid-July to late August, are designed for prearranged groups, but individuals can tag along ($16 per person; reservations essential).

off the
beaten
path

LA FERME MARTINETTE – In the heart of Québec's dairy country, this farm, which doubles as a modest B&B, hosts "sugaring off" parties with traditional menus in March and April. Lisa Nadeau and her husband, Gérald Martineau, have 2,500 maple trees as well as a herd of 50 Holsteins. You can tour the farm in a trailer pulled by the tractor that belonged to Gérald's grandfather and fill up on the C$20.95 all-you-can-eat traditional meal. Coaticook is 32 km (20 mi) south of Sherbrooke. ⊠ *1728 chemin Martineau, Coaticook* ☎ *819/ 849–7089 or 888/881–4561* ⊕ *www.lafermemartinette.com.*

Where to Stay & Eat

$$$–$$$$ ✕ **Restaurant au P'tit Sabot.** The adventurous menus here use local ingredients such as wild boar, quail, sweetbreads, venison, and bison in many dishes, in which the emphasis is on classical French cuisine. The serene decor and the small dining area (it seats around 35 people) make it a pleasant refuge from the busy and not very attractive shopping mall it's in. ⊠ *1410 rue King Ouest* ☎ *819/563–0262* ▤ *AE, DC, MC, V.*

$$–$$$$ ✕ **La Falaise St-Michel.** A warmly decorated redbrick-and-wood room takes the chill off even before you sit down. The superb French offerings at this restaurant, considered to be one of the best in town, include sautéed kidneys, veal sweetbreads, escargots, and warm duck salad. A large selection of wines complements the table d'hôte. ⊠ *100 rue Webster* ☎ *819/346–6339* ▤ *AE, DC, MC, V.*

¢ ▦ **Bishop's University.** If you're on a budget, these students' residences are a great place to stay in mid-May through August. The prices can't be beat, and the location—5 km (3 mi) south of Sherbrooke—is good for touring. The university's lovely grounds have architecture reminiscent of stately New England campuses. The 1857 Gothic-style chapel, paneled with richly carved ash, shows fine local craftsmanship. Reservations for summer are accepted as early as the previous September, and it's a good idea to book far in advance. ⊠ *rue College, Box 5000, Lennoxville, J1M 1Z7* ☎ *819/822–9651* ▤ *819/822–9615* ⊕ *www. ubishops.ca* ⤳ *438 rooms with shared baths, 40 apartments with bath* ♨ *Restaurant, 9-hole golf course, tennis court, 2 pools (1 indoors), gym; no a/c, no room TVs* ▤ *MC, V* ☉ *Closed Sept.–mid-May.*

Nightlife & the Arts

The 600-seat **Centennial Theatre** (⊠ Bishop's University, rue College, Lennoxville ☎ 819/822–9692), 5 km (3 mi) south of Sherbrooke, presents a roster of jazz, classical, and rock concerts, as well as opera, dance, mime, and children's theater. **Le Vieux Clocher de Sherbrooke** (⊠ 1590 rue Galt Ouest ☎ 819/822–2102 ⊕ www.vieuxclocher.com), in a converted church, presents music, from classical to jazz, and a variety of theater and comedy.

Notre-Dame-des-Bois

㉑ *100 km (62 mi) east of Sherbrooke, 204 km (127 mi) east of Montréal.*

The big draw here is the observatory. Both amateur stargazers and serious astronomers head to the **Astrolab du Mont-Mégantic** (Mont-Mégantic's Observatory), in a beautifully wild and mountainous area. The observatory is at the summit of the Townships' second-highest mountain (3,601 feet), whose northern face records annual snowfalls rivaling any in North America. A joint venture of the University of Montréal and Laval University, the observatory has a powerful telescope, the largest on the East Coast. At the welcome center on the mountain's base, you can view an exhibition and a multimedia show to learn about the night sky. ⊠ *Parc Megantic, 189 Rte. du Parc* ☎ *819/888–2941* ⊕ *www.astrolab. qc.ca* ⊡ *C$10.50, summit tour C$19; additional C$3.50 to enter Parc Megantic* ☉ *Mid-May–mid-June and mid-Aug.–mid-Oct., Sat. noon–5 and 8 PM–11 PM, Sun. noon–5; mid-June–mid-Aug., daily noon–7:30 and 8 PM–11 PM.*

Where to Stay & Eat

$ ✕▥⚏ **Aux Berges de l'Aurore.** Although this tiny B&B has attractive furnishings and spectacular views (it's at the foot of Mont-Mégantic), the food is the main attraction. The restaurant ($$$$) serves a six-course meal using produce from the inn's huge garden, as well as local wild game: boar, fish, hare, and caribou. ⊠ *139 route du Parc* ☎ *819/888–2715* ⊕ *www.auberge-aurore.qc.ca* ⟿ *5 rooms* ⚬ *Restaurant, meeting rooms; no a/c, no room TVs, no kids under 12* ▤ *MC, V* ☉ *Closed Jan.–May* ⦿ *EP.*

FodorsChoice
★

CHARLEVOIX

Updated by
Mark Cardwell

Stretching along the St. Lawrence River's north shore east of Québec City to the Saguenay River, Charlevoix embraces mountains rising from the sea and a succession of valleys, plateaus, and cliffs cut by waterfalls, brooks, and streams. UNESCO named it the first populated World Biosphere Reserve in recognition of its unique combination of nature and culture. The roads wind into villages of houses and churches, which often have bright tin roofs. The area has attracted summer visitors and artists for more than a century. Winter activities include downhill and cross-country skiing.

New France's first historian, the Jesuit priest François-Xavier de Charlevoix, is the region's namesake. The first white to explore Charlevoix (pronounced sharle-*vwah*) was Jacques Cartier, who landed in 1535, but the first colonists didn't arrive until well into the 1600s. They developed a thriving shipbuilding industry, specializing in the sturdy schooner called a *goélette*, which they used to haul everything from logs to lobsters up and down the coast in the days before rail and paved roads. By the early 20th century, however, tourism had overtaken shipbuilding as the backbone of the provincial economy; today wrecked and forgotten goélettes lie along beaches in the region.

Ste-Anne-de-Beaupré

㉒ *33 km (20 mi) east of Québec City.*

On Route 138 approaching Charlevoix from Québec City is the tiny town of Ste-Anne-de-Beaupré. Each year more than a million pilgrims
★ visit the region's famous religious site, the **Basilique Ste-Anne-de-Beaupré,** dedicated to the mother of the Virgin Mary and Québec's patron saint.

The French brought their devotion to St. Anne with them when they sailed across the Atlantic to New France. According to local legend, St. Anne was responsible for saving voyagers from shipwrecks in the harsh waters of the St. Lawrence. In 1650 Breton sailors caught in a storm vowed to erect a chapel at the spot where they landed.

The present neo-Roman basilica, constructed in 1923 and designed by architects Maxime Rosin from Paris and Louis N. Audet from Québec province, is the fifth to be built where the sailors first touched ground. The gigantic cross-shape structure has two imposing granite steeples. The interior has 22 chapels and 18 altars, as well as rounded arches and numerous ornaments in the Romanesque style. The 214 stained-glass windows, completed in 1949 by Frenchmen Auguste Labouret and Pierre Chaudière, tell a story of salvation through people believed to be instruments of God over the centuries. Other features of the shrine include wooden pews decorated with intricate carvings of animals and several smaller altars (behind the main altar) dedicated to saints.

Tributes to St. Anne can be seen in the shrine's mosaics, murals, altars, and ceilings. A bas-relief at the entrance depicts St. Anne welcoming pilgrims, and ceiling mosaics depict events that took place in her life. Numerous crutches and braces posted on the back pillars have been left by those who have felt the saint's healing powers.

The **Musée de Sainte Anne** (☎ 418/827–6873 ⊠ C$2), in the basilica parking lot, exhibits church treasures as well as donations made by pilgrims. The museum is open 10–5 daily from early June through August. *⊠ 10018 av. Royale ☎ 418/827–3781 ⊠ Free ☉ Reception booth daily 8:30–5. Guided tours: early June–Aug., daily at 1; Sept.–early June, by appointment.*

The **Commemorative Chapel,** across from Basilique Ste-Anne-de-Beaupré, was designed by Claude Bailiff and built in 1878. The chapel, constructed on the transept of a church built in 1676 with stones from that church, contains the old building's foundations. Among the remnants is a white-and-gold-trimmed pulpit designed by François Baillargé in 1807 and adorned with a sculpture depicting Moses and the Ten Commandments. The small chapel of **Scala Santa,** adjacent to the Commemorative Chapel, resembles a wedding cake. On bended knees, pilgrims climb its replica of the Holy Stairs, representing the steps Jesus climbed to meet Pontius Pilate. *⊠ av. Royale ☎ No phone ☉ Early May–mid-Oct., daily 8–4:30.*

At the **Réserve Faunique du Cap Tourmente** (Cap Tourmente Wildlife Reserve), about 8 km (5 mi) northeast of Ste-Anne-de-Beaupré, more than

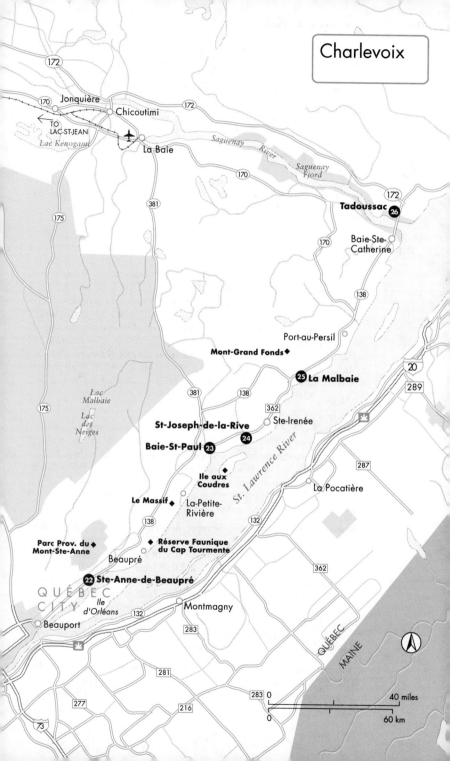

Charlevoix

172

170 Jonquière

Chicoutimi

172

TO LAC-ST-JEAN

Lac Kenogami

La Baie

Saguenay River

Saguenay Fjord

170

381

172

Tadoussac **26**

175

170

Baie-Ste-Catherine

138

Port-au-Persil

Mont-Grand Fonds ◆

25 **La Malbaie**

20

289

381

138

362

Lac Malbaie

175

Lac des Neiges

St-Joseph-de-la-Rive

Ste-Irenée

24

Baie-St-Paul **23**

287

Ile aux Coudres ◆

St. Lawrence River

La Pocatière

Le Massif ◆

La-Petite-Rivière

138

132

◆ **Réserve Faunique du Cap Tourmente**

362

Parc Prov. du Mont-Ste-Anne ◆

Beaupré

22 **Ste-Anne-de-Beaupré**

Q U É B E C C I T Y

Ile d'Orléans

132

Montmagny

287

Beauport

281

283

QUÉBEC

MAINE

277

283

0

281

216

0

40 miles

60 km

73

800,000 greater snow geese gather every October and May, with an average of 100,000 per day. The park harbors hundreds of kinds of birds and mammals and more than 700 plant species. This enclave on the north shore of the St. Lawrence River also has 18 km (11 mi) of hiking trails; naturalists give guided tours. ✉ *570 chemin du Cap Tourmente, St-Joachim* ☎ *418/827–4591 Apr.–Oct., 418/827–3776 Nov.–Mar.* 💳 *C$5* ⏰ *Jan.–Oct., daily 8:30–5.*

---

off the
beaten
path

RÉSERVE FAUNIQUE DES LAURENTIDES – The wildlife reserve, approximately 48 km (30 mi) north of Québec City via Route 175, has good lakes for fishing. It's a good idea to reserve a slot 48 hours ahead by phone or fax. ☎ *418/528–6868, 418/890–6527 for fishing reservations* 🖷 *418/528–8833.*

Where to Eat

★ **$$–$$$$** ✕ **Auberge Baker.** The best of old and new blend at this restaurant in a 1840 French-Canadian farmhouse built by the present owners' ancestors. Antiques and old-fashioned woodstoves decorate the dining rooms, where you can sample traditional Québecois fare, from tourtière and pork hocks to maple-sugar pie. Or opt for contemporary dishes such as the excellent herbed-and-breaded grilled lamb loin, and exotic choices such as minced wapiti (elk) with pesto sauce. The lower-priced lunch menu is served until 6. Upstairs is a five-room B&B, also decorated in Canadiana; two exterior buildings hold two additional rooms. Château-Richer is 4 km (2.5 mi) west of Ste-Anne-de-Beaupré. ✉ *8790 chemin Royale, Château-Richer* ☎ *418/824–4478 or 866/824–4478* ⊕ *www.auberge-baker.qc.ca* 🍴 *AE, DC, MC, V.*

Sports & the Outdoors

Le Massif (✉ 1350 rue Principale, Petite-Rivière-St-François ☎ 418/632–5876 or 877/536–2774 ⊕ www.lemassif.com) is a three-peak ski resort that has the province's longest vertical drop—2,526 feet. The resort, now owned by Daniel Gauthier, a founder of Le Cirque du Soleil, is in the midst of an expansion. Four lifts service the 36 trails, which are divided into runs for different levels; the longest run is 3.8 km (2.36 mi). Equipment can be rented on-site.

Mont-Ste-Anne (✉ 2000 blvd. Beaupré, Beaupré ☎ 418/827–4561 or 800/463–1568 ⊕ www.mont-sainte-anne.com), outside Québec City, is on the World Cup downhill circuit. It's one of the largest resorts in eastern Canada, with a vertical drop of 2,050 feet, 56 downhill trails, two half-pipes for snowboarders, a terrain park, and 13 lifts including a gondola. Cross-country skiing is also a draw here, with 21 trails totaling 224 km (139 mi). When the weather warms, mountain biking becomes the sport of choice. Enthusiasts can choose from 150 km (93 mi) of mountain-bike trails and 14 downhill runs (with a gondola up to the top). Three bike runs are designated as "extreme zones."

You can rent snowmobiles at **Centre de Location de Motoneiges du Québec** (✉ 15 blvd. Beaupré, Beaupré ☎ 418/827–8478 ⊕ www.locationmotoneiges.com), near Mont Ste-Anne, starting at C$40 per person (two to a snowmobile) for an hour or C$100 per person per day, including equipment.

Baie-St-Paul

㉓ *60 km (37 mi) northeast of Ste-Anne-de-Beaupré.*

Baie-St-Paul, one of the oldest towns in the province, is popular with craftspeople and artists. The village, full of centuries-old mansard-roofed houses, is by a river on a wide plain encircled by high hills. Boutiques and a handful of commercial galleries line the historic narrow streets in the town center; most have original artwork and handicrafts for sale. In addition, each August, more than a dozen artists from across Canada take part in "Symposium of Modern Art." Drawing on the theme that year, the artists create a giant canvas.

Jean-Paul Lemieux, Clarence Gagnon, and many more of Québec's greatest landscape artists have depicted the area, and some of these works are for sale at **Maison René Richard** (⊠ 58 rue St-Jean-Baptiste ☎ 418/435–5571 ☉ Daily 10–6). On the grounds is Gagnon's old studio.

The **Centre d'Art Baie-St-Paul** (⊠ 4 rue Ambroise-Fafard ☎ 418/435–3681), adjacent to the city's main church, displays a diverse collection of works by more than 20 Charlevoix artists. In the tapestry workshop, weavers create traditional and contemporary pieces and demonstrate techniques. The center is open from April to late June and early September to mid-November, Tuesday through Sunday 10–5; late June to early September, Tuesday through Sunday 10–6; and mid-November through March, Friday through Sunday 10–5. Admission is free.

The mandate of the **Centre d'Exposition de Baie-St-Paul** (⊠ 23 rue Ambroise-Fafard ☎ 418/435–3681 ☎ C$3) is to promote modern and contemporary art created by Charlevoix artists from 1920 to 1970. The center is in a modern building that was awarded a provincial architecture prize in 1992. It's open Tuesday through Sunday 10–6 (10–5 from early September to late June).

Where to Stay & Eat

★ **$$$–$$$$** ✕🖼 **Auberge la Maison Otis.** Three buildings in the village center house the calm, romantic accommodations of this inn. Some guest rooms, decorated in traditional or country styles, have whirlpools, fireplaces, and antique furnishings. There are also four apartments. The restaurant ($$$$), in an elegant, Norman-style house that dates to the mid-1850s, serves creative, regionally oriented French cuisine, such as *ballotine de faisan*, pheasant stuffed with quail and served in venison sauce. Dinner is a four-course, fixed-price affair. Rates for Monday and Tuesday stays can be based on a breakfast-only plan. ⊠ *23 rue St-Jean-Baptiste, G0A 1B0* ☎ *418/435–2255 or 800/267–2254* 🖷 *418/435–2464* ⊕ *www. maisonotis.com* 🛏 *26 rooms, 4 suites, 4 apartments* ♿ *2 restaurants, some fans, cable TV, some in-room VCRs, indoor pool, sauna, spa, bar, lounge, Internet, meeting rooms, some pets allowed (fee); no a/c in some rooms* ☐ *MC, V* ⊙I *MAP.*

> **en route** From Baie-St-Paul, instead of the faster Route 138 to La Malbaie, you can take the open coastal drive on **Route 362.** This section of road has memorable views of the hills—green, white, or ablaze with fiery hues, depending on the season—meeting the broad expanse of the "sea," as the locals call the St. Lawrence estuary.

St-Joseph-de-la-Rive

㉔ *19 km (12 mi) northeast of Baie-St-Paul.*

A secondary road descends sharply into St-Joseph-de-la-Rive, with a line of old houses that hugs the mountain base on a narrow shore route. The town has a number of peaceful inns and inviting restaurants. The small **Exposition Maritime** (Maritime Museum), in an old, still active shipyard, commemorates the days of the St. Lawrence goélettes, the feisty little schooners that, until the 1950s, were the lifeblood of the region. In the mid-20th century, the roads through Charlevoix were little more than rugged tracks. (Indeed, they are still narrow and winding.) Very large families lived in cramped conditions aboard the boats. To modern eyes, it doesn't look like it was a comfortable existence, but the folklore of the goélettes, celebrated in poetry, paintings, and song, is part of the region's identity. ⊠ *305 place de l'Église* ☎ *418/635–1131* ⊠ *C$3* ⊙ *Mid-May–mid-June and early Sept.–mid-Oct., weekdays 9–4 and weekends 11–4; mid-June–early Sept., daily 9–5.*

A free, government-run ferry from the wharf in St-Joseph-de-la-Rive takes you on the 15-minute trip to **L'Île-aux-Coudres** (☎ 418/438–2743 ferry information), an island where Jacques Cartier's men gathered *coudres* (hazelnuts) in 1535. Since then, the island has produced many a goélette, and the families of former captains now run several small inns. Larger inns have folk-dance evenings. You can bike around the island (26 km/16 mi) and see windmills and water mills, or stop at boutiques selling paintings and handicrafts such as traditional handwoven household linens.

Where to Stay

$–$$ ⊡ **Hôtel Cap-aux-Pierres.** The traditionally Canadian main building of this hotel has a long veranda with river views. Comfortable accommodations also are available in a motel section, open only in summer. About a third of the rooms have river views. The restaurant serves a mix of Québec standards and French cuisine; summer entertainment includes folk dancing on Saturday evening. ⊠ *246 chemin la Baleine, Île-aux-Coudres, La Baleine, G0A 2A0* ☎ *418/438–2711 or 800/463–5250* ⊟ *418/438–2127* ⊕ *www.hotelcapauxpierres.com* ⊅ *98 rooms* ⬧ *Restaurant, snack bar, cable TV with movies, driving range, miniature golf, tennis court, indoor-outdoor pool, hot tub, spa, badminton, croquet, lawn bowling, shuffleboard, softball, volleyball, bar, lounge, recreation room, shop, babysitting, playground, Internet, meeting rooms, some pets allowed (fee), no-smoking floors; no a/c in some rooms* ⊟ *AE, D, DC, MC, V* ⊙ *Closed mid-Oct.–Apr.* ⦿⧠ *EP.*

Shopping

Papeterie St-Gilles (⊠ 354 rue F. A. Savard ☎ 418/635–2430 or 866/635-2430) produces handcrafted stationery using a 17th-century process. The paper factory, which is also a small museum, explains through photographs and demonstrations how paper is manufactured the old-fashioned way. Slivers of wood and flower petals are pressed into the paper sheets, which are as thick as the covers of a paperback book. The finished products—made into writing paper, greeting cards, and one-page poems or quotations—make beautiful but pricey gifts.

La Malbaie

25 *35 km (22 mi) northeast of St-Joseph-de-la-Rive.*

La Malbaie, one of the province's most elegant and historically interesting resort towns, was known as Murray Bay when wealthy Anglophones summered here. The area became popular with American and Canadian politicians in the late 1800s when Ottawa Liberals and Washington Republicans partied decorously all summer with members of the Québec judiciary. William Howard Taft built the "summer White House," the first of his three summer residences here, in 1894, when he was the American civil governor of the Philippines. He became the 27th president of the United States in 1908.

Many Taft-era homes now serve as handsome inns, offering old-fashioned coddling with such extras as breakfast in bed, whirlpool baths, and free shuttles to the ski areas in winter. Many serve lunch and dinner to nonresidents, so you can tour the area going from one gourmet delight to the next. The cuisine, as elsewhere in Québec, is genuine French or regional fare.

The **Musée de Charlevoix** traces the region's history through a major permanent exhibit called *Appartenances* (Belonging), installed in 2003. Folk art, paintings, and artifacts recount the past, starting with the French, then the Scottish settlers, and the area's evolution into a vacation spot and artists' haven. ☒ *10 chemin du Havre, Pointe-au-Pic* ☎ *418/665–4411* ☜ *C$4* ☉ *Late June–early Sept., daily 10–6; early Sept.–late June, Tues.–Fri. 10–5, weekends 1–5.*

The **Casino de Charlevoix** is one of three highly profitable gaming halls in Québec. The smallest of the three, it still draws more than 1 million visitors a year—some of whom stay at the Fairmont Le Manoir Richelieu, which is connected to the casino by a tunnel. There are 22 gaming tables and 780 slot machines. Minimum age is 18. ☒ *183 rue Richelieu, Pointe-au-Pic* ☎ *418/665–5300 or 800/665–2274* ⊕ *www.casino-de-charlevoix. com* ☉ *Mid-June–Aug., Sun.–Thurs. 10 AM–2 AM, Fri. and Sat. 10 AM–3 AM; Sept.–mid-June, Sun.–Thurs. 11 AM–1 AM, Fri. and Sat. 11 AM–3 AM.*

off the beaten path

POTERIE DE PORT-AU-PERSIL – Visiting potters, many from France, study Canadian ceramic techniques at this studio, about 25 km (15½ mi) east of La Malbaie. Classes for amateurs are available from late June through August (by the hour or longer, starting at C$12). Half of the bright-yellow barn housing the studio is a store, with ceramics and other crafts made by Québec artists. ☒ *1001 rue Saint-Laurent (Rte. 138), Saint-Siméon* ☎ *418/638–2349* ⊕ *www. poteriedeportaupersil.com* ☉ *Mid-May–Sept., daily 9–6.*

Where to Stay & Eat

★ **$$–$$$$** ✕⊡ **Auberge la Pinsonnière.** An atmosphere of country luxury prevails at this Relais & Châteaux inn, which has an impressive art collection. Every guest room is different—some have fireplaces, whirlpools, and king-size four-poster beds—and half overlook Murray Bay on the St. Lawrence River. The restaurant ($$$$) is excellent, with one of the largest wine cellars in North America, housing 12,000 bottles. The haute cuisine doesn't come cheap; appetizers, including foie gras with pear confit, duck ravioli, warm smoked-salmon salad, and braised sweetbreads, cost as much as the entrées in other area establishments—this is an impressive dining experience. ⊠ *124 rue St-Raphaël, Cap-à-l'Aigle G5A 1X9* ☎ *418/665–4431 or 800/387–4431* ⧠ *418/665–7156* ⊕ *www. lapinsonniere.com* ⇨ *25 rooms, 1 suite* ⅋ *Restaurant, fans, in-room data ports, some in-room hot tubs, cable TV, tennis court, indoor pool, spa, beach, bar, 2 lounges, meeting rooms, no-smoking rooms; no a/c in some rooms* ⊟ *AE, MC, V* ⅋⊙⅋ *BP.*

$$–$$$ ✕⊡ **Auberge des Peupliers.** About half the guest rooms at this hilltop inn overlook the St. Lawrence River. Accommodations, outfitted in country-style furnishings, are spread among three buildings, including a farmhouse more than two centuries old. A former barn holds more-luxurious rooms, some with terraces; a stone house has rooms with fireplaces and balconies. At the restaurant, chef Dominique Truchon earns high marks for dishes such as Arctic trout in Pastis-and-raspberry sauce. For an extra C$60, you can choose the evening five-course table d'hôte for two. ⊠ *381 rue St-Raphaël, Cap-à-l'Aigle, G5A 2N8* ☎ *418/665– 4423 or 888/282–3743* ⧠ *418/665–3179* ⊕ *www.aubergedespeupliers. com* ⇨ *22 rooms* ⅋ *Restaurant, fans, cable TV, tennis court, hot tub, massage, sauna, badminton, croquet, lounge, piano bar, recreation room, babysitting, meeting room, no-smoking rooms; no a/c in some rooms* ⊟ *AE, DC, MC, V* ⊙ *No lunch* ⅋⊙⅋ *BP.*

★ **$$–$$$$** ⊡ **Fairmont Le Manoir Richelieu.** From the front lawn of this castlelike building, the cannons point to the St. Lawrence River below. Constructed in 1929 on the site of an earlier hotel, the Manoir is an elegant reminder of the past. At the clubby after-dinner lounge, you may smoke a cigar and sip a single malt or vintage port. The full-service spa has 22 treatment rooms, and the links-style golf course overlooks the St. Lawrence. A tunnel connects the hotel with the Casino de Charlevoix. ⊠ *181 rue Richelieu, Pointe-au-Pic, G5A 1X7* ☎ *418/665–3703 or 800/ 463–2613* ⧠ *418/665–3093* ⊕ *www.fairmont.com* ⇨ *390 rooms, 15 suites* ⅋ *3 restaurants, room service, in-room data ports, in-room safes, some in-room hot tubs, minibars, cable TV with movies and video games, driving range, 18-hole golf course, 9-hole golf course, miniature golf, 3 tennis courts, indoor pool, saltwater pool, health club, spa, mountain bikes, croquet, hiking, horseback riding, Ping-Pong, shuffle-board, volleyball, cross-country skiing, ice-skating, sleigh rides, snow-mobiling, tobogganing, 2 bars, lounge, casino, piano, recreation room, babysitting, children's programs (ages 4–12), dry cleaning, laundry service, concierge, concierge floor, Internet, convention center, some pets allowed (fee), no-smoking floors* ⊟ *AE, DC, MC, V* ⅋⊙⅋ *BP.*

The Arts

The music and dance academy **Domaine Forget** (⊠ 5 St-Antoine, Ste-Irenée ☎ 418/452-3535 or 888/336–7438 ⊕ www.domaineforget.com) has a 600-seat hall in Ste-Irenée, 15 km (9 mi) south of La Malbaie. Fine musicians from around the world, many of whom teach or study at the school, perform during its International Festival. The festival, which runs from mid-June to late August, includes Sunday musical brunches.

Sports & the Outdoors

Club de Golf de Manoir Richelieu (⊠ 595 côte Bellevue, Pointe-au-Pic ☎ 418/665–2526 or 800/463–2613 ⊕ www.fairmont.com) is a par-71, 6,225-yard, links-style course with 18 holes. Greens fees start at C$125. The resort also has a 9-hole course.

Mont-Grand Fonds (⊠ 1000 chemin des Loisirs ☎ 418/665–0095 or 877/665–0095 ⊕ www.quebecweb.com/montgrandfonds), 10 km (6 mi) north of La Malbaie, has 14 downhill slopes, a 1,105-foot vertical drop, and two lifts. It also has 160 km (99 mi) of cross-country trails. Two trails meet International Ski Federation standards, and the ski center occasionally hosts major competitions. You may also go dogsledding, sleigh-riding, ice-skating, and tobogganing here.

Tadoussac

 71 km (44 mi) north of La Malbaie.

The small town of Tadoussac shares the view up the magnificent Saguenay Fjord with Baie-Ste-Catherine, across the Saguenay River. The drive here from La Malbaie, along Route 138, leads past lovely villages and views along the St. Lawrence. Jacques Cartier made a stop at this point in 1535, and from 1600 to the mid-19th century it was an important meeting site for fur traders. Whale-watching excursions and fjord cruises now depart from Tadoussac, as well as from Chicoutimi, farther up the deep fjord.

As the Saguenay River flows from Lac St-Jean south toward the St. Lawrence, it has a dual character: between Alma and Chicoutimi, the once rapidly flowing river has been harnessed for hydroelectric power; in its lower section, it becomes wider and deeper and flows by steep mountains and cliffs. The small white beluga whale, which lives here year-round, breeds in the lower portion of the Saguenay in summer. The many marine species that live in the confluence of the fjord and the seaway attract other whales, too, including pilots, finbacks, humpbacks, and blues.

The beluga is an endangered species; the whales, with 27 other species of mammals and birds and 17 species of fish, are being threatened by pollution in the St. Lawrence River. This has spurred a C$100-million project funded by the federal and provincial governments. The 800-square-km (309-square-mi) **Parc Marine du Saguenay–St-Laurent** (⊠ park office: 182 rue de l'Église ☎ 418/235–4703 or 800/463–6769), a marine park at the confluence of the Saguenay and St. Lawrence rivers, has been created to protect the latter's ecosystem.

You can learn more about the whales and their habitat at the **Centre d'Interprétation des Mammifères Marins.** The interpretation center is run by members of a locally based research team, and they're only too glad to answer questions. In addition, explanatory videos and exhibits (including a collection of whale skeletons) tell you everything there is to know about the mighty cetaceans. ⊠ *108 rue de la Cale-Sèche* ☎ *418/235–4701* ⊕ *www.whales-online.net* ☜ *C$6.25* ☯ *Mid-May–mid-June and mid-Sept.–mid-Oct., daily noon–5; mid-June–mid-Sept., daily 9–8.*

Where to Stay

$$–$$$$ ⊡ **Hôtel Tadoussac.** The rambling white Victorian-style hotel with a red mansard roof is as much a symbol of Tadoussac as the Château Frontenac is of Québec City. The 1942 wood building has retained its gracefulness over the years. The spacious lobby has a stone fireplace, and sofas for relaxing. Long corridors lead to rooms, furnished in a country style; half the rooms overlook the bay, the starting point for whale-watching and fjord tours. Hand-painted murals and wood paneling from the 1852 hotel that stood on this site encircle the oldest dining room. ⊠ *165 rue Bord d'Eau, G0T 4A0* ☎ *418/235–4421 or 800/561–0718* ☐ *418/235–4607* ⊕ *www.hoteltadoussac.com* ☜ *149 rooms* ⚄ *3 restaurants, cable TV, miniature golf, tennis court, pool, spa, horseshoes, bar, recreation room, convention center, no-smoking floor; no a/c* ▭ *AE, D, DC, MC, V* ☯ *Closed late Oct.–late May* ﺷ *EP.*

Sports & the Outdoors

The best period for seeing whales is July through September, although some operators extend the season at either end if whales are around. **Croisières AML** (☎ 418/692–1159, 800/463–1292 July–Sept. ⊕ www. croisieresaml.com) has two- to three-hour whale-watching tours for C$45–C$55. The tours, in Zodiacs or larger boats, depart from Baie-Ste-Catherine and Tadoussac. Fjord tours are also available. **Croisières Dufour** (☎ 800/463–5250 ⊕ www.dufour.ca) offers day-long cruises combined with whale-watching from Québec City as well as 2¼- and 3-hour whale-watching cruises (C$50) from Baie-Ste-Catherine and Tadoussac. Tours, some of which cruise up the Saguenay Fjord, use Zodiacs or larger boats.

THE GASPÉ PENINSULA

Updated by Mark Cardwell

Jutting into the stormy Gulf of St. Lawrence like the battered prow of a ship, the Gaspé Peninsula (Gaspésie in French) remains an isolated region of wild natural beauty. Sheer cliffs tower above broad beaches, and tiny coastal fishing communities cling to the shoreline. Inland rise the Chic-Chocs, eastern Canada's highest mountains and the realm of bears, deer, and moose.

The Gaspé was on Jacques Cartier's itinerary—his first step in North America was here in 1534—but Vikings, Basques, and Portuguese fishermen had come before. Acadians, displaced by the British from New Brunswick in 1755, settled Bonaventure; Paspébiac still has a gunpowder shed that was built in the 1770s to help defend the peninsula from

American ships; and Empire Loyalists settled New Carlisle in 1784. Towns-people in some areas speak mainly English.

Today the area still seems unspoiled and timeless, a blessing for anyone driving along the spectacular coastal highways or venturing on river-valley roads to the interior. A vast, mainly uninhabited forest covers the hilly hinterland.

The Gaspé has many parks, nature trails, and wildlife sanctuaries. The most accessible include Parc de l'Île Bonaventure-et-du-Rocher-Percé (Bonaventure Island), a sanctuary for 250,000 birds; Parc National Forillon, at the tip of the peninsula, with 50 km (31 mi) of trails and an interesting boardwalk; and the Parc Provincial de la Gaspésie. The provincial park includes the Chic-Choc Mountains and has terrain ranging from tundra to subalpine forest.

Carleton

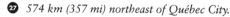

574 km (357 mi) northeast of Québec City.

The beaches are one of the main draws of this bayside town on the Gaspé Peninsula's south shore. Windsurfers and sailors enjoy the breezes here. Each summer, windsurfing marathons are held in the Baie des Chaleurs (Chaleur Bay), which separates the Gaspé from the province of New Brunswick to the south. *Chaleur* means heat in French; according to one version of the story, Jacques Cartier gave the bay this name because he discovered it on a warm day. Many locals find this funny, though, because the water temperature is lukewarm at best.

Other draws include the marina, eateries, and an immensely popular annual blues music festival, held in early August. In summer, take a stroll along the dock and watch folks fish for mackerel when the tide comes in.

The **Oratoire Notre-Dame-du-Mont Saint-Joseph** (Notre Dame Oratory), a chapel on Mont-St-Joseph, dominates this French-speaking town. Mass is celebrated on special holidays. Lookout points and hiking trails surround the site. The views from 2,000 feet high overlooking the town of Carleton and the Baie des Chaleurs are worth the wear on your brakes coming down. ⊠ *837 rue de la Montagne* ☎ *418/364–3723* 🎫 *C$4* ☉ *Late June–early Oct., daily 9–5.*

off the beaten path

PARC NATIONAL DE MIGUASHA – A UNESCO World Heritage Site, the 215-acre park includes cliffs riddled with fish and plant fossils dating back nearly 400 million years. The fossils are important in understanding how aquatic animals evolved into four-legged land creatures. The grounds include the Natural History Museum, where paleontology is the focus, as well as a restaurant, gift shop, and picnic tables. Guided tours of the museum and park show how fossils are uncovered, studied, and exhibited. The park is 22 km (14 mi) west of Carleton. ⊠ *231 Rte. Miguasha Ouest, Nouvelle* ☎ *418/794–2475, 866/644–8274 within Québec* ⊕ *www.sepaq.com* 🎫 *C$8.50 for museum and park* ☉ *June–Aug., daily 9–6; Sept.–mid-Oct., daily 9–5; mid-Oct.–June, weekdays 8:30–4:30.*

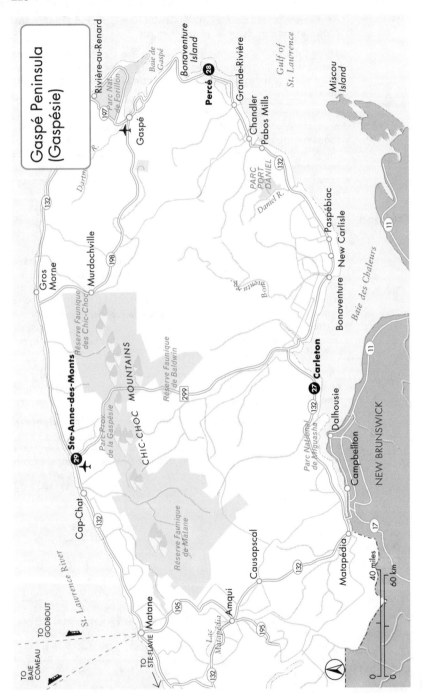

Gaspé Peninsula (Gaspésie)

Where to Stay & Eat

$–$$$ ✕⊞ **Hostellerie Baie Bleue.** The beachfront rooms make this hotel, within walking distance of the dock and a few craft stores, feel a bit like a resort. All guest rooms have bay views. Daily guided bus tours leave from the hotel June through September. Seafood is a specialty of the restaurant, La Seigneurie ($$–$$$$), where regional dishes and the table d'hôte won't break your budget; the wine list is extensive and well chosen. ⊠ *482 blvd. Perron, G0C 1J0* ☎ *418/364-3355 or 800/463–9099* 🖷*418/364–6165* ⊕*www.baiebleue.com* ⟳*92 rooms, 3 suites* ⏚*Restaurant, cable TV, tennis court, pool, beach, Internet, meeting rooms, some pets allowed, no-smoking rooms; no a/c* ⊟ *AE, DC, MC, V* ⊗ *Restaurant closed Nov.–Apr.*

¢ 🏕 **Camping de Carleton.** At a unique location on a peninsula, the campground is completely surrounded by sand beaches and the waters of the Chaleur Bay. At the foot of Mont-St-Joseph, the campground is a five-minute car ride from the town center of Carleton. ⏚ *Flush toilets, full hookups, drinking water, guest laundry, showers, electricity, public telephone, general store, swimming (ocean)* ⟳ *282 tent sites, 69 sites with partial hookups, 74 with full hookups* ⊠ *Banc de Larocque, C.P. 237, Carleton, G0C 1J0* ☎ *418/364–3992* 🖷 *418/364–7314* ⊕ *www.carletonsurmer.com* ⊟ *MC, V* ⊗ *Mid-June–mid-Sept.*

Percé

★ ❷❽ *193 km (120 mi) east of Carleton.*

Once known for its fishing, Percé, and its current attractions, are usually crowded in summer. The most famous sight in the region is Percé Rock, the huge, fossil-embedded, hole-riddled offshore ridge that the sea "pierced" thousands of years ago. (Don't be fooled by teasing locals who claim the hole was made by a stray cannon ball during a naval battle.)

★ Beyond Percé Rock 3½ km off the coast (2 mi, or a 15-minute boat ride from the main wharf) is l'**Île Bonaventure** (Bonaventure Island). The small park is the summertime home of an estimated 300,000 marine birds. The most impressive are the pelican-billed blue-eyed gannets, which number around 60,000, making this the second-largest (and most easily accessible) colony of its kind in the world. You can get to within a few feet of the nesting area, which is straight from the pages of *National Geographic*. Other species here include seagulls, terns, cormorants, petrels, and puffins—and seals. Several tour-boat operators are available at the main dock, as are high-sea-fishing outfitters. Depending on the season, you can buy lobsters and a variety of sea fish on the main pier, from fishermen returning with their day's catch. Other attractions include hiking trails and a maritime museum.

off the beaten path

FORILLON NATIONAL PARK – Stretching like a huge bow from Alabama to Newfoundland, the Appalachian Mountains abruptly end at the water's edge on the northern tip of the Gaspé Peninsula, resurfacing again on the far-off opposite shore of the Gulf of the St. Lawrence. This enchanting federal park offers visitors more than 70 km (44 mi) of trails, where everything from whales and seals to bears and birds can be spotted. The only accommodations within the park are campsites. ⊠ *122 Gaspé Blvd., Gaspé* ☎ *418/368–5505* ⊕ *www. parkscanada.gc.ca/forillon* ☜ *C$5* ☉ *Park June–mid-Oct., daily 7 AM–11 PM. Visitor center June–Aug., daily 9–7; Sept.–Oct., daily 9–5.*

Where to Stay & Eat

$$$–$$$$ ✕ **La Maison du Pêcheur.** The food and service at this casual seafood restaurant, a stone's throw from the wharf, earn high marks. A dish called the Trident combines lobster meat (from the restaurant's own lobster farm) with Cointreau sauce, scallops dipped in melted local goat cheese, and salmon coated with maple syrup. *Homard nu à la Chimo* (Naked Lobster) is a de-shelled lobster served with yogurt from Chimo, a local farm. Early birds and nighthawks can find nourishment in the Café de l'Atlantique, a bistro-style restaurant under the same roof that's open from 8 AM to midnight. The menu is more down-home (strong coffee and croissants), but also includes some surprises, such as an eggs Benedict–style *homard à l'oeuf* (lobster and eggs). ⊠ *155 place du Quai* ☎ *418/ 782–5331* ☐ *AE, DC, MC, V* ☉ *Closed Oct.–May.*

$$–$$$ ▦ **Hôtel La Normandie.** All but eight rooms here face the ocean and have views of both Percé Rock and Bonaventure Island. Third-floor rooms are the most spacious. A boardwalk gives you access to the beach. The views also get top billing in the restaurant, which is romantic and serves fine French and regional fare. Shops and activities are within walking distance. ⊠ *221 Rte. 132 Ouest, C.P. 129, G0C 2L0* ☎ *418/782–2112 or 800/ 463–0820* ☐ *418/782–2337* ⊕ *www.normandieperce.com* ⊷ *44 rooms, 1 suite* ☌ *Restaurant, cable TV, lounge, Internet, meeting rooms, some pets allowed; no a/c, no smoking* ☐ *MC, V* ☉ *Closed Nov.–mid-May* ⦿ *EP.*

$$ ▦ **Hôtel-Motel Le Mirage.** Thanks to its hilltop perch, this well-established family-owned hotel has the best views of Percé Rock and Bonaventure Island. All rooms face the water and have private balconies. Breakfast is the only meal served in the dining room, which also has splendid water views. ⊠ *288 Rte. 132 Ouest, G0C 2L0* ☎ *418/782–5151 or 800/463– 9011* ☐ *418/782–5536* ⊕ *www.hotellemirage.com* ⊷ *66 rooms, 2 suites* ☌ *Dining room, cable TV, tennis court, pool, babysitting, laundry facilities, travel services, no-smoking rooms; no a/c in some rooms* ☐ *AE, MC, V* ☉ *Closed Nov.–mid-May* ⦿ *EP.*

¢–$$ ▦ **Manoir de Percé.** Boutiques, art galleries, and the wharf and other sights are about a five-minute walk from this hotel-motel in the heart of town. Most rooms have picture windows and terraces with views of Bonaventure Island. ⊠ *212 Rte. 132 Ouest, G0C 2L0* ☎ *418/782–2022, 800/ 463–0858 in Canada* ☐ *418/782–5195* ⊕ *www.info-gaspesie.com/ manoirperce* ⊷ *38 rooms, 2 suites* ☌ *Restaurant, cable TV, bar, babysitting, laundry facilities, meeting room, car rental, travel services, some pets allowed, no-smoking rooms* ☐ *AE, MC, V* ☉ *Closed Nov.–mid-May* ⦿ *EP.*

¢–$ ▦ **Auberge Le Coin du Banc.** The warm hospitality at this inn 10 km (5 mi) north of Percé is expressed partly through fresh-baked breads and sweets. Antiques, paintings, and interesting trinkets fill the main lodge; four of the six cabins are on a sandy beach. Some pets are allowed in the cabins, which are spacious. Make a reservation if you intend to visit be-

tween October and May. ✉ *315 Rte. 132, G0C 2L0* ☎ *418/645–2907*
🛏 *11 rooms, 4 with private bath; 6 cabins ⚒ Restaurant, lounge, some
pets allowed; no a/c, no room phones, no TV in some rooms* ☱ *V* ⦿ *EP.*

Ste-Anne-des-Monts

㉙ *282 km (175 mi) northwest of Percé.*

With a population of 6,900, Ste-Anne-des-Monts is the largest community in the area and thus has more services than the smaller towns.
It's also a gateway to Parc Provinçial de la Gaspésie. The area south
of this coastal town includes eastern Canada's highest peaks, the Chic-
Choc Mountains.

Parc Provinçial de la Gaspésie (Gaspé Peninsula Provincial Park; ✉ Rte.
299 ☎ 418/763–3301 or 866/727–2427 ⦿ www.sepaq.com) has climbing, heli-skiing, mountain hiking, fishing, and canoeing. Nature-inter-
pretation programs include moose- and caribou-watching. Overnight
accommodation is available in cabins that sleep two to eight people and
are heated by wood-burning stoves. More-primitive huts and campsites
are available along the longer trails. The park is also accessible from
the south shore by taking Rte. 299 out of New Richmond.

Where to Stay & Eat

$–$$$$ ✕⊞ **Gîte du Mont-Albert.** In the middle of the Chic-Choc Mountains, this
property is 40 km (25 mi) south of Ste-Anne-des-Monts. It's a large mod-
ern hotel at the base of snow-capped mountains—a luxurious retreat
well positioned for hiking, biking, horseback riding, and canoeing or
salmon fishing on the Ste-Anne River. The beautifully presented meals
at the restaurant ($$$) are an opportunity to taste local fare with a re-
fined touch. Cottages are also available. ✉ *Parc Provinçial de la Gaspésie,
2001 Rte. du Parc, Box 1150, G4V 2E4* ☎ *418/763–2288, 888/270–
4483, or 866/727–2427* 🛏 *53 rooms, 19 cottages ⚒ Restaurant, pool,
sauna, hiking, cross-country skiing, bar, meeting rooms; no a/c in some
rooms, no TV in some rooms* ☱ *AE, DC, MC, V* ⦿ *EP, MAP.*

¢–$ ⊞ **Riôtel Monaco-des-Monts.** The motel, a 25-minute drive from the
provincial park's entrance, has an early-morning shuttle to take you there
in the early morning. Rooms are plain but comfortable; the beach is a
10-minute walk away, and the municipal golf course and other local services are about 20 minutes away by car. The restaurant is open 6:30 AM–10
PM. ✉ *90 blvd. Ste-Anne, G4V 1R3* ☎ *418/763–3321 or 800/463–7468*
⦿ *www.riotel.com* 🛏 *46 rooms ⚒ Restaurant, cable TV with movies
and video games, bicycles, bar, meeting rooms, no-smoking rooms; no
a/c in some rooms* ☱ *AE, DC, MC, V* ⦿ *BP, EP, MAP.*

PROVINCE OF QUÉBEC A TO Z

*To research prices, get advice from other travelers, and book travel ar-
rangements, visit www.fodors.com.*

AIR TRAVEL

Montréal and Québec City are the gateway cities.

BIKE TRAVEL

Québec is in the middle of developing the Route Verte, or the Green Route, a 3,500-km (2,170-mi) network of trails covering the southern half of the province, which will eventually link with trails in New England and New York. More than half of the marked bikeways are already open. For information and a map, contact Vélo Québec.

▊ **Vélo Québec** ☎ 514/521-8356 or 800/567-8356 ⊕ www.routeverte.com.

BUS TRAVEL

Daily service to Granby, Lac-Mégantic, Magog, and Sherbrooke in the Eastern Townships leaves from the Montréal central bus station. Greyhound's Canada Coach Pass Plus gives you access to Québec as well as the Maritime Provinces. Passes must be purchased in Canada at a Greyhound terminal or online before leaving home. They are an excellent value for travelers who want to wander the highways and byways of the country, packing a lot of miles into a relatively short period of time. However, for occasional day-trips (from Montréal to Québec City, for example) they're hardly worth it.

Voyageur is a province-wide bus line. Several smaller private companies also serve the regions and connect with Voyageur. The trip to Gaspé Peninsula from Montréal takes 15 hours.

Limocar service in the area covers the Laurentians: stops include Mont-Laurier, Ste-Adèle, Ste-Agathe-des-Monts, and St-Jovite. Limocar has a service to the Lower Laurentians region (including St-Jérôme), departing from the Laval Bus Terminal at the Henri-Bourassa Métro stop in north Montréal; Limocar also services Lanaudiere, Monteregie, and the Eastern Townships.

▊ **Greyhound Lines** ☎ 800/661-8747 in Canada, 800/231-2222 in the U.S. ⊕ www. greyhound.ca. **Limocar** ☎ 450/435-8899 ⊕ www.limocar.ca. **Station Central d'Autobus Montréal** ✉ 505 blvd. de Maisonneuve Est, Montréal ☎ 514/842-2281. **Gare du Palais** (Québec bus terminal) ✉ 320 rue Abraham-Martin, Québec City ☎ 418/525-3000. **Voyageur** ☎ 514/842-2281 ⊕ www.voyageur.com.

CAR TRAVEL

Major entry points are Ottawa/Hull; U.S. 87 from New York State south of Montréal; U.S. 91; U.S. 89 from Vermont into the Eastern Townships area; and the Trans-Canada Highway (Highway 40 to the west of Montréal, Highway 20 to the east).

Québec has fine roads—and speedy drivers. The major highways are Autoroute des Laurentides 15 North, a six-lane highway from Montréal to the Laurentians; Autoroute 10 East from Montréal to the Eastern Townships; U.S. 91 from New England, which becomes Autoroute 55 as it crosses the border to the Eastern Townships; Autoroutes Jean-Lesage 20 and Félix-LeClerc 40 between Montréal and Québec; and the scenic Route 138 (called the chemin de Roy between St. Barthélémy and Québec City), which runs from Montréal along the north shore of the St. Lawrence River. Road maps are available at Québec tourist offices.

Autoroute des Laurentides 15 North and Route 117—a slower but more scenic secondary road at its northern end—lead to the Laurentians.

Exit numbers on Autoroute 15 are the distance in kilometers from the U.S. border. Try to avoid traveling to and from the region Friday evening or Sunday afternoon, because you're likely to sit in traffic for hours.

Autoroute 10 East heads from Montréal through the Eastern Townships; from New England, U.S. 91 becomes Autoroute 55, a major road.

The main roads through the Charlevoix region are the scenic Route 362 and the faster Route 138.

On the Gaspé Peninsula, the Trans-Canada Highway (Highway 185 in Northern Québec) runs northeast along the southern shore of the St. Lawrence River to just south of Rivière-du-Loup, where the 270-km (167-mi) Route 132 hugs the dramatic coastline. At Ste-Flavie, follow the southern leg of Route 132. The entire distance around the peninsula is 848 km (526 mi). Consider touring the peninsula in a counterclockwise direction—you remain directly on the river (without a lane of cars between you and the shore), and you might encounter less traffic.

EMERGENCIES

🚩 **Ambulance, fire, police** ☎ 911.

🚩 Hospitals **Centre Hospitalier de Charlevoix** ✉ 74 blvd. Ambroise-Fafard, Baie-St-Paul ☎418/435-5150. **Centre Hospitalier de Gaspé** ✉215 blvd. York Ouest, Gaspé ☎418/368-3301. **Centre Hospitalier Laurentien** ✉ 234 rue St-Vincent, Ste-Agathe-des-Monts ☎ 819/324-4000. **Centre Universitaire de Santé de l'Estrie** (CUSE) ✉ 580 rue Bowen Sud, Sherbrooke ☎ 819/346-1110.

LODGING

CAMPING For information about Québec's national parks contact Canadian Heritage Parks Canada. Contact the individual park administration about camping in provincial parks. For information on camping in the province's private trailer parks and campgrounds, request the free publication "Québec Camping," from Tourisme Québec.

🚩 **Canadian Heritage Parks Canada** ✑ Box 6060, Passage du Chien d'Or, Québec City, G1R 4V7 ☎ 418/648-4177 or 800/463-6769 ⊕ www.parkscanada.gc.ca. **Tourisme Québec** ✑ Box 979, Montréal, H3C 2W3 ☎ 514/873-2015, 800/363-7777, or 877/266-5687 ⊕ www.bonjourquebec.com.

GUEST FARMS Agricotours, the Québec farm-vacation association, can provide lists of guest farms in the province.

🚩 **Agricotours** ✉ 4545 av. Pierre-de-Coubertin, C.P. 1000, Succursale M, Montréal, H1V 3R2 ☎ 514/252-3138 ⊕ www.agricotours.qc.ca.

SPORTS & OUTDOORS

FISHING The Fédération des Pourvoyeurs du Québec (Québec Outfitters Federation) has a list of outfitters (in French) that is available through tourist offices. Fishing requires a permit, available from the regional offices of the Ministère de l'Environnement et de la Faune (Ministry of the Environment and Wildlife), or at regional sporting-goods stores displaying an "authorized agent" sticker.

🚩 **Fédération des Pourvoyeurs du Québec** ✑ 5237 blvd. Hamel, Bureau 270, Québec City, G2E 2H2 ☎ 418/877-5191 ⊕ www.fpq.com. **Ministère de l'Environnement et de** la Faune ✉ 675 blvd. René-Lévesque Est, Québec City, G1R 5V7 ☎ 418/521-3830 or 800/561-1616 🌐 www.menv.gouv.qc.ca.

MOUNTAIN CLIMBING The Fédération Québécoise de la Montagne (Québec Mountain-Climbing Federation) has information about climbing, as do the province's tourist offices.

🛈 **Fédération Québécoise de la Montagne** ✉ 4545 av. Pierre-de-Coubertin, C.P. 1000, Succursale M, Montréal, H1V 3R2 ☎ 514/252-3004.

RIVER RAFTING Aventure en Eau Vive, New World River Expeditions, and Aventure Rivière Rouge—specializing in white-water rafting at Rivière Rouge—are on-site at a departure point near Calumet. (To get here, take Route 148 past Calumet; turn onto chemin de la Rivière Rouge until you see signs for the access road to each rafter's headquarters.) All offer four- to five-hour rafting trips and provide transportation to and from the river site, as well as guides, helmets, life jackets, and, at the end of the trip, a much-anticipated meal. Most have facilities on-site or nearby for dining, drinking, camping, bathing, swimming, hiking, and horseback riding.

🛈 **Aventure en Eau Vive** ☎ 819/242-6084 or 800/567-6881. **Aventure Rivière Rouge** ☎ 888/723-8464. **New World River Expeditions** ☎ 819/242-7238 or 800/361-5033 🌐 www.newworld.ca.

SKIING Lift tickets range from C$30 to C$52. For information about ski conditions, call Tourisme Québec and ask for the ski report.

🛈 **Tourisme Québec** ☎ 800/363-7777.

SNOWMOBILING Regional tourist offices have information about snowmobiling, including snowmobile maps and lists of essential services. Snowmobilers who use trails in Québec must obtain an access pass or day user's pass for the trails, which are regulated by the Québec Federation of Snowmobiling Clubs.

Jonview Canada offers snowmobile tours in the Laurentians, in Charlevoix, and as far north as the James Bay region. Other weeklong packages may include dogsledding and ice fishing.

🛈 **Jonview Canada** ✉ 1134 rue Ste-Catherine Ouest, 12th fl, Montréal, H3B 1H4 ☎ 514/861-9190. **Québec Federation of Snowmobiling Clubs** ✍ Box 1000, 4545 av. Pierre-de-Coubertin, Montréal, H1V 3R2 ☎ 514/252-3076.

TOURS

The Zoological Society of Montréal is a nature-oriented group that runs lectures, field trips, and weekend excursions. Tours include whale-watching in the St. Lawrence estuary and hiking and bird-watching in national parks throughout Québec, Canada, and the northern United States.

Autocar Dupont-Gray Line leads day excursions along the Côte de Beaupré, with stops at Montmorency Falls and the Ste-Anne-de-Beaupré basilica. The cost is about C$44 per person.

Trips from Percé to Bonaventure Island off the Gaspé Peninsula are offered by Les Bateliers de Percé; Croisières Baie de Gaspé offers 2½-hour whale-watching tours from Forillon National Park, at the eastern tip of the peninsula.

⚡ Autocar Dupont-Gray Line ☎ 418/649-9226. **Les Bateliers de Percé** ☎ 418/782-2974. **Croisières Baie de Gaspé** ☎418/892-5500. **Zoological Society of Montréal** ☎514/845-8317 ⊕ www.zoologicalsocietymtl.org.

TRAIN TRAVEL
The railway line follows the coast. On the south shore, the VIA Rail–operated *Chaleur* train stops at Rimouski, Mont-Joli, Matapédia, Carleton, Percé, and Gaspé.
⚡ Train Information VIA Rail ☎ 514/989-2626 or 888/842-7245 ⊕ www.viarail.ca.

VISITOR INFORMATION
Tourisme Québec can provide information on specific towns' tourist bureaus.

In the Laurentians, the major tourist office is the Association Touristique des Laurentides, just off the Autoroute des Laurentides 15 North at Exit 39. The office is open mid-June through August, daily 9–8:30; September to mid-June it's open Saturday through Thursday 9–5 and Friday 9–7. Mont-Tremblant, Piedmont/Saint-Sauveur, Sainte-Adèle, St-Jovite, Ste-Agathe-des-Monts, St-Eustache, St-Adolphe-d'Howard, and Val-David have regional tourist offices that are open year-round. Seasonal tourist offices (open mid-June to early September) are in Grenville, Labelle, Lachute, St-Jérôme, Oka, Notre-Dame-du-Laus, St-Sauveur, Ste-Marguerite-Estérel, Nominique, Lac-du-Cerf, and Ferme Neuve.

In the Eastern Townships, year-round regional provincial tourist offices are in Bromont, Coaticook, Lac-Mégantic, Magog-Orford, Sherbrooke, Sutton, and Granby. Seasonal tourist offices (open June to early September) are in Danville, Dunham, Eastman, Frelighsburg, Granby, Lambton, Masonville, Birchton, Dudswell, Lac-Brome (Foster), Ulverton, Waterloo, and Pike River. The schedules of seasonal bureaus are irregular, so it's a good idea to contact the Association Touristique des Cantons de l'Est before visiting. This association also provides lodging information.

On the way from Québec City to Charlevoix, look for the Beaupré Coast Interpretation Center off Highway 360 in Château-Richer. The old convent of Château-Richer (built in 1907) serves as the backdrop for guides in New France costumes to explain displays on the history of the region. Admission is C$4. The center is open from mid-June to mid-October, daily 10–5 (by reservation only the rest of the year).
⚡ Tourist Information Association Touristique des Cantons de l'Est ✉ 20 rue Don Bosco Sud, Sherbrooke, J1L 1W4 ☎ 819/820-2020 or 800/355-5755 ⊕ www.easterntownships.cc. **Association Touristique de la Gaspésie** ✉ 357 rte. de la Mer, Ste-Flavie, G0J 2L0 ☎ 418/775-2223 or 800/463-0323 ⊕ www.tourisme-gaspesie.com. **Association Touristique des Laurentides** ✉ 14142 rue de la Chapelle, Mirabel, J7J 2C8 ☎ 450/436-8532 or 800/561-6673 ⊕ www.laurentides.com. **Association Touristique Régionale de Charlevoix** ✉495 blvd. de Comporté, C.P. 275, La Malbaie, G5A 3G3 ☎418/665-4454 or 800/667-2276 ⊕ www.tourisme-charlevoix.com. **Beaupré Coast Interpretation Center** ✉ 7977 av. Royale, Château-Richer, G0A 1N0 ☎ 418/824-3677. **Tourisme Québec** ✉ 1001 rue du Square-Dorchester, No. 100, C.P. 979, Montréal, H3C 2W3 ☎ 800/363-7777.

UNDERSTANDING
QUÉBEC

QUÉBEC AT A GLANCE

Fast Facts

Nickname: La Belle Province (The Beautiful Province)
Capital: Québec City
Motto: Je me souviens (I remember)
Province bird: Snowy owl
Province flower: Blue flag iris
Province tree: Yellow birch
Administrative divisions: 17
Entered the Confederation: July 1, 1867
Population: 7.5 million
Population density: 5 people per square km (13 people per square mi)
Median age: 38.8
Infant mortality rate: 4.9 deaths per 1,000 live births
Ethnic groups: White 93%; black 2%; South Asian 1%; Chinese 1%; Southeast Asian 1%; Arab/West Asian 1%; Latin American 1%
Religion: Roman Catholic 83%; unaffiliated 6%; Protestant 5%; other 3%; Muslim 2%; Jewish 1%

Some say that no one ever leaves Montréal, for that city, like Canada itself, is designed to preserve the past, a past that happened somewhere else.

— Leonard Cohen

Why should Canada, wild and unsettled as it is, impress us as an older country than the States, unless because her institutions are old? All things appeared to contend there with a certain rust of antiquity, such as forms on old armor and iron guns— the rust of conventions and formalities. It is said that the metallic roofs of Montréal and Québec keep sound and bright for 40 years in some cases. But if the rust was not on the tinned roofs and spires, it was on the inhabitants and their institutions.

— Henry David Thoreau

Geography & Environment

Land area: 1.6 million square km (594,860 square mi); Canada's largest province
Terrain: Rocky, forested hills, including the Laurentian Mountains, with many rivers and lakes to the north and the population centered in the south, along the northern bank of the St. Lawrence River
Natural resources: Aluminum, asbestos, copper, gold, iron, silver, wood, zinc
Natural hazards: Earthquakes, forest fires, ice storms, landslides, tornados

Environmental issues: Effluent from textiles, pulp and paper, and wastewater treatment are a problem in Québec's rivers; volatile organic compounds such as benzene and sulfur oxide are closely monitored in the air on the east end of Montréal; 10 of Canada's 11 aluminum smelters are located in Québec and the province is working to reduce the output of industry pollutants; wood burning in Montréal and other big cities is affecting air quality and is discouraged.

Economy

GSP: C$221.8 billion ($162.1 billion U.S. dollars)
Per capita income: C$34,275 ($25,044 U.S. dollars)
Unemployment: 8.4%

Work force: 3.7 million: manufacturing 17%; trade 16%; health care and social assistance 13%; other 8%; finance, insurance, real estate and leasing 6%; professional, scientific and technical

services 6%; educational services 6%; accommodation and food services 6%; public administration 6%; transportation and warehousing 5%; construction 4%; information, culture, and recreation 4%; business, building, and other support services 3%
Major industries: Aircraft, beverages, chemicals, clothing, fishing, food products, fur, furniture, iron, motor vehicles, paper, refined petroleum, steel, tourism
Agricultural products: Dairy products, sugar beets, tobacco
Exports: C$5.2 billion ($3.8 billion U.S. dollars)
Major export products: Aircraft, machinery, paper products

Did You Know?

• Québec's vast water resources generate much of Canada's electricity. Using the La Grande River and other waterways, Hydro-Québec has created an underground set of spillways three times the height of Niagara Falls. This and other massive projects make it the largest generator in the country.

• Québec is three times the size of France, but at 6 million has just one-tenth the number of French speakers.

• The world's largest edible fungi was found in Québec in 1987. The giant puffball (Calvatia gigantea) was more than 8 feet in circumference and weighed 48 pounds.

• According to Canada's 2001 census, the majority of immigrants to Montréal are from Italy. Haitian immigrants are the second largest group.

• There are 380 islands inside the borders of metropolitan Montréal.

• While the rest of Canada uses English common law, Québec's civil law is based on old French laws. All of Canada has one criminal code.

• How much cheese does 540,000 pounds of milk make? Québec's Agropur turned exactly that much milk into a cheddar weighing 57,508 pounds in 1995.

• Eighty-four percent of Québec is covered by the Canadian Shield, a geographical area believed to be the nucleus of North America. Geologic evidence shows rock in Québec was the first in North America to be permanently elevated above sea level, leaving formations millions of years old unaltered since ice sheets drifted across the continent.

• Québec was the sports capital of North America in the 19th century. Here the rules for ice hockey were invented, and lacrosse, football, and curling were all altered here. Snowshoes, canoes, and toboggans were adapted from versions the Native Americans used here.

• Michael Barski made Québec the sit-up capital of the world in 2003 when he completed 7,203 abdominal crunches in an hour. That's two sit-ups every second.

• Québec City is the only city in North America to have preserved its surrounding ramparts, bastions, gates, and defenses. For that, it was named a World Heritage Site by UNESCO.

VOCABULARY

One of the trickiest French sounds to pronounce is the nasal final *n* sound (whether or not the *n* is actually the last letter of the word). You should try to pronounce it as a sort of nasal grunt—as in "huh." The vowel that precedes the *n* will govern the vowel sound of the word, and in this list we precede the final *n* with an *h* to remind you to be nasal.

Another problem sound is the ubiquitous but untransliterable *eu,* as in *bleu* (blue) or *deux* (two), and the very similar sound in *je* (I), *ce* (this), and *de* (of). The closest equivalent might be the vowel sound in "put," but rounded. The famous rolled *r* is a glottal sound. Consonants at the ends of words are usually silent; when the following word begins with a vowel, however, the two are run together by sounding the consonant. There are two forms of "you" in French: *vous* (formal and plural) and *tu* (a singular, personal form). When addressing an adult you don't know, *vous* is always best.

English	French	Pronunciation

Basics

Yes/no	Oui/non	wee/nohn
Please	S'il vous plaît	seel voo play
Thank you	Merci	mair-**see**
You're welcome	De rien	deh ree-**ehn**
Excuse me, sorry	Pardon	pahr-**don**
Good morning/ afternoon	Bonjour	bohn-**zhoor**
Good evening	Bonsoir	bohn-**swahr**
Goodbye	Au revoir	o ruh-**vwahr**
Mr. (Sir)	Monsieur	muh-**syuh**
Mrs. (Ma'am)	Madame	ma-**dam**
Miss	Mademoiselle	mad-mwa-**zel**
Pleased to meet you	Enchanté(e)	ohn-shahn-**tay**
How are you?	Comment allez-vous?	kuh-mahn-tahl-ay **voo**
Very well, thanks	Très bien, merci	tray bee-ehn, mair-**see**
And you?	Et vous?	ay voo?

Numbers

one	un	uhn
two	deux	deuh
three	trois	twah

four	quatre	**kaht**-ruh
five	cinq	sank
six	six	seess
seven	sept	set
eight	huit	wheat
nine	neuf	nuf
ten	dix	deess
eleven	onze	ohnz
twelve	douze	dooz
thirteen	treize	trehz
fourteen	quatorze	kah-torz
fifteen	quinze	kanz
sixteen	seize	sez
seventeen	dix-sept	deez-**set**
eighteen	dix-huit	deez-**wheat**
nineteen	dix-neuf	deez-**nuf**
twenty	vingt	vehn
twenty-one	vingt-et-un	vehnt-ay-**uhn**
thirty	trente	trahnt
forty	quarante	ka-**rahnt**
fifty	cinquante	sang-**kahnt**
sixty	soixante	swa-**sahnt**
seventy	soixante-dix	swa-sahnt-**deess**
eighty	quatre-vingts	kaht-ruh-**vehn**
ninety	quatre-vingt-dix	kaht-ruh-vehn-**deess**
one hundred	cent	sahn
one thousand	mille	meel

Colors

black	noir	nwahr
blue	bleu	bleuh
brown	brun/marron	bruhn/mar-**rohn**
green	vert	vair
orange	orange	o-**rahnj**
pink	rose	rose
red	rouge	rouge
violet	violette	vee-o-**let**

white	blanc	blahnk
yellow	jaune	zhone

Days of the Week

Sunday	dimanche	dee-**mahnsh**
Monday	lundi	luhn-**dee**
Tuesday	mardi	mahr-**dee**
Wednesday	mercredi	mair-kruh-**dee**
Thursday	jeudi	zhuh-**dee**
Friday	vendredi	vawn-druh-**dee**
Saturday	samedi	sahm-**dee**

Months

January	janvier	zhahn-vee-**ay**
February	février	feh-vree-**ay**
March	mars	marce
April	avril	a-**vreel**
May	mai	meh
June	juin	zhwehn
July	juillet	zhwee-**ay**
August	août	ah-**oo**
September	septembre	sep-**tahm**-bruh
October	octobre	awk-**to**-bruh
November	novembre	no-**vahm**-bruh
December	décembre	day-**sahm**-bruh

Useful Phrases

Do you speak English?	Parlez-vous anglais?	par-lay **voo** **ahn**-glay
I don't speak . . . French	Je ne parle pas . . . français	zhuh nuh parl pah frahn-**say**
I don't understand	Je ne comprends pas	zhuh nuh kohm-**prahn** pah
I understand	Je comprends	zhuh kohm-**prahn**
I don't know	Je ne sais pas	zhuh nuh say **pah**
I'm American/ British	Je suis américain/ anglais	zhuh sweez a-may-ree-**kehn**/ ahn-**glay**
What's your name?	Comment vous ap-pelez-vous?	ko-mahn voo za-pell-ay-**voo**

English	French	Pronunciation
My name is . . .	Je m'appelle . . .	zhuh ma-**pell** . . .
What time is it?	Quelle heure est-il?	kel air eh-**teel**
How?	Comment?	ko-**mahn**
When?	Quand?	kahn
Yesterday	Hier	yair
Today	Aujourd'hui	o-zhoor-**dwee**
Tomorrow	Demain	duh-**mehn**
Tonight	Ce soir	suh **swahr**
What?	Quoi?	kwah
What is it?	Qu'est-ce que c'est?	kess-kuh-**say**
Why?	Pourquoi?	**poor**-kwa
Who?	Qui?	kee
Where is . . .	Où est . . .	oo ay
the train station?	la gare?	la gar
the subway station?	la station de métro?	la sta-**syon** duh may-**tro**
the bus stop?	l'arrêt de bus?	la-**ray** duh **booss**
the post office?	la poste?	la post
the bank?	la banque?	la bahnk
the . . . hotel?	l'hôtel . . .?	lo-**tel**
the store?	le magasin?	luh ma-ga-**zehn**
the cashier?	la caisse?	la **kess**
the . . . museum?	le musée . . .?	luh mew-**zay**
the hospital?	l'hôpital?	lo-pee-**tahl**
the elevator?	l'ascenseur?	la-sahn-**seuhr**
the telephone?	le téléphone?	luh tay-lay-**phone**
Where are the restrooms? (men/women)	Où sont les toilettes? (hommes/femmes)	oo sohn lay twah-**let** (**oh**-mm/**fah**-mm)
Here/there	Ici/là	ee-**see**/la
Left/right	A gauche/à droite	a goash/a draht
Straight ahead	Tout droit	too drwah
Is it near/far?	C'est près/loin?	say pray/lwehn
I'd like . . .	Je voudrais . . .	zhuh voo-**dray**
a room	une chambre	ewn **shahm**-bruh
the key	la clé	la clay
a newspaper	un journal	uhn zhoor-**nahl**
a stamp	un timbre	uhn **tam**-bruh
I'd like to buy . . .	Je voudrais acheter . . .	zhuh voo-**dray** **ahsh**-tay
cigarettes	des cigarettes	day see-ga-**ret**

matches	des allumettes	days a-loo-**met**
soap	du savon	dew sah-**vohn**
city map	un plan de ville	uhn plahn de **veel**
road map	une carte routière	ewn cart roo-tee-**air**
magazine	une revue	ewn reh-**vu**
envelopes	des enveloppes	dayz ahn-veh-**lope**
writing paper	du papier à lettres	dew pa-pee-ay a **let**-ruh
postcard	une carte postale	ewn cart pos-**tal**
How much is it?	C'est combien?	say comb-bee-**ehn**

A little/a lot	Un peu/beaucoup	uhn peuh/bo-**koo**
More/less	Plus/moins	plu/mwehn
Enough/too (much)	Assez/trop	a-say/tro
I am ill/sick	Je suis malade	zhuh swee ma-**lahd**
Call a . . .	Appelez un . . .	a-play uhn
doctor	docteur	dohk-**tehr**
Help!	Au secours!	o suh-**koor**
Stop!	Arrêtez!	a-reh-**tay**
Fire!	Au feu!	o fuh
Caution!/Look out!	Attention!	a-tahn-see-**ohn**

Dining Out

A bottle of . . .	une bouteille de . . .	ewn boo-**tay** duh
A cup of . . .	une tasse de . . .	ewn tass duh
A glass of . . .	un verre de . . .	uhn vair duh
Bill/check	l'addition	la-dee-see-**ohn**
Bread	du pain	dew pan
Breakfast	le petit-déjeuner	luh puh-**tee** day-zhuh-**nay**
Butter	du beurre	dew burr
Cheers!	A votre santé!	ah vo-truh sahn-**tay**
Cocktail/aperitif	un apéritif	uhn ah-pay-ree-**teef**
Dinner	le dîner	luh dee-**nay**
Dish of the day	le plat du jour	luh plah dew **zhoor**
Enjoy!	Bon appétit!	bohn a-pay-**tee**
Fixed-price menu	le menu	luh may-**new**
Fork	une fourchette	ewn four-**shet**
I am diabetic	Je suis diabétique	zhuh swee dee-ah-bay-**teek**

I am on a diet	Je suis au régime	zhuh sweez oray-**jeem**
I am vegetarian	Je suis végé-tarien(ne)	zhuh swee vay-zhay-ta-ree-**en**
I cannot eat . . .	Je ne peux pas manger de . . .	zhuh nuh **puh** pah mahn-**jay** deh
I'd like to order	Je voudrais commander	zhuh voo-**dray** ko-mahn-**day**
Is service/the tip included?	Est-ce que le service est compris?	ess kuh luh sair-**veess** ay comb-**pree**
It's good/bad	C'est bon/mauvais	say bohn/ mo-**vay**
It's hot/cold	C'est chaud/froid	say sho/frwah
Knife	un couteau	uhn koo-**toe**
Lunch	le déjeuner	luh day-zhuh-**nay**
Menu	la carte	la cart
Napkin	une serviette	ewn sair-vee-**et**
Pepper	du poivre	dew **pwah**-vruh
Plate	une assiette	ewn a-see-**et**
Please give me . . .	Donnez-moi . . .	doe-nay-**mwah**
Salt	du sel	dew sell
Spoon	une cuillère	ewn kwee-**air**
Sugar	du sucre	dew **sook**-ruh
Waiter!/Waitress!	Monsieur!/ Mademoiselle!	muh-**syuh**/ mad-mwa-**zel**
Wine list	la carte des vins	la cart day vehn

MENU GUIDE

General Dining

French	English
Entrée	Appetizer/Starter
Garniture au choix	Choice of vegetable side
Plat du jour	Dish of the day
Selon arrivage	When available
Supplément/En sus	Extra charge
Sur commande	Made to order

Petit Déjeuner (Breakfast)

French	English
Confiture	Jam
Miel	Honey
Oeuf à la coque	Boiled egg
Oeufs sur le plat	Fried eggs
Oeufs brouillés	Scrambled eggs
Tartine	Bread with butter

Poissons/Fruits de Mer (Fish/Seafood)

French	English
Anchois	Anchovies
Bar	Bass
Brandade de morue	Creamed salt cod
Brochet	Pike
Cabillaud/Morue	Fresh cod
Calmar	Squid
Coquilles St-Jacques	Scallops
Crevettes	Shrimp
Daurade	Sea bream
Ecrevisses	Prawns/Crayfish
Harengs	Herring
Homard	Lobster
Huîtres	Oysters
Langoustine	Prawn/Lobster
Lotte	Monkfish
Maquereau	Mackerel
Moules	Mussels
Palourdes	Clams
Saumon	Salmon
Thon	Tuna
Truite	Trout

Viande (Meat)

French	English
Agneau	Lamb
Boeuf	Beef
Boudin	Sausage

Boulettes de viande	Meatballs
Brochettes	Kabobs
Cassoulet	Casserole of white beans, meat
Cervelle	Brains
Chateaubriand	Double fillet steak
Choucroute garnie	Sausages with sauerkraut
Côtelettes	Chops
Côte/Côte de boeuf	Rib/T-bone steak
Cuisses de grenouilles	Frogs' legs
Entrecôte	Rib or rib-eye steak
Épaule	Shoulder
Escalope	Cutlet
Foie	Liver
Gigot	Leg
Porc	Pork
Ris de veau	Veal sweetbreads
Rognons	Kidneys
Saucisses	Sausages
Selle	Saddle
Tournedos	Tenderloin of T-bone steak
Veau	Veal

Methods of Preparation

A point	Medium
A l'étouffée	Stewed
Au four	Baked
Ballotine	Boned, stuffed, and rolled
Bien cuit	Well-done
Bleu	Very rare
Frit	Fried
Grillé	Grilled
Rôti	Roast
Saignant	Rare
Sauté/Poêlée	Sautéed

Volailles/Gibier (Poultry/Game)

Blanc de volaille	Chicken breast
Canard/Caneton	Duck/Duckling
Cerf/Chevreuil	Venison (red/roe)
Coq au vin	Chicken stewed in red wine
Dinde/Dindonneau	Turkey/Young turkey
Faisan	Pheasant
Lapin/Lièvre	Rabbit/Wild hare
Oie	Goose
Pintade/Pintadeau	Guinea fowl/Young guinea fowl
Poulet/Poussin	Chicken/Spring chicken

Légumes (Vegetables)

Artichaut	Artichoke
Asperge	Asparagus
Aubergine	Eggplant
Carottes	Carrots
Champignons	Mushrooms
Chou-fleur	Cauliflower
Chou (rouge)	Cabbage (red)
Laitue	Lettuce
Oignons	Onions
Petits pois	Peas
Pomme de terre	Potato
Tomates	Tomatoes

Fruits/Noix (Fruits/Nuts)

Abricot	Apricot
Amandes	Almonds
Ananas	Pineapple
Cassis	Blackcurrants
Cerises	Cherries
Citron/Citron vert	Lemon/Lime
Fraises	Strawberries
Framboises	Raspberries
Pamplemousse	Grapefruit
Pêche	Peach
Poire	Pear
Pomme	Apple
Prunes/Pruneaux	Plums/Prunes
Raisins/Raisins secs	Grapes/Raisins

Desserts

Coupe (glacée)	Sundae
Crème Chantilly	Whipped cream
Gâteau au chocolat	Chocolate cake
Glace	Ice cream
Tarte tatin	Caramelized apple tart
Tourte	Layer cake

Drinks

A l'eau	With water
Avec des glaçons	On the rocks
Bière	Beer
Blonde/brune	Light/dark
Café noir/crème	Black coffee/with steamed milk
Chocolat chaud	Hot chocolate
Eau-de-vie	Brandy

Eau minérale	Mineral water
gazeuse/non gazeuse	*carbonated/still*
Jus de . . .	. . . juice
Lait	Milk
Sec	Straight or dry
Thé	Tea
au lait/au citron	*with milk/lemon*
Vin	Wine
blanc	*white*
doux	*sweet*
léger	*light*
brut	*very dry*
rouge	*red*

INDEX